CONTENTS

VOLUME ONE CONTINUED

MANAGEMENT OF MENTAL DISORDERS

Volume 2

* Schizophrenic Disorders
* Dieting Disorders
* Substance Use Disorders
* Sleep Disorders
* Sexual Dysfunction
* Personality Disorders

EDITED BY
GAVIN ANDREWS & RACHEL JENKINS

UK EDITION - VOLUME TWO

WORLD HEALTH ORGANIZATION COLLABORATING CENTRES
IN MENTAL HEALTH,
SYDNEY AND LONDON

Published by the World Health Organization
Collaborating Centre for Mental Health and Substance Abuse
299 Forbes Street, Darlinghurst, Sydney, NSW, 2010
Australia
Fax (612) 9332 4316

Australian Edition
First published 1995
Second edition 1997

United Kingdom Edition
First Published 1999 in 2 volumes

Distributed for the Publishers in the United Kingdom by Datamail Direct Ltd.
Unit 3, Gresham Industrial Estate, Eastern Road, Aldershot, Hants, GU12 4YD, UK
Fax: +44 1252 322315

Reference this book as:
Andrews, G. & Jenkins, R.(Eds) (1999). *Management of Mental Disorders*
(UK Edition). Sydney: World Health Organization Collaborating Centre
for Mental Health and Substance Abuse.

Printed and Bound in the United Kingdom by
Bridge Offset Ltd., Headway House, Ivy Road
Aldershot, Hampshire, GU12 4TX

VOLUME ONE CONTINUED

VOLUME ONE CONTINUED

VOLUME TWO CONTINUED

VOLUME TWO CONTINUED

VOLUME TWO CONTINUED

TREATMENT PROTOCOL PROJECT

Staff: First Edition

Gavin Andrews MD, FRANZCP, FRCPsych
Caroline Hunt PhD
Heidi Sumich BSc (Psychol.) (Hons.)

Staff: Second Edition

Gavin Andrews MD, FRANZCP, FRCPsych
Caroline Hunt PhD
Malinda Jarry BSc (Psychol.) (Hons.)

Staff: UK Edition

Gavin Andrews MD, FRANZCP, FRCPsych
Rachel Jenkins MD, FRCPsych
Malinda Jarry BSc (Psychol.) (Hons.)

Consultants: UK Edition

Paul Bebbington, Terry Brugha, Mike Crawford, Michael Farrell, Dilys Jones, David Kingdon, Anthony Mann, Paul Moran, Graham Thornicroft.

Consultants: Australian Edition

Chapters 1, 2, and 11.

Bill Andrews, Stuart Baker, Neil Buhrich, Anne Butchart, Peter Daniels, Michael Dudley, Stewart Einfeld, Peter Ellis, Robert Finlay-Jones, Alan Garrity, Paul Jacobsen, John Lam Po Tang, Lisa Lampe, Neil McConaghy, Phil Mitchell, Helen Molony, Hugh Morgan, Saxby Pridmore, Ursula Ptok, Vivienne Schnieden, Donald Scott-Orr, Robert Sprague, Maree Teesson, Michael Williamson.

Chapter 3

Jill Ball, John Bardon, Philip Boyce, Claire Croumbie-Brown and Wentworth Area Health Service, Judy Kennedy and Hunter Area Health Service, Lisa Lampe, Phil Mitchell, Myra Murray and Dubbo Community Health Centre, Conrad Newman, Sagar Parikh, Gordon Parker, Michael Saville, Noel Wilton.

Chapter 4

Andrew Baillie, Rocco Crino, John Franklin, Jonathan Gaston, Lisa Lampe, Brian O'Grady, Gordon Parker, Raymond Way, Judy Westerway, Noel Wilton.

Chapter 5

Jane Chalmers, David Corby and Wollongong Community Psychiatric Centre, Jane Edwards, Ian Falloon, Judy Frost and Manning-Great Lakes Health Service, Katrina Hazelton and Ashfield Community Health Centre, Rob Hines and the SHIPS Programme, Cathy Issakidis, Marko Klobas and Northern Territory Department of Health and Community Services, Patrick McGorry and staff at EPPIC, Kim O'Brien, Louise O'Brien, Maryanne O'Donnell, Simon Richards, Alan Rosen, Grant Sara, Peter Schaecken, Donald Scott-Orr, Maree Teesson and Inner City Mental Health Service, Noel Wilton.

Chapter 6, 9 and 10

Jillian Ball, Helen Bearpark, Dieting Disorders Centre, University of Sydney, and the Royal Prince Alfred, Westmead, and Lynton Hospitals (R Griffiths, K. Lowinger, M. Sheridan, H. Williams, S.W. Touyz & P.J.V. Beumont), Owen Foster-Jones, John Franklin, Raphael Fraser, Ron Grunstein, Tamara Kitson, Merran Lindsay, Rosie McInnes, Andrea Mant, Kate Raffle, Barbara Roche, Louise Shepherd, David Schotte.

Chapter 7

Andrew Baillie, Amanda Baker, Margaret Eagers, Wayne Hall, Richard Mattick, Katy O'Neill, John Saunders, Maree Teesson.

Chapter 8

Michelle Singh, Joe Rey.

FORWARD

If obtaining international agreement about the definition of diagnostic concepts was an early achievement of the Mental Health Division of WHO, this book represents an even greater achievement – setting forth plans for the best management of a wide range of disorders, while avoiding controversial treatment methods. The common ground of the team of authors is common sense and a refreshingly pragmatic approach, paying attention not only to treatment strategies, but also to the assessment of severity of disorder, and the information which should be given to the patient and his or her carers.

The inclusion of assessment instruments with information about their scoring, and the provision of examples of "early warning" documents to be given to patients are both excellent developments, which mark the book out as being unusually useful. Psychiatrists of my generation will read the book with some envy, since clinical wisdom accumulated the hard way over many years is here set forth by a team of experts whose collective experience is enormous.

Dr Rachel Jenkins and her colleagues are to be congratulated in adapting the book for the British scene by replacing the sections dealing with legal aspects of psychiatry with their local equivalents; by describing the Care Programme Approach, and by making numerous minor amendments throughout.

We may congratulate ourselves on adapting our usually arbitrary local diagnostic systems to achieve international consensus; we satisfy our intellectual curiosity by improving our understanding of the social variables which release or exacerbate episodes of disorder; we improve our knowledge about the biological systems whose malfunctions underlie most serious disorders in order to find better ways of restoring homeostasis – but at the end of the say, our value to our patients is determined by our knowledge of the treatment strategies which prevent or abort episodes of disorder. And that is what this book is about. If a young doctor could only read one text – it would have to be this one.

Sir David Goldberg
Director of Research & Development
Institute of Psychiatry, King's College, London

PREFACE

Radical changes in mental health care have occurred over the past ten years. There is a lower proportion of people with mental disorders in hospital than at any time this century. It is not that we have suddenly become healthier, but rather that we have learned to manage people in the community who would once have been in hospital. This shift to community care has meant that we have had to develop new management methods.

This text encapsulates the best of current practice in mental health care. It is directed specifically towards those who are new to community mental health (e.g., new graduates, or clinicians who are transferring out of hospital inpatient services into community-based services), professionals who work in rural and isolated areas in which resources and specialist referral options may be limited, general practitioners, experienced community mental health clinicians who would like to refresh their knowledge about specific or infrequently used management techniques, and undergraduate or post-graduate university students. This text is not intended to be a substitute for training, supervision, or consultation with peers. A good clinician would use this text to supplement his or her ongoing education and would actively seek supervision, consultation, or referral if unsure about his or her expertise in a particular area.

This book was begun in 1991 when Professor Gavin Andrews returned from work with the World Health Organization Scientific Group on the Treatment of Psychiatric Disorders.It was funded by the NSW Institute of Psychiatry, Sydney, and the first edition was prepared at the Clinical Research Unit for Anxiety Disorders, St Vincent's Hospital, Sydney, with Gavin Andrews co-ordinating the project and Caroline Hunt and Heidi Sumich researching and writing the text. Both the NSW Institute of Psychiatry and the Clinical Research Unit for Anxiety Disorders are part of the Australian Multisite World Health Organization Collaborating Centre for Mental Health and Substance Abuse, which owns the copyright, and is the publisher of the book. The role of the WHO Collaborating Centre at the Clinical Research Unit for Anxiety Disorders is to prepare assessment instruments and treatment protocols. This text is therefore central to those activities. The book is derivative, and contains little that is truly new. It is simply a compilation of the best practice in mental health circa 1999. The UK edition has two new chapters, one on child and adolescent disorders drafted by Professor Joe Rey, and one on Substance use disorders drafted by Dr Maree Teesson. The chapters have been revised in the context of practice in the United Kingdom. The editors would be pleased to know of errata or omissions.

Gavin Andrews
World Health Organization Collaborating Centre for Mental Health and Substance Abuse
299 Forbes Street, Darlinghurst, Sydney, NSW, 2010, Australia.

Rachel Jenkins
World Health Organization Collaborating Centre for Mental Health Training and Research
Institute of Psychiatry, De Crespigny Park, London, SE5 8AF, United Kingdom.

5

SCHIZOPHRENIC DISORDERS

5.1 SCHIZOPHRENIA: GENERAL INFORMATION

5.1.1 DESCRIPTION

Schizophrenia is characterised by distortions of thinking and perception and is usually accompanied by emotions that are inappropriate or blunted. Typically there is a disturbance of the most basic functions that give a person the feeling of individuality, uniqueness and self-direction. For example, an individual may believe that intimate thoughts are known by others or that supernatural forces are influencing his or her actions in ways that are often bizarre. Additionally, the individual may lack insight and may not appreciate that there is anything wrong with his or her mental state.

Mood is usually shallow, frivolous, or inappropriate for the situation. Social withdrawal and emotional detachment are common. In addition, there is often a disturbance in self-initiated, goal-directed activity with inadequate interests or ability to follow a course of action to its logical conclusion.

Clear consciousness and intellectual capacity are usually maintained, although certain cognitive deficits (such as in memory or concentration) may evolve during the course of time.

Listed below is a summary of common complaints given by individuals or their families:

Individuals may have problems with:
- Hearing voices when no-one is around
- Strange beliefs
- Disturbances with thinking or concentration
- Managing daily activities
- Managing social interactions, work or studies

Families may ask for help with the individual's:
- Strange, frightening, or annoying behaviour (e.g., irritability, suspiciousness)
- Apathy, withdrawal or poor living skills

There is evidence that genetic factors play a role in the disorder. Psychosocial factors such as stress are likely to be involved in triggering the initial and subsequent episodes in vulnerable people, although other factors may also act as triggers (e.g., substance abuse). Episodes of schizophrenia appear to involve biological disturbances in the brain.

5.1.2 DIAGNOSIS

According to the World Health Organization's (WHO) International Classification of Diseases (ICD)-10th Edition, the signs and symptoms for this diagnosis must be present for *most of the time* during an episode which lasts *at least one month*.

The most important symptoms and signs include:
- **Hallucinations** (i.e., seeing, hearing, smelling, sensing, or tasting things that other people do not see, hear, smell, sense, or taste; for example, the person may hear voices which command him or her to behave in certain ways).
- **Delusions** (i.e., false beliefs that are firmly held despite objective and contradictory evidence, and despite the fact that other members of the culture do not share the same beliefs; for example, the person may believe that he or she is Jesus Christ, or that he or she is being followed, poisoned, or experimented upon).

- **Thought disturbances** in which the person believes that thoughts are being inserted into or withdrawn from the mind; are being broadcast to others; or are being echoed in the mind.
- **Disordered thinking** which results in incoherent or irrelevant speech.
- **Negative symptoms** such as extreme apathy, lack of spontaneous speech, and blunted or inappropriate affect, leading to disturbances in social or occupational functioning (or, if onset is in childhood or adolescence, a failure to reach expected academic, occupational or interpersonal achievement).

There is no single *specific* symptom that is required for a diagnosis of schizophrenia. In other words, the symptoms experienced by one person may not be exactly the same as the symptoms experienced by another person. However, *as a group,* people with schizophrenia display an identifiable *set* of symptoms. If someone exhibits one or more of these symptoms for a specified length of time, he or she may then be regarded as having a diagnosis of schizophrenia.

The American Psychiatric Association's (APA) Diagnostic and Statistical Manual of Mental Disorders, Fourth Edition (DSM-IV) is the alternative major diagnostic classificatory system to ICD-10. In DSM-IV, the diagnostic criteria for schizophrenia differ slightly from ICD-10 in relation to the duration of time for which symptoms are required to have been present prior to diagnosis. DSM-IV requires a minimum duration of six months, including a prodromal or residual phase, while ICD-10 requires the persistence of symptoms for only one month. Although acknowledging the existence of a prodromal phase to the disorder, ICD-10 states that the symptoms of the prodrome are not specific to schizophrenia, and hence the inclusion of a prodrome as part of the diagnosis is not justified.

Both DSM-IV and ICD-10 allow the diagnosis to be broken down into the pattern of course of the illness (e.g., chronic or continuous, episodic or with acute exacerbation, in remission, etc.). This breakdown may add further depth to the clinical picture. Individuals wishing to know more about the classification of the course of the illness are advised to consult ICD-10 or DSM-IV.

SUBTYPES OF SCHIZOPHRENIA

Many attempts have been made to classify schizophrenia into various subtypes although to date there is no consensus about the best system for subtyping schizophrenia. The most widely accepted form of subtyping is that used in both ICD-10 and DSM-IV. The subtypes describe a number of symptom patterns that are, or have been, commonly observed (e.g., paranoia, catatonia, hebephrenia, undifferentiated symptoms, etc.). See ICD-10 or DSM-IV for further details about these subtypes.

5.1.3 DIFFERENTIAL DIAGNOSIS

The diagnosis of schizophrenia can only be made when there is no evidence that an organic factor initiated and maintained the disturbance. A neurobiological assessment is usually considered for individuals who are experiencing their first episode of schizophrenia. This assessment will help rule out the possibility of an **organic mental disorder**.

Psychosis resulting from **psychoactive substance abuse** (e.g., LSD, cocaine, amphetamines, alcohol, L-dopa, etc.) shares many of the symptoms of schizophrenia, such as hallucinations, delusions, and abnormal speech. Before a provisional diagnosis of schizophrenia can be made, it is best if the individual is free from the effects of drug or alcohol intoxication or withdrawal. Urine sample will detect amphetamines as individuals will not always admit to drug use. Particular attention needs to be given to young people who have a psychosis of sudden onset with no evidence of the usual prodromal symptoms.

Psychotic phenomena such as delusions and hallucinations may be present in **severe (psychotic) depression** and in **mania**, thus causing diagnostic confusion. Schizophrenia should not be diagnosed if psychotic and affective symptoms are present simultaneously unless it is clear that the symptoms of schizophrenia occurred before the affective symptoms. A manic episode can be differentiated according to the presence of elevated mood and the absence of a gradual accumulation of residual symptoms. In addition, psychotic experiences in the affective disorders are usually consistent with the underlying mood (e.g., delusions that one does not exist in depression and delusions related to self-importance in mania). (See also Chapter 3: Affective Disorders).

RELATED DISORDERS

Following are a number of diagnostic categories which may be confused with schizophrenia.

Schizoaffective disorder is diagnosed when schizophrenic and affective symptoms (depressive or manic) are both prominent in the same episode of illness, usually simultaneously, but at least within a few days of each other. A diagnosis of schizophrenia alone is not appropriate here (even though criteria for schizophrenia are met) since the diagnosis of schizophrenia would not give a *complete* picture of the disorder. (See Schizoaffective Disorder in Section 5.5).

Acute and transient psychotic disorder is the appropriate diagnosis when psychotic symptoms are present for less than one month. The onset of symptoms is usually associated with acute psychological stress and occurs over a matter of days (one to two weeks at most), resolving within two to three weeks. (See Section 5.4).

Schizotypal personality disorder and other **personality disorders** need to be differentiated from schizophrenia. A schizotypal personality disorder should not be diagnosed if the criteria for schizophrenia are met. Schizotypal disorder is characterised by a chronic disturbance (at least two years duration) which includes eccentric behaviour or appearance, odd beliefs and 'magical' thinking, cold and aloof affect, social withdrawal, and unusual speech (e.g., vague, digressive, or impoverished). Although transient psychotic symptoms may be present, these symptoms usually disappear within hours or days.

Schizophrenia may be confused with **persistent delusional disorder** in which a single delusion or set of related delusions is the only, or most conspicuous, characteristic. The content may be persecutory, hypochondriacal, grandiose, or may concern litigation or jealousy. Hallucinations are *not* typical symptoms of persistent delusional disorder, and there are usually no disturbances in affect, speech, or behaviour.

5.1.4 EPIDEMIOLOGY

Approximately one in 100 individuals will develop schizophrenia. Most of these individuals will present as young adults between the ages of 15 and 25, however, schizophrenia may develop at any age. Men and women from all cultures are equally likely to develop schizophrenia although there is a tendency for men to develop the disorder slightly earlier in their lives than women.

5.1.5 COURSE

Schizophrenia can be divided into three major phases: the prodromal state, an active phase, and a residual phase.

During the *prodromal state* it is not uncommon for a number of non-specific symptoms to be present in the weeks or months preceding the first onset of typical symptoms of schizophrenia, particularly in young people. These symptoms include:

- A general loss of interest
- Avoidance of social interactions
- Avoidance of work or study (e.g., dropping out of school, college or university)
- Being irritable and oversensitive
- Odd beliefs (e.g., superstitiousness)
- Odd behaviour (e.g., talking to self in public)

These changes will often be incapacitating for the individual and distressing for the family. Friends or relatives may describe the individual as "no longer the same person". The length of the prodromal phase is extremely variable and prognosis is less favourable when the prodromal phase has had a lengthy course.

During the *active phase* of the illness, psychotic symptoms such as delusions, odd behaviour and hallucinations are prominent and are often accompanied by strong affect such as distress, anxiety, depression, and fear. If untreated, the active phase may resolve spontaneously or may continue indefinitely. With appropriate treatment (primarily medication) the active phase is usually able to be brought under control. It is during the active phase that most individuals present for treatment, whether it is their first presentation or an exacerbation of their symptoms.

The active phase of the illness is usually followed by a *residual phase*. The residual phase is similar to the prodromal phase although during the residual phase blunted affect and impairment in role functioning are more common. While psychotic symptoms may persist into the residual phase, the psychotic symptoms are less likely to be accompanied by such strong affect as experienced during the active phase. There is great variation in the severity of the residual phase from one person to the next. Some individuals will function extremely well while others may be considerably more impaired.

The most common course of the disorder generally involves numerous active phases of illness with residual phases of impairment between episodes. The extent of residual impairment often increases between episodes during the initial years of the disorder although may possibly become less severe during the later phases of the illness.

5.1.6 PROGNOSIS

While full remissions from schizophrenia do occur, most people have at least some residual symptoms of varying severity. Generally, 25% of people experience a complete recovery, 40% experience recurrent episodes of psychosis with some degree of social disability and periods of unemployment, while 35% may remain chronically disabled.

Research suggests that, rather than being a deteriorating illness, schizophrenia may in fact be viewed as a progressively ameliorating illness in which the frequency of episodes declines over time. Once again, however, the severity and outcome of the disorder varies greatly from one individual to the next.

As yet there is no accurate method for predicting who will or will not recover from this illness. Individual prognosis is never certain, however, some factors that are associated with a good prognosis include:

- Abrupt onset
- An absence of premorbid disturbance
- Onset in mid-life
- Presence of acute and resolvable life stressors
- A family history of affective disturbance
- Presence of florid symptoms, confusion or perplexity during acute phase
- Appropriate early treatment and care
- A favourable, non-critical attitude from family members
- Absence of blunted or flat affect

5.2 SCHIZOPHRENIA: THE ACUTE EPISODE

5.2.1 MANAGEMENT OF AN ACUTE EPISODE

The acute or active phase of schizophrenia is when symptoms of psychosis such as delusions, hallucinations, and odd behaviour are most prominent. It is during this phase of the disorder that individuals are most likely to be brought to the attention of mental health workers. During the acute phase the individual's behaviour is likely to be at its most disruptive, leading family, friends or others to seek assistance on behalf of the individual. Sometimes the individual may realise that he or she is quite unwell and will voluntarily seek help. At other times, however, the individual may not see the need for intervention and will choose not to accept assistance from health professionals.

An acute episode of schizophrenia will always require medical assessment. The need for assessment will be *particularly* urgent if the individual is at high risk of self harm or harm to others. (Note however, that people who have schizophrenia are no more dangerous or violent than people who do *not* have schizophrenia).

The major components for the management of an acute episode, which are discussed on the following pages, are:

1. To maximise the safety of the individual and others.
2. To reduce symptoms of psychosis and disturbed behaviour.
3. To build a therapeutic relationship with the individual and carers (see Chapter 1: Core Management Skills).
4. To develop a management plan to aid recovery from the acute episode.

5.2.2 MAXIMISING SAFETY

Regardless of the manner in which the individual is brought to the attention of health workers, the first step in the management of an acute episode is to ensure the safety of all involved.

ASSESS THE RISK OF SELF HARM

An acute episode of psychosis, especially the first episode, is terrifying and confusing. Frequently this psychosis may lead to the development of suicidal ideas and behaviours. It has been estimated that about 10% of individuals with schizophrenia will commit suicide within five years of the onset of the disorder. Suicidal ideas are especially likely if the individual is hearing voices which are *commanding* self-harm or suicide. The strength of these thoughts and the individual's ability to act on them must be assessed. Additionally, other more general factors such as depression and disappointment may also contribute to the risk of suicide (see p. 374). The questions on the following page will assist with the assessment of self harm.

Questions for assessing the risk of self harm (positive responses indicate increased risk)

- Has the individual attempted suicide in the past?
- Do voices command the individual to harm himself or herself? (What exactly are the voices saying?)
- Is the individual unable to resist the commands at present?
- Is it likely that the individual will *continue* to be unable to resist the commands?
- Is the individual extremely depressed or expressing suicidal ideation?
- Was the individual recently diagnosed or recently discharged from hospital?
- Does the individual live alone or unsupervised?
- Is the individual also using illegal drugs?
- Does the individual have a plan of action?
- Does the individual have the skills or weapons to carry out this plan?
- Is there evidence of impulsive behaviour?

For more detailed information see Section 1.1.3: Suicide Assessment and Management in Volume 1.

ASSESS THE RISK OF HARM TO OTHERS

Acutely psychotic individuals, especially those who are paranoid, tend to believe that an individual, a group, or a bureaucratic body is persecuting them. The persecution is resented by the individual who sometimes makes the decision to take matters into his or her own hands so as to stop the perceived persecution. Sometimes the individual can become homicidal. The homicidal ideas may also occur if the individual hears hallucinatory voices which command him or her to harm others. The strength of such homicidal drives and the ability to act on these drives must be assessed. The following questions may assist with this assessment.

Questions for assessing the risk of harm to others (positive responses indicate increased risk)

- Does the individual blame a specific person or group for his or her problem?
- Does the individual believe the persecutor should be punished?
- Are hallucinatory voices responsible for the individual's desire to harm others? (What exactly are the voices saying?)
- Is the individual unable to resist the voices at present?
- Is it likely that the individual will continue to be unable to resist the voices?
- Has the individual reported an intent to act on these beliefs?
- Does the individual have a plan of action?
- Does the individual have the skills or weapons to carry out this plan? (e.g., combat training, firearms experience, access to a gun or knife, a past history of violence, etc.)
- Is there evidence of impulsive behaviour?

Assess the risk of *unintentional* harm to others

More infrequently, individuals who are acutely psychotic may be a danger to others who are under their care, such as children or other dependants. The nature of the danger is usually through neglect of physical or emotional needs. If the individual is in a position of caring for others, the individual's self-report of his or her ability to maintain appropriate care must be confirmed through others. If children are involved it may be necessary to contact the local child protection and family crisis service if there is any doubt about the children's well-being.

WHERE TO TREAT?

Psychotic individuals who pose a substantial risk of danger to themselves or others may need hospital care. However, if other less restrictive alternatives can adequately ensure the safety of all concerned, these alternatives are preferable and result in better outcome for the individual. In community mental health the development of extended hours teams, crisis teams, and other intensive treatment programmes have made less restrictive treatment options more viable. With co-operation, both the individual and the individual's support network can be provided with expert care in the home while the psychosis is brought under control with medication.

For situations where there is inadequate support and there is a high risk of self harm or harm to others, voluntary or involuntary hospital admission may be necessary. When assessing the adequacy of support you will need to consider first the attitudes and desires of the family and friends and then the following issues:

- Where does the individual live? (e.g., at home with family or friends, alone, supervised or unsupervised hostel or boarding home, homeless, nursing home).
- What support services are available? (e.g., 24-hour crisis teams, telephone counselling services, general practitioner, voluntary care workers like Meals-on-Wheels).
- How far will the individual be situated from medical and emergency services?
- Do the individual and carers have easy access to a telephone?

REDUCING SYMPTOMS AND DISTURBED BEHAVIOUR

Biological interventions

In acute episodes of schizophrenia, antipsychotic medication is an essential starting point for treatment since the first step is to speed recovery from the impairment of severe psychotic symptoms. Antipsychotic medication is generally an effective method for decreasing psychotic symptoms such as agitation, hallucinations, and delusions. With these psychotic symptoms reduced, other unpleasant symptoms and disturbed behaviour may cease to be as extreme (e.g., confusion, perplexity, withdrawal, suicidal or homicidal thoughts, and lack of concentration). A list of antipsychotic medications is given in Section 2.1.3.

It will be important for non-prescribing clinicians to be familiar with the medications used by individuals with schizophrenia. Non-prescribing clinicians may be required to administer prescribed drugs, monitor side effects, answer questions about medication, encourage adherence, and so forth.

Psychological interventions

The needs of individuals in the acute phase of illness will be determined by the severity of symptoms. Individuals with severe impairment who may be experiencing florid psychotic symptoms will generally require an environment characterised by:

- Low stimulation
- Low stress
- High levels of support

Support

The best context for the care of an acute episode is one of empathy and concern for the distress of the individual and his or her family. Of course it is also at this time that interaction with floridly psychotic individuals is extremely difficult.

Collusion with the individual's delusional system (humouring) is rarely appropriate. A better strategy is to empathise and feed in some reality as early as possible (e.g., *"I can understand how frightening this must be the way you see it. However, you're not well at the moment. I think you may be a little confused about things just now."*).

During the acute phase of the disorder, the individual and his or her family will have particular needs when the individual is being cared for in the community. Community clinicians have enormous potential to fulfil these needs through:

- The provision of reassurance and support for the family so as to help share some of the burden of responsibility of caring for an individual who is psychotic.
- Regular assessment (at least daily) of the needs of both the individual and his or her carers, and review of the carer's ability to manage the current crisis in that setting.
- Provision of regular contact with, and immediate access to, professional mental health resources, either through the key worker, crisis or extended hours teams, or primary care services (general practitioners). It is essential that carers be given written instructions outlining who they can contact (at any time of the day or night) in a range of emergency situations (e.g., threatened suicide, aggression, etc.).
- Assistance with ongoing problem solving for the individual and carers regarding strategies that best aid recovery from the episode.
- Provision of medical and psychological strategies for the best treatment of symptoms or other targeted problems.
- Regular consultation with members of the mental health team to review the current crisis and management plan.
- It is recommended that the management plan and the exact roles and responsibilities of the individual, carers, and clinicians be clearly defined and written down.

Education during an acute episode

While the main educational input is best conducted *after* recovery from an acute episode when the individual will be thinking more clearly, information will also be required *during* the acute episode. The aim of the education is to minimise anxiety and confusion, particularly among family members, and particularly if the current episode is the first episode of illness.

Information needs to be *simple, clear, concise* and *relevant*. The minimum information for families at this stage is contained in the following box. If the family requests more detailed information, an educational brochure is contained in Section 5.7.1 ("What is Schizophrenia?"). Also useful is advice for families about how to deal with their relative's difficult behaviour. See Section 5.7.2: Coping with Difficult Behaviour.

Agitation, strange beliefs, and strange behaviour are symptoms of the illness.

Appropriate medication usually reduces psychotic symptoms (i.e., delusions and hallucinations).

No-one is to blame for the illness - families DO NOT CAUSE schizophrenia.

Symptoms of recent onset which are preceded by a severe stressor usually resolve, but MAY recur at a later date.

It is important to minimise stress and stimulation during the acute episode.

Do not argue with strange beliefs. You may disagree with an individual's beliefs but you should not try to convince the individual that he or she is wrong.

Avoid confrontation or criticism unless necessary for preventing harmful or disruptive behaviour.

Education immediately after an acute episode

Individuals and their families will take some time to adjust following the experience of an acute episode of psychosis. Practical advice about how to cope during this time of high stress may take precedence over detailed factual information about schizophrenia and its treatment. A handout for families entitled "What You May Expect After an Acute Episode of Psychosis" is provided in Section 5.7.3. Further information about the disorder and available support groups may be obtained by contacting SANELINE – Telephone:0345 678 000, or contacting MIND – National Association for Mental Health, 22 Harley Street, London, W1N 2ED. Telephone: 0171 637 0741..

Further information about structuring and conducting education sessions can be found in Section 5.3.3.

Protecting social relationships

The importance of social support and of building and maintaining social relationships in the recovery and maintenance phases of schizophrenia is described in Section 5.3.7.

Patrick McGorry, an expert in the treatment of early onset psychosis, states that *"Psychotic illness puts social and professional relationships under great strain and many of these (relationships) are likely to be damaged or lost over time if preventive action is not taken."* Therefore, strategies may need to be implemented to protect the individual's social networks and to prevent the development of stigma from the wider community. There is no doubt that community development strategies including public education are needed in order to tackle the wider social issues of mental illness as seen by the community. However, in terms of direct practical assistance for individuals in the overtly psychotic, acute stage of the disorder, it may be sensible for them to avoid or minimise interactions with too many other people if it is likely that strange or disruptive behaviour may damage these relationships.

Reduction of disturbed behaviour

Specific behavioural strategies may be employed to reduce or eliminate disturbed or disruptive behaviours. The application of such programmes will require a detailed behavioural analysis and knowledge of behavioural concepts. Specialist consultation may be useful.

Social interventions

During an acute episode of schizophrenia, social stressors may emerge or existing stressors may worsen. These social stressors include: housing and financial difficulties; needing time off work; legal problems (including possible disputes over involuntary hospitalisation); inadequate childcare facilities; lack of support from family, friends or others; lack of availability of medical care (especially 24 hour care), and so on. The provision of practical assistance with these difficulties and structured problem solving for the individual and carers will be important. (See Chapter 1: Core Management Skills for information about these strategies). Social interventions will be extremely important for individuals who are being cared for in the community.

FIRST-EPISODE PSYCHOSIS

There is a growing body of evidence that early detection of psychosis followed by intensive and assertive intervention results in improved outcomes for the individual, their family and mental health services. The considerable delay (up to 1-2 years) between the onset of psychotic symptoms and contact with specialist mental health care is a cause for concern. This delay has been shown to be a strong predictor of later poor outcome. It is therefore important that schools or other educational facilities, primary health care professionals and community agencies in contact with young people, are assertive in starting the process of referral to specialist mental health services as soon as symptoms are evident, rather than taking a 'wait and see' approach.

It is also clear that the earliest symptoms of psychosis may be non-specific (e.g., vague perceptual abnormalities, mood and behaviour disturbances), so agencies dealing with young people should be encouraged to seek early referral even in the absence of typical psychotic symptoms. This is especially true in young people who may have additional risk factors for the development of psychosis, such as a family history of schizophrenia or significant drug abuse. Once individuals who are experiencing first-episode psychosis come into contact with mental health professionals, there are a number of special issues to keep in mind. These issues are outlined below:

Developing a collaborative relationship

The development of a collaborative team approach involving the client, his or her family and mental health professionals is the cornerstone of successful management of first-episode psychosis. As soon as possible, attempts should be made to establish a therapeutic alliance with a single responsible clinician who can co-ordinate the person's care, whether treatment is in hospital or community setting. This clinician can assist the client and family deal with the trauma and distress that is associated with first-episode psychosis.

The diagnosis of psychosis is a time of crisis when people feel vulnerable and unable to cope. It is also a time when people are more open to accepting assistance from mental health professionals and when lasting alliances are formed. Interventions at this point should be supportive and provide basic information about what is happening. More detailed education can be provided after the crisis has passed for then people are more able to take in information

Unfortunately some people will refuse engagement. In those situations it is important to continue to provide support to the person's family. This may provide a pathway to later engagement as well as preventing the breakdown of the person's family support systems.

Recognise the potential trauma of hospital admission

If hospital admission is necessary, the trauma produces additional feelings of confusion, depression, or even post-traumatic stress. This experience may be worse if the admission is made to a locked or 'intensive care' ward where the individual is in a closed environment with other highly disturbed people. Such involuntary admission has been shown to be associated with poor longer term outcome. Several studies have shown that even very severe psychoses can be successfully treated outside of hospital. Wherever possible the least restrictive treatment setting needs to be sought.

Assist with recovery and adaptation to the disorder

First-episode psychosis usually occurs at a critical developmental stage of life in terms of personality, social role, or educational or vocational achievement. It is also a stage where the family's hopes and dreams for their child are usually beginning to be realised. Specific counselling and practical assistance may be required in each of these areas. The Early Psychosis Prevention and Intervention Centre (EPPIC) have developed Cognitive Oriented Psychotherapy (COPE) which merges cognitive therapeutic strategies with the consideration of the developmental difficulties associated with first-episode psychosis. This involves a particular focus on the way in which the individual and family make sense of the experience of psychosis and integrates it into their view of themselves. A range of Cognitive Behavioural strategies are also used to deal with positive and negative symptoms associated with psychosis, for example help with realistic goal planning and with problem solving or skills training to enable the individual to achieve these goals.

Recognise the absence of a firm diagnosis

It is vital to recognise that diagnosis at this stage of illness is frequently unclear and unstable. Even illnesses that initially appear to fit one classic pattern (e.g., mania, schizophrenia) may evolve and change. Consequently, the educational programme and discussion about prognostic issues should stress the uncertainty of precise diagnosis and inability to be definite about the course or prognosis of the disorder at this early stage. It should always be stressed to the individual, and to the family, that complete recovery is probable.

5.3 SCHIZOPHRENIA: SPECIFIC INTERVENTIONS

5.3.1 ASSESSMENT

The aim of assessment is to:

> 1. Identify the main diagnosis and any other comorbid disorders or problems.
> 2. Highlight the areas that require intervention so that goals can be set and a management plan can be devised.
> 3. Identify a baseline against which improvement or deterioration can be measured.

Ideally, assessment will occur not only at the beginning of treatment but will be repeated at appropriate points *during* treatment and at the *conclusion* of treatment. In this way, progress can be measured and the management plan can be adapted accordingly. Some planned interventions may not bring about change and will need to be reviewed. Other interventions may be detrimental. For example, the individual may take on a new full-time job and may be unable to cope with the stress so soon after recovery. A new plan may be implemented which involves part-time or voluntary work. Alternatively, if interventions are successful, measuring the extent of success will allow new goals to be set and positive reinforcement to be provided.

WHAT TYPE OF ASSESSMENT IS NEEDED?

A psychiatric history and mental state examination (see Chapter 1: Core Management Skills) are standard components of assessment for all psychiatric disorders. This clinical history is especially important in people with schizophrenia because there may, in the acute case, be difficultly in completing more structured assessments. In addition, most individual will require assessment in the following areas:

1. Extent and severity of symptoms
2. Social and living skills
3. Overall level of functioning
4. Satisfaction with treatment
5. Assessment of medication side effects

Extent and severity of symptoms

The monitoring of symptoms is covered in "Symptom Monitoring" on page 332.

Social and living skills

A brief social and living skills checklist was developed for this textbook to help the clinician think about areas in which intervention may be required (see Section 5.7.4). This checklist is not a psychometrically valid assessment tool but simply a checklist of areas that need to be considered. Negative responses will require intervention of some kind.

Life Skills Profile

In terms of conducting assessment using psychometrically valid measuring tools, social skills deficits can also be assessed using the Life Skills Profile (LSP) which was developed by Rosen, Hadzi-Pavlovic & Parker for use among individuals with schizophrenia. The LSP contains 39 questions covering five domains (self-care; non-turbulence; social contact; communication; responsibility). This questionnaire can be filled out by the clinician, regular doctor, a family member, or a close friend or carer of the individual. High scores on each of the five domains indicate high functioning, and scores for each domain can be summed to give an overall rating of functioning.

The LSP allows the clinician to determine whether an intervention has resulted in an improvement in one *specific* area of functioning (e.g., self care) and to determine whether this improvement was associated with an increase or decrease in the *overall* level of functioning. Sometimes one area can be improved but another area may consequently deteriorate. Thus, an assessment tool like the LSP allows the clinician to make a more informed assessment of the usefulness of particular interventions.

Other assessment tools

- *The Health of the Nation Outcome Scales* (HoNOS) are a set of 12 scales to be completed by a trained mental health care clinician on the basis of all available information about the patient. All scales have a glossary with anchor points for the four point ratings which can be completed in a matter of minutes for a well known patient. The scales have satisfactory reliability when used with patients with whom the clinician is familiar. The scales are sensitive to change in clinical status and hence are suitable for the routine and repeated assessment of patients with severe mental illnesses. This form and scoring information are reproduced in Section 1.3.4.

- *Social Behaviour Schedule* (SBS) which covers areas such as: conversational skills; social mixing; hostility; and habits or manners. This schedule is not designed specifically for the assessment of schizophrenia hence some questions are not entirely relevant. The schedule is filled out by clinicians or other direct care staff. This schedule is probably a bit too long for routine use, however, it is not necessary to administer the entire schedule at once. Specific sections of the schedule may be used as required. The SBS can be obtained by writing to Dr Til Wykes, Psychologist, Department of Psychology, Institute of Psychiatry, De Crespigny Park, London, SE5 8AF.

- Clinicians who would like to assess social relationships and social networks are referred to: Jackson, H.J. & Edwards, J. (1992). Social networks and social support in schizophrenia: correlates and assessment. In Kavanagh, D.J. (Ed.) *Schizophrenia: An Overview and Practical Handbook*, 275-292. London: Chapman & Hall.

Overall level of functioning : Mental Health Inventory-5 (MHI-5)

The MHI-5 (short form), developed by Veit and Ware, is a 5 item scale that is used for measuring well-being and psychological distress. This short form of the scale was developed from a longer 38-item instrument. The MHI-5 and the MHI-38 correlate highly (0.95) indicating that there is a strong association or agreement between the short and the long versions (i.e., the short version, which is quicker to use, produces a similar result to the long version). The MHI, although developed for use in the general population, may also be used for individuals with schizophrenia. A copy of the MHI-5 and the scoring manual is provided in Section 5.7.5.

Satisfaction with treatment

The most straightforward way of assessing satisfaction with treatment is simply to ask the individual. A range of assessment instruments have been developed, however, these instruments have a number of problems associated with them. Asking the individual and his or her family about their level of satisfaction, responding constructively to their comments, and recording their comments in the file is a simple and useful assessment and management technique.

Assessment of medication side effects

For any individual who is on medication, the assessment of the presence and severity of side effects (e.g., sedation, extrapyramidal symptoms) will be important. Assessment is discussed in Chapter 2: Medication, together with strategies for managing a number of side effects.

SYMPTOM MONITORING

Why monitor symptoms?

Regular monitoring will allow the clinician and doctor to establish whether symptoms are *improving, stabilising*, or *worsening*. Assessment is important for answering the following questions:

- *What is the individual's usual level of symptoms?*
  The identification of a baseline level of symptoms will allow for the monitoring of improvement or worsening of symptoms over time. Establishing a baseline may be particularly important for individuals who have residual symptoms (as compared to those individuals who have no residual symptoms between episodes).

Case Study 1

When Joan was first seen in the hospital, she was totally preoccupied with messages from the TV, radio and computers. On the Brief Psychiatric Rating Scale she was rated a 7 on Unusual Thought Content, the highest possible rating. She also reported hallucinations several times a day, thereby warranting a 6 on that item. She was taking oral fluphenazine 20 mg daily. By hospital discharge, her hallucinations had remitted totally. When she came to the outpatient clinic for her visit two days after discharge from the hospital, Joan told her key worker that she still was getting messages but only from the radio. She did not think about them and they did not interfere with her functioning (this warrants a 4 on the Unusual Thought Content item of the Brief Psychiatric Rating Scale). After Joan had been seen for four weeks as an outpatient, the key worker was concerned about the persistence of Joan's delusions of reference about messages from the radio, even though they were at a low level of intensity. The findng of persisting delusional thinking was discussed with the clinic's psychiatrist, and a decision was reached to increase Joan's daily fluphenazine dosage to 30 mg. Six weeks later, another administration of the Brief Psychiatric Rating Scale revealed no change in Joan's ratings, however, her motor retardation had increased to a moderately severe level. With her agreement, she was switched to biweekly 20 mg IM fluphenazine decanoate to rule out non-adherence as a factor in her persisting symptomatology. When Joan came in for her third injection, she announced that she would not take her shot. She stated that the shots were painful and that she wanted pills. Review of the Brief Psychiatric Rating Scale ratings revealed no additional therapeutic impact from the increased dosage or from IM administration; indeed, the only change was an increase in motor retardation and akathisia, both likely side effects of the antipsychotic drug. On the basis of this re-evaluation, the key worker and the psychiatrist agreed to place Joan back on oral fluphenazine at the original discharge dosage. Two weeks later, Joan's unusual thoughts were no longer of delusional proportions, and her extrapyramidal side effects had begun to lessen. Her maintenance fluphenazine dose was further decreased to 10 mg daily with continued improvement in her thinking and functioning. The serial ratings using the Brief Psychiatric Rating Scale enabled Joan's psychiatrist to titrate her antipsychotic drug therapy to the lowest effective dose compatible with the least side effects.

From Lukoff, D. & Ventura, J. (1988). Psychiatric diagnosis. In Liberman, R.P., *Psychiatric Rehabilitation of Chronic Mental Patients*. Washington, D.C.: American Psychiatric Press, Inc. Reprinted with permission.

- *What is the most effective and lowest dosage medication needed?*
  The monitoring of symptoms and side effects can inform the doctor about the choice and dose of antipsychotic medication. Symptom monitoring allows the benefits of medication (reduction in symptoms) to be weighed against the risks and costs of medication (medication side effects). Case study 1, highlights how symptom monitoring can be useful for assessing medication requirements.

- *How have life changes affected symptoms?*
  As individuals recover from acute episodes of schizophrenia they can be encouraged to take on new tasks and activities. However, it will be important that such changes do not significantly increase stress levels and the subsequent risk of relapse. Monitoring changes in symptoms following significant life changes such as a new home or new job will be important for establishing whether or not the individual is coping with such changes (see case study 2 following). It will also be important to monitor early warning signs of relapse at this time and to instigate strategies to help the individual deal with stress should these signs be present. (See "Early warning signs" in Section 5.3.4)

- *What further strategies are needed?*
  A thorough knowledge of the symptoms experienced and the distress caused by these symptoms can provide important information regarding areas in which intervention may be required (e.g., strategies for control of residual psychotic symptoms; anxiety management; or improving sleep).

- *How effective are these strategies?*
  Symptom monitoring will also allow the effectiveness of various strategies to be evaluated. For example, the clinician may wish to assess whether or not strategies that specifically target symptoms are actually successful in reducing the experience of those symptoms. Alternatively, it may be desirable to determine whether other programmes, such as skills training, problem solving, or educational programmes affect the level of symptoms in a positive or negative manner.

Case Study 2

A male patient at an outpatient clinic requested that the social worker help him move from a small board-and-care facility where he had been living for the past two years to a board-and-care closer to his parents. The social worker arranged a transfer to a much larger facility in the neighbourhood where his parents lived. One month after the move, the social worker had a session with the patient and asked him how he was doing. He replied that he enjoyed being able to spend some evenings and weekends with his parents. If she had stopped the interview at that point, everything would have seemed fine. however, the social worker continued to ask questions from the Brief Psychiatric Rating Scale, a standardised rating scale. These questions uncovered a marked increase in anxiety, difficulty in sleeping, and the belief that others at the board-and-care were staring at him and talking about him. These prodromal symptoms concerned the social worker because they represented a definite exacerbation from the level of smptomatology present before the patient moved. Additional questioning revealed that the patient felt overwhelmed at the new larger placement and had not made any even casual friendships. However, he did not want to move further away from his parents. The social worker immediately scheduled an appointment that afternoon with his psychiatrist to determine if an increase in medication was warranted. With the patient's consent, the social worker notified the board-and-care manager and suggested that he pay some special attention to the patient. Then she contacted other board-and-care homes in the area to locate one that housed a smaller number of residents. Through the social worker's careful monitoring of the patient's symptomatology and her efforts to alter the stressful situation, a potential relapse was averted.

From Lukoff, D. & Ventura, J. (1988). Psychiatric diagnosis. In Liberman, R.P., *Psychiatric Rehabilitation of Chronic Mental* Patients. Washington, D.C.: American Psychiatric Press, Inc. Reprinted with permission.

How often do symptoms need to be formally monitored?

Symptom monitoring is ideally used as a routine part of the regular review process. The review date will vary from service to service depending on policy and procedure, however, every three months is usually considered sufficient for individuals whose symptoms are stable. Symptoms may need to be monitored more frequently under the following circumstances:

- During and following an acute episode or exacerbation of the illness.
- When establishing a baseline of symptoms against which change can be measured.
- Whenever changes to medication occur.
- Whenever significant life changes occur (e.g., change of job or housing, loss of a relationship).
- When evaluating specific interventions.
- Whenever early warning signs of relapse have been noted.

How can symptoms best be monitored?

Standardised rating scales are the best tools for monitoring symptoms because:
- Standardised scales are objective (i.e., the same questions are asked every time and scored the same way every time, thus reducing bias).
- These scales are reliable (i.e., the scales give similar ratings when used by different members of the team).
- They can pinpoint important information quickly and efficiently.
- They provide a permanent, easily understood record that can be kept in an individual's notes for all treating clinicians to see.

It is particularly useful to graph symptom severity over time so as to recognise how the symptoms are related to other events such as changes in medication, psychological strategies, or life events. Some useful ratings scales are listed below:

- The *Brief Psychiatric Rating Scale* (BPRS) is a widely used and easy to administer rating scale appropriate for symptom monitoring among individuals with schizophrenia. A copy of this scale and a manual outlining how to use the scale are included in Section 5.7.6.

- The *Symptom Checklist 90 Revised* (SCL-90R), is a list of 90 self-report questions relating solely to the individual's experience of specific physical symptoms. It is mainly used as an initial screening instrument but is also useful for measuring progress throughout treatment.

- For those wanting more specific and in-depth scales for assessing symptoms of schizophrenia, the *SAPS* (Schedule for the Assessment of Positive Symptoms) and the *SANS* (Schedule for the Assessment of Negative Symptoms) may be useful. Both scales, however, are probably not suitable for untrained raters since clinical judgement is required. These scales may be obtained by writing to Dr Andreasen, Department of Psychiatry, University of Iowa, Iowa City, IA, 52242.

5.3.2 MANAGEMENT PLAN

The experience of an acute psychotic episode with possible inpatient admission can be an extremely threatening and stressful event. It is not surprising that following the initial improvement of some of the more severe and incapacitating symptoms of the disorder the recovery process can be long and difficult. However, clinicians play an important role in facilitating this process of recovery by:

1. Developing a therapeutic relationship with the individual
2. Involving individuals and their carers in the management plan
3. Recognising and reinforcing the strengths of individuals and their families
4. Building upon effective strategies that individuals may use in the recovery process
5. Introducing specific strategies, information, and new means of coping

The process of recovery is influenced by multiple factors including medical, psychological, and social issues. The problems individuals face as a consequence of the disorder have likewise been differentiated into three factors by the World Health Organisation (WHO), namely: impairments; disabilities; and handicaps. 'Impairments' refers to problems at the symptom or disease level, 'disabilities' refers to the problems that these symptoms cause to the individual's level of functioning, and 'handicaps' refers to the effects of these disabilities on the individual's role in the environment.

Examples of this system of defining the range of consequences of a disorder are listed below.

IMPAIRMENTS (symptoms)	DISABILITIES (functioning)	HANDICAPS (environment)
Hallucinations	Poor concentration	Unemployment
Thought interference	Poor problem solving	Poor housing
Reduced drive	Inactivity	Lack of leisure activity
Agitation	Feelings of fear or inadequacy	Loss of social support

For example, an individual who experiences hallucinations (impairment) is likely to have poor concentration (disability) which may then lead to unemployment (handicap).

Consequently, the interventions that are used to help individuals with recovery from an episode and with continued maintenance of well-being need to be focused broadly on all three levels (i.e., impairment, disability and handicap). Examples of some useful interventions are outlined in the following table:

IMPAIRMENTS (symptoms)	DISABILITIES (functioning)	HANDICAPS (environment)
Antipsychotic medication	Structured problem solving	Work skills
Self control strategies for residual symptoms	Increasing effective coping responses	Building social relationships

In the previous example, treatment of the impairment (antipsychotic medication for the hallucinations) will improve concentration and then work skills can be developed to enhance employment prospects.

GENERAL MANAGEMENT PRINCIPLES

Outlined below are the main principles of care during recovery from an acute episode of psychosis.

Conduct regular and thorough assessment

An adequate assessment of premorbid functioning (i.e., before the episode) across the levels of impairment, disability and handicap is vital. The level of premorbid functioning will provide important information about the potential level of functioning that may be expected after the recovery period. It is unrealistic to anticipate a level of functioning during or after recovery which is higher than the premorbid level of functioning.

Secondly, regular assessment over this time period will allow interventions to be better targeted to the individual's needs and will also provide the necessary information required for an evaluation of outcome. (See Chapter 1 for a discussion of outcome measurement).

Specialist consultation may be helpful for the standardised assessment of psychotic and non-psychotic symptoms, and for the examination of behavioural and cognitive strengths and disabilities.

Encourage an active role in recovery

It will be important to encourage individuals who are recovering from an episode of psychosis to take an active role in their recovery. Ideally this role would be part of a collaborative relationship with health professionals and may involve the use of strategies such as: monitoring of early warning signs (Section 5.3.4); managing symptoms (Section 5.3.6), goal planning (Section 5.3.5), and adherence to treatment, structured problem solving, and communication skills training (see Chapter 1: Core Management Skills). Each person will have a different set of needs and will approach the recovery process with different attitudes, feelings, and motivations.

Provide encouragement, not pressure

As individuals recover from the acute or florid stage of the disorder they will gain more benefit from the range of psychological and social strategies that are available. However, it is important for individuals to be allowed to progress at their own pace, with consistent encouragement rather than a pressure to perform.

Build on strengths

The recovery period should build on the strengths and resources of the individual rather than focus exclusively on deficits in coping or functioning. In particular, it is useful to ask what has already been helpful for dealing with the huge stress associated with a psychotic episode. Many individuals possess important qualities such as courage, perseverance, resourcefulness, humour, spirituality, creative talents, as well as many practical skills. It will be useful to highlight, encourage, and praise these qualities.

Address concerns about integration into the community

If individuals have been hospitalised, the transition from hospital back to the community setting may cause much anxiety or embarrassment. Fears about leaving hospital (e.g., being stigmatised or unable to cope) may need to be specifically addressed. The individual and his or her family will require support and practical assistance. The development or consolidation of the therapeutic relationship, and the establishment of links with community support services and the individual's general practitioner, will be particularly important during any phases of hospital admission and will enhance the smooth transition back to the community.

Involvement of families or carers in management

At all stages of an individual's illness it is essential that his or her carers or relatives are involved in the management process. Hence, throughout this textbook, much reference will be made to the involvement of family or household members. The rationale for such involvement is based on the following factors:

1. All families have a right to information and most families *want* to be involved.
2. Most families when under stress will find it more difficult to cope. Families with a member who has schizophrenia may be particularly stressed. Perceived burden and difficulty with coping is well documented in such situations.

3. The family environment, particularly the expressed emotion of family members (i.e., critical or hostile remarks or emotional over-involvement) has a well established influence on the precipitation of relapse.
4. Family intervention programmes effectively improve relapse rates and social outcome among individuals with schizophrenia.

(N.B.: Family therapy and expressed emotion does not imply that families are responsible for the development of schizophrenia).

Family members could be encouraged to meet on a regular basis (every 1-2 weeks) to discuss important issues and the implementation of the strategies that are discussed in this textbook.

Further reading on family therapy for schizophrenia includes:

Barrowclough, C. & Tarrier, N. (1992). *Families of Schizophrenic Patients: Cognitive Behavioural Intervention.* London: Chapman Hall.

Falloon, I.R.H., Boyd, J.L. & McGill, C.W. (1984). *Family Care of Schizophrenia.* New York: Guildford Press.

BASIC STRUCTURE OF THE MANAGEMENT PLAN

There is no single management plan that will be suitable for every individual. Specific needs will differ from one individual to the next. However, it is important that the management of schizophrenia:

- Is planned following a thorough analysis of all relevant problems.
- Targets relevant symptoms (e.g., psychotic symptoms) and other psychosocial or medical problems (e.g., ensuring adequate social support, monitoring medication side effects).
- Is based upon specific strategies and theories, while remaining sufficiently flexible to suit each person's changing needs.
- Is understood by individuals and their families.
- Includes the family as much as is necessary or possible.
- Guarantees continuity of care over an extended period of time.
- Is evaluated regularly for positive and negative outcomes in the present and in the future.

An outline of a management plan is provided in the flowchart on the following pages.

Management plan flowchart

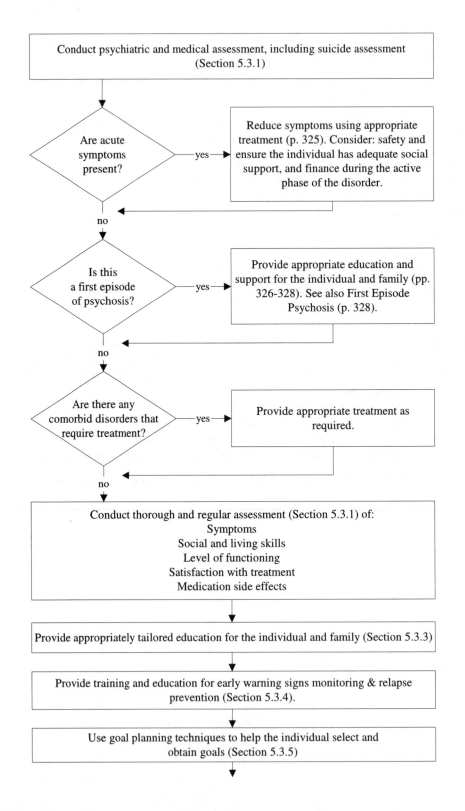

Management plan flowchart (continued)

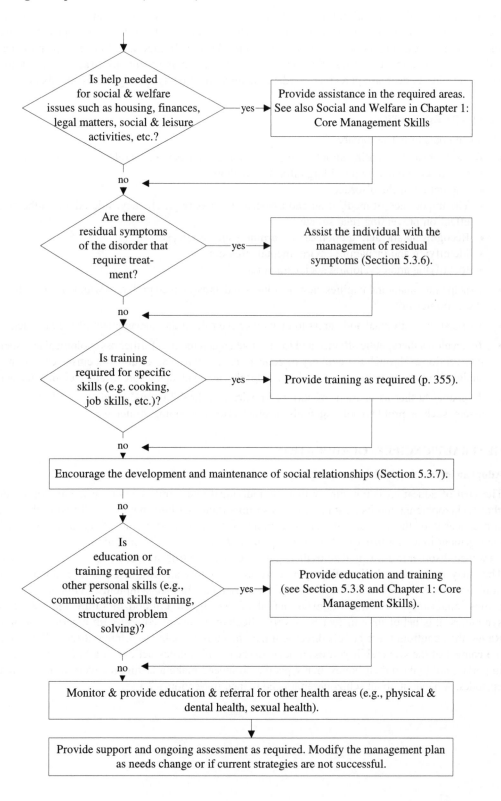

5.3.3 EDUCATION

There is no doubt that education for individuals and their families or carers is an extremely valuable feature of all good management programmes. While education alone does not appear to reduce relapse or produce changes in symptoms or behaviour, education is important for engaging individuals and families in treatment and for setting the scene for longer term interventions. In addition, education has been found to decrease perceived burden, distress, and anxiety among family members.

GOALS OF EDUCATION

The main goals of education are:

- To facilitate understanding about the disorder and its management as relevant to each individual and his or her family by providing information about:
  - The nature of the disorder
  - The importance of medication and associated issues (e.g., efficacy, side effects, adherence, effect on preventing relapse, etc.)
  - Recognising and acting upon early warning signs of relapse
  - Identifying and managing environmental stressors
  - Identifying and developing social supports

- To help individuals and families view the illness and its associated problems within a vulnerability-stress framework.

- To assist the individual and carers to take an active role in the management of the disorder.

- To develop a therapeutic alliance and to promote engagement in further psychological and social interventions. Through the delivery of education, clinicians can establish themselves as honest, straightforward, supportive persons, knowledgeable about mental disorders and their management.

- To enable further assessment of current impairment, disability, and handicap, and of goals or assets, such as problem solving skills or other effective coping strategies.

GENERAL PRINCIPLES OF EDUCATION

Adopt an interactive model of education

The goal of education is not simply that the individual and family acquire academic knowledge about schizophrenia and its treatment. It is also important that information is tailored to the needs and concerns of the participants so as to increase their understanding of the disorder and its management in a way that will *facilitate coping and reduce stress*. For example, individuals may view their disorder in a way that helps them gain a sense of control and mastery over their experience. They may for instance believe that symptoms are caused by stressful life events and that if they minimise stress in the future they can avoid experiencing further symptoms. While some health professionals may view this belief as denial of the high likelihood of future recurrences of symptoms, this belief may in fact be a very effective means of coping with a serious disorder. Rather than confront these beliefs directly, it may be more valuable to reframe these beliefs within the context of the vulnerability-stress model. Likewise, if families believe in a 'miracle cure', it is important not to dash their hopes; many people do indeed make a lasting recovery from psychotic episodes. A handout about schizophrenia is contained in Section 5.7.1.

Provide information about the vulnerability-stress model

Developing and implementing effective management plans for individuals with mental disorders requires an understanding of the factors that contribute to the cause, course, and outcome of the disorder. The vulnerability-stress model of schizophrenia is one such model that can aid understanding and guide intervention strategies. The vulnerability-stress model involves three groups of factors:

1. *Vulnerability factors* which predispose an individual to develop schizophrenia. For example, biological abnormalities are believed to be responsible for many of the impairments associated with schizophrenia.

2. *Environmental factors* which, in conjunction with vulnerability factors, influence the onset and course of symptoms. Stressors that may trigger episodes of schizophrenia include the accumulation of day-to-day hassles in an individual's life, or more specific life events such as the loss of a job or the break-up of a close relationship.

3. *Protective factors* which act as a buffer against the effects of stress and biochemical vulnerabilities or which minimise the severity of symptoms. The most important protective factor is medication. Other protective factors include: stress management; social support; and effective problem solving skills.

The vulnerability-stress model (adapted from Falloon) is illustrated in the following diagram.

Diagram of Vulnerability-Stress Model

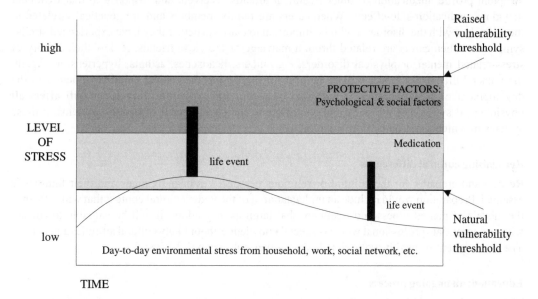

If environmental stress exceeds an individual's natural vulnerability threshold, symptoms of schizophrenia are likely to be experienced. However, protective factors such as medication or psychological and social factors raise the vulnerability threshold. This raised vulnerability threshold means that an individual has a greater capacity to cope with stress without experiencing a relapse of the symptoms of schizophrenia.

Adequate preparation for education sessions

Prior to the education sessions it will be important to have a thorough understanding of each family member's current knowledge, beliefs, attitudes, and expectations regarding the disorder and its treatment. Much of this information can be gained through the use of an Individual Family Member Interview such as the one developed by Ian Falloon. A copy of this interview form is included with permission in Section 5.7.7.

A detailed understanding of the way individuals and carers view the disorder and its treatment can help educational material be appropriately targeted. For example, family members may understand that delusions are symptoms of schizophrenia, but may interpret their relative's withdrawal as a reluctance to 'face up to reality' rather than as a consequence of delusional thinking. If families are unrealistic in their expectations of how much an individual is able to achieve (e.g., getting back to study or work, participating fully in family activities), then their expectations may require some adjustment. This adjustment is best made slowly. Goals may need to be presented as achievable in the long-term, and able to be broken down into smaller steps. (See also goal planning in Section 5.3.5.

Generally, individuals and their families will already have formulated some explanatory model of their experiences and of the disorder so as to help them cope. It will be important to assess existing beliefs and expectations before presenting a contradictory model that individuals may find difficult to accept.

On a more practical level, it is also important for clinicians to be fully informed about an individual's symptom profile, medication or other treatment already received, and response to that treatment including medication side-effects. When carers are family members and are genetically related to the individual with the disorder, it will be important to clarify whether they have experienced similar symptoms. When carers are related through marriage or are close friends, review their history of stress-related mental or physical disorders, e.g., ulcers, headaches, asthma, hypertension. Again, the vulnerability-stress model will be helpful for explaining the role of hereditary factors in the development of schizophrenia. It will also be useful for explaining that stress will affect all physiological systems of the body and contribute to the development of health problems in those systems in which a person is more vulnerable.

Recognising cultural differences

Respect and empathy for the cultural or religious perspectives of individuals and their families is essential. Preparation would include an understanding of the wider cultural context that will influence the models of mental illness and treatment that families may adopt. It will be valuable to consult with an appropriate professional who has special knowledge about likely cultural attitudes and beliefs. The employment of health professionals from other cultures will be helpful.

Education: an ongoing process

The main educational input usually takes place over a number of sessions during the early stages of recovery from an acute episode. The sessions are best arranged for a time when all family members are able to attend and contribute to the discussion, and are capable of processing the information provided. While such education sessions may well promote engagement and set the scene for further interventions, it is important that education be seen as a process that is carried out whenever necessary throughout all phases of the illness. Research has shown that short-term education programmes tend to produce short-term benefits.

Involving the individual in education

Involvement can be facilitated by an invitation to describe first hand experiences of the disorder and its treatment. In other words, the individual with the illness is regarded as an expert. However, you may need to gently encourage a reluctant individual to contribute to the session. Praise all efforts, no matter how small. You may provide prompts by describing the general features of an issue and inviting participants to describe their specific experiences and link these experiences with behaviours that others may find odd or criticise. For example, *"I have just described how hearing voices is one of the symptoms of this illness. Has anyone here experienced anything like that?"*, or, *"What happens when you hear those voices, Jane? Does keeping to yourself help you cope better with those voices?"*.

Pinpoint coping attempts

Education sessions provide a good opportunity to highlight the fact that many behaviours which may seem strange are really attempts to cope with symptoms of the disorder. Pinpointing successful coping attempts in this way may aid in developing effective strategies for coping with distressing symptoms of the disorder.

Special issues following first-episode psychosis

Of particular relevance to education is the recognition that diagnosis is frequently unclear and unstable in most first presentations. It may be useful to point out that a diagnosis cannot be made in the absence of longitudinal information. Educational material in the early stages is best framed in terms of 'a psychotic episode' rather than 'schizophrenia'. Schizophrenia will often have poor prognostic implications for the individual and his or her family, thus reducing hope and inhibiting positive coping attempts. This may often based on media portrayals, or on contact with health professionals who maintain a pessimistic view of schizophrenia not informed by the more recent evidence that full or partial recovery is probable. The individual's own experience of psychosis, the symptoms experienced, and the resultant behaviours are a better focus of education in the first episode than a focus on diagnostic labels.

It can be extremely difficult for family members to accept that no specific diagnosis can be given, as it would be in other illnesses they may have had experience with. Families are often searching for answers as part of a grieving process. They will often feel that mental health professionals are being evasive in not giving them definite answers, protecting them from 'bad news'. It is extremely important to be very clear and concise in answering questions and it may also assist to frame the fact that there is no definite diagnosis in positive terms (*"We expect that the person may recover from the episode"*).

After recovery some individuals will deny the presence of any residual problems or abnormalities that have followed their first episode. This denial may partly be due to difficulties in information processing which may make individuals unaware of the abnormal nature of their own experiences or behaviours. Alternatively, an individual and his or her family may not want to acknowledge the existence of the disorder. While this denial may be protective in the short term, the denial may ultimately compromise further contact with mental health professionals, and hence further preclude helpful interventions. Consequently, it will be all the more difficult for individuals and their families to cope if severe symptoms are indeed experienced in the future. Again, it is important to tailor information to specific needs and to use the sessions to foster further engagement. In the case of denial of illness, the following points may be useful:

1. Focus on problems as defined by the individual or family. For example, it may be helpful to focus on feelings (unmotivated or 'down') or behaviours (inactivity) rather than symptoms of a disorder.

2. Focus on recovery of function in terms of disability and handicap (e.g., offering help with meeting people or getting back into the workforce).
3. Focus on preventing the problem from recurring (e.g., *"Perhaps we can work together to prevent you from having to go to hospital again"*).

It may also be helpful to use video education materials. For example, the Early Psychosis Prevention and Intervention Centre (EPPIC) has produced an educational video about the early detection of psychosis, which also includes support materials such as information sheets explaining psychosis. This video (and others) is available from EPPIC in the *Early Psychosis Information Kit* (EPIK). More recently EPPIC has produced two Early Psychosis Manuals, *Psychoeducation in Early Psychosis* and *Working With Families in Early Psychosis*.

Information about medication

Providing clear information about the benefits and drawbacks of medication is an important component for encouraging adherence to medication. Chapter 2 contains information about medication and about where to obtain brochures for specific medications. Some important aspects to discuss with regard to medication are outlined below.

- Ensure the individual understands that regular medication will help control symptoms and minimise the risk of relapse.

- Explain (or ensure that the individual's doctor explains) the various medications that are available and the benefits and drawbacks of each.

- Discuss (or ensure the individual's doctor discusses) side effects that may be experienced so that the individual is able to discriminate between medication side effects and symptoms of the disorder. Many individuals wrongly attribute unpleasant side effects to the disorder and do not realise that some side effects can be reduced or eliminated by changing medications or doses. It will also be important to acknowledge the unpleasant nature of the side effects, and to encourage the individual to discuss troublesome side effects as they arise, rather than just ceasing medication without talking to anyone about this decision.

- Explain the importance of determining the optimal dose of medication (i.e., the dose at which maximal benefits are obtained with the least possible side effects). It will also be helpful to emphasise that a smaller maintenance dose is usually required once the acute phase of the disorder has passed.

- Wherever possible individuals are to be encouraged to take an active role in assessing the effect of medication on their level of symptoms. (See "Early warning signs of relapse" in Section 3.5.4 and "Symptom monitoring" in Section 5.3.1).

- Discuss (or ask the individual's doctor to discuss) all available alternatives to medication and the associated benefits and drawbacks of each alternative. It is important that the individual is provided with information about the various treatment options so that he or she can make an informed choice about whether or not to take medication, and if so, the type of medication that is preferred. Such decisions cannot realistically be made during the acute psychotic stages of illness. However, once the episode has stabilised, this information will be necessary for making decisions about maintenance treatment.

- Discuss strategies that might be useful (or have already been useful) for minimising side effects (see Chapter 2: Medication).

- Discuss strategies for improving adherence to medication (see Chapter 1: Core Management Skills).

- Ensure that the individual understands how to take his or her medication. It will also be helpful to ensure other household members are aware of the medication regimen.
- It will be important to elicit any fears or misconceptions that individuals or their families may hold about medication. For example, they may believe that the drugs are addictive, or that taking drugs is a sign of weakness.

Further interventions or resources

As stated earlier, the education sessions encourage engagement in further psychological or social strategies. These strategies can be discussed with the individual and family at the education sessions. Information about services (e.g., crisis teams, living skills centres), community resources (respite housing, dental health care) or local self-help groups can also be provided.

CONDUCTING EDUCATION SESSIONS

Preparation
- Review participants' understanding of the disorder and its treatment
- Read further material on relevant issues if necessary

Level of material
- Information is best kept simple, tailored to your audience, and consistent with the model of the disorder you wish to present (e.g., the vulnerability-stress model).
- Discuss issues in everyday language. Avoid technical detail, medical jargon, or complex explanations. Avoid debates or arguments about diagnosis, causes, alternative therapies, and so on.
- If you do not have an answer to an individual's question, say that you do not know but that you are prepared to consult experts and *get back to the individual*.

Handouts
- Prepare and review all handouts that you may be planning to use.
- Ensure that handouts are consistent with the information you want to impart and that they are written in a style that the participants will comprehend.
- Take care in recommending professional material such as books or journal articles. These materials are seldom written in a way that can be easily understood by the lay-person and may only serve to confuse the issues.

Structure of sessions

As far as possible try to make it explicit that the session is to be devoted to education. Try to maximise time spent discussing issues of specific relevance to those present.

Maintaining attention
- Present each point in no more than five minute segments.
- Encourage participants to describe their own experiences, voice their concerns, and ask questions.

- At the end of each segment, encourage participants to summarise the key points they have understood. For example, *"We have discussed the main side effects that people can experience with this medication. Would you tell me what you have understood these side effects to be. You can refer to your handout if you like."* Involve all participants by directing questions at them in turn throughout the session.
- Repeat important points throughout the session.

Controlling the emotional climate

- Present the information in a calm, neutral manner.
- Avoid taking sides or getting into arguments over issues.
- *Halt accusatory or hostile exchanges immediately.*

Between session tasks

- It is useful to ask participants to discuss the material covered in education sessions among themselves outside of these sessions, perhaps at a specially arranged family meeting.
- Encourage participants to read the handouts and to make a note of any questions or concerns that arise during the time between sessions.
- Encourage participants to seek out additional information, for example, from relevant resource organisations such as the SANELINE (phone: 0345 678 000).

Review of information at next session

- Begin the next session with a review of information discussed in the last session. Ask questions to assess understanding.
- Go over important issues that have not been clearly understood.

Suggested readings for the clinician

Barrowclough, C. & Tarrier, N. (1992). *Families of Schizophrenic Patients: Cognitive Behavioural Intervention.* London: Chapman & Hall.

Birchwood, M. & Tarrier, N. (1992). *Innovations in the Psychological Management of Schizophrenia: Assessment, Treatment and Services.* Chichester, West Sussex: John Wiley & Sons Ltd.

Falloon, I.R.H., Laporta, M., Fadden, G. & Graham-Hole, V. (1993). *Managing Stress in Families: Cognitive and Behavioural Strategies for Enhancing Coping Skills.* London: Routledge.

Kavanagh, D.J. (1992) (Ed.). *Schizophrenia: An Overview and Practical Handbook.* London: Chapman & Hall.

5.3.4 EARLY WARNING SIGNS OF RELAPSE

The most effective management of schizophrenia requires that episodes are treated at the earliest possible time. Early intervention will not only limit the severity of acute episodes but will also help prevent the development of disability and handicap. Additionally, there is evidence to suggest that further episodes of schizophrenia may be *prevented* if optimal management is provided when the earliest warning signs of relapse are detected.

Such relapse prevention strategies include:
- Engagement and education about early warning signs
- Identification of each individual's particular pattern of early warning signs

- Monitoring and early detection of early warning signs
- Planning optimal pharmacological and psychological strategies
- Implementing strategies immediately if early warning signs occur

The vulnerability-stress model suggests that any increase in stress will play a major role in the onset or exacerbation of symptoms of schizophrenia. The vulnerability-stress model is therefore important for understanding the process of relapse.

It has been argued that increased stress levels will lead to the onset of characteristic stress responses. These stress responses precede the development of schizophrenic symptoms. If stress levels remain high the individual may experience an exacerbation of symptoms.

An alternative hypothesis is that early cognitive-perceptual changes (which occur at the onset of relapse) cause an individual to feel anxious and perplexed. The anxiety and perplexity leads to increased stress, which in turn may accelerate the relapse process. In other words, the alternative hypothesis suggests that stress *itself* does not initiate the relapse process but merely facilitates the process once relapse has begun.

Further research will increase our understanding of the factors associated with relapse. However, the most important finding to date is that many individuals who experience recurrent episodes of schizophrenia exhibit characteristic changes in their mood or behaviour in the days or weeks prior to relapse. In other words, each individual usually has a characteristic set of behavioural or mood changes which can be identified as early warning signs of relapse. By identifying and acting on these early warning signs, relapse may be prevented or the severity minimised.

COMMON EARLY WARNING SIGNS

The most commonly reported early warning signs are listed below:

Mood changes
Depression and lack of interest or drive
Fear, anxiety and tension
Irritability, quick temperedness or aggression

Behavioural changes
Decreased appetite
Social withdrawal
Sleeping problems

Cognitive changes
Concentration or memory problems
Preoccupation with one or two things
Loss of control of mental processes

Early psychotic symptoms
Hearing voices
Talking in a nonsensical way
Suspiciousness or magical thinking
The feeling of being controlled

STEPS IN RELAPSE PREVENTION

1. Engagement and education

Effective relapse prevention and monitoring of early warning signs requires close co-operation among individuals with the disorder, family or carers, and health professionals. The following principles and strategies are therefore important:

- *A trusting and co-operative relationship* between the individual, carers, and professionals.
- *Continuing education* about the advantages of monitoring early warning signs, predicting relapse, and the early implementation of preventive strategies.
- Reinforcement of the notion of *shared responsibility* in detecting early warning signs and initiating the treatment plan. In other words, while it is important for health professionals to check early warning signs at each contact and to take an active role in the planned intervention strategies, the individual and family members can also take responsibility for the regular monitoring of signs.

2. Identification of early warning signs

The aim is to identify early warning signs of relapse that are:

- *Individualised*
- *Specific* and if possible defined in behavioural terms (e.g., 'stays in room for over half the day' is better than 'withdrawal')
- Described in terms that are *understandable* to the individual and his or her carers (e.g., 'unable to read without thoughts crowding into head' is better than 'difficulty concentrating')

In some cases, particularly if the course of the illness has been episodic and there has been a recent re-emergence of symptoms, early warning signs can be identified retrospectively. In other words, if an individual relapses, the individual and his or her carers can look back at the individual's behaviour prior to relapse in an attempt to identify any characteristic early warning signs that may have been present.

The following individuals may be helpful in identifying specific early warning signs:

- The individual with the disorder
- Family members, carers, or other household members
- The clinician, living skills staff, or other mental health professionals who regularly interact with the individual
- The individual's regular general practitioner/psychiatrist
- Any other person who is in regular contact with the individual

Questions for identifying early warning signs

For example, you might ask individuals and their carers:

- *Can you think back to when you (your relative) first began having difficulties with ... [symptom/s of illness].*
- *What exactly was going on at the time?*
- *What thoughts, feelings, or behaviours did you notice?*
- *Did you notice anything unusual or different before that time?*
- *How long did you (your relative) have these changes in behaviour before becoming unwell?*
- *What was the first thing you noticed that was different about your (your relative's) thoughts, feelings or behaviours?*
- *After first noticing ... [the symptoms], how long was it before the illness started?*

If the individual or family cannot identify any changes, you may want to prompt for common signs. For example:

- *Did you feel nervous, or on edge, or more cranky than usual?*
- *Did your relative begin to act suspiciously or say or do strange things?*
- *Did you (your relative) stop seeing friends and start spending long periods of time alone?*

Specific early warning signs should then be documented clearly for future reference. In addition, a clearly specified plan of action will help the individual or family understand what to do if the early warning signs occur again.

The form below, developed by Ian Falloon, is a useful way of documenting early warning signs. The immediate action plan is best developed in consultation with the individual, the family, any health professionals who might be involved (e.g., crisis team), or the individual's doctor if the plan involves any changes to medication. An example of a completed Early Warning Signs form is given below and a blank form for photocopying is provided in Section 5.7.8.

N.B.: It is important that the early warning signs document is modified if new information emerges with further episodes. It is likely that a list of early warning signs which has been compiled retrospectively will not be wholly accurate or complete.

EARLY WARNING SIGNS

Name: *Joy Allen*

I am at risk of developing episodes of: *Schizophrenia*

My early warning signs are:
1. *Reduction in my sleep of 2 hours for 3 nights in a row*
2. *Not able to read for more than 5 minutes at a time*
3. *Spending more than 4 hours alone in my room for 3 days running*

Whenever I have *any* of these signs I will respond by:
1. *Inform my doctor by phone immediately*

2. *Inform my therapist (James McDowell) by phone immediately*

3. *Pinpoint any stresses & arrange emergency problem solving discussion*

My doctor is: *Dr Fraser*   Phone: *5555 4682*

My home contact is: *Frank Allen*   Phone: *5555 6412*

If I have any concerns about my illness I will contact:
James McDowell   immediately.

Identifying early warning signs in the presence of residual symptoms or medication side effects

In some cases the identification of discrete early warning signs will be made difficult by the presence of residual symptoms or medication side effects which may obscure changes in thoughts, feelings, or behaviour. In such cases, subtle changes may be discriminated by establishing a baseline level of symptoms and regularly monitoring changes to this baseline.

One method has been developed by Birchwood and his colleagues and uses an Early Signs Scale. Each fortnight individuals plot their responses to the scale on a graph. In this way changes can be monitored on a regular basis. Additionally, this method assists with the identification of characteristic changes prior to exacerbation and also assists with the development of decision rules for early intervention. This method requires a relatively intensive and methodological approach. In addition, individuals with schizophrenia require training and rehearsal in the recognition of, and response to, complex and subtle changes in symptoms and behaviours. Therefore, in such cases, specialist consultation will be useful.

3. Monitoring of early warning signs

Once early warning signs of relapse have been identified it is important that the signs are *regularly* monitored. Some individuals may conceal changes in their behaviour if their insight declines or if the changes make them very fearful. Therefore it is important that the responsibility for regular monitoring is shared with family members and other health professionals.

Methods for enhancing the regular monitoring of early warning signs
- Health professionals can review the early warning signs at each contact.
- A copy of the Early Warning Signs form can be placed in a prominent position in the case records belonging to all appropriate health professionals including the family doctor's medical records and the community health centre case file. All health professionals who are in contact with the individual need to be fully aware of the signs to watch for and the plan which is to be implemented should these warning signs occur.
- A copy of the Early Warning Signs form can be given to family members who are encouraged to review signs at family meetings.
- The Early Warning Signs form could be summarised on a small card which the individual can carry around in his or her wallet at all times.

Routine assessment by the clinician will reinforce the importance of monitoring these signs and the importance of prompt action should these signs occur.

4. Early intervention strategies

Following the detection of early warning signs, strategies which aim to minimise the risk of an episode can be employed. These strategies include:

- *Increased contact and support for the individual and the family*
  The presence of signs which, in addition to being unpleasant in themselves are possibly indicative of an impending relapse, will place increased strain on individuals and their families. Regular contact and support is important for the purposes of: lessening anxiety; sharing the burden of responsibility; and ensuring quick access to services (specialist consultation, crisis or extended hours teams, inpatient care) should these services be required.

- *Regular symptom monitoring*
  Symptoms need to be monitored more closely when early warning signs are present.

- *Medication review*
  For individuals who are optimally managed with low targeted doses, an increase in medication may be the most important factor for preventing relapse. Psychiatric consultation and assessment will be required.

- *Implement stress management procedures*
  - Identify possible sources of stress which may have triggered early warning signs (especially life events such as moving, changing jobs, etc.)
  - Facilitate use of structured problem solving by the individual and family to resolve outstanding problems that may be increasing stress.
  - Reinforce those strategies that have been successful in the past for the management of stress or unpleasant symptoms.
  - Cease or decrease activities or interactions that increase stress levels.
  - Encourage the use of relaxation methods (and provide training in relaxation methods if needed).

- *Encourage discussion about the experience of early warning signs*
  It is important that individuals and their families do not catastrophise in response to the presence of early warning signs. It will be important to provide education informing the individual and family that, although the signs signify increased risk of relapse, the symptoms can often be controlled with appropriate assistance.

5.3.5 GOAL PLANNING

The following guidelines will help to structure and apply goal planning techniques more effectively. These guidelines have been written with family involvement in mind but can be equally useful when adapted for use with individuals alone.

ENGAGEMENT

The process of engagement begins early and relies on the development of a good therapeutic relationship (see Chapter 1: Core Management Skills). When assisting individuals to plan their goals, *offer rationales and suggestions* for behaviour change, such as trying to improve the individual's enjoyment of life, or increasing harmony within the household setting. In other words, reinforce and highlight the ways in which a particular behavioural change will be of benefit.

Encourage *discussion of pros and cons* of behaviour change. Let the individuals talk about their thoughts, fears, and hopes so that you know what they want and can provide reassurance or correct any misconceptions.

Make sure that everyone *understands* what has been said and agrees with the need for change.

IDENTIFYING PROBLEM AREAS AND NEEDS

This step incorporates step one of problem solving. Ask the individual and his or her family to *list problem areas* that need attention (see the box on the following page). For example, problem areas may include budgeting money, cooking meals, or other problems such as those outlined in the Social and Living Skills Checklist in Section 5.7.4. Combine input from all family members and help the individual and family decide collectively which goals are to be given priority.

Once the main problem areas have been gathered it is important to *rephrase the problems in positive terms and define the needs*. For example, the problem "spending too much time doing nothing" could be rephrased as "plan to spend more time doing activities", or, "doesn't have any time at home alone" could become "plan to spend more time at home alone". Defining the problems and needs in this way is the first step towards taking positive action to improve the situation.

IDENTIFYING STRENGTHS AND RESOURCES

On the same list, ask all participants to identify things that the individual does well, or any abilities, resources (e.g., names of people willing to help), or interests of the individual (see the box below). Include activities and skills that the individual used to do well before the onset of the illness (e.g., used to do a lot of aerobics and swimming), and simple skills that may otherwise be overlooked (e.g., having a driver's licence).

Problems
- Spends too much time doing nothing
- Rude to friends and visitors
- Doesn't take medication regularly
- Messy around the house
- Never left alone in house
- Parents nag too much
- Upset by voices

Strengths/resources
- Likes listening to music
- Enjoys movies
- Used to read a lot
- Belongs to the library
- Belongs to university sports club
- Can catch buses alone
- Paul, Jane and Tina happy to help in any way possible

Most important needs
- To spend more time doing enjoyable activities
- To take medication regularly
- To be able to spend time alone at home
- To be polite to friends and visitors

TIPS FOR SETTING SPECIFIC GOALS

Once needs have been defined, the next step in goal planning is to decide upon an appropriate goal. As outlined below, the goal needs to be realistic, achievable, specific, broken down into small steps, and 'owned'. The individual's strengths and resources listed earlier can be used as a means of helping the individual decide on appropriate goals. For example, if the identified need was to do more activities and the individual used to like swimming, perhaps the first goal could be to go swimming once a week.

Developing realistic and achievable goals

Sometimes people may set goals for themselves that are extremely high and practically impossible to achieve. Naturally, when they fail to achieve these goals they feel depressed and very disappointed. If they *do* achieve these goals they feel extremely delighted and proud, however, the chances of succeeding at these very high goals is quite low. Alternatively, sometimes people set no goals at all or set goals that are too easy. Achieving easy goals is not going to be very rewarding because success does not require much effort.

The best goals are those that are high enough to be motivating and rewarding yet are not so high that they are impossible to achieve. When the individual has decided on the exact goal to be set it is a good idea to monitor the individual's present level of functioning and to encourage him or her to set a goal which is at a slightly higher level - *a level which is attainable for that person*. (N.B.: It is important to be aware of the individual's premorbid level of functioning and the level of functioning prior to the most recent episode of illness. There is no point in the individual aiming for a goal that could not be achieved *before* becoming unwell!)

Once the set goal has been achieved, another slightly harder goal can be set. This form of stepwise goal setting may seem to be a slow process, however, it is important for the individual not to be rushed or placed in a situation in which failure is likely. Failure is demoralising and may lead to an increased likelihood of relapse or to feelings of hopelessness and apathy.

Developing specific goals

The goal that is set needs to be very specific so that everyone knows the exact nature of the goal and can identify when that goal has been achieved. For instance, setting the goal *I need to go out more often* is a bit too vague. It would be more useful for the individual to include information about where he or she intends to go, how often, and set a date by which time the goal is to be achieved. So, the individual may decide that by three weeks from now he or she plans to be able to go alone to visit a particular friend. Initially the individual may need an escort all the way or part of the way to the friend's house but could aim to make the trip alone within the three week period. After the first solo visit the individual can aim to visit his or her friend (or another friend) each week.

Break long-term goals down into smaller steps

While it is important to develop long-term goals so as to give direction for the future, long-term goals by themselves are quite unrewarding most of the time since it takes so long to reach the goal and receive the rewards or benefits. It is also difficult to maintain motivation when the goal does not have to be reached for a long period of time.

It is therefore a good idea to break the long-term goal into a series of short-term or stepwise goals. Help the individual decide which parts of the long-term goal can be begun *now*, and make these the specific short-term goals. For example, if an individual was aiming to move out of his parents' home and into a group home, he could make short-term goals such as: learning to do grocery shopping by himself by Christmas; learning how to cook five different meals by the end of February (one new meal per month); completing a 'course' in communications skills at the local mental health centre, and so on. These short-term goals provide rewards along the way and are evidence that the long-term goal is ultimately achievable.

'Owning' the goal

It is very easy for the family or health professional to set a goal for the individual. However, unless the individual agrees with the goal, it is unlikely that he or she will strive to achieve the goal. The individual needs to feel that the goal is important and that the goal is possible to achieve by the set date. Goal setting is much more effective if the individual 'owns' the goal and plays the central role in goal planning.

PUTTING GOAL PLANNING INTO PRACTICE

Once goals have been decided upon it may be useful to employ a structured problem solving approach for planning complicated goals (see Section 5.3.8). It will be important to determine the time frame and order of each phase of the goal. In some cases individuals will not have the skills necessary for achieving a specific step of a goal. In this instance it will be useful to provide individuals with skills training in specific areas. The main principles of skills training are outlined on page 355.

In the planning stage it is also important to consider issues such as:

- Who will remind the individual about the goal (if necessary)?
- The need for written instructions, perhaps stuck on the fridge for all participants to see.
- Planning what to do if something goes wrong.
- Deciding on possible rewards for when the goal is reached (e.g., a new CD, etc.).

REVIEWING PROGRESS

It is always important to monitor progress and to praise the individual for success or for attempts at achieving a goal.

Gaining reward from 'failure'

Sometimes people may not attain the goals they have set. Perhaps the failure is due to the goal being too advanced or difficult, or because success at the goal is not entirely in their hands. For example, the failure to move into a group home by a set date may be a result of a lack of available housing, a relapse of the illness, or too short a time frame for completion of the goal and relevant skills. It is important that the individual does not focus on the failures but instead focuses on what *has* been achieved or learned. During the course of the goal the individual may have learned to do the grocery shopping, cook three meals, and may have completed most of a communications skills course. These positive aspects need to be emphasised and praised. The individual could then be encouraged to set some new goals based on what has already been achieved.

Monitoring progress

There is no point setting goals unless the individual keeps track of whether or not the goals have been achieved. If a goal *has* been achieved, monitoring provides a chance for the individuals involved to receive praise and rewards from self or others. This praise and feedback will also help to maintain the new behaviours. If the goal has *not* been achieved, monitoring enables revision of goals and praise for partial success or for any *attempts* to achieve the goal. It may be useful to keep a progress chart of the goals that have been set and their completion dates. Encourage individuals to monitor their own progress daily, weekly, etc. depending on the time frame of the goal.

PROBLEMS ENCOUNTERED IN GOAL PLANNING

Some individuals and families have *difficulty with setting realistic goals*. This difficulty may be due to a reluctance to accept lower standards - standards which reinforce the fact that a family member is unwell. In these situations it is important to remind the participants that:

- Recovery may be slow and should not be rushed
- Excessive pressure may increase stress and lead to worsening of symptoms
- Goals need to be flexible
- More difficult goals can be set once previous goals have been achieved

Cultural expectations also need to be considered. These expectations include such things as: marriage; going into the family business; going to university, and so on. While it is important to respect and empathise with different cultural ideas and expectations, you can help the individual and family realise that their expectations may take longer than usual to achieve or in some cases may not be possible at all. Encourage everyone to work towards what is best for the individual, and what will be most effective for improving the individual's quality and enjoyment of life.

Repeated failure or high expectations may result in *feelings of helplessness, anxiety or pressure.* Ensure that the individual does not set goals which are too demanding. Remind everyone that if the goals are causing too much pressure or anxiety it is always possible to plan new goals which are less threatening. It is better to persevere at a slightly easier task than to give up on a harder task.

SPECIFIC SKILLS TRAINING

Each individual will have different needs and will progress at a different pace. Therefore, programmes need to be individualised for each person. The main principles of skills training are:

1. *Break tasks down into small steps*
   Individuals may become overwhelmed and confused if they are presented with too much information at the one time. The learning process is much easier if individuals are allowed to master one small task before being exposed to the next one. Start with the most simple task and work up to more difficult tasks later.

2. *Keep explanations as simple and clear as possible*
   Many individuals who require skills training may have difficulty concentrating or absorbing information. Use simple language and be specific and clear with your instructions. For example, instead of saying *"Put some tea-leaves into the pot"* say *"Put two spoonfuls of tea-leaves into the pot"*.

3. *Repeat instructions*
   You may need to repeat the instructions a number of times - in writing if necessary. Individuals may forget things quickly or may not understand your instructions the first time around.

4. *Link tasks in logical order*
   Once the individual has learned a few small tasks you may then begin to link the tasks together. Do not try to link too many tasks together too soon. Start with, say, two simple and associated tasks and link these together. At a later date you can begin to add extra tasks to the sequence. For example, if you are teaching an individual how to cook breakfast, filling the teapot could be linked with putting toast into the toaster.

5. *Individual versus group training*
   Depending on the individual's level of functioning, some tasks are better taught on a one-to-one basis (e.g., shopping). However, if the individual is functioning well, you may be able to provide group training by allocating different tasks to different members of the group. Other tasks such as catching a bus or buying stamps at the post office are more likely to be suitable for group training. Group training also has the advantage of enhancing the individual's social and communication skills.

The time frame for learning new skills varies enormously from one individual to the next. Some individuals master basic skills within a few weeks or months while others may take years to show any noticeable improvement.

In some cases it may be helpful to obtain consultation with someone who is specialised in the functional assessment and skill rehabilitation of individuals who experience residual effects of chronic mental illness.

Case example

Tony lives in a boarding house but is unhappy with his lack of privacy. He discusses this concern with his key worker and together they decide to work out how to solve this problem. They use the structured problem solving method and decide that the best solution is for Tony to work towards moving into a flat with his friend Rick who will have a spare room available in three months time. Therefore, Tony's long-term goal is to move in with Rick in three months time.

Next, Tony and his key worker consider Tony's strengths and weaknesses. Tony's strengths are that he is able to manage his personal needs such as medication and grooming, and that he has a small amount of money saved as well as a regular pension. However, Tony is unsure about his ability to carry out household tasks such as cooking and shopping.

Using the structured problem solving method again, Tony and his key worker work out how Tony can achieve his goal of moving in with Rick and sharing the household responsibilities. The solutions they come up with are:

1. Talk to Rick about the expenses involved in sharing the flat (e.g., rent, food, telephone, electricity, etc.).
2. Learn how to budget on the current income.
3. Learn some basic domestic skills such as cooking, shopping, and cleaning.

These three solutions are the short-term goals that will enable Tony to fulfil his long-term goal of moving in with Rick. Tony and his key worker then plan each step of these short-term goals by outlining a time frame for each and by specifying exactly how each goal is to be achieved. It is evident that the second and third goals require some skills training so Tony's key worker uses the principles of skills training to achieve these goals. Examples of two skills training exercises that he uses are outlined on the following page.

Tony achieves his goal of moving in with Rick but after a few months Tony tells his key worker that he is bored because Rick works long hours and he is home alone all day. Tony used to like swimming and decides that his new goal is to go down to the local pool every day. However, Tony has never been to this pool before and is a bit anxious about venturing out to a new place on his own. Tony and his key worker plan how Tony might break down his goal into smaller steps that are more easily achieved. The follow short-term goals are agreed upon:

1. Tony's key worker will accompany Tony to the pool. Together they will make a note of: where to pay; the location of the change rooms; pool hours; bus routes, etc. Neither of them will go for a swim on this occasion.
2. Tony and his key worker will make another visit to the pool and will go for a quick swim together. Tony will be 'in charge' of directions, paying, etc.
3. Tony will visit the pool alone and go for a swim.
4. Tony's key worker will reward Tony for achieving his goal by taking Tony out for a cappuccino.

Examples of two skills training exercises are given below

Example 1 - Cooking Breakfast (eggs, toast and tea)

These tasks can be learned separately and then linked together in logical order, step by step.

- Set the table with knives, forks, plates, salt and pepper, napkins.
- Organise the utensils needed for cooking: toaster, frying pan, egg flip, etc.
- Gather cooking ingredients: eggs, bread, butter, tea leaves, milk, sugar, etc.
- Boil water in jug
- Prepare the teapot by spooning some tea leaves into the pot
- Pour the boiling water into the pot
- Cook the toast
- Cook the egg
- Pour the tea and add sugar and/or milk if needed
- Serve the eggs, toast and tea and eat together
- Clear the dishes from the table and stack them on the sink
- Put away extras from table - pepper and salt, butter, etc.
- Prepare washing-up water
- Wash dishes
- Wipe dishes
- Put dishes away

Example 2 - Budgeting Money

- Ask the individual to make a list of essentials that must be budgeted for each fortnight.
- Check the individual's list for missing items such as toothpaste, bus fares, etc.
- Work out an estimated cost.

shopping	£ 30
bills	£ 20
fares	£ 5
miscellaneous	£ 10
TOTAL	£ 65

- Discuss how much money is left over and what the individual might want to do with that money (e.g., savings, cigarettes, hairdressers)

Suggested reading

For further information about skills training and rehabilitation, the following readings are suggested:

- Liberman, R.P. (1988). *Psychiatric Rehabilitation of Chronic Mental Patients.* Washington: American Psychiatric Press Inc.
- Wing, J.K. & Morris, B. (1981). *Handbook of Psychiatric Rehabilitation Practice.* Oxford: Oxford University Press.

5.3.6 MANAGING SYMPTOMS

Some individuals continue to experience residual symptoms as their acute episodes abate. Others may find that their symptoms are unresponsive to medication.

A number of naturalistic studies have looked at how individuals with schizophrenia attempt to control or master their symptoms. These studies suggest that a number of psychological strategies can add to the effect of medication by targeting both the 'positive' symptoms, such as delusions, hallucinations or bizarre behaviour, as well as the 'negative' symptoms, such as withdrawal or apathy, which are generally less responsive to antipsychotic medication.

PRINCIPLES OF SYMPTOM CONTROL STRATEGIES

Clinicians can play an important role in helping individuals manage their symptoms more effectively. However, a consistent and long-term approach is necessary if psychological interventions are to be effective; it will not suffice to just provide information and suggestions to these individuals because these individuals sometimes find new learning and new skill acquisition difficult.

Specialist consultation (e.g., with a clinical psychologist) will be useful in providing detailed behavioural analysis and advice, particularly if problems appear to be less than straightforward or if the psychological strategies presented here are unsuccessful. The following points outline a useful approach for helping individuals cope more effectively with their distressing symptoms.

1. Explain why various strategies may be helpful

Many individuals will be willing and able to contribute to the planning and implementation of specific strategies for managing their symptoms. Commitment and motivation will be needed for using the strategies and monitoring the effects. Therefore, explanation as to why the strategies might help and why it is important to use them in a regular and consistent manner will be vital for maintaining their use.

If individuals do not regard their symptoms such as delusions or hallucinations to be a problem then it may be helpful instead to focus on alleviating any distress that the symptoms may cause (e.g., anxiety, hostile reactions from others).

If, on the other hand, the individual appears apathetic and withdrawn, environmental factors (including the behaviour of relatives) could provide a more useful focus of intervention. For example, parents may complain that their son is withdrawn and not interested in participating in family activities. They may also complain that the more they try to get him involved, the less responsive the son becomes. An intervention that is directed at changing the behaviour of the parents (for example, encouraging the parents to replace nagging or hostile demands with low-key requests), may be more appropriate. Some of the simple behavioural strategies listed on pages 363-364 may be useful in these cases.

2. Identify symptoms that may be helped by intervention

Not all individuals readily talk about their symptoms. A detailed understanding of symptoms and the distress caused by these symptoms may be an important first step with this approach. Rating scales or other forms of assessment may be useful for eliciting troubling symptoms (see Symptom Monitoring on p. 332). Recognition that individuals' experiences are very real to them will also help to build rapport in this process.

One very important step in treatment is to ask what *the individual* would like to see changed. As mentioned in Section 5.3.5: Goal planning, the individual must *own* the goal if he or she is to strive to attain that particular goal.

It will be necessary to prioritise symptoms as it is advisable to tackle one symptom at a time. Symptoms are best prioritised according to ease of intervention (clearly specified symptom for which appropriate strategies are available) and level of distress (e.g., causing considerable disruption to functioning).

3. Conduct a problem analysis

It is important to understand the factors that influence the experience of symptoms. The clinician can assist the individual to use and build on appropriate coping methods that are already being used (e.g., talking to a friend) and help the individual decrease coping methods that are inappropriate (e.g., smoking dope).

The questioning format listed below, referred to as a problem or symptom analysis, can provide the necessary information about a symptom. Cognitive behaviour therapists routinely use this approach in their formulation of problems or difficulties and will therefore provide useful consultation for this process.

The answers to these questions can then be used to: .
- Help prioritise symptoms that are to be tackled
- Plan strategies to deal with symptoms
- Increase strategies that have been useful in the past
- Decrease behaviours that make the symptoms worse
- Change the external environment (e.g., increasing or decreasing stimulation) to reduce symptoms
- Change the individual (e.g., reduce anxiety) to reduce the symptoms
- Be prepared for any negative consequences that might result from reducing the symptoms

---

Problem analysis
- How often does the symptom occur?
- How much does this symptom interfere with your life and activities?
- How long have you been experiencing this symptom?
- What things happen before you experience the symptom that might trigger the symptom?
  (Can you tell when the symptom is going to occur?)
  (Who else is around? What are they doing?)
  (Where does the symptom start happening?)
- What happens as a result of experiencing this symptom? (How does this symptoms make you feel? What do you do?)
- What makes the symptom better?
- What makes the symptom worse?
- How have you tried to cope with the symptom up until now?
- What would you do or feel if you no longer had the symptom?

---

4. Problem solving

Effective symptom management strategies tend to be very individualised and therefore it is important that a range of techniques are considered. Structured problem solving (see Section 5.3.8) provides a very useful framework for encouraging individuals to pinpoint the problem, come up with a diversity of solutions, and put a plan into practice that has taken into account all practical constraints.

5. Real-life practice

The usefulness of symptom-control strategies is severely limited if these strategies are not put into practice in an individual's day-to-day life. Therefore it is very important that individuals are encouraged, prompted and rewarded for using the strategies, whenever and wherever they experience the symptom that has been targeted. This learning may take some time and the clinician needs to have patience, perseverance and some ingenuity for helping the individual in this procedure. Strategies will need to be adapted to the individual's circumstances and reminders can be arranged and used at appropriate moments. Current coping attempts may be built upon or adapted so as to reduce the occurrence of negative consequences (e.g., listening to music but using headphones so as to avoid disturbing others in the household).

6. Skills training

During the session many strategies may need to be taught to individuals through modelling, role play and rehearsal, especially those strategies that may be difficult to implement such as distraction or anxiety management techniques. For example, it will be useful to get the individual to simulate the symptom during the session and then practice the coping strategy. In addition, homework can require the individual to deliberately enter situations in which the symptom is likely to occur, with the aim being to practise the coping strategies in realistic situations. (See also Specific Skills Training on p. 355).

7. Monitor progress

To test the usefulness of these strategies it will be important to monitor the effect these strategies have on symptoms. It will be counterproductive to encourage individuals to continue to use techniques that do not work or that have some other aversive consequence. Ask the individual to keep a simple record of how successful the strategy has been for reducing the symptom or its associated distress and note any other consequences that might result. For example, you may ask the individual to use a rating system such as the one below:

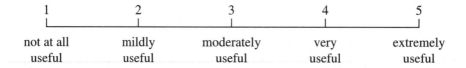

When strategies are found to be useful it is important to praise all efforts and encourage individuals to take credit for the control and mastery they have achieved over their symptoms.

STRATEGIES FOR SPECIFIC SYMPTOMS

There is now evidence that cognitive behaviour therapy is effective in improving adherence to medication regimes and in managing symptoms that have been resistant to medication.

Auditory hallucinations

Assisting patients in understanding that 'voices' are their own thoughts can reduce the distress caused by them and such 'insight' improves use of coping strategies and medication. This requires a structured approach:

- Discuss the nature of the voices with the patient.
- Establish that they sound like someone talking or shouting.

- Ask if they think that others hear their voices. If they are unsure, ask them to check this out with staff, caregivers or close friends. If they think others don't hear the voices, ask why they think such clear sounds are not heard by them.
- Discuss the reasons given:
  - if these seem delusional - use appropriate techniques as below
  - if the patient is uncertain, suggest alternative explanations, e.g., that, if someone is vulnerable, voices can occur in stressful circumstances such as in hostage situations or deprived of sleep or sensation, with drug intoxication or with illnesses such as schizophrenia or depression. They may also occur and relate to a particularly traumatic previous experience.

The aim is to assist the patient to understand that their voices originate within their own mind. Therefore have no more control over them than any other thoughts, and that things they themselves do, e.g., coping strategies, may help.

In a study that specifically examined the way individuals cope with auditory hallucinations, Falloon and Talbot found that patients who generally coped better with their disorder applied the same coping strategies as those who coped poorly. However, these individuals were able to apply the strategies more consistently, were better able to identify the stimuli associated with the onset of their symptoms, and had learned to avoid situations that often led to the experience of their symptoms. Specific strategies that may be useful for symptom reduction are listed below:

Changing the level of activity

- Relaxation
- Taking a walk
- Exercising
- Keeping busy through work
- Changing posture (e.g., sitting still, lying down)

Increased social activity

- Talking to others
- Phoning a friend

Distraction techniques

- Any activity, such as playing an instrument, reading, hobbies
- Watching television
- Listening to music
- Meditation, yoga, tai chi
- Snapping a rubber band around the wrist

Anxiety management (see also Anxiety Disorders in Chapter 4)

- Breathing control exercises to reduce hyperventilation (which can make symptoms worse)
- Relaxation or imagery techniques
- Gradual exposure to feared situations

Changing sensory input

- Using earplugs (available from chemists) in one or both ears
- Listening to music through a headset, etc.

Humming

The use of humming is based on a theory that subvocal activity (subtle movement of the larynx muscles) is causally related to the experience of auditory hallucinations. Research into the use of various procedures (such as humming) to create interference with this subvocal activity has shown mixed success. However, the use of quiet humming has reduced the frequency of auditory hallucinations in a number of individuals and therefore is worthy of consideration.

Delusions

There is growing evidence that, in certain cases, delusions that are unresponsive to medication may be amenable to psychological intervention.

Reality testing, or testing the validity of the individual's beliefs, may be useful. For example, individuals who believe that people look at them in a special way when they walk down the street might be encouraged to actually look at people to see if they take any notice of them each time they walk down the street. The clinician could accompany the individual on this exercise and later discuss both their observations, including possible reasons why some people might have looked.

Another strategy is the provision of hypothetical evidence that may be used to contradict delusional ideas. Consultation with or referral to professionals who have expertise in cognitive reframing strategies with delusional individuals is recommended.

There are also certain contraindications to the use of such reframing strategies with delusions. For example, the methods will be impossible to use among thought disordered individuals who have a high degree of conceptual disorganisation. It will also be very difficult and threatening for the patient to deal with delusions that produce high amounts of distress. The first step is therefore to understand how the delusion affects the individual, examining:
- The distress associated with the belief
- The degree of preoccupation with the belief
- The individual's reaction to evidence which is contradictory to delusions

In the absence of expert supervision these strategies are best reserved for overvalued ideas (i.e., ideas which are not held as strongly as delusions) that may interfere with an individual's life or activities, or the accomplishment of certain life goals, but which are not perceived as problematic by the individual. For example, an overvalued idea might involve the individual's reluctance to maintain a full-time job because he feels it may be possible that he is soon going to be selected to star in a major motion picture.

Where delusions do not seem to be responding to reality testing and reasoning, inference chaining has been shown in recent studies of 'treatment-resistant' symptoms to be a useful technique. On one level, this allows exploration of the practical consequences of delusional beliefs, e.g., *"What provides power to the transmitter that you are sure has been inserted into your brain? If it's electrical, how does power get to it. If it has batteries, wouldn't they have needed changing by now...etc"*. On another level, it may be possible to understand and then explore underlying beliefs (schemas), e.g., *"If people did believe that you were King David returned with the lost tribe of Israel, what would that mean to you? .... Why would that be important to you?"*

Thought disorder

Although thought disorder might be considered to be a contraindication to cognitive behaviour therapy, it simply requires different techniques. There are usually discernible themes that can be progressively explored through, sometimes repetitive and persistent, prompting and steering. These themes are usually emotionally pertinent and discussion leads back to relevant events that can then be explored.

UNHELPFUL COPING STRATEGIES

A number of authors have described strategies associated with a poor outcome. These strategies may have no effect on the symptoms, may worsen the symptoms, or may produce some other adverse consequence. For example, unhelpful coping strategies include:

- Angrily ordering the voices to "go away" or "keep quiet". This strategy is usually ineffective in reducing the distress associated with auditory hallucinations.
- Sleep is usually an ineffective coping method.
- Long term social avoidance resulting in withdrawal and isolation is not a useful strategy for symptom management.
- Alcohol or drug use. Individuals may be unaware that alcohol or drug use can actually worsen their symptoms and it may be helpful to instigate some simple experiments so that the individual can test this theory (e.g., assessing specific symptoms when drug or alcohol use is temporarily avoided or reduced). Further education about the problems associated with drug and alcohol use will also be important, particularly in regard to interactions with medication. If drug or alcohol abuse is pervasive and long-standing, a considered and structured approach to these problems will be required. A discussion of management issues associated with such dual diagnoses is provided in Section 5.3.10.
- Suicide. A drastic and irreversible coping strategy! But individuals may be particularly vulnerable if their auditory hallucinations are persistent, unpleasant, or of a threatening nature, or if hopelessness is a prominent feature of their depression. Furthermore, other factors that may be associated with depression and suicidal ideation include: the trauma of having a psychotic episode; negative experiences while in hospital; inappropriate treatment; not being listened to by the clinician; the feeling of not being in control of the situation; stigmatisation; or the fear of relapse or further hospital admission. It is crucial for clinicians to thoroughly assess suicide risk among individuals who seem depressed or who have made previous attempts. (See Section 1.1.3: Suicide Assessment and Management in Volume 1).

ADAPTIVE COPING ATTITUDES

Denial of illness and a 'combative' coping style (*"I can beat these symptoms"*) are not only normal coping responses to adversity (these responses are also found with individuals who discover that they have a life-threatening physical illness) but can be adaptive both in the short and long term. Just as people try to search for explanations of changes in their mood and general well-being, individuals with a psychotic illness will also try to seek the most plausible explanation for the rather more bizarre experiences of psychosis. Such explanations should be seen as part of the adjustment process rather than maladaptive attitudes to the disorder. As in the case of reactions to physical illness, the adjustment process can be seen to involve:

- A search for meaning: (*"Why me?" "It must have been those drugs I took at that party."*)
- An attempt to gain a sense of control and mastery over the experience: (*"If I take medication I won't get sick" "I can control my symptoms"*)
- A restoration of self-esteem through self-enhancing evaluations: (*"I'm actually coping much better than other people with this disorder"*).

BEHAVIOURAL STRATEGIES

Research indicates that behavioural strategies, such as rewards or punishment, may stop individuals from talking about their delusions and hallucinations, but will not prevent them from experiencing the anxiety, depression or anger that may result from being bombarded by voices, images or thoughts. Disregard for the experience of such symptoms may be harmful, as individuals will learn not to talk about their symptoms or their early warning signs of relapse. It is better to help individuals acquire skills to control and cope more effectively with their symptoms as outlined previously in this section.

Behavioural strategies are *not* useful for targeting distressing psychotic symptoms.

Dealing with unwanted behaviour or the absence of appropriate behaviour

The same approach for dealing with troublesome symptoms may also be applied to dealing with behavioural difficulties. Difficulties encountered may include unwanted behaviours (e.g., playing loud music at midnight, talking aloud to voices, shouting at family members) or the absence of appropriate behaviour (e.g., not getting out of bed, not getting involved in any activities).

The use of self-control strategies for unwanted behaviours has had mixed success as reported in the literature. Individuals who act upon their delusional beliefs in a manner that others define as 'deviant' or 'sick' are often aware that their behaviour is abnormal but find it difficult to inhibit these maladaptive coping techniques.

Self-control strategies require that individuals are able to:
1. Monitor and detect the unwanted behaviour.
2. Identify specific behaviours as abnormal and related to their illness.
3. Employ a procedure to counteract or reduce that behaviour.

These strategies require that individuals have the ability to monitor their own behaviour. If individuals are unable to appreciate that their behaviour may be related to their disorder, or if they deny the presence of symptoms, then self-control methods will fail. However, the literature does provide examples where individuals have been able to use self-control strategies with some success. For example, one individual who was experiencing delusions of reference was able to compare her own behaviour to that of others and could tell herself to "be responsible" when her behaviour became inappropriate. Or, another individual was able to get feedback from others about his behaviour when he was troubled by disorganised thinking. In the case of behavioural difficulties, the same approach is applied as for symptom management (see points 1 to 7 listed previously).

Managing behavioural problems
1. Explain how it may be helpful to use specific strategies to target behavioural difficulties
2. Target those behaviours that may be helped by the intervention (the principles of goal planning will be important here - see Section 5.3.5 for more detail)
3. Conduct a problem analysis
4. Use problem solving
5. Encourage real-life practice
6. Provide skills training for alternative behaviours
7. Monitor progress

Specific behavioural strategies will be familiar to clinicians who have been trained in these techniques (e.g., clinical psychologists) and consultation should be sought by those who are less familiar with these techniques.

Behavioural strategies include:

- The use of rewards to increase wanted behaviours (e.g., having breakfast cooked by a family member if the individual is up and dressed by 10 a.m., or, even better, intrinsic rewards such as thinking of the good things that certain behaviours can bring).

- Stopping rewards if unwanted behaviours are exhibited (e.g., friends or relatives cease giving the individual attention if the individual yells at them).

- Changing those things in the environment that may trigger unwanted behaviours (e.g., if withdrawn or inappropriate behaviours are associated with too many visitors then the number of visitors to the home at one time could be limited).

- Changing those things within the individual that may trigger unwanted behaviours (e.g., alcohol use, lack of sleep, or excessive tiredness may trigger aggressive behaviour).

- Use prompts as reminders for new skills (e.g., pin a note to the bedroom door as a reminder to shower before leaving the house; get family members to provide non-nagging reminders).

5.3.7 BUILDING SOCIAL RELATIONSHIPS

Social relationships are important factors in the recovery from episodes of psychosis. Individuals with large social networks tend to have fewer psychotic exacerbations and hospitalisations than those with smaller social networks, presumably because a larger social network is more likely to fulfil social needs, thus resulting in lower levels of stress.

Clinicians need to consider their own role, as well as the roles of others (such as family members and friends), in the assistance of recovery. The establishment of a supportive and ongoing psychotherapeutic relationship will be essential for helping an individual cope with the experience and consequences of a psychotic episode.

The aspects of social relationships which are most helpful for recovery vary from one individual to another, and from one phase of the illness to the next. However the following aspects of social relationships are particularly helpful for individuals who have experienced an acute episode of psychosis.

ROLE OF SOCIAL RELATIONSHIPS IN THE RECOVERY FROM AN ACUTE EPISODE

Expressing emotions and receiving reassurance

Talking about and expressing emotions with close friends, and the reassurance that usually follows, will help to reduce the anxiety that can often occur after an episode (e.g., concerns about getting back to usual activities, fears about relapse, and concerns about being stigmatised because of a mental illness).

Reality testing

Interacting with others provides a means of reality testing. Other people's behaviours (e.g., facial expressions) or verbal feedback from social interactions provide useful cues for distinguishing between reality and perceptual distortions or delusional thinking.

Practical feedback from others

Discussion of problems and practical feedback from others are important aspects of day-to-day problem solving, valuable for providing order in individuals' lives and for planning for the future.

Constancy in relationships

Constancy in relationships before and after the acute episode helps to remind individuals of their life and identity before the most recent episode, and that life can continue in much the same way as before.

Support from family

Family members are particularly important providers of social support at this stage of an individual's illness, providing 'unconditional love' as well as being the main source of material support (e.g., housing, finances, food, transportation, etc.).

BUILDING ON SOCIAL NETWORKS IN LONG-TERM MANAGEMENT

Once individuals have recovered from the acute episode they can focus on getting on with their lives. Life changes will inevitably bring increased stress and individuals may become more vulnerable to exacerbation of their symptoms or a recurrence or relapse of the disorder. Consequently, good social networks will be important at this time and the following aspects may become more apparent:

- Sharing, and providing support to others, increases self esteem and makes relationships generally more satisfying.
- *Motivation or encouragement* from others to achieve social or work goals is valuable.
- Other people are important for assisting with *symptom monitoring* (p. 332) or *early warning signs of relapse* (see Section 5.3.4), both of which can provide individuals with greater control over their disorder.

5.3.8 OTHER USEFUL PERSONAL SKILLS

STRUCTURED PROBLEM SOLVING

As described in the vulnerability-stress model (p. 341), high levels of stress will make an individual with schizophrenia more vulnerable to a worsening or re-emergence of symptoms. Effective problem solving will reduce, minimise, and help control stress and anxiety in daily living, thus providing the individual with a 'buffer' against relapse.

While structured problem solving is useful for handling the stress associated with daily living, problem solving may also be a helpful strategy for dealing with problems relating to schizophrenia itself. For example, structured problem solving may be used for finding better ways of coping with specific symptoms or medication side effects, for increasing adherence with treatment, improving living skills, rebuilding social networks, or for achieving personal goals (e.g., increasing leisure activities or returning to work).

There are rarely perfect or ideal solutions to problems, however, the structured problem solving approach aims to identify the most effective plans of action. The problem solving process includes:

- Defining problems or goals in an everyday manner
- Encouraging individuals to seek a wide range of ideas
- Defining solutions in terms of current strengths
- Careful consideration of the practical constraints that are involved in successfully applying a solution

One of the main aims of teaching structured problem solving to individuals or families is to assist people to incorporate the principles of efficient problem solving and goal achievement into their everyday lives. The aim is NOT for the clinician to solve everyone's problems for them but to give people skills so that they can effectively overcome problems and achieve goals for themselves. *Self-management* is a key goal, with the clinician adopting the role of a teacher or guide.

Further information about the steps involved in teaching structured problem solving is provided in Chapter 1: Core Management Skills.

COMMUNICATION SKILLS TRAINING

The aim of communication skills training is to help the individual and family express their thoughts and feelings in a productive way. When a member of the family is psychotic, or is recovering from an episode of psychosis, communication patterns within the family may become less productive due to high levels of stress, or else existing difficulties with communication may become more apparent. For example, family members may feel too irritable or may be too busy to express positive feelings about each other, or their negative feelings may be expressed bluntly during moments of frustration. Furthermore, the individual with the disorder may find it difficult to concentrate and may become confused if conversation or communication is complex or involves lengthy sentences.

Further information about facilitating effective communication is provided in Chapter 1.

5.3.9 PHYSICAL HEALTH

There is an increased incidence of physical disorder among people with chronic mental illness. Poverty and a failure to access mainstream medical services contribute to the increased incidence of physical illness.

It is important that individuals are encouraged to look after their physical health. Education and group discussions can highlight the importance of maintaining good health and nutrition. Health screening and prophylaxis of serious illness is recommended (e.g., pap smears, hepatitis shots). Regular exercise will help keep individuals fit and may have the added benefit of improving depressed mood and anxiety.

Regular check-ups can be organised with local general medical practitioners, dentists, and other relevant health professionals. The individual may find it helpful to use a calendar and fill in reminder notices showing when the next check-up is due. The clinician, family, and friends may help the individual by giving reminders and by assisting the individual to make and keep appointments. However, the individual will ideally be the one who takes responsibility for his or her own physical health.

The following check-ups may be particularly important:
- Regular examination of medication side effects, especially for signs of tardive dyskinesia which may be irreversible. (See Chapter 2: Medication for a discussion of the assessment of tardive dyskinesia and other side effects). Individuals are to be encouraged to monitor their own side effects on a regular basis.
- Dental care for tooth decay, gum disease, or other dental problems (see "Dental Care").
- Podiatry for injured or painful feet caused by poor footwear or absence of shoes.
- Pelvic examinations (pap smears) to detect early cervical changes or sexually transmitted diseases.
- Breast screening
- Prostate and testicular checks
- Blood tests for HIV if the individual uses intravenous drugs or engages in unsafe sex (see also Section 1.1.14: Sexual Health).

- Screening for skin cancers since some antipsychotic medication increases sensitivity to sunlight
- Diabetes
- Diet and nutrition
- Optometry

DENTAL CARE

Specific dental patterns have emerged among individuals with chronic schizophrenia. While these individuals are brushing their teeth and dentures quite well, there is still an obvious rapid increase in dental decay, especially root surface decay as compared with decay of the tooth crown. There is also an increase in chronic gum disease with increasing age. There are a number of factors related to mental illness that contribute to these patterns of dental disease.

Medication

Medication is the major cause of dental problems, particularly following long-term use. Nearly all drugs prescribed for treatment of mental illness (especially antipsychotics, antidepressants and lithium) cause side effects. The two side effects with particular implications for dental health are xerostomia (dry mouth) and tardive dyskinesia.

Xerostomia

Normally, saliva will buffer sugars and wash food and plaque from tooth and gum surfaces. If there is little or no saliva, sugars and plaque stay around the teeth and gums. As a result there is a much increased level of decay and gum disease. Problems associated with xerostomia include:

- Poor taste sensation
- Speech problems
- Soreness and burning of the mouth
- Dry, cracked lips (with frequent cold sores)
- Problems wearing dentures as there is little suction and the lining of the mouth is thin and easily damaged (thus ulcerating easily)
- Increased susceptibility to infections such as: Candida (thrush); Angular Chelitis (at corners of mouth); Denture Sore Mouth (fiery red mucosa under denture bearing surfaces); Acute Thrush (white removable layer, especially on tongue)

Tardive dyskinesia

Tardive dyskinesia is a movement disorder resulting from the prolonged use of antipsychotic medication. Due to the involuntary movements of tongue and facial muscles, dentures (especially lower dentures) do not sit well in the mouth. Unless medication side effects are closely monitored, tardive dyskinesia may develop to a damaging and irreversible extent thus causing life-long problems with speech and the wearing of dentures. Information about the assessment of tardive dyskinesia is provided in Chapter 2: Medication.

Dietary habits

Dietary habits often involve the frequent consumption of lollies, chewing gum and sugary soft drinks (Coca-Cola). Many individuals state that this is often to alleviate their dry mouth.

Smoking

Smoking will stain teeth and dentures and may alter taste sensations.

Lifestyle situations

The individual's lifestyle may not encourage regular dental care. Access to dentists may be difficult and thus individuals may only attend for treatment when in pain. Generally, hospitalised individuals and those living in supportive environments (e.g., with families) tend to have better dental care (and thus fewer dental problems) than those living in hostels or boarding houses.

---

5 tips for preventing dental problems

1. Educate the individual about diet: encourage sugar-free soft drinks, chewing gum and sweets, and decrease frequency of sugar consumption in between meals.
2. Encourage increased water consumption to help lubricate the mouth or use of an artificial saliva (Salube or Glandosane).
3. Encourage individuals to clean their teeth or dentures regularly.
4. Carefully monitor medication side effects (especially side effects such as tardive dyskinesia which may be prevented).
5. Encourage or assist the individual to organise regular dental checkups.

Regular dental check-ups

The specific dental patterns associated with chronic schizophrenia make it even more important that people with schizophrenia should have regular six monthly dental checks from an NHS dentist as part of their specific coverplan, and that dental treatment should promptly be instigated if needed.

5.3.10 COMORBIDITY AND OTHER SPECIAL POPULATIONS

Comorbid diagnoses and problems can sometimes complicate the management of schizophrenia. Where treatment exists the over-riding principle is to treat the comorbid problem, especially if the problem appears to have arisen independently of schizophrenia. For example, substance abuse, depression, and anxiety disorders can be directly targeted. Specific issues relevant to the management of these problems in individuals with schizophrenia are addressed in the following sections.

In some cases the experience of depression, anxiety, or the use of drugs or alcohol as coping strategies, may be secondary to the experience of schizophrenia. Here it may be equally effective to address the primary factors that have been identified during assessment (e.g., frightening psychotic symptoms, or lack of social activities).

The second class of comorbid problems with implications for management are those problems that are long-standing and not easily amenable to treatment (e.g., developmental disability and difficult personality traits). Developmental disability is discussed in Chapter 1 and the management of difficult personality traits is discussed in Chapter 11. Additionally, there are a number of other populations which may require specialised knowledge or treatment including: children with schizophrenia; parenthood and pregnancy; and schizophrenia in older populations.

SUBSTANCE ABUSE

Over 30% of individuals with schizophrenia abuse substances such as alcohol and street drugs and a large proportion smoke marijuana and cigarettes. There is suggestion that some psychoactive substances may facilitate the development of schizophrenia or other mental illnesses, although there is no clear evidence available. At the least, substance abuse tends to contribute to exacerbation of acute symptoms of schizophrenia, regardless of adherence to antipsychotic medication. Substance abusers are more likely to be rehospitalised and are more likely to display poor self care, disruptive behaviour, and non-adherence to treatment. However, although substance abuse has such negative consequences, many individuals can learn to manage this problem.

Despite the fact that many individuals are in need of specialised care and treatment for substance abuse problems, current programmes tend to be inadequate for their needs. Individuals with schizophrenia (or other serious psychiatric disorders) are often excluded from treatment at drug and alcohol agencies since the staff at these agencies are not trained to cope with mental illness. Similarly, many community mental health centres feel inadequate about dealing with the intricacies of substance abuse. Consequently, individuals with schizophrenia *and* a comorbid substance abuse problem can be shunted between agencies and frequently 'fall through the cracks'.

The present trend in treatment for these individuals is towards integration of services. Clinicians are being encouraged to take responsibility for the treatment of the individual's substance abuse problem as well as caring for all of the individual's other needs. These integrated services are more holistic in that the substance abuse is not seen as the only problem but rather as one problem which may affect the individual's life.

Ideally clinicians will be trained to deal with substance abuse problems, however, this training is generally not adequately provided at present. Some community teams are fortunate enough to have one or more members who have training and experience in drug and alcohol counselling, however, many teams do not have such a specifically skilled member. The following theory and practical advice highlights some useful strategies for altering substance abuse problems.

Treatment of substance abuse

Goal setting: abstinence or harm minimisation?

Most drug and alcohol programmes have abstinence as their goal of treatment. However, for some individuals who have schizophrenia *as well as* a substance abuse problem, abstinence may be too demanding a goal for which to strive. These individuals may perceive few positive aspects to their lives and may have little motivation to become abstinent. According to the harm minimisation model, perhaps for these individuals the goal of treatment should not be abstinence but reduction or minimisation of the harm caused by the substance abuse. Harm minimisation may include such things as: controlled drinking; recreational (rather than constant) drug use; or ensuring adequate nutrition, housing, and clothing. While the clinician is not expected to condone the use of drugs, and is advised to maintain an *abstinence-directed* programme, abstinence does not necessarily have to be the ultimate goal. Whether the goal is best defined as abstinence or harm minimisation depends on the individual concerned (e.g., his or her level of functioning; degree of substance abuse; motivation to achieve abstinence; extent of support from carers and friends). A flexible management approach will be required.

Reasons for substance abuse

In order to treat the substance abuse it is important to understand *why* the individual is engaging in this kind of behaviour. Perhaps the individual is experiencing particular problems (e.g., boredom, unpleasant medication side effects) which are contributing to substance abuse. Some possible reasons for substance abuse are listed below:

- To change or elevate mood, especially if the individual is depressed or frustrated
- To reduce anxiety
- To increase confidence in social situations
- Because of peer group pressure

- Because of low self-esteem
- For avoidance or escape from unpleasant life problems
- As a means of self-medication to overcome unpleasant side effects of medication (e.g., drowsiness, dystonia) or to minimise unpleasant symptoms of illness (e.g., loss of emotion, interest and energy)
- To aid creativity
- To help with sleep
- For the purpose of experimentation
- For attention or as a form of rebellion
- To reduce pain (physical or emotional)
- Demoralisation through lack of appropriate support
- To assume the identity of a drunk or a drug addict, both of which tend to carry less social stigma than that of a mentally ill person
- Dependence

By identifying *why* the individual is abusing substances it may be possible to help the individual change aspects of his or her life so that substance abuse ceases to become so necessary or 'appealing'.

Is hospital admission required?

Hospital admission may be required if the individual is aiming for abstinence and is heavily addicted to a substance. Careful supervision may be needed in this situation. Antipsychotic medication makes it more likely that an individual may experience seizures during the detoxification process. Additionally, depression is common in the weeks following withdrawal, and the risk of suicide is thus increased.

If a person *does* need to be admitted to hospital for the withdrawal process, it may also be possible to use this opportunity to adjust the dose of antipsychotic medication so as to achieve an optimal dose. Many individuals with schizophrenia may be over-medicated and consequently feel 'drugged' (a side effect which is exacerbated by the use of alcohol). Other individuals may be under-medicated so they use alcohol or other substances to drown the voices or other unpleasant symptoms associated with schizophrenia. Adjustment of medication may help to alleviate some of these problems.

If the individual is hospitalised, ongoing support and reassurance will be needed. Preparations need to be made for the individual's return to the community, with attention given to ensuring that the individual has adequate social supports and that his or her environment is modified in such a way so as to minimise the possibility of relapse (e.g., not returning to a drug-abusing peer group or household).

The four phases of treatment

The four steps in treatment are: engagement; persuasion; active treatment; and relapse prevention. These steps are outlined below.

Phase 1: Engagement

Before the individual can learn to manage his or her substance abuse problem, he or she must first be attracted to the treatment programme. This attraction may be facilitated by providing the individual with a range of useful and non-threatening services (e.g., assistance with housing, food and clothing; health care; provision of legal advice or referral; social and vocational opportunities).

The engagement process is also the time during which a relationship is established between the clinician and the individual. If the individual learns to trust and like the clinician, and believes that the clinician is acting in his or her best interests, the individual may become more interested in the notion of behavioural change.

During the engagement phase it is important that the clinician does not make strong demands on the individual to stop or reduce drug taking behaviours. The engagement phase needs to be alluring and non-threatening. It is acceptable for the clinician to indicate his or her disapproval of excessive alcohol intake and drugs (not for moral reasons but because the alcohol and drugs make the individual's illness worse), however, at this stage the clinician is advised not to push the individual to change his or her behaviour. The engagement phase may take a long time to develop to the point where phase two can be implemented.

Phase 2: Persuasion

The aim here is to help the individual realise that he or she has a drug problem and to encourage the individual to do something about this problem. Unfortunately, denial of the problem is a very strong defence mechanism and some individuals with schizophrenia may find it difficult to assess and alter their beliefs. Thought disorder, suspiciousness, and depression may all influence the individual's ability to adopt a new and more objective viewpoint. The persuasion phase of the programme can be very challenging for the clinician. The following guidelines may be useful for persuading the individual to accept help.

Express concern for the individual's well-being. The clinician (who will have gained the individual's trust by this stage) is in a position to express genuine concern for the individual's well-being. It may be useful to start with gentle persuasion such as: *"I'm not really happy about you drinking so much because the alcohol makes your schizophrenia worse. It probably makes you feel sleepy as well. I know you may feel OK as soon as you have a drink but you always end up feeling really lousy afterwards. Maybe you could stop drinking during the daytime. Then you'd feel less sleepy and you could buy a hot lunch with the money you save."*

Provide education. The role of education in substance abuse is very important. Individuals may not realise how the alcohol or drugs are affecting their illness. Educational material may be presented informally in passing conversation or may be discussed in greater detail over a cup of coffee at the drop-in centre or during a visit to the doctor. Information may include (in simple language):

- Discussion of the effects of alcohol or other drugs on the body and on schizophrenia.
- Feedback from objective tests (e.g., Breathalyser tests, urine tests, changes in weight, other physical examinations or tests).
- Highlighting other negative effects of the alcohol or other drugs (e.g., frequent trouble with the police; worsening of symptoms; social problems such as relationship breakups, loss of housing, lack of money).
- Discussion about the kinds of substances the individual is abusing and why the individual may be abusing these substances (positive and negative reasons – see p. 370).
- Discussion of what can be done to help the individual deal with problems in his or her life which may be making him or her turn to alcohol or other drugs.
- Indicating how the individual's life can be improved without drugs.
- Talking about what is involved in dealing with a substance abuse problem.
- Encouraging the individual to attend group meetings with other individuals who have both schizophrenia and a substance abuse problem who are also thinking about or addressing a substance abuse problem (if such meetings exist or can be arranged).

Capitalise on hospital admissions. If the individual is admitted to hospital because of serious psychotic symptoms, the individual is more likely to be abstinent (probably involuntarily) and is more likely to be in a position where he or she realises that things are not 'right' and help is needed.

Assess the individual's commitment to change. The individual may well be persuaded to accept treatment for substance abuse, however, if the individual is not very committed to the treatment programme, failure is likely. Failure leads to frustration and loss of self-esteem thus making it less likely that the individual will try again at a later date. If the individual readily accepts assistance it is important that he or she realises that support and respect will not be withdrawn if early relapses occur. Relapse is to be expected and should be viewed as a minor setback, not as a failure.

Discussion with others. Other individuals with schizophrenia who are coping well and have learned to manage a substance abuse problem may be a source of support and wise advise, perhaps making it easier for the individual to make the decision to accept help at this time.

Phase 3: Active treatment

Once the individual has decided that he or she wants to try giving up alcohol or other drugs, the active treatment phase may begin. A thorough assessment is required, followed by an individually tailored treatment plan, devised ideally in conjunction with the individual and his or her family, and other members of the treatment team.

Assessment. The individual will need an assessment of physical, mental, and social well-being. It is important to find out:
- What drugs or medications the individual is using.
- Why the individual is abusing substances (refer to list provided earlier).
- Whether there are any co-existing disorders that may be contributing to the substance abuse problem and which need to be treated (e.g., physical illnesses, anxiety, mood disorders).
- Specific cues that trigger cravings or drug use (e.g., going to the pub, living or associating with particular people).
- Which skills the individual will need to acquire (e.g., survival skills, communication skills, structured problem solving).

Encourage substitute behaviours or environments. If the substance abuse problem is to be eliminated, alternative behaviours or environments will have to be substituted for those that are presently associated with drug use. Consultation with a cognitive behavioural therapist (e.g., a clinical psychologist) may be helpful here. Substitute behaviours may include:
- Interacting with a different (non-drug abusing) peer group or, where possible, encouraging the individual's peer group to also accept help for substance abuse.
- Engaging in enjoyable recreational activities.
- Spending quality time with friends, family or others.
- Changing the environment or particular behaviours that have come to be associated with alcohol or other drugs (e.g., stop going to the pub, move house away from substance-abusing peers, take up a sport or activity).
- Ensuring that the individual is rewarded (by self, family or others) for abstinence or attempts at abstinence. Possible rewards may include such things as smiles; praise; presents; attention; time; outings; handshakes; special meals.
- Ensuring that the individual does not receive attention for drug-related behaviours.
- Encouraging the individual to talk to family, trusted friends or his or her clinician if day-to-day problems arise rather than turning immediately to drugs.

Skills training. The individual may require retraining of personal, vocational, or social skills such as structured problem solving, goal planning, communication skills, job skills, and assertiveness training. The acquisition of these skills will help to improve the individual's self-esteem and confidence. The individual may also expand his or her peer group and interests through attendance at these programmes. See relevant sections in this chapter and Chapter 1: Core Management Skills for more information.

Support. Throughout all stages of treatment, it is important for the clinician to act like a 'coach' and provide the individual with pep talks and support. Progress will occur one step at a time and cannot be rushed. Relapses are inevitable and, as mentioned previously, should be viewed as minor setbacks in a difficult task rather than as indicators of failure. Regular attention and praise for all efforts, no matter how small, will be important motivators. The clinician can enhance the individual's self-esteem and help the individual gain a sense of control over his or her life. Support and encouragement from the individual's family may also be extremely beneficial. Family education about both mental illness and substance abuse may be helpful.

Attend to other needs. The needs that were attended to during the engagement phase (e.g., housing, welfare) should continue to be cared for during the active treatment phase.

Monitoring. Symptoms and signs of relapse can be monitored, perhaps with the use of regular urine tests, Breathalyser tests, and so on. Satisfactory test results provide extra opportunity for feedback and praise of the individual's new and adaptive behaviours.

Phase 4:   Relapse prevention

Once the individual has been drug free for six months to a year, he or she graduates to the relapse prevention phase. During this phase the individual will require ongoing contact and support from mental health staff, family, and friends. Success needs to be highlighted and praised. Regular or sporadic monitoring may be used (with the individual's consent) to provide opportunities for positive feedback and to deter or identify relapse.

It will be useful for the individual and the clinician to discuss how the individual may feel and respond if relapse occurs, and what action could be taken in such a situation (e.g., reintroduction of useful coping strategies, education sessions, hospitalisation).

Other important tips

- Often, if individuals with schizophrenia are advised not to mix medication and other drugs, the individuals simply refrain from taking medication on days when they drink. It is important that individuals understand the importance of taking regular medication, as well as being informed about which drugs do and do not mix.
- Some individuals object to attending Alcoholics Anonymous because of the religious basis of the programme. Perhaps an alternative group exists in your area.
- Do not allow the individual to behave violently or aggressively, especially in group programmes. The individual should be removed from the programme, although not removed from care.

DEPRESSION AND SUICIDE

Up to 50% of individuals with schizophrenia will be clinically depressed within the first six months after the acute episode. The risk of suicide is particularly high during this period. Furthermore, for individuals with chronic schizophrenia, clinical depression may *continue* to be a problem during the course of the illness.

Overall, the rate of suicide among individuals with schizophrenia is approximately 10% in the first five years following diagnosis. Suicide is often related to depression but may occur in the absence of depression. Sometimes suicide is in direct response to hallucinations or delusions. Other factors that increase the risk of suicide include: the absence of negative symptoms, awareness and insight into one's deficit, and alcohol and drug abuse/dependence. Suicide assessment and management is discussed in Chapter 1: Core Management Skills.

The management of depression in schizophrenia follows the same basic principles as for any other depressed population. It is important to consider the possible effects of life stressors and biochemical disturbance. Some individuals with schizophrenia may have low self-confidence and low self-esteem, leading to the development of very real fears about future levels of functioning. Additionally, the fear of relapse of the acute phase of the illness may also contribute to the development of depressive symptoms. These reactive aspects of schizophrenia will require support and reassurance from the clinician and carers. Stresses need to be minimised using individual and family counselling (e.g., stress management, communication skills training, goal planning, early warning sign monitoring).

During the acute phase of the illness, antipsychotic drugs may need to be increased. If the individual's depressive symptoms do not respond to this increased medication, antidepressants may be required. Atypical depressive symptoms such as akinetic depression (absence of spontaneous movement), may respond to a *decrease* in antipsychotic medication. If depression is severe and the individual is suicidal, electroconvulsive therapy (ECT) may also be useful.

Management strategies for depression and associated problems (e.g., increasing activity levels, relaxation training for reducing anxiety) are covered in Chapter 3: Affective Disorders.

ANXIETY

As with depression, anxiety is a common experience associated with schizophrenia. Schizophrenia may result in a loss of self-confidence and self-esteem and a perceived loss of control over life, thus leading to anxiety. The fear associated with delusions and hallucinations may also contribute to anxiety, often leading to withdrawal and social isolation. Symptoms of anxiety may include breathlessness, sweating, palpitations, difficulty getting to sleep, and restlessness.

The best treatment for anxiety involves psychological therapies, however, drug treatments may also be useful in some situations. Treatment information is contained in Chapter 4.

CHILDREN WITH SCHIZOPHRENIA

Schizophrenia is known to occur in children and can be differentiated from childhood autism, in which the child shows impaired development including abnormal functioning in social interaction, communication, and repetition of behaviour. Generally, as the child becomes older, the symptoms become more like those displayed by an adult with schizophrenia.

Children with schizophrenia are managed in much the same way as adults with schizophrenia. Antipsychotic medication is used, as are family management programmes. However, rehabilitation programmes differ slightly since these programmes for children require a greater emphasis on academic education so as to maximise the child's future level of functioning.

The prognosis of childhood schizophrenia appears to be poor.

PARENTHOOD AND PREGNANCY

Parenthood

Many women and men with schizophrenia find parenthood and childbirth most fulfilling. However, fulfilling as pregnancy may be, many pregnant women and their partners may also find pregnancy and childbirth to be a somewhat stressful experience. Given the relationship between stress and relapse of schizophrenia, extra support from family and health professionals will be required at this time.

Pregnancy

It is not always easy to detect early pregnancy in women with schizophrenia because of the cessation of menstruation which frequently occurs as a result of antipsychotic medication. For women with schizophrenia, problems associated with pregnancy depend partly on whether or not the schizophrenia is adequately controlled. The greatest risk of relapse occurs during the last three months of pregnancy and the first two months after birth. Relapse may occur even if the woman is functioning well and has been adhering to medication prior to pregnancy.

If symptoms are not well controlled, early hospitalisation prior to delivery may be needed, postnatal follow-up will need to be more frequent, and medication may need to be prescribed or increased after delivery providing the mother does not breastfeed. Following birth, mother and child will need to be supervised carefully due to the possibility of relapse of the mother's schizophrenia which, among other things, may lead to neglect of the baby or other children. Assistance will be particularly important for single mothers and those who do not have an adequate support network.

Support following childbirth

If the symptoms of schizophrenia are not well controlled, or if other social or psychological difficulties are present (e.g., financial or housing difficulties, an inadequate supportive social network, substance abuse, personality problems), individuals may find it difficult to provide suitable care for their children. The clinician can play an extremely important role by organising appropriate support and opportunities for these individuals. For example, individuals could be helped to find employment, new housing can be located, social security options can be explored, social networking can be fostered, and so on.

Contraception and safe sex

Schizophrenia usually has its onset during adolescence, a time when individuals are learning about themselves, their bodies, and life in general. Sometimes, due to the social withdrawal and disturbance in thinking and behaviour that is characteristic of the prodromal phase of this disorder, individuals may have reduced interaction with their peers or family, and may miss out on learning about important issues such as contraception and safe sex. A lot of what we know about sex and sexuality is gained from interaction with our peers and family during our adolescent years.

It is important for all couples to have access to accurate information about contraception and safe sex if their knowledge in this area is lacking. This statement is true not only for couples in which one or both members has schizophrenia, but for all couples. There are a number of different methods of contraception. The decision about which method to use is up to the individual and his or her partner, and can be discussed with the couple's doctor or family planning advisor. (See also Section 1.1.14: Sexual Health).

Fear of passing the disorder to potential offspring

Some couples who are contemplating parenthood and have an illness like schizophrenia which appears to have a genetic component may express concern or fear about passing the disorder onto their offspring. Schizophrenia does appear to run in families so it is understandable that some couples may have concerns in this area. It will be important to reassure couples that schizophrenia is not inevitable, even if one or both parents has the disorder. A genetic vulnerability is only one factor that is associated with the development of this disorder. However, it will also be important that individuals understand that there *is* a risk that one or all children will develop the disorder. This risk is increased if both parents have schizophrenia. If individuals wish to obtain more detailed information about this issue of family planning they can be referred to their psychiatrist or general medical practitioner who can provide them with the information they desire, or refer them to someone else who can.

SCHIZOPHRENIA IN OLDER POPULATIONS

Although schizophrenia usually begins in adolescence or early adulthood, schizophrenia-like symptoms can also occur in older populations. Late-onset schizophrenia is characterised by: paranoia; a higher frequency in females than males; a higher prevalence of hearing loss and eye disease; schizoid or paranoid personality traits prior to the illness; a tendency towards chronic illness with a poor prognosis; and improvement of symptoms with antipsychotic medication.

If psychotic symptoms appear suddenly in later life it is necessary to examine all possible causes. Nutritional problems such as B12 and folic acid deficiency, endocrine problems such as myxoedema, iatrogenic syndromes induced by drugs, tumours, chronic infections, and Huntington's chorea can all present with schizophrenia-like symptoms and should therefore be identified and treated appropriately. Additionally, affective disorders and dementia may also involve a psychotic component.

Treatment for schizophrenia in the elderly involves the use of antipsychotic medication. It needs to be noted, however, that symptoms usually recur if medication is ceased. If individuals are paranoid, live alone, and have poor adherence to medication, low dose depot injections can be considered. Many elderly people are very sensitive to side-effects so great caution must be exercised and initial doses need to be low.

5.4 ACUTE AND TRANSIENT PSYCHOTIC DISORDER

5.4.1 DESCRIPTION

Acute and transient psychotic disorders are similar in appearance to acute episodes of schizophrenia. Hallucinations, delusions, and other 'positive' symptoms of schizophrenia are usually most prominent and there may be fluctuations in emotional state.

Listed below is a summary of the presenting complaints given by individuals or their families during initial or ongoing treatment.

Individuals may have problems with:
- Hearing voices when no-one is around
- Strange beliefs
- Confusion and perplexity
- Perceptual disturbances
- Agitation or emotional turmoil

Families may ask for help with the individual's:
- Changes in behaviour that cannot be explained (e.g., withdrawal, irritability, confusion, suspiciousness)

5.4.2 DIAGNOSIS

The main diagnostic feature is the acute onset of symptoms, where the individual progresses from a non-psychotic state to a clearly abnormal psychotic state within a period of two weeks. Onset is usually preceded by acute stress from life events although acute stress is not an essential requirement for diagnosis.

According to the World Health Organisation's (WHO) International Classification of Diseases (ICD)-10th Edition, the most important signs and symptoms include:

- **Hallucinations** (i.e., seeing, hearing, smelling, sensing, or tasting things that other people do not see, hear, smell, sense, or taste; for example, the person may hear voices which command him or her to behave in certain ways).
- **Delusions** (i.e., false beliefs that are firmly held despite objective and contradictory evidence, and despite the fact that other members of the culture do not share the same beliefs; for example, the person may believe that he or she is Jesus Christ, or that he or she is being followed, poisoned, or experimented upon).
- **Disordered thinking** resulting in incoherent or irrelevant speech.

For further details about diagnostic criteria, see ICD-10 or DSM-IV.

5.4.3 DIFFERENTIAL DIAGNOSIS

This diagnosis *should not be made* if:
- The criteria for schizophrenia are fulfilled.
- There are extensive depressive or manic symptoms.
- There is evidence of an organic cause such as with states of concussion, delirium, epilepsy, drug or alcohol intoxication or withdrawal.

5.4.4 EPIDEMIOLOGY

There is no adequate information about the prevalence or sex ratios of acute and transient psychotic disorders. As with schizophrenia, acute and transient psychotic disorders also seem most likely to occur during adolescence or early adulthood.

5.4.5 COURSE AND PROGNOSIS

By definition, the course of acute and transient psychotic disorders is brief. If symptoms endure for longer than one month, the diagnosis should be changed to something more appropriate (e.g., schizophrenia or delusional disorder).

Recovery is usually complete within two to three months, and often within a few days or weeks. Only rarely do persistent and disabling states develop. There is some indication that the more acute the onset, the better the prognosis. An onset of less than 48 hours is especially likely to have a promising and rapid outcome.

5.4.6 MANAGEMENT GUIDELINES

Acute and transient psychotic disorder is usually treated as for acute episodes of schizophrenia. The medical treatment focuses on:
- Ensuring the safety of the individual and others
- Antipsychotic medication

Psychosocial interventions include:
- Education
- Monitoring early warning signs of relapse
- Structured problem solving
- Stress management such as relaxation exercises (see Chapter 4: Anxiety Disorders)

These interventions are covered in detail in the Schizophrenia sections of this chapter.

5.5 SCHIZOAFFECTIVE DISORDER

5.5.1 DESCRIPTION

Schizoaffective disorder is characterised by the presence of affective (depressive or manic) symptoms and schizophrenic symptoms within the same, uninterrupted episode of illness.

Schizoaffective disorder (depressive type) is accompanied by depressive symptoms such as: psychomotor retardation; insomnia; loss of energy, appetite, or weight; reduction of normal interests; impairment of concentration; guilt; feelings of hopelessness; and suicidal thoughts. Within the same period of illness schizophrenic symptoms are also present such as: thought broadcast or interference; the belief of being controlled by alien forces; paranoid delusions of being plotted against or spied upon by someone else; hearing voices that talk about killing the individual or which make unpleasant remarks about the individual. The depressive type of schizoaffective disorder is usually less florid and alarming than the manic type.

In schizoaffective disorder (manic type), the disturbance of mood usually takes the form of elation, with increased self-esteem and grandiosity. Sometimes excitement and irritability may be more obvious and may be accompanied by aggressive behaviour and persecutory ideas. Also apparent is: an increase in energy and hyperactivity; impaired concentration; and a loss of normal social inhibition. The schizophrenic symptoms may include: delusions of grandeur, reference, or persecution; thought broadcast or insertion; the belief of being controlled by alien forces; hearing voices. The manic type of schizoaffective disorder is usually very florid with an acute onset and grossly disturbed behaviour. Individuals may have problems with:

- Hearing voices when no-one else is around
- Strange beliefs
- Disturbances with thinking or concentration

AND

- Depressed mood
- Depressive symptoms (retardation, insomnia, suicidal ideation, hopelessness)
  OR
- Elated or irritable mood
- Manic symptoms (increased energy, overactivity, decreased need for sleep, racing thoughts, loss of normal social inhibition)

Although the relationships between schizoaffective disorder and affective disorders, and between schizoaffective disorder and schizophrenia are uncertain, schizoaffective disorder is given a separate diagnostic category in ICD-10 because the occurrence of this syndrome is too common to be ignored.

5.5.2 DIAGNOSIS

Both affective and schizophrenic symptoms are prominent *within* the same episode of illness, and are present simultaneously at some point during that episode, or at least within a few days of each other. The DSM-IV criteria require that during the episode there have been delusions or hallucinations for at least two weeks *in the absence of prominent mood symptoms*, while ICD-10 does not require the absence of prominent mood symptoms within this two week period.

Within the same episode there must be:

- At least one, preferably two, symptoms of schizophrenia
- Prominent elevation of mood, or increased irritability or excitement (manic type) OR
  A prominent depressed mood with at least two characteristic depressive symptoms (depressive type).

5.5.3 DIFFERENTIAL DIAGNOSIS

The diagnosis of schizoaffective disorder *should not be made* if:

- The episode of illness meets criteria for either **schizophrenia**, or a **depressive or manic episode**. For example, exclude individuals who present with depressive symptoms following their recovery from an episode of schizophrenia, or in whom the affective disturbance is brief relative to the total duration of the psychotic episode.
- There is evidence of an **organic disturbance** such as epilepsy, or states of chronic alcohol intoxication or withdrawal.

5.5.4 EPIDEMIOLOGY

There is no detailed information regarding the prevalence of schizoaffective disorder, however, this disorder is believed to be less common than schizophrenia. Those affected are generally young people who have acute onsets, good premorbid functioning, a family history of affective disorder, and the presence of environmental precipitants. There is no information regarding sex ratio.

5.5.5 COURSE AND PROGNOSIS

Schizoaffective disorder usually has an acute onset, with symptoms that tend to remit spontaneously or in response to lithium. Prognosis may be variable. Some individuals may recovery completely with little residual deficit between attacks, especially if the affective symptoms are of the manic kind. Recovery from schizoaffective disorder, manic type is usually within a few weeks. Schizoaffective disorder, depressive type generally lasts longer and has a less favourable prognosis. Some individuals eventually develop residual schizophrenic symptoms.

5.5.6 MANAGEMENT GUIDELINES

Individuals with schizoaffective disorder experience the symptoms of both schizophrenia and affective disorder (manic and/or depressive). Hence these individuals will require the specific treatments for each disorder.

The decision about where to treat and other aspects of acute management encompass the same issues as for schizophrenia (see p. 328). Medical treatment usually always involves the use of antipsychotics. Antidepressants or electroconvulsive therapy may also be used for depressive mood and mood stabilising drugs are generally used for symptoms of mania. (See also Chapter 2: Medication).

An educational handout is contained in Section 5.7.9. For specific information about assessment techniques and management strategies, see Schizophrenia in this chapter and Affective Disorders in Chapter 3.

5.6 BIBLIOGRAPHY

American Psychiatric Association (1994). *Diagnostic and Statistical Manual of Mental Disorders (4th ed.)*. Washington: American Psychiatric Press.

Andreasen, N.S. (1983). *The scale for the assessment of negative symptoms (SANS)*. Iowa City: The University of Iowa.

Andreasen, N.S. (1984*). The scale for the assessment of positive symptoms (SAPS)*. Iowa City: The University of Iowa.

Anthony, W.A. & Liberman, R.P. (1986). The practice of psychiatric rehabilitation: historical, conceptual, and research base. *Schizophrenia Bulletin, 12*, 542-559.

Barrowclough, C. & Tarrier, N. (1992). *Families of Schizophrenic Patients: Cognitive Behavioural Intervention*. London: Chapman Hall.

Birchwood, M. (1992). Early intervention in schizophrenia: theoretical background and clinical strategies. *British Journal of Clinical Psychology, 31*, 257-278.

Bleuler, M. (1988). Prognosis of Schizophrenic Psychoses. In F. Flach (Ed.), *The Schizophrenias*. New York: W.W. Norton & Company.

Breier, A. & Strauss, J.S. (1983). Self-control in psychotic disorders. *Archives of General Psychiatry, 40*, 1141-45.

Breier, A. & Strauss, J.S. (1984). The role of social relationships in the recovery from psychotic disorders. *American Journal of Psychiatry, 141*, 949-55.

Carr, V. (1988). Patients' techniques for coping with schizophrenia: an exploratory study. *British Journal of Medical Psychology, 61*, 339-52.

Cohen, C.I. & Sokolovsky, J. (1978). Schizophrenia and social networks: ex-patients in the inner city. *Schizophrenia Bulletin, 4*, 546-560.

Corrigan, P.W. & Storzbach, D.M. (1993). Behavioural interventions for alleviating psychotic symptoms. *Hospital and Community Psychiatry, 44*, 341-347.

Derogatis, L, Lipman, R. & Covi, L. (1973). SCL-90: an outpatient psychiatric rating scale - preliminary report. *Psychopharmacology Bulletin, 9*, 13-17.

Drake, R.E. & Wallach, M.A. (1989). Substance abuse among the chronic mentally ill. *Hospital and Community Psychiatry, 40*, 1041-1046.

Eaton, W.W., Bilker, W., Haro, J.M., Herrman, H., Mortensen, P.B., Freeman, H. & Burgess, P. (1992). The long-term course of hospitalization for schizophrenia part II: change with passage of time. *Schizophrenia Bulletin, 18*, 229-241.

Fadden, G., Bebbington, P. & Kuipers, L. (1987). Caring and its burdens: a study of the spouses of depressed patients. *British Journal of Psychiatry, 151*, 660-667.

Falloon, I.R.H. (1986). Family stress and schizophrenia. *Psychiatric Clinics of North America, 9*, 165-182.

Falloon, I.R.H. (1993). *The clinical management of major mental disorders: a strategy for assessment and intervention*. Unpublished manuscript.

Falloon, I.R.H., McGill, C. & Boyd, J. (1980). *Treatment of schizophrenia: Medication*. Family Aftercare Program, University of Southern California, LA.

Falloon, I.R.H., McGill, C. & Boyd, J. (1980). *What is schizophrenia?* Family Aftercare Program, University of Southern California, LA.

Falloon, I.R.H., Mueser, K., Gingerich, S., Rappaport, S., McGill, C. & Hole, V. (1988). *Behavioural Family Therapy: A Workbook*. Buckingham: Buckingham Mental Health Service.

Falloon, I.R.H. & Talbot, R.E. (1981). Persistent auditory hallucinations: coping mechanisms and implications for management. *Psychological Medicine*, *11*, 329-39.

Falloon, I.R.H., Boyd, J.L. & McGill, C.W. (1984). *Family Care Of Schizophrenia: A Problem Solving Approach to the Treatment of Mental Illness*. New York & London: Guildford Press.

Family Education Programme in Schizophrenia (1988). Department of Health, NSW and Family Interventions Forum of NSW. Sydney: State Health Publication No. (MH) 88-053, Department of Health, NSW.

Hall, J. & Baker, R. (1983). *REHAB: A Users Manual*. Aberdeen: Vine Publishing.

Harris, M.J. & Jeste, D.V. (1988). Late-onset schizophrenia: an overview. *Schizophrenia Bulletin*, *14*, 39-55.

Hoult, J., Reynolds, I. , Charbonneau-Powis, M., Weekes, P. & Briggs, L. (1983). Psychiatric hospital versus community treatment. *Australian & New Zealand Journal of Psychiatry*, *17*, 160-167.

Jackson, H.J. & Edwards, J. (1992). Social networks and social support in schizophrenia: correlates and assessment. In D.J. Kavanagh (Ed.), *Schizophrenia: An Overview and Practical Handbook* (pp. 275-292). London: Chapman & Hall.

Kaplan, H.I., Freedman, A.M. & Sadock, B.J. (1980). *Comprehensive Textbook of Psychiatry/III, Volume 3* (3rd ed.). Williams & Wilkins Company: Baltimore.

Kaplan, H.I. & Sadock, B.J. (1991). *Synopsis of Psychiatry: behavioural sciences clinical psychiatry* (6th ed.). Williams & Wilkins: Baltimore.

Kavanagh, D.J. (1992). *Schizophrenia: An Overview and Practical Handbook*. London: Chapman Hall.

Kemp R., Hayward P., Applewhaite G., Everitt B. & David A. (1996) Compliance therapy in psychotic patients: randomised controlled trial. *British Medical Journal*, *312*, 345-349.

Kingdon, D.G. & Turkington, D. (1994) *Cognitive-Behavioral Therapy of Schizophrenia*. New York: Guilford Press & London: Psychology Press.

Kuipers, L., Leff, J. & Lam, D. (1992). *Family Work for Schizophrenia - A Practical Guide*. London: Gaskell, Royal College of Psychiatrists.

Leff, J. & Vaughn, C. (1985). *Expressed emotion in families: its significance for mental illness*. New York: Guildford Press.

Liberman, R.P. (1988). *Psychiatric Rehabilitation of Chronic Mental Patients*. Washington: American Psychiatric Press.

Lukoff, D., Lieberman, R.P. & Nuechterein, K.H. (1986). Symptom monitoring in the rehabilitation of schizophrenic patients. *Schizophrenia Bulletin*, *12*, 578-593.

Lukoff, D. & Ventura, J. (1988). Psychiatric diagnosis. In R.P. Liberman (Ed.), *Psychiatric Rehabilitation of Chronic Mental Patients*. Washington: American Psychiatric Press.

McDermott, F. & Pyett, P. (1993). *Not Welcome Anywhere: People who have both a serious psychiatric disorder and problematic drug or alcohol use*. Melbourne: Victorian Community Managed Mental Health Services (VICSERV).

McGorry, P.D. (1992). The concept of recovery and secondary prevention in psychotic disorders. *Australian & New Zealand Journal of Psychiatry*, *26*, 3-17.

McGorry, P.D. (1993). Early psychosis prevention and intervention centre. *Australian Psychiatry*, *1*, 32-34.

McGorry, P.D. (Ed.) (1998). Verging on reality: Preventative strategies in early psychosis. *British Journal of Psychiatry*, *172 (Suppl. 33)*, 1-136.

Muijen, M., Marks, I.M., Connolly, J. & Audini, B. (1992). Home based care and standard hospital care for patients with severe mental illness: a randomised controlled trial. *British Medical Journal, 304*, 749-754.

Muijen, M., Marks, I.M., Connolly, J., Audini, B. & McNamee, G. (1992). The daily living programme. *British Journal of Psychiatry, 160*, 379-384.

Osher, F.C. & Kofoed, L.L. (1989). Treatment of patients with psychiatric and psychoactive substance abuse disorders. *Hospital and Community Psychiatry, 40*, 1025-1030.

Piatkowska, O., Visotina, M., Brecht, G. & Urwyler, M.J. (1987). *Guidelines on Medication Adherence: Adult Mental Health Services.* Publication No. (RUI) 87-034. Sydney: Dept of Health, NSW.

Quality Assurance Project (1984). Treatment outlines for the management of schizophrenia. *Australian and New Zealand Journal of Psychiatry, 18*, 19-38.

Rosen, A., Hadzi-Pavlovic, D. & Parker, G. (1989). The life skills profile: a measure assessing function and disability in schizophrenia. *Schizophrenia Bulletin, 15*, 325-337.

Rosenthal, R.N., Hellerstein, D.J. & Miner, C.R. (1992). Integrated services for treatment of schizophrenic substance abusers: demographics, symptoms, and substance abuse patterns. *Psychiatric Quarterly, 63*, 3-26.

Shaffer, D., Gould, M.S., Brasic, J., Ambrosini, P., Fisher, P., Bird, H. & Aluwahlia, S. (1983). Children's global assessment scale (CGAS). *Archives of General Psychiatry, 40*, 1228-1231.

Siris, S.G. & Docherty, J.P. (1990). Psychosocial management of substance abuse in schizophrenia. In M.I. Herz, S.J. Keith & J.P. Docherty (Eds.), *Handbook of Schizophrenia: Psychosocial Treatment of Schizophrenia.* Amsterdam: Elsevier Science Publishers B.V.

Smith, J.V. & Birchwood, M.J. (1987). Specific and non-specific effects of educational intervention with families living with a schizophrenic relative. *British Journal of Psychiatry, 150*, 645-652.

Stein, L.I. & Test, M.A. (1980). Alternative to mental hospital treatment. I: conceptual model treatment programme and clinical evaluation. *Archives of General Psychiatry, 37*, 392-397.

Tarrier, N., Barrowclough, C., Vaughn, C., Bamrah, J.S., Porceddu, K., Watts, S. & Freeman, H. (1988). The community management of schizophrenia: a controlled trial of a behavioural intervention with families to reduce relapse. *British Journal of Psychiatry, 153*, 532-542.

Tucker, P. (1991). Paper presented at "Winter School in the Sun". Annual conference of Alcohol and Drug Foundation - Brisbane, Queensland.

Veit, C.T. & Ware, J.E. (1983). The structure of psychological distress and well-being in general populations. *Journal of Consulting & Clinical Psychology, 51*, 730-742.

Warner, R. (1985). *Recovery from Schizophrenia: Psychiatry and Political Economy.* New York: Routledge & Kegan Paul Inc.

Weleminsky, J. (1991). Schizophrenia and the family - the customer's view. *International Review of Psychiatry, 3*, 119-124.

World Health Organisation (1992). *ICD-10 Classification of Mental and Behavioural Disorders: clinical descriptions and diagnostic guidelines.* Geneva: World Health Organisation

World Health Organisation (1992). *International Classification of Impairments, Disabilities and Handicaps.* Geneva: World Health Organisation.

Wykes, T. & Sturt, E. (1986). The measurement of social behaviour in psychiatric patients: an assessment of the reliability and validity of SBS. *British Journal of Psychiatry, 148*, 1-11.

5.7 RESOURCE MATERIALS

5.7.1 WHAT IS SCHIZOPHRENIA? [1]

COMMON BELIEFS ABOUT SCHIZOPHRENIA

Schizophrenia is a term just about everyone has heard. However, most people do not know what schizophrenia really is, or what causes schizophrenia, or what can be done for individuals who have this illness.

Q. What do you understand by the term 'schizophrenia'?

Many people have the wrong idea about schizophrenia. Firstly there is the common belief that schizophrenia means you have more than one personality, like Dr Jekyll and Mr Hyde! This is NOT the case. People with schizophrenia have only one personality, although their personality may be disturbed in some way. Schizophrenia refers to personality problems where the individual may have difficulty deciding what is real and what is not real. Schizophrenia is a bit like having a dream when you are wide awake - you are unsure whether the events in the dream are really happening to you or not.

Schizophrenia does not mean you have more than one personality

Another confusion is that many people think schizophrenia means you are 'mad'. While it is true that individuals with schizophrenia will sometimes act in strange or irrational ways, more often they will behave quite normally most of the time.

Another common belief is that people with mental illness are violent and dangerous. Some individuals with schizophrenia may have violent outbursts if they become very frustrated or angry, but they are more likely to be quiet, timid and fearful. In fact, some people who do NOT have schizophrenia have violent outbursts when they are frustrated or angry.

People with schizophrenia are no more violent than people without schizophrenia.

SO WHAT IS SCHIZOPHRENIA?

Schizophrenia is a major mental illness that affects people in all countries of the world. About one person in every hundred is likely to develop this disorder. The number of hospital beds filled by people with schizophrenia is much greater than the number of beds filled by people with any other single illness.

We describe schizophrenia as a major mental illness because schizophrenia has a great effect on nearly every aspect of a person's life. Everything that is important in life may be affected by schizophrenia.

Although the symptoms of schizophrenia are not the same for every person, the symptoms often cause problems in everyday living at some stage of the illness. People with schizophrenia may have difficulty handling problems because their thinking may be jumbled and unclear. It may become difficult for people to work as well as they did before because they may have trouble concentrating or thinking quickly and clearly. There may also be similar difficulties with leisure activities. In

---

[1] Adapted with permission from Falloon, I., McGill, C. & Boyd, J. (1980). *What is Schizophrenia?* L.A.: Family Aftercare Program, University of Southern California.

addition, relationships with other people may become troubled because of difficulties in conversations, or because of problems with their feelings. At times individuals may be so preoccupied with their thoughts and feelings that they cannot take care of even the most basic needs (for example, sleeping and eating).

Not everyone who has schizophrenia will display exactly the same symptoms

Q. What areas of your life have been affected by schizophrenia?

HOW DO WE KNOW WHEN A PERSON HAS SCHIZOPHRENIA?

Schizophrenia is diagnosed when a person displays a specific group of symptoms. These symptoms involve unusual changes in a person's thoughts, feelings, and behaviours. There are no special x-rays or blood tests that tell the doctor that you have schizophrenia. Your doctor will depend almost entirely on what you say you have been experiencing over the past weeks. It is important to tell your doctor exactly what has been going on. Psychiatrists cannot read people's minds even though popular belief suggests that they can! Doctors can only make a diagnosis from what you tell them.

The main symptoms of schizophrenia include:

Disturbances of thinking

You may have difficulty organising your thoughts or difficulty concentrating. Your thoughts may seem jumbled and unusual. People may comment that you are not making sense. They may also say that you drift off the topic of conversation and talk about irrelevant things.

You may also experience thoughts are being put into your head which are not your own thoughts. The thoughts may seem to come from other people or may seem to be put there as a result of telepathy, radio-waves, or laser beams. Thoughts may seem to disappear from your head, as if they are being taken out by somebody. Your mind may go quite blank and you may feel that you are unable to think about anything.

Thoughts may seem to be spoken out loud as if somebody close by could hear them. Sometimes it may feel as if your thoughts are being broadcast from your head so that everybody knows what you are thinking and none of your thoughts seem to be private anymore.

Schizophrenia leads to jumbled thinking.
People may comment that your conversation does not make sense.
Your may feel as if thoughts are put into or taken out of your head, or are escaping and are available to people around you.

Q. Have you experienced any of these difficulties in your thinking?

Delusions

Another difficulty in your thinking is called a 'delusion'. A delusion is a false belief that may seem quite real to you but does not seem real to other people. Delusions can be very frightening at times. Some examples of these delusions are:

- The belief that some other person or force is controlling your thoughts or your actions. You may feel like a zombie with no free will whose body and brain has been taken over by another person.
- The belief that somebody is trying to harm you or perhaps actually trying to kill you.
- The belief that things you see or hear have a special message for you. For example, seeing a red car may mean the world is about to end.

- The belief that you are a special person or have special abilities. For example, that you are a king or a queen, or that you can cause earthquakes, floods or other natural disasters.

A delusion is a false belief which may seem real to you but does not seem real to other people

These ideas often come on suddenly and are quite unusual. Because the ideas are so unusual your family and friends are able to realise that you are not well. When you are a bit better you may be surprised about what you believed when you were ill. Some people say it is a bit like waking up from a dream.

Q. Have you experienced any of these unusual ideas? What did you think was going on?

Hallucinations

An hallucination is the experience of hearing things, seeing things, or smelling things that are not seen, heard, or smelt by other people. Hearing voices when nobody is in the room is a very common symptom of schizophrenia. The voices seem quite real and may appear to come from outside your head or from the next room. Sometimes the voices may seem to come from inside a person's head or, more rarely, from a part of the body.

An hallucination is hearing, seeing or smelling things that are not seen, heard, or smelt by other people

Q. Have you heard voices when there is nobody around? What did the voices say?

Unusual speech

Sometimes people with schizophrenia will talk in a way that is difficult to follow. Occasionally people will make up unusual words or use unusual expressions. Sometimes they may speak very little and be almost impossible to communicate with.

Strange behaviour

Some people with schizophrenia may hold their arms and legs in unusual positions and may not move their arms and legs for long periods of time. However, this behaviour is quite rare with modern treatments. It is more likely that you may have unusual facial expressions or that your body movements may be a bit restless or repetitive. These movements are often a side effect of antipsychotic medications.

Changed feelings

The experience that your feelings or emotions have disappeared, or are much less intense, is a common symptom of schizophrenia. Both happy and sad feelings may be affected. Sometimes you may feel quite depressed and at other times you may feel quite excited. You may also find that your feelings are unusual at times so that you may laugh or cry when you are not feeling happy or sad.

Lack of energy or motivation

Things that you used to do very easily may now seem to require much more effort. Perhaps you may find it difficult to complete tasks or to start the tasks at all. Making conversation with people may also take a lot of effort. It is possible that you may feel the need to withdraw from other people and spend time alone.

Lack of insight

Although your behaviour may seem very unusual to other people, it is possible that you do not believe there is anything wrong with you. This denial of your illness may lead you to refuse treatment. People who care about you may be very distressed by your lack of insight. They would prefer to see you accept treatment and get better. Sometimes you may need to trust the judgement of those who care about you.

Q. Have you noticed any unusual features of your behaviour when you have been ill with schizophrenia?

WHAT CAUSES SCHIZOPHRENIA?

Schizophrenia is probably caused by a combination of life stress and problems with brain functioning. The brain works by using special chemicals called neurotransmitters. Although it is not exactly clear what goes wrong when a person develops schizophrenia, it seems that these chemicals in the brain are affected. This chemical change usually occurs at times in people's lives when they are experiencing a great deal of stress. The chemicals in the brain do not seem to be properly balanced which results in the symptoms of hallucinations, delusions and thinking difficulties.

Schizophrenia is a disturbance of the brain chemicals which may be brought on by stress

It has also been noted that certain types of medication which act like the special chemicals in the brain can help to correct this chemical problem and decrease the symptoms of schizophrenia. These medicines are called antipsychotics.

Many scientists have been trying to find the cause of schizophrenia but have not reached any general agreement. New theories appear every few months and it is easy to become confused. At present we still do not know what causes schizophrenia, nor do we have a total cure. We do, however, have treatment that can reduce many of the symptoms of schizophrenia and help you to live a more fulfilling life.

Although schizophrenia cannot be cured, many of the unpleasant symptoms can be reduced with medication

DOES SCHIZOPHRENIA RUN IN FAMILIES?

Yes, schizophrenia does tend to run in families. However, this does not mean that if somebody in your family has schizophrenia then everybody else will get schizophrenia. Nor does it mean that an individual who has schizophrenia should not marry and have children. We mentioned before that people in the general population have a chance of about 1 in 100 of developing schizophrenia. Well, if a close relative like a mother, father, brother or sister has experienced schizophrenia then your chances of developing schizophrenia are now about 1 in 10 . If both your parents have schizophrenia, or if you have an identical twin who has schizophrenia, your chances are even greater - something like 1 in 2.

The risk of developing schizophrenia is greater if you have a parent, brother, sister or identical twin who has schizophrenia

It does not seem to be schizophrenia itself that is inherited but merely the tendency to develop schizophrenia. People who inherit this tendency possibly lack some chemical in the brain which makes it more likely that they will develop schizophrenia. However, schizophrenia probably only develops when the person who has this tendency experiences a major period of stress.

ENVIRONMENTAL STRESS & SCHIZOPHRENIA

It has been noted that schizophrenia is most likely to develop when people are under a lot of stress. One of the most stressful periods of life is early adult life. At this time individuals are striving to get a good job, to develop close friendships, and to establish independence. This period of life is the most common time for schizophrenia to begin in men. In women, the period of major life stress is usually around the time of childbirth and child-rearing. We find that the age at which schizophrenia starts in women is generally later.

Schizophrenia often develops following periods of stress

Several studies show that major stressful events such as a death in the family, loss of a job, or break-up of a relationship tend to make schizophrenia worse. Other studies show that once a person has schizophrenia, the environment in which he or she lives (that is, family, work, etc.) can help the individual get better if people in that environment provide plenty of support and encourage the individual to gradually regain former skills. If family and friends tend to push, nag, or criticise, these behaviours may make things worse. On the other hand, allowing the individual to lie around all day doing nothing may also make things worse.

It is impossible to totally avoid stress, but family members are most helpful when they assist one another to cope with difficulties in their lives. Your family will need to help you aim for realistic goals step-by-step.

Q. Can you remember whether you were particularly stressed just before you became unwell?

It is clear that family members can be very helpful but that occasionally they can also make things more stressful. However, there is no evidence that families can actually cause schizophrenia. A few years ago it was believed that schizophrenia was caused entirely by the way parents communicated their thoughts and feelings to their children. While we all know how important it is for parents to communicate their thoughts and feelings clearly, there is NO scientific evidence that child-rearing techniques, or family communication patterns cause schizophrenia.

Families do not CAUSE schizophrenia

WILL I GET BETTER?

Schizophrenia usually begins in early adult life but may occur at any time in an individual's life. Individuals who develop schizophrenia at a very early age do not tend to do as well as those individuals whose illness begins in middle or old age. However, many people experience only one episode of the illness and never have a further episode. Generally, 25% of people recover completely, 40% have further episodes of psychosis with some degree of social disability, and 35% may have more severe long-term disability. There is a tendency for schizophrenia to gradually get better over the years, however, for many people schizophrenia will be a life-long concern.

Schizophrenia is often a recurring illness

BRIEF SUMMARY OF SCHIZOPHRENIA

- Schizophrenia is a major illness which affects 1 in 100 people.
- The symptoms include: disturbances in thinking; delusions (false ideas); hallucinations (false sensations which are usually in the form of voices); problems with feelings, behaviours, motivation, and speech.
- The exact cause is not known but appears to have something to do with the balance of chemicals in the brain.
- Stress makes the symptoms worse and possibly triggers the illness.
- Your chance of developing schizophrenia is greater if you have close relatives who have schizophrenia.
- Some people may recover completely from schizophrenia while others will have symptoms which occur from time to time or which are present all the time.
- Relapses can often be prevented and life difficulties overcome.
- Family members and friends can be most helpful by encouraging the individual to gradually regain former skills and to cope with stress more effectively.

5.7.2 COPING WITH DIFFICULT BEHAVIOUR [1]

There are many ways of coping with behaviour that annoys or upsets you. There are also ways of making yourself feel better about the difficult behaviour, even if you cannot *change* the other person's behaviour.

It is important to encourage the other person to control his or her own behaviour. Before working out the best thing to do, it is important to understand what is happening to your mentally ill relative. In this way you will know what to expect of your relative, and to accept your own feelings and not blame yourself. Your relative may not be able to help doing some things because these behaviours may be a part of the illness itself. However, many behaviours can be changed with good management. With your help, the individual may be able to improve his or her self control.

The following suggestions are made to help you cope with certain behaviours associated with schizophrenia. Remember though that every person is different and everyone's circumstances are different. On the following pages are some suggestions you may like to try, but if these suggestions do not work for you make sure you consult with your mental health professional to find other strategies which may work instead. Perhaps the particular suggestion needs to be used differently in your situation. Or, maybe a different method may work better. Do not assume that nothing can be done.

(N.B.: For simplicity, the following has been written using the masculine gender.)

HALLUCINATIONS - e.g., when your relative sees or hears things that you do not see or hear, or when he talks to himself or to 'voices'.

Do

- Do keep calm.
- Do distract the person if you can by: Involving the person in something interesting; Offering something to look at (e.g., newspaper article); Asking the person to help you find something (e.g., to find the newspaper); Engaging the person in pleasant conversation; Encouraging the person to be with other people he knows well.

Don't

- Don't panic or assume that another breakdown is occurring.
- Don't act horrified.
- Don't try and figure out what he is talking about or to whom he is talking.
- Don't let others laugh about these hallucinations or strange talk.
- Don't ask him to try to *force* the voices to stop.

[1] Adapted from Piatkowska & Visotina (1989). Mental Health Information Manual: a self-help guide for relatives and carers.

SLEEPING OR WITHDRAWING a lot of the time, or sleeping at odd times.

In the first 6-12 months:

Do

- Do leave the person alone but make contact whenever he comes out of his room to let him know you are there if he needs you.
- Do remember that he needs to sleep and withdraw while he is recovering.
- Do gently encourage other activities which are not too demanding (e.g., watching TV, washing dishes, etc.).
- Do go out and enjoy yourself with other people.
- Do occasionally offer a cup of tea or coffee.

Don't

- Don't take it personally or blame yourself.
- Don't keep trying to drag him out of his room
- Don't wear yourself out trying to change him
- Don't worry or fuss too much over him.
- Don't invite a lot of visitors home - it may be too overwhelming.
- Don't force him to talk to people

After 6-12 months:

Do

- Do slowly ask the person to get up earlier in the day and to do more things.
- Do offer something to enjoy when he gets up, like a tempting breakfast or pleasant music.
- Do praise him for getting up.

Don't

- Don't think you always have to be protective.

Note

If your relative has been well for some time and develops sleeping difficulties or begins to withdraw again, contact his or her clinician. These behaviours may be a sign that your relative is relapsing.

INACTIVITY and not feeling like doing anything.

In the first 6-12 months:

Do

- Do leave him alone if he does not want to do anything.
- If he says he's bored, offer or suggest some simple activity such as watching TV, listening to music, going for a walk, etc.
- Do experiment with different activities to find out what the person will enjoy. At first try activities that are passive (e.g., listening to or watching something).
- Do try to have a regular daily routine so that things are predictable.
- Do encourage him to join in or follow this daily routine.
- When he starts getting better, give him simple daily chores to do. *Break chores into small steps if they are difficult.*
- Do try to make allowances for him if he needs to do things like eating at unusual times. (You can leave healthy snacks in the fridge.)

- Do offer rewards and praise for the times when your relative does the chores, even if the chores are not done perfectly.
- Do remember that your relative may be distractible and may make mistakes or find it hard to finish long jobs.
- Do talk with your relative's clinician or doctor about rehabilitation programmes. Get advice about when he is ready to do various things and how to encourage him to do these things.

Don't

- Don't insist on your relative doing much or going out.
- Don't overwhelm him with too many suggestions at once.
- Don't suggest activities or chores that are too complicated (e.g., a game of Scrabble or grocery shopping).
- Don't nag or criticise him.
- Don't expect him to do things he is afraid of doing (e.g., going out to a party) or which he finds too confusing (e.g., writing letters or rearranging the furniture).
- Don't give too many instructions at the one time.
- Don't label your relative as 'lazy' - this label doesn't help either of you.
- Don't expect things to be done perfectly.
- Don't wear yourself out doing everything for your relative.

MANIPULATIVE BEHAVIOUR

If your relative feels helpless, left out, or suspicious and threatened, he may start to use manipulative behaviour. For example, he may try to get the members of the family to do everything that he wants them to do, or he may try to set one family member against another, or he may try to get attention at any cost. Note that these behaviours and situations can also happen in most 'ordinary' families at some time.

If your relative tries to manipulate you into doing things you don't want to do, or tries to get you to do things that are unreasonable:

Do

- Do be firm by saying, *"No, this is something you can do for yourself."*
- Do be firm by saying, *"I don't like this behaviour. Please stop."*

Don't

- Don't do things for your relative which he can do for himself, or which you feel are too much for you.
- Don't let yourself give in through feelings of guilt - there is nothing you *have* to do.

If your relative seems to do inappropriate things to get attention:

Do

- Do say you want him to stop the behaviour.
- Do pay attention and give praise when your relative does something nice and helpful.
- Do, if possible, avoid paying attention to the inappropriate behaviour.
- Do make it part of the routine to spend time doing something with your relative (e.g., chatting over coffee, walking, gardening, etc.)

If your relative tells you negative things about other people:

Do

- Do check out any negative 'stories' your relative tells you about others (in the family or outside such as the clinician).
- Do ask why he feels/thinks that way.
- Do remember your relative may be confused and may misinterpret what people say.
- Do have open family problem solving discussions if behaviours bother the family.
- Do discuss your relatives concerns with the clinician to sort out any misunderstandings or to see whether your relative may need to change his treatment in some way.
- Do seek another opinion if you are not happy with your relative's treatment.

Don't

- Don't make accusations against other family members.
- Don't jump to conclusions if your relative says negative things about others (including family, clinicians, doctors, etc.).
- Don't allow your relative to stop attending treatment without first discussing it with the doctor.

AGGRESSIVE BEHAVIOUR

People with schizophrenia are usually shy and withdrawn. Aggression is no more common among these people than in the general community. However, if you're living with someone who does tend to be aggressive, you will need to know what to do when he becomes aggressive so that you feel more able to cope in these situations.

Do

- Do give a firm command such as *"stop please"*.
- If he doesn't stop, leave the room or the house quickly.
- Do leave the person alone until they've calmed down. If you've left the house, a phone call may tell you if he is calmer.
- Do call your relative's clinician, or if the clinician is not available, call the Crisis Team if one is available in your area. (Your local hospital or community mental health centre will inform you.)
- Do take any threats or warnings seriously and contact the clinician or doctor, particularly if your relative has ideas of being persecuted and talks about *"Getting them before they get me"*, etc.
- Afterwards you can say, *"I know you were upset but we won't put up with violence - EVER"*, or *"You can tell us what you're angry about, but cannot hit anybody"*.
- If you're afraid for your safety over a period of time you may need to arrange to have someone else stay with you or be available on the phone, or to arrange for your relative to stay elsewhere.
- Do discuss any threats and violence openly in the family and with the clinician.
- Try to see what triggers the aggression and stop or avoid that behaviour/situation (e.g., over-crowding in the house, criticism, doing too much for the person, etc.).
- If all else fails, it's OK to call the police if you or your family need protection.

Don't

- Don't say angry, critical things which will provoke more aggression.
- Don't argue.
- Don't stay around if the person doesn't calm down.
- Don't ignore verbal threats or warnings of violence made to you or about others.
- Don't tolerate aggression or violence to you or your family.
- Don't try to battle it out on your own - ask for help.
- Don't let yourself or the family become the only ones your relative depends on - this can create anger.

STRANGE TALK OR BELIEFS

Do

- Do gently and matter-of-factly disagree with strange ideas.
- Do show some understanding of the person's feelings (e.g., fear of the voices).
- Do encourage the person to talk normally or 'sensibly'.
- Do change the subject to something routine, simple, or pleasant in real life (e.g., what you're making for dinner).
- Do say you don't understand and you'd like him to talk clearly.
- Do say when you think something is not real (e.g., 'the voices'), while acknowledging that they *seem* real to your relative.
- Do help your relative to tell the difference between reality and fantasy by saying you think *"It's your brain playing a trick on you just now - it's not really out there"*.
- Do tell your relative that if he feels he *must* talk about the strange ideas, to do this only to certain people who are not worried by these ideas (e.g., the clinician or doctor).

Don't

- Don't allow the family to make jokes or criticise the person.
- Don't argue about the strange ideas - arguing never changes the ideas and only upsets both of you.
- Don't spend much time listening to talk that makes no sense to you.
- Don't pretend to agree with strange ideas or talk you can't understand.
- Don't keep looking at the person or nodding your head if they are speaking strangely.
- Don't try to enter his world and follow everything he says.
- Don't keep up a conversation that you feel is distressing, or annoying, or too confusing for you. It's OK to say, *"I'll talk to you later when you're making more sense"*.
- Don't look horrified or embarrassed by strange talk. It's better to say clearly that you don't like the strange talk.

NOT TAKING PRESCRIBED MEDICATION

Do

- If the problem is a result of forgetting, gently remind him when it is time to take the medicine. Find a daily routine (e.g., breakfast, tooth brushing) when tablet taking can become a habit.
- Do remind him calmly that medication helps to keep/make him well.
- Do ask if he is having any side effects.
- Do talk to his doctor about his difficulty with remembering to take medication.
- If he refuses to take medication, let the doctor know if symptoms get worse or reappear.

FEARS OF SUICIDE

Do

- Do listen to all your relative's feelings of depression but also point out that help is available.
- Do show appreciation of your relative's feelings and the fact that he confided in you.
- Do contact the clinician or doctor if suicidal ideas persist.
- Do distract your relative by involving him in pleasant, low key activities with someone he knows well.
- Do help the person to be with someone by whom they feel accepted so they don't feel isolated.
- Do let the person know you accept and care about him.
- Do consider whether any stressors can be removed which might be depressing your relative (e.g., too much pressure to go back to work, etc.).

Don't

- Don't panic if your relative talks about suicide, but do take his feelings seriously.
- Don't tell the person things like, *"Pull yourself together"*.

ODD OR EMBARRASSING BEHAVIOUR

Do

- Do remember that you are not responsible for this behaviour.
- Do ignore this behaviour if you can, especially if the behaviour is not serious.
- If you can't ignore the behaviour, ask the person clearly and pleasantly not to do that particular behaviour.
- If the person can't help the behaviour, ask him to do it only in his room.
- Do state clearly that the behaviour is not acceptable to others.
- If you can, rearrange the house or change the environment so as to lessen the behaviour (e.g., remove mirror from living room if he stands talking to himself in the mirror in front of visitors.)
- Do find times to praise the person for acting normally.
- If the behaviour seems to be set off by stress (e.g., too many visitors, being criticised, upsetting events, etc.) see if the stress can be reduced or stopped.

Don't

- Don't tell yourself that the behaviour is a reflection on you or your family.
- Don't act upset.
- Don't get into long discussions.
- Don't let the family pay attention to the behaviours or laugh at the behaviours.
- Don't nag the person about the behaviour.

ALCOHOL OR STREET DRUGS

Alcohol can be taken in small amounts - not more than one or two drinks a day, depending on the individual.

Drugs such as marijuana, L.S.D., amphetamines ('speed') and ecstasy are like poison to a person with schizophrenia. These drugs can make symptoms worse and can trigger a relapse. If your relative takes these drugs or too much alcohol:

Do

- Do remind him firmly that the drugs are harmful.
- Do remind him about how much alcohol he can safely drink.
- Do ask your relative why he takes these drugs/excess alcohol. If he takes the drugs to lessen tension or to be accepted by his peers, encourage him to explore other alternatives.
- Do discuss his drug-taking with his doctor or clinician. Look for any stressors that may lead to drinking or drug-taking (e.g., fights with family, job pressures) and discuss ways of solving these stressors.
- Do discuss alternative ways of 'being happy' or 'getting high', such as making new friends, music, sport, etc. Your relative may need to learn new things (e.g., socialising with people who don't drink or take drugs, a new satisfying hobby, or doing voluntary work to gain a sense of achievement).

- Do make a firm rule about no drug taking or excessive drinking. Support this rule by:
  a. Giving rewards or special privileges (perhaps each week) if your relative keeps the rule (e.g., a trip to the movies, a special meal, money, or anything else he values).
  b. If your relative breaks the rule, take away the drugs or drink if possible and take away a privilege immediately (e.g., pocket money, records, video, ban a favourite TV programme, or anything else he values). Make sure you choose something he can't get some other way (e.g., from a friend).

Don't

- Don't give him the promised reward if he didn't stick to the rule.
- Don't nag or criticise since this may make things worse.
- Don't get into arguments about your decisions.
- Don't set an example of heavy drinking or drug-taking yourself.
- Don't let the family encourage heavy drinking or drug-taking by making these behaviours sound good. (e.g., *"Boy, I had a great night - got really pissed"* or *"Had a great party - we all got stoned"*).
- Don't allow yourself to be talked out of enforcing the rule - it's important to be consistent.

5.7.3 WHAT YOU MAY EXPECT AFTER AN ACUTE EPISODE OF PSYCHOSIS [1]

When someone in the family has symptoms of psychosis, it is very frightening, confusing and distressing for the family. In this time of stress it can be helpful to learn what to expect and what to do.

A psychotic illness makes it hard to tell what is real from what is not real. This illness also makes the person feel overwhelmed by things going on around them.

Individuals are likely to feel very confused, distressed, afraid, and lacking in self confidence, not only during any time spent in hospital but often for a long time afterwards. They have been through a frightening experience. The illness has probably caused them to lose control of their thoughts and feel overwhelmed by the world around them. They may have frightening ideas that someone is persecuting them or talking about them, or they may also hear voices or feel depressed.

The person has had a serious shock. The body and brain need rest to be able to cope, just as we need rest to get over the flu. With a psychotic illness, however, recovery usually takes longer.

It is common for individuals who have just experienced a psychotic illness to:
- Sleep long hours every night (or even during the day) for 6-12 months.
- Feel the need to be quiet and alone more often than other people.
- Be inactive and feel that they *cannot* or do not *want* to do much.

These behaviours are natural ways of slowing down so as to help the body and brain recover. It is best to let the person be like this instead of expecting them to get back to normal straight away. It may take several months or a year to recover. Putting too much pressure on the person to get up or go out and do things can make them worse during this time of recovery.

On the other hand, this DOES NOT MEAN the person needs to lie down all day, have everything done for them, or never do any household chores. It is a good idea to gently encourage the individual to help with simple chores, chat with the family, or ask if they would like to go out on some outing they used to like. If the person says no at this stage you should leave him or her alone, saying *"Okay, but you are welcome to come when you want to"*.

It is not a good idea to do everything for your relative, or to do so much that you feel worn out. For example, some families, especially mothers, feel they have to tidy up after their relative or make all the cups of coffee they ask for. It is important to encourage your relative to take responsibility for such tasks, but perhaps offer to help if necessary.

It is important for your recovering relative to have a quiet place to go. This is usually a deep need and is often helpful. It is NOT a personal rejection of you or the family if the person withdraws to his or her bedroom quite frequently. It is only if your relative stays there all the time for many days that you need to be concerned. If the withdrawal is excessive, it can mean the illness might be getting worse again.

For the same reason (the need for calm, quiet and simplicity) you may find your relative being emotionally distant, not very affectionate, or expressing very little feeling. This is part of the disorder, and is NOT a personal insult to you. In the same way as the need for quiet withdrawal, this emotional distance is simply the need to cut down on all the confusing stimulation.

---

[1] Adapted from Visotina & Piatkowska (1988). *Mental Illness Information Manual: a self-help guide for relatives and carers.* Sydney: Department of Health, NSW.

Often the person may like to just sit in company and watch or listen to people. These behaviours can be helpful. It is good to accept these behaviours and not be worried by your relative saying nothing when in the company of others.

You may find the person likes to listen to loud music a lot of the time. This music may be a way of drowning out the distressing 'voices' or thoughts. Earphones or a walkman may be helpful.

Your relative may sometimes talk in a strange way which you may find hard to follow. The talk may seem unconnected or irrelevant to the conversation at times. Or your relative may make unexpected remarks that do not make sense. This 'odd' conversation happens because the imbalance of brain chemical makes it hard to think clearly. Sometimes it is because the person is hearing voices that seem very real, although they are not there.

The person may have unusual patterns of sleeping or eating (e.g., getting up for meals in the middle of the night).

Your relative may sometimes behave in unusual, odd, or embarrassing ways. These behaviours are also a part of the disorder and do NOT mean that he or she is stupid or trying to embarrass you.

It is important to remember that the person with a psychotic illness often acts and speaks quite normally as well. Symptoms often get better and may re-appear only under stress. It is helpful to treat the person normally, except when you are dealing with fairly severe symptoms.

5.7.4 SOCIAL AND LIVING SKILLS CHECKLIST

Basic living skills   *Please circle*

1. Is basic self-care adequate?
   a. Personal hygiene and appearance   Yes   No
   b. Clothing   Yes   No
   c. Preparation of meals   Yes   No
   d. Diet   Yes   No
   e. Housework (e.g., washing dishes, laundry, household hygiene, etc.)   Yes   No
   f. Survival skills in community (e.g., shopping, transport, crossing roads, etc.)   Yes   No

(If skills are inadequate, see Goal Planning and Skills Training in Section 5.3.5)

Physical health & medications / treatment

1. Has individual recently had a medical check-up?
   (e.g., general health, optometry, dentistry, podiatry, etc.)   Yes   No
2. Are medication and health problems managed appropriately?
   (e.g., non-adherence, side effects, expenses, etc.)   Yes   No
3. Is current medication (type and dose) satisfactory for:
   a. Individual?   Yes   No
   b. Key worker?   Yes   No
   c. Doctor?   Yes   No

(See Physical Health in Section 5.3.9, plus Sexual Health & Medication in Volume 1)

Housing

1. Is the housing situation adequate? (e.g., electricity / gas, clean water, rent,
   heating, phone, furniture, appliances, disputes with landlord / housemates, etc.)   Yes   No
2. Is supervision adequate for this individual?   Yes   No
3. a. Is individual happy with his or her current housing situation?   Yes   No
   b. Is Key worker happy?   Yes   No
   c. Are carers happy?   Yes   No
4. If not happy with housing, what kind of housing is preferred?   Yes   No

(See Housing in Chapter 1: Core Management Skills)

Finances

1. Is individual receiving all benefits to which he or she is entitled?   Yes   No
2. Is the individual's income adequate?   Yes   No
3. Can the individual budget and handle money effectively?   Yes   No
4. Can individual handle financial commitments without assistance?   Yes   No

(See Finances in Chapter 1: Core Management Skills)

Family and social supports

1. Are the individual's family and social supports adequate?   Yes   No
2. Do the individual and his or her family have:
   a. Clear ideas about roles and responsibilities? (Who does what?)   Yes   No
   b. Adequate decision making skills? (Who decides and how?)   Yes   No
   c. Skills for managing difficult behaviour?   Yes   No
   d. Satisfactory communication of feelings? (Content & expression)   Yes   No
   e. Realistic expectations of one another?   Yes   No
   f. Receptive attitudes to outside assistance? (Accepting help)   Yes   No
3. Do the individual and his or her family have adequate:
   a. Communication skills? (Section 5.3.8)   Yes   No
   b. Problem solving skills? (Section 5.3.8)   Yes   No

(See Social Support in Chapter 1: Core Management Skills)

Employment

1. If employed, is the work situation satisfactory?
   (e.g., punctuality, attendance, performance, social interactions, etc.)   Yes   No
2. If unemployed, is individual suitable for employment?   Yes   No
3. If unemployed, can the individual find work without assistance?   Yes   No

(See Employment in Chapter 1: Core Management Skills)

Legal

1. If subject to the Mental Health Act or legal proceedings, is the matter
   being handled appropriately?   Yes   No

(See Legal Matters in Chapter 1: Core Management Skills)

Leisure and social activities

1. Is individual happy with the way spare time is spent?   Yes   No
2. Is the key worker happy?   Yes   No
3. Is individual happy with present friendships? (quantity & quality)   Yes   No
4. Is individual happy with present leisure activities? (quantity & quality)   Yes   No

(See Leisure & Social Activities in Chapter 1: Core Management Skills)

Education

1. If the individual is currently undertaking a course of study, is he or she
   coping with the demands of this study?   Yes   No
2. If a current course of study has been interrupted, has the university
   (or other) been notified and supplied with supportive the documentation
   for deferral of the course, etc.?   Yes   No
3. Is the individual satisfied with his or her current educational status or situation?
   (e.g., further education may be desired).   Yes   No

Mental Health Services

1. Is the individual happy with the services?   Yes   No
2. Is the individual happy with:
   a. Key worker?   Yes   No
   b. Psychiatrist?   Yes   No
   c. Other mental health workers?   Yes   No
   d. Choice of treatment?   Yes   No
3. Is the individual aware of his or her options re treatment and services?   Yes   No

(See Social Support in Chapter 1: Core Management Skills)

N.B.: Negative responses on this checklist indicate that intervention of some kind will be necessary.

5.7.5 MENTAL HEALTH INVENTORY-5 (MHI-5) [1]

1. During the past month, how much of the time were you a happy person?

    All of the time 1
    Most of the time 2
    A good bit of the time 3
    Some of the time 4
    A little of the time 5
    None of the time 6

2. How much of the time, during the past month, have you felt calm and peaceful?

    All of the time 1
    Most of the time 2
    A good bit of the time 3
    Some of the time 4
    A little of the time 5
    None of the time 6

3. How much of the time, during the past month, have you been a very nervous person?

    All of the time 1
    Most of the time 2
    A good bit of the time 3
    Some of the time 4
    A little of the time 5
    None of the time 6

4. How much of the time, during the past month, have you felt downhearted and blue?

    All of the time 1
    Most of the time 2
    A good bit of the time 3
    Some of the time 4
    A little of the time 5
    None of the time 6

5. How much of the time, during the past month, did you feel so down in the dumps that nothing
    could cheer you up?

    Always 1
    Very often 2
    Fairly often 3
    Sometimes 4
    Almost never 5
    Never 6

[1] The MHI was developed by Veit, C.T. & Ware, Jnr, J.E. (1983). The structure of psychological distress and well-being in general populations. *Journal of Consulting and Clinical Psychology, 51*, 730-742.

SCORING THE MHI-5

Items 1 and 2 are reverse scored as shown below:

1 - score as 6 points
2 - score as 5 points
3 - score as 4 points
4 - score as 3 points
5 - score as 2 points
6 - score as 1 point

Items 3, 4, and 5 are scored as they appear.

The MHI-5 has a maximum score of 30 and a minimum score of 5. Higher scores are desirable in that they indicate the experience of psychological well-being and the absence of psychological distress during the past month.

For further information see:

Veit, C.T. & Ware, Jnr, J.E. (1983). The structure of psychological distress and well-being in general populations. *Journal of Consulting and Clinical Psychology*, *51*, 730-742.

Davies, A.R., Sherbourne, C.D., Peterson, J.R., & Ware, J.E. (1988). *Scoring manual: Adult health status and patient satisfaction measures used in RAND's Health Insurance Experiment*. Santa Monica, CA: RAND Corporation.

5.7.6 BRIEF PSYCHIATRIC RATING SCALE (BPRS) [1]

Individual's name _____   Date _____

Rater's name _____

INSTRUCTIONS

This form consists of 24 symptom constructs, each to be rated on a 7-point scale of severity ranging from 'not present' to 'extremely severe.' If a specific symptom is not rated, mark 'NA' (not assessed). Circle the number headed by the term that best describes the patient's present condition.

1	2	3	4	5	6	7
not present	very mild	mild	moderate	moderately severe	severe	extremely severe

		NA	1	2	3	4	5	6	7
1.	Somatic concern	NA	1	2	3	4	5	6	7
2.	Anxiety	NA	1	2	3	4	5	6	7
3.	Depression	NA	1	2	3	4	5	6	7
4.	Suicidality	NA	1	2	3	4	5	6	7
5.	Guilt	NA	1	2	3	4	5	6	7
6.	Hostility	NA	1	2	3	4	5	6	7
7.	Elated mood	NA	1	2	3	4	5	6	7
8.	Grandiosity	NA	1	2	3	4	5	6	7
9.	Suspiciousness	NA	1	2	3	4	5	6	7
10.	Hallucinations	NA	1	2	3	4	5	6	7
11.	Unusual thought content	NA	1	2	3	4	5	6	7
12.	Bizarre behaviour	NA	1	2	3	4	5	6	7
13.	Self-neglect	NA	1	2	3	4	5	6	7
14.	Disorientation	NA	1	2	3	4	5	6	7
15.	Conceptual disorganization	NA	1	2	3	4	5	6	7
16.	Blunted affect	NA	1	2	3	4	5	6	7
17.	Emotional withdrawal	NA	1	2	3	4	5	6	7
18.	Motor retardation	NA	1	2	3	4	5	6	7
19.	Tension	NA	1	2	3	4	5	6	7
20.	Uncooperativeness	NA	1	2	3	4	5	6	7
21.	Excitement	NA	1	2	3	4	5	6	7
22.	Distractibility	NA	1	2	3	4	5	6	7
23.	Motor hyperactivity	NA	1	2	3	4	5	6	7
24.	Mannerisms and posturing	NA	1	2	3	4	5	6	7

[1] This version was adapted by Ventura, M.A., Green, M.F., Shaner, A. & Liberman, R.P. (1993). Training and quality assurance with the brief psychiatric rating scale: "The drift buster". *International Journal of Methods in Psychiatric Research*, 3, 221-244.

BRIEF PSYCHIATRIC RATING SCALE (BPRS) EXPANDED VERSION (4.0)

This section reproduces an interview schedule, symptom definitions, and specific anchor points for rating symptoms on the BPRS. Clinicians intending to use the BPRS should also consult the detailed guidelines for administration contained in the reference below.

Scale Items and Anchor Points

Rate items 1-14 on the basis of individual's self-report. Note items 7, 12 and 13 are also rated on the basis of observed behaviour. Items 15-24 are rated on the basis of observed behaviour and speech.

1. SOMATIC CONCERN: Degree of concern over present bodily health. Rate the degree to which physical health is perceived as a problem by the individual, whether complaints have realistic bases or not. Somatic delusions should be rated in the severe range with or without somatic concern. Note: be sure to assess the degree of impairment due to somatic concerns only and not other symptoms, e.g., depression. In addition, if the individual rates 6 or 7 due to somatic delusions, then you must rate Unusual Thought Content at least 4 or above.

2 **Very mild** Occasional somatic concerns that tend to be kept to self.

3 **Mild** Occasional somatic concerns that tend to be voiced to others (e.g., family, doctor).

4 **Moderate** Frequent expressions of somatic concern or exaggerations of existing ills OR some preoccupation, but no impairment in functioning. Not delusional.

5 **Moderately severe** Frequent expressions of somatic concern or exaggerations of existing ills OR some preoccupation and moderate impairment of functioning. Not delusional.

6 **Severe** Preoccupation with somatic complaints with much impairment in functioning OR somatic delusions without acting on them or disclosing to others.

7 **Extremely severe** Preoccupation with somatic complaints with severe impairment in functioning OR somatic delusions that tend to be acted on or disclosed to others.

"Have you been concerned about your physical health?" "Have you had any physical illness or seen a medical doctor lately? (What does your doctor say is wrong? How serious is it?)"
"Has anything changed regarding your appearance?"
"Has it interfered with your ability to perform your usual activities and/or work?"
"Did you ever feel that parts of your body had changed or stopped working?"

[If individual reports any somatic concerns/delusions, ask the following]:
"How often are you concerned about [use individual's description]?"
"Have you expressed any of these concerns to others?"

2. ANXIETY: Reported apprehension, tension, fear, panic or worry. Rate only the individual's statements - not observed anxiety which is rated under Tension.

2   **Very mild**   Reports some discomfort due to worry OR infrequent worries that occur more than usual for most normal individuals.

3   **Mild**   Worried frequently but can readily turn attention to other things.

4   **Moderate**   Worried most of the time and cannot turn attention to other things easily but no impairment in functioning OR occasional anxiety with autonomic accompaniment but no impairment in functioning.

5   **Moderately Severe**   Frequent, but not daily, periods of anxiety with autonomic accompaniment OR some areas of functioning are disrupted by anxiety or worry.

6   **Severe**   Anxiety with autonomic accompaniment daily but not persisting throughout the day OR many areas of functioning are disrupted by anxiety or constant worry.

7   **Extremely Severe**   Anxiety with autonomic accompaniment persisting throughout the day OR most areas of functioning are disrupted by anxiety or constant worry.

"Have you been worried a lot during [mention time frame]? Have you been nervous or apprehensive? (What do you worry about?)"
"Are you concerned about anything? How about finances or the future?"
"When you are feeling nervous, do your palms sweat or does your heart beat fast (or shortness of breath, trembling, choking)?"

[If individual reports anxiety or autonomic accompaniment, ask the following]:
"How much of the time have you been [use individual's description]?"
"Has it interfered with your ability to perform your usual activities/work?"

3. DEPRESSION: Include sadness, unhappiness, anhedonia and preoccupation with depressing topics (can't attend to TV or conversations due to depression), hopeless, loss of self-esteem (dissatisfied or disgusted with self or feelings of worthlessness). Do not include vegetative symptoms, e.g., motor retardation, early waking or the amotivation that accompanies the deficit syndrome.

2   **Very mild**   Occasionally feels sad, unhappy or depressed.

3   **Mild**   Frequently feels sad or unhappy but can readily turn attention to other things.

4   **Moderate**   Frequent periods of feeling very sad, unhappy, moderately depressed, but able to function with extra effort.

5   **Moderately Severe**   Frequent, but not daily, periods of deep depression OR some areas of functioning are disrupted by depression.

6   **Severe**   Deeply depressed daily but not persisting throughout the day OR many areas of functioning are disrupted by depression.

7   **Extremely Severe**   Deeply depressed daily OR most areas of functioning are disrupted by depression.

"How has your mood been recently? Have you felt depressed (sad, down, unhappy, as if you didn't care)?"
"Are you able to switch your attention to more pleasant topics when you want to?"
"Do you find that you have lost interest in or get less pleasure from things you used to enjoy, like family, friends, hobbies, watching TV, eating?"

[If individual reports feelings of depression, ask the following]:
"How long do these feelings last?"   *"Has it interfered with your ability to perform your usual activities?"*

4. SUICIDALITY: Expressed desire, intent, or actions to harm or kill self.

2   **Very mild** Occasional feelings of being tired of living. No overt suicidal thoughts.

3   **Mild** Occasional suicidal thoughts without intent or specific plan OR he/she feels they would be better off dead.

4   **Moderate** Suicidal thoughts frequent without intent or plan.

5   **Moderately Severe** Many fantasies of suicide by various methods. May seriously consider making an attempt with specific time and plan OR impulsive suicide attempt using non-lethal method or in full view of potential saviours.

6   **Severe** Clearly wants to kill self. Searches for appropriate means and time, OR potentially serious suicide attempt with individual knowledge of possible rescue.

7   **Extremely Severe** Specific suicidal plan and intent (e.g., "as soon as _____ I will do it by doing X"), OR suicide attempt characterised by plan individual thought was lethal or attempt in secluded environment.

"Have you felt that life wasn't worth living? Have you thought about harming or killing yourself? Have you felt tired of living or as though you would be better off dead? Have you ever felt like ending it all?"

[If individual reports suicidal ideation, ask the following]:
"How often have you thought about [use individual's description]?"
"Did you (Do you) have a specific plan?"

5. GUILT: Overconcern or remorse for past behaviour. Rate only individual's statements, do not infer guilt feelings from depression, anxiety, or neurotic defences. Note: if the individual rates 6 or 7 due to delusions of guilt, then you must rate Unusual Thought Content at least 4 or above, depending on level of preoccupation and impairment.

2   **Very mild** Concerned about having failed someone, or at something, but not preoccupied. Can shift thoughts to other matters easily.

3   **Mild** Concerned about having failed someone, or at something, with some preoccupation. Tends to voice guilt to others.

4   **Moderate** Disproportionate preoccupation with guilt, having done wrong, injured others by doing or failing to do something, but can readily turn attention to other things.

5   **Moderately Severe** Preoccupation with guilt, having failed someone or at something, can turn attention to other things, but only with great effort. Not delusional.

6   **Severe** Delusional guilt OR unreasonable self-reproach very out of proportion to circumstances. Moderate preoccupation present.

7   **Extremely Severe** Delusional guilt OR unreasonable self-reproach grossly out of proportion to circumstances. Individual is very preoccupied with guilt and is likely to disclose to others or act on delusions.

"Is there anything you feel guilty about? Have you been thinking about past problems?"
"Do you tend to blame yourself for things that have happened?"
"Have you done anything you're still ashamed of?"

[If individual reports guilt/remorse/delusions, ask the following]:
"How often have you been thinking about [use individual's description]?"
"Have you disclosed your feelings of guilt to others?"

6. HOSTILITY: Animosity, contempt, belligerence, threats, arguments, tantrums, property destruction, fights, and any other expression of hostile attitudes or actions. Do not infer hostility from neurotic defences, anxiety or somatic complaints. Do not include incidents of appropriate anger or obvious self-defence.

2   **Very mild** Irritable or grumpy, but not overtly expressed.
3   **Mild** Argumentative or sarcastic.
4   **Moderate** Overtly angry on several occasions OR yelled at others excessively.
5   **Moderately Severe** Has threatened, slammed about or thrown things.
6   **Severe** Has assaulted others but with no harm likely, e.g., slapped or pushed, OR destroyed property, e.g., knocked over furniture, broken windows.
7   **Extremely Severe** Has attacked others with definite possibility of harming them or with actual harm, e.g., assault with hammer or weapon.

"How have you been getting along with people (family, co-workers, etc.)?"
"Have you been irritable or grumpy lately? (How do you show it? Do you keep it to yourself?"
"Were you ever so irritable that you would shout at people or start fights or arguments? (Have you found yourself yelling at people you didn't know?)"
"Have you hit anyone recently?"

7. ELEVATED MOOD: A pervasive, sustained and exaggerated feeling of well-being, cheerfulness, euphoria (implying a pathological mood), optimism that is out of proportion to the circumstances. Do not infer elation from increased activity or from grandiose statements alone.

2   **Very mild** Seems to be very happy, cheerful without much reason.
3   **Mild** Some unaccountable feelings of well-being that persist.
4   **Moderate** Reports excessive or unrealistic feelings of well-being, cheerfulness, confidence or optimism inappropriate to circumstances, some of the time. May frequently joke, smile, be giddy, or overly enthusiastic OR few instances of marked elevated mood with euphoria.
5   **Moderately Severe** Reports excessive or unrealistic feelings of well-being, confidence or optimism inappropriate to circumstances, much of the time. May describe feeling 'on top of the world', 'like everything is falling into place', or 'better than ever before', OR several instances of marked elevated mood with euphoria.
6   **Severe** Reports many instances of marked elevated mood with euphoria OR mood definitely elevated almost constantly throughout interview and inappropriate to content.
7   **Extremely Severe** Individual reports being elated or appears almost intoxicated, laughing, joking, giggling, constantly euphoric, feeling invulnerable, all inappropriate to immediate circumstances.

"Have you felt so good or high that other people thought that you were not your normal self?"
"Have you been feeling cheerful and 'on top of the world' without any reason?"

[If individual reports elevated mood/euphoria, ask the following]:
"Did it seem like more than just feeling good?"
"How long did that last?"

8. GRANDIOSITY: Exaggerated self-opinion, self-enhancing conviction of special abilities or powers or identity as someone rich or famous. Rate only individual's statements about himself, not his/her demeanour. Note: if the individual rates 6 or 7 due to grandiose delusions, you must rate Unusual Thought Content at least 4 or above.

2   Very mild Feels great and denies obvious problems, but not unrealistic.

3   Mild Exaggerated self-opinion beyond abilities and training.

4   Moderate Inappropriate boastfulness, e.g., claims to be brilliant, insightful or gifted beyond realistic proportions, but rarely self-discloses or acts on these inflated self-concepts. Does not claim that grandiose accomplishments have actually occurred.

5   Moderately Severe Same as 4 but often self-discloses and acts on these grandiose ideas. May have doubts about the reality of the grandiose ideas. Not delusional.

6   Severe Delusional - claims to have special powers like ESP, to have millions of dollars, invented new machines, worked at jobs when it is known that he/she was never employed in these capacities, be Jesus Christ, or the Prime Minister. Individual may not be very preoccupied.

7   Extremely Severe Delusional - same as 6 but individual seems very preoccupied and tends to disclose or act on grandiose delusions.

"Is there anything special about you? Do you have any special abilities or powers? Have you thought that you might be somebody rich or famous?"

[If the individual reports any grandiose ideas/delusions, ask the following]:
"How often have you been thinking about [use individuals description]? Have you told anyone about what you have been thinking? Have you acted on any of these ideas?"

9. SUSPICIOUSNESS: Expressed or apparent belief that other persons have acted maliciously or with discriminatory intent. Include persecution by supernatural or other non-human agencies (e.g., the devil). Note: ratings of 3 or above should also be rated under Unusual Thought Content.

2   Very mild Seems on guard. Reluctant to respond to some 'personal' questions. Reports being overly self-conscious in public.

3   Mild Describes incidents in which others have harmed or wanted to harm him/her that sound plausible. Individual feels as if others are watching, laughing or criticising him/her in public, but this occurs only occasionally or rarely. Little or no preoccupation.

4   Moderate Says other persons are talking about him/her maliciously, have negative intentions or may harm him/her. Beyond the likelihood of plausibility, but not delusional. Incidents of suspected persecution occur occasionally (less than once per week) with some preoccupation.

5   Moderately Severe Same as 4, but incidents occur frequently, such as more than once per week. Individual is moderately preoccupied with ideas of persecution OR individual reports persecutory delusions expressed with much doubt (e.g., partial delusion).

6   Severe Delusional - speaks of Mafia plots, the FBI or others poisoning his/her food, persecution by supernatural forces.

7   Extremely Severe Same as 6, but the beliefs are bizarre or more preoccupying. Individual tends to disclose or act on persecutory delusions.

"Do you ever feel uncomfortable in public? Does it seem as though others are watching you? Are you concerned about anyone's intentions toward you? Is anyone going out of their way to give you a hard time, or trying to hurt you? Do you feel in any danger?"

[If individual reports any persecutory ideas/delusions, ask the following]:
"How often have you been concerned that [use individual's description]? Have you told anyone about these experiences?"

10. HALLUCINATIONS: Reports of perceptual experiences in the absence of relevant external stimuli. When rating degree to which functioning is disrupted by hallucinations, include preoccupation with the content and experience of the hallucinations, as well as functioning disrupted by acting out on the hallucinatory content (e.g., engaging in deviant behaviour due to command hallucinations). Include thoughts aloud ('gedenkenlautwerden') or pseudohallucinations (e.g., hears a voice inside head) if a voice quality is present.

2 **Very mild** While resting or going to sleep, sees visions, smells odours or hears voices, sounds, or whispers in the absence of external stimulation, but no impairment in functioning.

3 **Mild** While in a clear state of consciousness, hears a voice calling the individual's name, experiences non-verbal auditory hallucinations (e.g., sounds or whispers), formless visual hallucinations or has sensory experiences in the presence of a modality-relevant stimulus (e.g., visual illusions) infrequently (e.g., 1-2 times per week) and with no functional impairment.

4 **Moderate** Occasional verbal, visual, gustatory, olfactory or tactile hallucinations with no functional impairment OR non-verbal auditory hallucinations/visual illusions more than infrequently or with impairment.

5 **Moderately Severe** Experiences daily hallucinations OR some areas of functioning are disrupted by hallucinations.

6 **Severe** Experiences verbal or visual hallucinations several times a day OR many areas of functioning are disrupted by these hallucinations.

7 **Extremely Severe** Persistent verbal or visual hallucinations throughout the day OR most areas of functioning are disrupted by these hallucinations.

"Do you ever seem to hear your name being called?"
"Have you heard any sounds or people talking to you or about you when there has been nobody around?

[If hears voices]:
"What does the voice/voices say? Did it have a voice quality?"
"Do you ever have visions or see things that others do not see? What about smell odours that others do not smell?"

[If the individual reports hallucinations, ask the following]:
"Have these experiences interfered with your ability to perform your usual activities/work? How do you explain them? How often do they occur?"

11. UNUSUAL THOUGHT CONTENT: Unusual, odd, strange, or bizarre thought content. Rate the degree of unusualness, not the degree of disorganisation of speech. Delusions are patently absurd, clearly false or bizarre ideas that are expressed with full conviction. Consider the individual to have full conviction if he/she has acted as though the delusional belief was true. Ideas of reference/ persecution can be differentiated from delusions in that ideas are expressed with much doubt and contain more elements of reality. Include thought insertion, withdrawal and broadcast. Include grandiose, somatic and persecutory delusions even if rated elsewhere. Note: if Somatic Concern, Guilt, Suspiciousness or Grandiosity are rated 6 or 7 due to delusions, then Unusual Thought Content must be rated 4 or above.

2 **Very mild** Ideas of reference (people may stare or may laugh at him), ideas of persecution (people may mistreat him). Unusual beliefs in psychic powers, spirits, UFOs, or unrealistic beliefs in one's own abilities. Not strongly held. Some doubt.

3 **Mild** Same as 2, but degree of reality distortion is more severe as indicated by highly unusual ideas or greater conviction. Content may be typical of delusions (even bizarre), but without full conviction. The delusion does not seem to have fully formed, but is considered as one possible explanation for an unusual experience.

4 **Moderate** Delusion present but no preoccupation or functional impairment. May be an encapsulated delusion or a firmly endorsed absurd belief about past delusional circumstances.

5 **Moderately Severe** Full delusion(s) present with some preoccupation OR some areas of functioning disrupted by delusional thinking.

6 **Severe** Full delusion(s) present with much preoccupation OR many areas of functioning are disrupted by delusional thinking.

7 **Extremely Severe** Full delusion(s) present with almost total preoccupation OR most areas of functioning disrupted by delusional thinking.

"Have you been receiving any special messages from people or from the way things are arranged around you? Have you seen any references to yourself on TV or in the newspapers?"
"Can anyone read your mind?"
"Do you have a special relationship with God?"
"Is anything like electricity, X-rays, or radio waves affecting you?"
"Are thoughts put into your head that are not your own?"
"Have you felt that you were under the control of another person or force?"

[If individual reports any odd ideas/delusions, ask the following]:
"How often do you think about [use individual's description]?"
"Have you told anyone about these experiences? How do you explain the things that have been happening [specify]?"

Rate items 12-13 on the basis of individual's self-report and observed behaviour.

12. BIZARRE BEHAVIOUR: Reports of behaviours which are odd, unusual, or psychotically criminal. Not limited to interview period. Include inappropriate sexual behaviour and inappropriate affect.

2   **Very mild** Slightly odd or eccentric public behaviour, e.g., occasionally giggles to self, fails to make appropriate eye contact, that does not seem to attract the attention of others OR unusual behaviour conducted in private, e.g., innocuous rituals, that would not attract the attention of others.

3   **Mild** Noticeably peculiar public behaviour, e.g., inappropriately loud talking, makes inappropriate eye contact, OR private behaviour that occasionally, but not always, attracts the attention of others, e.g., hoards food, conducts unusual rituals, wears gloves indoors.

4   **Moderate** Clearly bizarre behaviour that attracts or would attract (if done privately) the attention or concern of others, but with no corrective intervention necessary. Behaviour occurs occasionally, e.g., fixated staring into space for several minutes, talks back to voices once, inappropriate giggling/laughter on 1-2 occasions, talking loudly to self.

5   **Moderately Severe** Clearly bizarre behaviour that attracts or would attract (if done privately) the attention of others or the authorities, e.g., fixated staring in a socially disruptive way, frequent inappropriate giggling/laughter, occasionally responds to voices, or eats non-foods.

6   **Severe** Bizarre behaviour that attracts attention of others and intervention by authorities, e.g., directing traffic, public nudity, staring into space for long periods, carrying on a conversation with hallucinations, frequent inappropriate giggling/laughter.

7   **Extremely Severe** Serious crimes committed in a bizarre way that attract the attention of others and the control of authorities, e.g., sets fires and stares at flames OR almost constant bizarre behaviour, e.g., inappropriate giggling/laughter, responds only to hallucinations and cannot be engaged in interaction.

"Have you done anything that has attracted the attention of others?"
"Have you done anything that could have gotten you into trouble with the police?"
"Have you done anything that seemed unusual or disturbing to others?"

13. SELF-NEGLECT: Hygiene, appearance, or eating behaviour below usual expectations, below socially acceptable standards or life threatening.

2   **Very mild** Hygiene/appearance slightly below usual community standards, e.g., shirt out of pants, buttons unbuttoned, shoe laces untied, but no social or medical consequences.

3   **Mild** Hygiene/appearance occasionally below usual community standards, e.g., irregular bathing, clothing is stained, hair uncombed, occasionally skips an important meal. No social or medical consequences.

4   **Moderate** Hygiene/appearance is noticeably below usual community standards, e.g., fails to bathe or change clothes, clothing very soiled, hair unkempt, needs prompting, noticeable by others OR irregular eating and drinking with minimal medical concerns and consequences.

5   **Moderately Severe** Several areas of hygiene/appearance are below usual community standards OR poor grooming draws criticism by others and requires regular prompting. Eating or hydration are irregular and poor, causing some medical problems.

6   **Severe** Many areas of hygiene/appearance are below usual community standards, does not always bathe or change clothes even if prompted. Poor grooming has caused social ostracism at school/ residence/work, or required intervention. Eating erratic and poor, may require medical intervention.

7   **Extremely Severe** Most areas of hygiene/appearance/nutrition are extremely poor and easily noticed as below usual community standards OR hygiene/appearance/nutrition require urgent and immediate medical intervention.

"How has your grooming been lately? How often do you change your clothes? How often do you take showers? Has anyone (parents/staff) complained about your grooming or dress? Do you eat regular meals?"

14. DISORIENTATION: Does not comprehend situations or communications, such as questions asked during the entire BPRS interview. Confusion regarding person, place, or time. Do not rate if incorrect responses are due to delusions.

2   **Very mild** Seems muddled or mildly confused 1-2 times during interview. Oriented to person, place and time.

3   **Mild** Occasionally muddled or mildly confused 3-4 times during interview. Minor inaccuracies in person, place, or time, e.g., date off by more than 2 days, or gives wrong division of hospital or community centre.

4   **Moderate** Frequently confused during interview. Minor inaccuracies in person, place, or time are noted, as in 3 above. In addition, may have difficulty remembering general information, e.g., name of Prime Minister.

5   **Moderately Severe** Markedly confused during interview, or to person, place, or time. Significant inaccuracies are noted, e.g., date off by more than one week, or cannot give correct name of hospital. Has difficulty remembering personal information, e.g., where he/she was born or recognising familiar people.

6   **Severe** Disoriented as to person, place, or time, e.g., cannot give correct month and year. Disoriented in 2 out of 3 spheres.

7   **Extremely Severe** Grossly disoriented as to person, place, or time, e.g., cannot give name or age. Disoriented in all three spheres.

"May I ask you some standard questions we ask everybody?"
"How old are you? What is the date [allow 2 days]"
"What is this place called? What year were you born? Who is the Prime Minister?"

Rate items 15-24 on the basis of observed behaviour and speech.

15. CONCEPTUAL DISORGANISATION: Degree to which speech is confused, disconnected, vague or disorganised. Rate tangentiality, circumstantiality, sudden topic shifts, incoherence, derailment, blocking, neologisms, and other speech disorders. Do not rate content of speech.

2   **Very mild** Peculiar use of words or rambling but speech is comprehensible.

3   **Mild** Speech a bit hard to understand or make sense of due to tangentiality, circumstantiality, or sudden topic shifts.

4   **Moderate** Speech difficult to understand due to tangentiality, circumstantiality, idiosyncratic speech, or topic shifts on many occasions OR 1-2 instances of incoherent phrases.

5   **Moderately Severe** Speech difficult to understand due to circumstantiality, tangentiality, neologisms, blocking or topic shifts most of the time, OR 3-5 instances of incoherent phrases.

6   **Severe** Speech is incomprehensible due to severe impairment most of the time. Many BPRS items cannot be rated by self-report alone.

7   **Extremely Severe** Speech is incomprehensible throughout interview.

16. BLUNTED AFFECT: Restricted range in emotional expressiveness of face, voice, and gestures. Marked indifference or flatness even when discussing distressing topics. In the case of euphoric or dysphoric individuals, rate Blunted Affect if a flat quality is also clearly present.

2   **Very mild** Emotional range is slightly subdued or reserved but displays appropriate facial expressions and tone of voice that are within normal limits.

3   **Mild** Emotional range overall is diminished, subdued or reserved, without many spontaneous and appropriate emotional responses. Voice tone is slightly monotonous.

4   **Moderate** Emotional range is noticeably diminished, individual doesn't show emotion, smile or react to distressing topics except infrequently. Voice tone is monotonous or there is noticeable decrease in spontaneous movements. Displays of emotion or gestures are usually followed by a return to flattened affect.

5   **Moderately Severe** Emotional range very diminished, individual doesn't show emotion, smile, or react to distressing topics except minimally, few gestures, facial expression does not change very often. Voice tone is monotonous much of the time.

6   **Severe** Very little emotional range or expression. Mechanical in speech and gestures most of the time. Unchanging facial expression. Voice tone is monotonous most of the time.

7   **Extremely Severe** Virtually no emotional range or expressiveness, stiff movements. Voice tone is monotonous all of the time.

Use the following probes at end of interview to assess emotional responsivity:
"Have you heard any good jokes lately? Would you like to hear a joke?"

17. EMOTIONAL WITHDRAWAL: Deficiency in individual's ability to relate emotionally during interview situation. Use your own feeling as to the presence of an 'invisible barrier' between individual and interviewer. Include withdrawal apparently due to psychotic processes.

2   **Very mild** Lack of emotional involvement shown by occasional failure to make reciprocal comments, appearing preoccupied, or smiling in a stilted manner, but spontaneously engages the interviewer most of the time.

3   **Mild** Lack of emotional involvement shown by noticeable failure to make reciprocal comments, appearing preoccupied, or lacking in warmth, but responds to interviewer when approached.

4   **Moderate** Emotional contact not present much of the interview because individual does not elaborate responses, fails to make eye contact, doesn't seem to care if interviewer is listening, or may be preoccupied with psychotic material.

5   **Moderately Severe** Same as 4 but emotional contact not present most of the interview.

6   **Severe** Actively avoids emotional participation. Frequently unresponsive or responds with yes/ no answers (not solely due to persecutory delusions). Responds with only minimal affect.

7   **Extremely Severe** Consistently avoids emotional participation. Unresponsive or responds with yes/no answers (not solely due to persecutory delusions). May leave during interview or just not respond at all.

18. MOTOR RETARDATION: Reduction in energy level evidenced by slowed movements and speech, reduced body tone, decreased number of spontaneous body movements. Rate on the basis of observed behaviour of the individual only. Do not rate on the basis of individual's subjective impression of his own energy level. Rate regardless of medication effects.

2 **Very mild** Slightly slowed or reduced movements or speech compared to most people.
3 **Mild** Noticeably slowed or reduced movements or speech compared to most people.
4 **Moderate** Large reduction or slowness in movements or speech.
5 **Moderately Severe** Seldom moves or speaks spontaneously OR very mechanical or stiff movements
6 **Severe** Does not move or speak unless prodded or urged.
7 **Extremely Severe** Frozen, catatonic.

19. TENSION: Observable physical and motor manifestations of tension, 'nervousness' and agitation. Self-reported experiences of tension should be rated under the item on anxiety. Do not rate if restlessness is solely akathisia, but do rate if akathisia is exacerbated by tension.

2 **Very mild** More fidgety than most but within normal range. A few transient signs of tension, e.g., picking at fingernails, foot wagging, scratching scalp several times or finger tapping.
3 **Mild** Same as 2, but with more frequent or exaggerated signs of tension.
4 **Moderate** Many and frequent signs of motor tension with one or more signs sometimes occurring simultaneously, e.g., wagging one's foot while wringing hands together. There are times when no signs of tension are present.
5 **Moderately Severe** Many and frequent signs of motor tension with one or more signs often occurring simultaneously. There are still rare times when no signs of tension are present.
6 **Severe** Same as 5, but signs of tension are continuous.
7 **Extremely Severe** Multiple motor manifestations of tension are continuously present, e.g., continuous pacing and hand wringing.

20. UNCO-OPERATIVENESS: Resistance and lack of willingness to co-operate with the interview. The unco-operativeness might result from suspiciousness. Rate only unco-operativeness in relation to the interview, not behaviours involving peers and relatives.

2 **Very mild** Shows non-verbal signs of reluctance, but does not complain or argue.
3 **Mild** Gripes or tries to avoid complying, but goes ahead without argument.
4 **Moderate** Verbally resists but eventually complies after questions are rephrased or repeated.
5 **Moderately Severe** Same as 4, but some information necessary for accurate ratings is withheld.
6 **Severe** Refuses to co-operate with interview, but remains in interview situation.
7 **Extremely Severe** Same as 6, with active efforts to escape the interview

21. EXCITEMENT: Heightened emotional tone or increased emotional reactivity to interviewer or topics being discussed, as evidenced by increased intensity of facial expressions, voice tone, expressive gestures or increase in speech quantity and speed.

2 **Very mild** Subtle and fleeting or questionable increase in emotional intensity. For example, at times seems keyed-up or overly alert.
3 **Mild** Subtle but persistent increase in emotional intensity. For example, lively use of gestures and variation in voice tone.
4 **Moderate** Definite but occasional increase in emotional intensity. For example, reacts to interviewer or topics that are discussed with noticeable emotional intensity. Some pressured speech.

5 Moderately Severe Definite and persistent increase in emotional intensity. For example, reacts to many stimuli, whether relevant or not, with considerable emotional intensity. Frequent pressured speech.

6 Severe Marked increase in emotional intensity. For example, reacts to most stimuli with inappropriate emotional intensity. Has difficulty settling down or staying on task. Often restless, impulsive, or speech is often pressured.

7 Extremely Severe Marked and persistent increase in emotional intensity. Reacts to all stimuli with inappropriate intensity, impulsiveness. Cannot settle down or stay on task. Very restless and impulsive most of the time. Constant pressured speech.

22. DISTRACTIBILITY: Degree to which observed sequences of speech and actions are interrupted by stimuli unrelated to the interview. Distractibility is rated when the individual shows a change in the focus of attention as characterised by a pause in speech or a marked shift in gaze. Individual's attention may be drawn to noise in adjoining room, books on a shelf, interviewer's clothing, etc. Do not rate circumstantiality, tangentiality or flight of ideas. Also, do not rate rumination with delusional material. Rate even if the distracting stimulus cannot be identified.

2 Very mild Generally can focus on interviewer's questions with only 1 distraction or inappropriate shift of attention of brief duration.

3 Mild Individual shifts focus of attention to matters unrelated to the interview 2-3 times.

4 Moderate Often responsive to irrelevant stimuli in the room, e.g., averts gaze from the interviewer.

5 Moderately Severe Same as above, but now distractibility clearly interferes with the flow of the interview.

6 Severe Extremely difficult to conduct interview or pursue a topic due to preoccupation with irrelevant stimuli.

7 Extremely Severe Impossible to conduct interview due to preoccupation with irrelevant stimuli.

23. MOTOR HYPERACTIVITY: Increase in energy level evidenced in more frequent movement and/or rapid speech. Do not rate if restlessness is due to akathisia.

2 Very mild Some restlessness, difficulty sitting still, lively facial expressions, or somewhat talkative

3 Mild Occasionally very restless, definite increase in motor activity, lively gestures, 1-3 brief instances of pressured speech.

4 Moderate Very restless, fidgety, excessive facial expressions, or non-productive and repetitious motor movements. Much pressured speech, up to one-third of the interview.

5 Moderately Severe Frequently restless, fidgety. Many instances of excessive non-productive and repetitious motor movements. On the move most of the time. Frequent pressured speech, difficult to interrupt. Rises on 1-2 occasions to pace.

6 Severe Excessive motor activity, restlessness, fidgety, loud tapping, noisy, etc., throughout most of the interview. Speech can only be interrupted with much effort. Rises on 3-4 occasions to pace.

7 Extremely Severe Constant excessive motor activity throughout entire interview, e.g., constant pacing, constant pressured speech with no pauses, individual can only be interrupted briefly and only small amounts of relevant information can be obtained.

24. MANNERISMS AND POSTURING: Unusual and bizarre behaviour, stylised movements or acts, or any postures which are clearly uncomfortable or inappropriate. Exclude obvious manifestations of medication side effects. Do not include nervous mannerisms that are not odd or unusual.

2   **Very mild** Eccentric or odd mannerisms or activity that ordinary persons would have difficulty explaining, e.g., grimacing, picking. Observed once for a brief period.

3   **Mild** Same as 2, but occurring on two occasions of brief duration.

4   **Moderate** Mannerisms or posturing, e.g., stylised movements or acts, rocking, nodding, rubbing, or grimacing, observed on several occasions for brief periods or infrequently but very odd. For example, uncomfortable posture maintained for 5 seconds more than twice.

5   **Moderately Severe** Same as 4, but occurring often, or several examples of very odd mannerisms or posturing that are idiosyncratic to the individual.

6   **Severe** Frequent stereotyped behaviour, assumes and maintains uncomfortable or inappropriate postures, intense rocking, smearing, strange rituals or foetal posturing. Individual can interact with people and the environment for brief periods despite these behaviours.

7   **Extremely Severe** Same as 6, but individual cannot interact with people or the environment due to these behaviours.

5.7.7 INDIVIDUAL FAMILY MEMBER INTERVIEW

This semi-structured interview is adapted with permission from an interview developed by Ian Falloon. The interview is designed to elicit very specific information about the current goals, problems, and problem-solving functions of each family member. The relative contribution by each member of the family unit is also assessed. The specific problems listed below are to be used in a flexible way in order to gather all relevant details.

Introduction

"I would like to spend some time getting to know you better. I am going to ask you about situations that you find stressful in your life, and how your family helps you overcome these problems. Also, I would like to get an idea of your own goals, and how your family helps you to achieve these goals. This information will help me to decide the best way we can help your family to work together for everyone's benefit. Do you have any questions before we start?"

1. Background Information

Relevant information is gathered about the individual's social and medical background (i.e., education, occupation, past medical and psychiatric treatment)

2. Knowledge Of Index Individual's Disorder

Make particular note of environmental (e.g., stressors) and biological (e.g., medication) factors that lead to improvement or worsening of the disorder.

- What do you understand about ....'s problem?
- What is the problem called?
- What do you think causes it?
- What do you think seems to help?
- What do you do that seems to make things worse?
- What do you know about the medication he/she is currently receiving (e.g., type, dosage, etc.)?
- What do you see as the benefits of the medication?
- What are the undesirable effects of the medication?

3. Impact Of Disorder

- What are the main difficulties you have had with the individual (experienced)?
- How do you cope with his/her (your) symptoms or behaviour (as described by above answer)?
- All things considered, how much of a burden is the individual to you (how much of a burden is your illness)?

4. Activity Survey

Disability may prevent individuals from getting the most out of their environment, hence dissatisfaction and frustration may result. Discovering what individuals find rewarding and what they find unpleasant may provide a focus for change.

- What activities take up most of your time? (e.g., work, chores, hobbies, doing nothing, etc.) What activities would you like to spend more time doing?
- What prevents you from doing the things you like?
- Where do you spend most of your time? (e.g., work, home, bedroom, garden, parks, etc.)
- Where would you like to be able to spend more time?
- Who do you spend most of your time with? (e.g., workmates, friends, family, alone, etc.)

- Who would you like to be able to spend more time with?
- Do you have a person you can discuss your problems with? How often?
- Do you need more privacy? Do you have your own bedroom?
- Do you have a sexual partner? (choose appropriate wording)
- How would you like your friendships to be better? (more/less intimate)
- What situations (activities, people, places) do you dislike/avoid?
- Does anyone in the family bother/concern you? How much time do you spend with them? How would you like them to be different?

5. Personal Goals

- If your current problems were removed or reduced, what would you like to be doing in three months time? (pinpoint 1-2 goals)
- What people (family, friends, etc.) could help you to achieve this goal? (specify)
- What may prevent you from achieving this goal? (specify)
- What steps have you achieved already? (specify)

6. Other Problems

Designed to gain a picture of the typical activities of the family member, specific problems encountered, and desire for specific changes.

- What other problems do you have in your everyday life? Specify problems that may not be identified by the family member as current limitations of functioning:
  (e.g., marital conflict, medical or psychiatric symptoms, lack of friendship, social skills deficits, substance abuse, financial stress, housing problems, work related problems, cultural conflicts, etc.)

Note: Whenever a problem is described:
1. Ask for a clear example.
2. Ask family member how he/she feels about the problem.
3. Ask family member how he/she and the family have attempted to resolve the problem.

5.7.8 EARLY WARNING SIGNS FORM [1]

EARLY WARNING SIGNS

Name: _____

I am at risk of developing episodes of: _____

My early warning signs are:

1. _____

2. _____

3. _____

Whenever I have *any* of these signs I will respond by:

1. _____

   _____

2. _____

   _____

   _____

3. _____

My doctor is: _____Phone: _____

My home contact is: _____Phone: _____

If I have any concerns about my illness I will contact:

_____ immediately.

---

[1] Reprinted with permission from Falloon, I.R.H., Laporta, M., Fadden, G. & Graham-Hole, V. (1993). Managing Stress in Families: Cognitive and Behavioural Strategies for Enhancing Coping Skills. London: Routledge.

5.7.9 WHAT IS SCHIZOAFFECTIVE DISORDER?

Schizoaffective disorder is an illness in which the individual has symptoms of schizophrenia and symptoms of affective disorder *at the same time.*

A description of schizoaffective disorder

Episodes of schizoaffective disorder may be of a depressive type or a manic type. These 'types' are described below.

Schizoaffective disorder (depressive type) involves symptoms of depression such as: loss of sleep; loss of energy; loss of appetite or weight; feeling less interested in things; poor concentration; feelings of guilt and hopelessness; and suicidal thoughts. Within the same period of illness, symptoms of schizophrenia are also present. These symptoms may include such things as: the feeling that one's thoughts are being broadcast to the world or interfered with in some way; the belief that one is controlled by alien forces or is being plotted against or spied upon by someone else; hearing voices that talk about killing the individual or which make unpleasant remarks about the individual, for example, that the individual is worthless and should be punished.

In *schizoaffective disorder (manic type)* the disturbance of mood usually takes the form of elation, with increased self-esteem and unrealistically high opinions of oneself and one's abilities. Sometimes excitement and irritability may be more obvious and individuals may behave more aggressively. Also present is: an increase in energy and overactivity; poor concentration; and socially inappropriate behaviour (e.g., increased sexual activity towards friends or strangers, or overspending). During the same period of illness, symptoms of schizophrenia are also present. These symptoms may include such things as: the feeling that thoughts are being broadcast to the world, inserted into the mind, or interfered with in some way; the belief that one is controlled by alien forces; paranoid ideas (e.g., that someone is trying to steal the individual's magical powers or that assassination is likely because of the individual's fame or special talents); or hearing voices that may comment on the individual's talents and fame.

What causes schizoaffective disorder?

No-one knows exactly what causes this illness although we do know that the illness is associated with a disturbance of the balance of chemicals in the brain. Those affected are generally young people who were functioning well before the onset of the disorder and who have relatives who have suffered from depression or mania. Episodes of illness usually occur following life stress. Therefore, the picture seems to suggest that individuals who have a genetic or family vulnerability towards developing this illness tend to have episodes of illness that are triggered by life stress and which cause the chemicals in the brain to become unbalanced.

Will I get better?

After reading the previous descriptions you will see that schizoaffective disorder is a bit like having two illnesses rolled into one. Many individuals make a complete recovery after a schizoaffective episode. Recovery from a manic-type episode tends to be quicker than recovery from a depressive-type episode. Symptoms disappear on their own or after treatment with lithium, or antidepressant or antipsychotic medication. Additionally, by taking regular medication individuals may prevent or reduce the likelihood of further episodes of illness in the future. Over a lifetime, some individuals will have only one episode of illness while others will have multiple episodes of the manic and/or depressive type. Although the likelihood of recovery from a schizoaffective episode is quite promising, some individuals may develop long-lasting problems such as difficulty concentrating or thinking clearly, or a lower ability to 'feel' strong emotions.

Schizoaffective disorder is usually treated with techniques that have been developed for schizophrenia and for depression or mania. For further information please refer to the handouts on schizophrenia, depression, and mania. Your clinician can give you these handouts.

6

DIETING DISORDERS

6.1 DIETING DISORDERS

6.1.1 ABOUT DIETING DISORDERS

The dieting disorders include anorexia nervosa and bulimia nervosa, both of which involve serious psychiatric and physical disturbances. As individuals with both disorders adopt restricted eating patterns and excessive dieting behaviours, they are perhaps more appropriately referred to as dieting disorders rather than eating disorders. The term dieting disorder will therefore be used throughout this text.

It is important that clinicians can recognise clinical and subclinical presentations of dieting disorders, and also have some knowledge about simple management strategies. While some people experience severe forms of one or other of these disorders, many experience incomplete forms or may sporadically exhibit only a few of the relevant symptoms (e.g., occasional episodes of binge-eating with or without vomiting). If an individual presents with severe disturbances in dieting behaviour or a dieting disorder, it is negligent not to refer that person to a clinician or unit specialised in the treatment of these disorders, if such services are available. If specialist clinicians are not available, the generalist clinician may choose either to refer the person further afield or to commence treatment with the aid of the strategies outlined in this chapter. The clinician is advised to seek consultation with an expert over the telephone to obtain assistance and guidance throughout the management process.

Clinicians choosing to treat dieting problems need to be aware of the following issues:
- Medical supervision is imperative. If this is not possible, the individual will need to be referred to a health centre or specialist who has access to an appropriate medical practitioner.
- Liaison with a dietician who is experienced in the area of dieting disorders is strongly recommended. If no such experienced clinician is available, consultation via telephone is recommended.
- It is common for people to deny their dieting behaviours and to downplay the severity of their symptoms. Clinicians should maintain a high index of suspicion for this disorder in any person who is underweight, losing weight rapidly, or who presents with any of the other symptoms of anorexia or bulimia nervosa.
- Be suspicious of women whose children are not gaining weight or developing at the expected rate. Often these mothers have a dieting disorder and may consequently underfeed their children.
- If a person is brought to the clinician's attention via a parent or spouse who is concerned that their loved one has a dieting disorder, it is generally the case that the relative is correct.
- Most people with anorexia nervosa do not cut their wrists or take overdoses, but people with bulimia nervosa often do. These people may be extremely difficult to treat and will often need referral to someone who is specialised in dealing with such behaviours.

6.1.2 ANOREXIA NERVOSA

DIAGNOSIS

The World Health Organization's (WHO) International Classification of Disease (ICD) 10th Edition requires the following features for a diagnosis of anorexia nervosa:

- The individual's body-mass index (BMI) is 17.5 or less, or body weight is maintained at least 15% below the expected or average body weight for the individual's age and sex. If prepubertal, the expected weight gain does not occur during the growth period.
- Weight loss is self-induced and/or sustained through the avoidance of 'fattening' foods and through the utilisation of other weight loss tactics such as self-induced vomiting, laxative or diuretic abuse, excessive exercise, and appetite suppressants.
- Body-image distortion and a morbid dread of fatness is present.
- There is evidence of an endocrine disorder in the form of amenorrhoea among women and loss of sexual desire and potency among men. There may also be elevated levels of growth hormone and cortisol, alterations to the metabolism of the thyroid hormone, and abnormal insulin secretion.

Body-Mass Index (BMI)

A calculation of the BMI is the best way to measure the extent to which an individual is underweight or overweight. The BMI can be calculated by dividing the individual's weight by the square of his or her height, as indicated in the following formula. For adults, a healthy BMI is in the range of 20-25. A healthy BMI for adolescents is lower, at about 18.5.

$$BMI = \frac{weight\ (kgs)}{[height\ (m)]^2}$$

When weighing individuals, keep the following points in mind:

- Use the same scales each time (preferably a scale with sliding weights along the top, as used in hospitals and gymnasiums since these scales are the most accurate).
- Ensure the scales are calibrated accurately at zero before use.
- Occasionally, some individuals with anorexia nervosa may try to make themselves appear heavier than they really are by strapping weights close to their body or carrying heavy objects in their pockets or will drink low calorie fluids and avoid toileting before weighing.
- Excess clothing should be removed, such as coats, jumpers, scarves, shoes, belts, watches, etc.

DIFFERENTIAL DIAGNOSIS

In the absence of indicators of anorexia nervosa, the clinician may suspect a **somatic cause of weight loss** such as Crohn's disease, a brain tumour, a malabsorption syndrome, or another chronic debilitating disease. People who are experiencing a **major depressive episode** may lose weight following the loss of appetite or motivation to eat. However, people with anorexia nervosa do not experience a loss of appetite; rather, they *choose* not to eat despite great hunger and desire for food (although they may deny being hungry if asked). Also, unlike people with anorexia nervosa, depressed people do not exhibit an excessive concern about their body shape or the caloric content of food, unless the depression is secondary to a diagnosis of anorexia or bulimia nervosa. Furthermore, unlike those who are depressed, people with anorexia nervosa will be pleased about their weight loss. **Obsessional symptoms** (e.g., fear of eating contaminated food, or decreased food intake due to the urge to chew each mouthful a specific number of times, etc.) may also account for weight loss. As always, a thorough psychiatric history will need to be taken prior to making a firm diagnosis.

DESCRIPTION

Physical symptoms of anorexia nervosa

Some of the physical symptoms of anorexia nervosa are directly related to the effects of starvation while other physical symptoms are mainly associated with behavioural problems such as excessive exercising, vomiting, or purging. The table below lists the most common physical symptoms.

Physical symptoms caused mainly by starvation

- Amenorrhoea
- Dry skin
- Lanugo hair (fine downy hair) on exterior surfaces of the body such as the back, face, arms
- Fatigue
- Abdominal discomfort on eating (from shrunken stomach)
- Dizziness and ringing in the ears
- Headaches
- Stunting of growth in younger people
- Hypothermia (low body temperature) and sensitivity to cold and heat due to diminished layers of fat
- Hypotension (low blood pressure)
- Bradycardia (pulse rate < 60) and heart arrhythmias
- Reduced gastric motility
- Brittle hair or hair loss
- Constipation due to lack of bulk in bowels and the abuse of laxatives
- Hyperactivity
- Brittle bones and osteoporosis resulting from low oestrogens (amenorrhoea) and calcium depletion, often leading to stress fractures in those who overexercise

Physical symptoms caused mainly by behavioural problems

- Dental decay (caused by the high acid content in vomit)
- Polyuria (excessive urine secretion often due to excessive water consumption)
- Paresthesias (abnormal sensations of burning, prickling, or tingling arising from biochemical disturbances)
- Disturbed blood chemistry (from vomiting and laxative abuse)
- Stress fractures from excessive exercise and brittle bones
- Swollen salivary glands from excessive vomiting

From the clinical viewpoint, the most concerning of these symptoms are the biochemical and cardiac complications which may be life-threatening, and the osteoporosis which may have irreversible effects.

Psychological symptoms of anorexia nervosa

As with physical symptoms, psychological symptoms may be caused directly by starvation or may be independent and/or premorbid. The most common psychological symptoms are listed in the table on the following page.

Physical symptoms caused by starvation
- Depression
- Loss of concentration
- Preoccupation with thoughts of food
- Anxiety
- Labile mood (i.e., fluctuating from one extreme to another)
- Irritability
- Feelings of inadequacy
- Hypersensitivity to noise
- Obsessional thinking
- Increased perfectionism
- Social withdrawal so as to avoid situations involving eating
- Depression/suicidal ideation

Psychological symptoms that are premorbid or unrelated to starvation
- Low self-esteem
- Obsessional traits
- A tendency towards perfectionism

Abnormal eating-related behaviours

People with anorexia nervosa exhibit abnormal patterns of eating, and may also engage in unusual behaviours *during* meals. Some of these abnormal behaviours are listed in the following box. Not every person will exhibit all of these behaviours.

Abnormal eating-related behaviours include
- A refusal to eat
- Obsessional calorie counting or measurement of food quantities
- A reluctance to eat with other people and minimal conversation during meals
- Eating different food from the rest of the family
- Eating at different times from the rest of the family
- Leaving the table frequently during meals, especially to go to the bathroom
- Eating extremely slowly
- Cutting food into tiny pieces
- Secretly disposing of food during meals (e.g., feeding the food to a pet under the table, wrapping food in a napkin, or putting food in pockets)
- Excessive water consumption
- Excessive use of condiments (e.g., mustard)
- Unusual or inappropriate combinations of food
- Using inappropriate eating utensils
- Eating food in a specific sequence
- Fussiness about food or claiming to have a dislike of, or a 'reaction' to particular foods, especially red meat, sweets, and fatty foods
- Difficulty choosing what to eat
- Excessive interest in what other people are eating
- Feeling full after eating only a small amount of food
- Excessive use of diet foods (e.g., those that are low-fat or artificially sweetened)
- A desire to talk about food all the time
- Excessive handling of food, desire to do the shopping, and take over the preparation of meals

Anorexia nervosa is different from normal dieting in the following ways:
- Weight loss goals are constantly changing such that once a weight loss goal has been reached, a new, lower goal is set.
- The dieting behaviour is solitary. Most dieters discuss their dieting progress and tactics with their peers. Determined, solitary dieting should be regarded warily.
- The individual is usually dissatisfied with success. Most dieters are pleased if they lose a few kilograms. Successful dieters who remain self-critical may be at risk.
- Menstruation ceases (amenorrhoea).

COURSE AND PROGNOSIS

Approximately 70% of people with anorexia nervosa return to the normal range of body weight within about six months of intervention. However, 15-25% of people later relapse, and some eventually die from the disorder as a result of cardiac arrhythmias, opportunistic infections, suicide, or starvation, and approximately the same proportion remain chronically ill. In fact, follow-up studies conducted four years after the onset of illness indicate that about 50% of people have an apparently good outcome (weight within normal range and a return of menstruation), 25% have an intermediate outcome, and 25% have a poor outcome. At 20 year follow-up, studies indicate a mortality rate of almost 20%, suggesting that most patients who retain chronic morbid preoccupations with food and weight go on to serious physical morbidity. Those people whose illness is less severe and who are treated as outpatients tend to have better outcomes although the chronic nature of the disorder makes long-term maintenance programmes necessary for the prevention of relapse.

Among those people who are receiving outpatient treatment, a good prognosis is indicated by:
- An absence of severe emaciation (i.e., body-mass index > 17)
- An absence of serious medical complications
- The motivation to change present behaviours
- The presence of supportive family and friends

Poor prognosis is indicated by:
- A later age of onset
- A history of neurotic and personality disturbances
- Disturbed family relationships
- A longer duration of illness

Generally, early recognition and intervention are highly desirable and are likely to lead to improved outcome. However, recovery is possible even after a long duration of illness and it is never too late to attempt vigorous treatment.

6.1.3 BULIMIA NERVOSA

DIAGNOSIS

According to the World Health Organization's (WHO) International Classification of Diseases (ICD) 10th Edition, bulimia nervosa is diagnosed when:

- An individual consumes large quantities of food in short periods of time, following irresistible food cravings and a persistent preoccupation with eating.
- The individual engages in compensatory weight loss behaviours such as self-induced vomiting, purging, intermittent periods of starvation, the use of appetite suppressants, thyroid preparations, diuretics, or excessive exercise. People with diabetes may choose to neglect their insulin treatment.
- The individual has a morbid fear of fatness and strives to attain or maintain a weight that is below his or her optimum weight, as determined by the physician. Anorexia nervosa may have been diagnosed at some stage in the past.

The Diagnostic and Statistical Manual for Mental Disorders, 4th Edition (DSM-IV) diagnostic criteria also includes a time frame for these behaviours whereby binge-eating and compensatory weight loss behaviours are engaged in at least twice a week for three months. DSM-IV also requires that the individual experiences a lack of control during binge-eating episodes such that he or she cannot stop eating and cannot control the type or quantity of food that is eaten. Additionally, DSM-IV also distinguishes between purging and non-purging subtypes of bulimia nervosa. This diagnosis is excluded if the disturbance occurs only during episodes of anorexia nervosa.

DIFFERENTIAL DIAGNOSIS

The clinician will need to differentiate between bulimia nervosa and **anorexia nervosa**. The main distinguishing feature is body weight - people with bulimia nervosa are usually at, or near, normal weight while anorexics are severely underweight. If all the criteria for anorexia nervosa are met then the individual should be given this diagnosis rather than bulimia nervosa, even if binge-eating and purging are present. **Gastrointestinal disorders** may involve repeated vomiting and as such needs to be considered as a differential diagnosis. People who have the central nervous system disorder called **Kleine-Levin syndrome** exhibit disturbed eating behaviour, however, they do not report excessive concern about body shape and weight. Symptoms of bulimia nervosa such as binge-eating may be present in individuals who have **major depressive episodes** and **personality disturbances**. Careful history taking and assessment will help to differentiate these disorders.

DESCRIPTION

Binge-eating episodes

Binge-eating is when an individual eats, during a short period of time, quantities of food that are definitely larger than most people would eat during a similar time frame and in similar circumstances. During a binge-eating episode, individuals report a sense of loss of control over their eating behaviour. The episodes usually occur in secret and are often a source of disgust and self-loathing.

Most people with bulimia nervosa binge-eat at least once a day and the sessions generally occur at weekends or during the evening. For many people, binge-eating becomes a part of the daily routine. Binges may be planned in advance, and food will be bought, prepared, and hoarded in a ritualised way.

A typical binge will usually involve the consumption of high-carbohydrate and high-fat foods, and 'junk food' may also be eaten. Interestingly, these are the foods that would otherwise have been avoided because they are viewed as being 'fattening'. The texture of the food is chosen on the basis that it is easy to swallow and regurgitate. Fluids may also be ingested to facilitate vomiting. During the early stages of binge-eating, the food tends to be consumed rapidly. However, during later binge-eating sessions the individual may eat more slowly and 'pick' or graze throughout the day. The duration of a binge-eating episode is variable but typically lasts for about an hour.

Binge-eating may be precipitated by a number of factors including:
- Cravings for a particular kind of food
- A reaction to eating 'forbidden' or 'fattening' foods
- A reaction to restricted eating or total fasting
- Mood states such as depression, anxiety, frustration, hostility, boredom, and excitement
- Being alone
- Stressful life events
- A reaction to specific situations or interpersonal difficulties

A binge-eating episode is usually terminated in response to:
- Abdominal fullness, pain, and distension
- Social interruptions
- The need to sleep
- 'Running out of steam'

Physical symptoms of bulimia nervosa
- Swollen salivary glands from recurrent vomiting, often confused with mumps
- Amenorrhoea (cessation of menstruation for at least 3 months) or irregular menstruation caused by energy deficiency during periods of starvation
- Dental decay (caused by the high acid content of vomit)
- Acute stretching or dilatation of the stomach due to overeating, often associated with abdominal pain
- Irritable bowel, dark mucus in the colon (melanosis coli), and disturbed bowel motions from chronic laxative abuse
- Electrolyte imbalances from purging, possibly leading to heart arrhythmias, brain seizures, abnormal EEGs, muscle cramps and stiffness, liver disease, and kidney failure
- Swollen hands and feet, swollen salivary glands
- Fatigue
- Nausea
- Headaches
- Hair loss
- Bruising
- Insomnia
- Chronic hoarseness of the voice
- Urinary tract infections
- Callused knuckles
- Hypokalemia (low potassium) as revealed by blood tests

COURSE AND PROGNOSIS

Very little is known about the natural course of bulimia nervosa. There is research to suggest that untreated bulimia nervosa runs a chronic course, however, this is based on short-term follow-up (< 2 years) only. In the short-term, the outcome following treatment appears to be good with approximately 70% of individuals reporting a substantial reduction of symptoms of bulimia nervosa.

Individuals who have milder symptoms at the commencement of treatment tend to have a better prognosis than those individuals who are disabled and functioning poorly at the start of treatment. Additionally, other indicators of poor prognosis include premorbid personality disturbance, low self-esteem, impulsivity and persistent body image dissatisfaction.

Given that dieting disorders appear to be more difficult to overcome once they are well established, it is essential that clinicians are able to recognise this disorder while it is still in the early stages. Immediate intervention for any person who only binges or purges on odd occasions may help to prevent the development of a chronic and dangerous illness.

6.1.4 ASSESSMENT

The assessment of dieting disorders will involve both a psychiatric assessment and a medical assessment. Ideally, assessment of symptoms will occur not only at the beginning of treatment but should be repeated at appropriate points *during and after* treatment. In this way progress can be measured and the management plan can be adapted accordingly. An important aspect of assessment is to feed the results back to the individual. Feedback is useful for enhancing motivation, especially if the feedback shows evidence of positive progress.

PSYCHIATRIC ASSESSMENT

The aim of a psychiatric assessment is to:

1. Identify the main diagnosis and any other comorbid disorders or problems.
2. Highlight the areas that require intervention (e.g., encouraging weight gain, or controlling binge-eating) so that goals can be set and a management plan can be devised.
3. Identify a baseline against which improvement or deterioration can be measured.

A psychiatric history and mental state examination (see Chapter 1: Core Management Skills) are standard components of assessment for all psychiatric disorders. In addition, the following assessment procedures will also be useful.

Eating Behaviour Assessment Interview

This interview (see Section 6.3.1) was designed for this textbook to help clinicians obtain relevant and detailed information about the dieting disorder. This form is not a diagnostic interview but is used simply for information gathering purposes. Clinicians who are experienced in this area may choose to use their own interview procedure.

Eating Attitudes Test (EAT)

This test, designed by Garner and Garfinkel (see bibliography), is one of the most extensively used self-rating scales for dieting disorders. The EAT was designed to assess a range of eating behaviours and attitudes that are associated with anorexia nervosa. The EAT is also useful for assessing bulimia nervosa, even though it was not originally designed for this disorder. Regular use of the EAT will highlight improvement or deterioration of symptoms over time and will enable clinicians to adapt their management strategies accordingly. Other psychological tests (e.g., the Eating Disorders Inventory) are available for use with this population and may be better for assessing bulimia nervosa.

Food and behaviour diary

During the assessment and engagement phase it may be useful to ask the individual to keep a food and behaviour diary (see example opposite, and Section 6.3.2). In this diary the individual records:

- The time of day at which food is eaten
- The type and amount of food that is eaten
- Where the food was eaten
- Whether binge-eating, vomiting, or purging occurred
- The context of eating (e.g., what prompted the individual to eat, what feelings or thoughts occurred at that time)
- The type and duration of exercise

A food and behaviour diary can be used for self-monitoring during the engagement phase and it allows both the individual and the clinician obtain a clearer view of current behaviours. Such information will be important when it comes to identifying the times of day and situations during which there is the highest risk of problem eating. By identifying high risk situations the individual can take steps to reduce the risk of at such times through the use of alternative coping strategies (see Section 6.1.10). Once treatment has commenced, the food diary can also be used to monitor progress.

Not everyone will keep accurate diaries. Some individuals will resent having to record all their eating behaviours while others will forget to do so or will not appreciate the usefulness of keeping such a diary. Generally, individuals with anorexia nervosa tend to be quite obsessional and are therefore more likely to keep food diaries. As the clinician is attempting to help the individual focus away from obsessional monitoring of food consumed, having individuals with anorexia nervosa keep a food diary for longer than one week can be counterproductive.

Binge Monitoring Form

This form was designed for this text for the purpose of obtaining detailed information about binge-eating episodes. While a food diary is useful for obtaining an overall picture of binge-eating episodes, the Binge Monitoring Form will allow a more thorough examination of the emotions, behaviours, and thoughts that precede, accompany, and follow binge-eating episodes (e.g., the presence of unrealistic or negative beliefs; the use of laxatives, vomiting, diuretics; factors that trigger episodes of binge-eating; high-risk situations). Such information may enhance the individual's insight and will allow the clinician to tailor the management plan to suit each person (e.g., education about laxative abuse; activity scheduling and goal planning if the individual eats out of boredom; relaxation training and structured problem solving if the individual eats as a means of coping with stress and life problems).

The Binge Monitoring Form is best filled out as soon as possible after a binge. This form is likely to be most useful when the number of binge-eating episodes each day or week is low. Therefore, if the individual initially binges very frequently each day, it would be best to introduce this form during a later stage of treatment, after the number of binge-eating episodes has decreased somewhat. The Binge Monitoring Form can be found in Section 6.3.3.

PHYSICAL ASSESSMENT

Body Mass Index (BMI)

Anorexics will need to have their BMI monitored on a regular (weekly) basis. Individuals with bulimia nervosa may also wish to monitor their weight. Multiple daily weighing sessions are to be avoided since fluctuations in body fluid content can cause weight to vary slightly throughout the day and from one day to the next. The gain or loss of fat or muscle tissue is more accurately determined by regular weekly weight measurements.

Sample Food and Behaviour Diary

Day and Date: _____

*B = Binge   V/P = Vomiting or Purging

Time	Food and liquid consumed	Place	*B	*V/P	Context	Exercise Type	Exercise Duration
7.54	1 apple 1 black coffee	kitchen	no	no	Breakfast. Felt good and slim.		
10.45	1 black coffee	work	no	no			
12.45						swimming	40 mins
1.45	2 black coffees fruit salad (medium) 1 unbuttered roll	desk at work	no	yes (V)	Felt OK till I had the bread roll - then I knew I had to vomit.		
3.45	5 Tim Tams	work tearoom	yes	yes (V)	I couldn't resist them & no-one was around - then I felt guilty & fat & had to vomit.		
4.00	1 black coffee	desk at work	no	no			
6.10	1 bowl cereal & low fat milk 1 manderin salad & vinegar (no oil)	kitchen	no	no	I felt really hungry. Still feel really hungry but must not put on weight.		
7.30						aerobics	1 hour
9.55	8-9 peanut wafer biscuits 3 bowls chocolate ice cream 1 packet (500gm) oven french fries & tomato sauce 2 cups orange juice 2 cups water	kitchen	yes	yes (V&P)	Couldn't stop thinking about food. Hungry - kind of knew I was going to binge, ever since dinner time. Took 18 Ford pills. Felt disgusted with myself. Why am I so weak?		

Advise individuals that if they wish to weigh themselves, the best time to do so is on the same day each week, before getting dressed in the morning. If individuals feel unable to avoid multiple weighing sessions, perhaps they could be encouraged to remove their scales from sight or give the scales to a friend or family member for safe-keeping.

Medical assessment

Section 6.3.4 contains a minimum list of investigations to be conducted by the individual's doctor. This handout may be photocopied and sent to the treating doctor prior to medical assessment or taken to the appointment by the individual.

ASSESSMENT OF CHILDREN AND ADOLESCENTS

Young people with dieting disorders are usually brought to the attention of health workers by concerned relatives, typically mothers. With the child's permission, it is important during the early stage of the interview for the mother to be given the opportunity to explain her concerns in front of her child. The mother's account of her child's eating and/or dieting behaviours would also be elicited at this time (e.g., how the child behaves at the dinner table, how she responds when asked to finish a meal, indications of food disposal or vomiting). Confrontation is to be avoided and the child should be given the chance to reply calmly to her mother's concerns. After this point the mother leaves the room so that the clinician and child can continue with the interview and explore these claims further in private.

WHEN IS HOSPITAL ADMISSION REQUIRED?

Under most Mental Health Acts, a dieting disorder is not recognised as a mental illness that requires involuntary hospital admission. As such it is difficult or impossible to section someone on the basis of his or her refusal to eat, or refusal to cease binge-eating, vomiting, or purging. However, if it is felt that hospital based care is required and the individual will not accept such care on a voluntary basis, liaison with the local Department of Health may be helpful for securing hospital admission.

Hospital admission may be required for anorexia nervosa if:
- The Body Mass Index falls below 16.
- Weight loss is rapid (e.g., 4-5 kgs in one week or 1kg per week over a number of weeks).
- There are abnormal electrocardiogram, liver function, haematology, or biochemistry test results.
- There is marked dehydration with hypotension less than 90mmHg systolic blood pressure.
- There is bradycardia in which the heart rate is less than 40 beats per minute with symptoms of faintness.
- The individual is felt to be a serious suicide risk.
- The individual has been severely underweight for a long period of time and has not responded to outpatient treatment.
- Outpatient treatment has not been successful for interrupting the vicious cycle of binge-eating followed by purging or vomiting.

Hospital admission for bulimia nervosa is recommended under the following circumstances:
- Well-designed outpatient treatment has not been effective and the bulimic behaviour is severe or life-threatening due to electrolyte or cardiac problems.
- Antidepressant medication is required but safe monitoring or adequate compliance cannot be guaranteed in outpatient treatment.
- The individual is suicidal.

6.1.5 MANAGEMENT GUIDELINES

Anorexia nervosa and bulimia nervosa have much in common. In fact, it is argued that the two disorders lie on a continuum. The management of the two disorders therefore has much in common and the plan outlined below is relevant to both anorexia nervosa and bulimia nervosa. The clinician, however, needs to adapt this management plan depending on the specific symptom profile. Treatment would ideally:

1. Be planned following a thorough analysis of all relevant problems.
2. Target both the symptoms of the dieting disorder (e.g., weight loss, binge-eating) and other psychosocial problems.
3. Be based upon specific rules while remaining sufficiently flexible to suit each person's changing needs.
4. Be understood by individuals and their families.
5. Include the family as much as is necessary or possible.
6. Guarantee continuity of care over an extended period of time.
7. Be evaluated regularly for positive and negative outcomes in the present and in the future, at least for 3 months in bulimia nervosa and at least for a year in anorexia nervosa.

The initial stage of management aims to restore normal eating patterns so as to correct any biological and psychological consequences of malnutrition that may perpetuate disordered eating behaviour. Subsequent treatment aims to resolve associated psychological, social, family, and behavioural problems that may contribute to the disorder. Such treatments also act to help prevent relapse.

The main aims and stages of treatment are:

1. To conduct a thorough psychiatric assessment (Section 6.1.4) (including suicide assessment, see Core Management Skills in Chapter 1)
2. To conduct a thorough physical assessment (Section 6.1.4)
3. To gain the individual's co-operation (Section 6.1.6) through:
   - The establishment of a therapeutic relationship
   - Acknowledgement and empathy for the individual's distress
   - Basic education (Section 6.1.7)
   - Insight gained through the use of a food diary (pp. 434-435)
4. To help the individual plan appropriate and desirable goals (Section 6.1.8)
5. To restore weight (in the case of anorexia nervosa) and normal eating patterns (Section 6.1.9) by:
   - Developing a well-balanced, nutritious, and regular eating plan
   - Providing education about nutrition
   - Rewarding and encouraging adaptive behaviours (Section 6.1.11)
6. To modify bulimic behaviours (Section 6.1.10) by:
   - Monitoring bulimic behaviours
   - Restoring normal eating patterns
   - Providing education about binge-eating and compensatory weight loss behaviours (Section 6.1.7)
   - Encouraging the use of alternative coping strategies (Section 6.1.10)
   - Rewarding and encouraging adaptive behaviours (Section 6.1.11)
7. To foster healthy thoughts, beliefs, and values about body shape, body weight, and eating by:
   - Challenging unrealistic beliefs (Section 6.1.12)
   - Providing education (Section 6.1.7)
   - Providing or referring for further psychotherapy as needed

8. To enhance the individual's psychological and physical well-being (Section 6.1.13) through:
   - Psychotherapy
   - Fostering interests and achievements in other domains of the individual's life (goal planning)
   - Stress management strategies
   - The enhancement of family support and communication
9. To prevent or effectively manage relapse (Section 6.1.15) with the aid of:
   - Education about relapse
   - Follow-up assessment

6.1.6 GAINING CO-OPERATION

People with anorexia nervosa are often reluctant to present for treatment. They may deny that they are ill and often only enter the mental health system after being brought in by doctors or distressed relatives. Others may present with problems that they believe are unrelated to the dieting disorder, such as sleeping problems.

People with bulimia nervosa are more likely to recognise that their behaviour is out of control and therefore will often self-present. However, they generally want treatment to be on their terms as they fear that once they start eating they will not be able to stop and that they will gain weight.

It is likely that individuals will be guarded about certain aspects of their behaviour, such as how little they eat, or the methods they use to control their weight. Their guardedness is likely to stem from a desire to keep their dieting behaviours 'undiscovered' so that future weight loss will not be jeopardised, or may stem from embarrassment about specific dieting behaviours. The clinician will need to be accepting, non-judgemental, honest, tolerant, and empathic. For people with anorexia nervosa, the perception of being fat is very real to the individual and it is important that the clinician recognises this to be the case. One of the most important tasks is to motivate the individual to make the decision to take control of the dieting disorder. The following strategies will be important during the engagement phase of management.

ESTABLISH A THERAPEUTIC RELATIONSHIP

The quality of the relationship between the clinician and the individual is an important component of treatment. A clinician who is regarded as trustworthy, interested, helpful and understanding is more likely to engage the individual in ongoing and beneficial treatment. Principles for establishing a therapeutic relationship are discussed in Core Management Skills in Chapter 1.

ACKNOWLEDGE AND EMPATHISE WITH THE INDIVIDUAL'S DISTRESS

One thing is almost certain - people with dieting disturbances will be experiencing a wide range of physical and psychological problems that may cause severe distress and discomfort. By acknowledging distress and by attempting to understand the individual's view of the problem, rapport may be enhanced. A trusting, co-operative and optimistic relationship may be fostered by the open expression of concern about the individual's physical and emotional health, and by the expressed desire to help the individual regain control over his or her life and dieting behaviours.

Flowchart of management plan

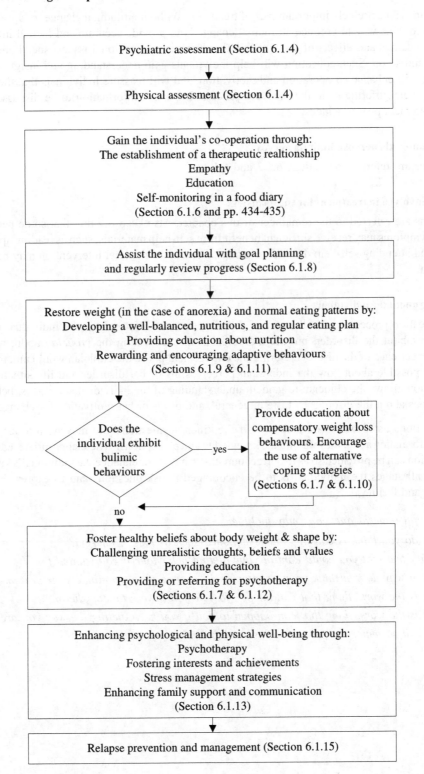

6.1.7 EDUCATION

Education is an extremely important part of treatment. Without attitudinal change, relapse is almost guaranteed. One way to produce attitudinal change is to provide accurate and factual information about the causes and effects of disturbed dieting behaviour, nutritional issues, social and cultural factors, and so on. Such education will help individuals gain understanding and insight into their disorder, will enhance co-operation and motivation, and will reassure individuals that they are not alone in their suffering or in the recovery process. Important information to be discussed during the engagement phase includes:

What is anorexia nervosa/bulimia nervosa?

Clinicians are referred to Sections 6.1.2 and 6.1.3.

What is involved in treatment for the disorder?

Clinicians are referred to the remainder of this chapter. Also keep in mind that some people with milder symptoms may receive sufficient benefit from self-help materials, such as reading appropriate books and attending self-help discussion groups. Sometimes minimal intervention may be the best approach.

Learning about the individual

The education process can be thought of as being two-way. Not only is the individual receiving education about the disorder, but the individual is also educating the *clinician* about his or her unique experience of the disorder. During the engagement phase the clinician would aim to learn as much as possible about how the individual perceives his or her disorder and life situation. Such information allows the clinician to gain an understanding of the individual's attitudes, beliefs, and perceptions about the disorder and life in general, and of his or her motivation for change.

The questions listed below are a *sample* of the kinds of questions you may wish to ask so as to obtain information about the individual's knowledge and perceptions. Where appropriate, educational information can be provided so as to correct unrealistic beliefs or enhance the individual's knowledge base. At all stages the individual is to be encouraged to ask questions and to express his or her thoughts and feelings.

Some useful general questions may include:
- *What do you think is causing your symptoms (such as loss of energy)?*
- *Do you feel that you could control your dieting behaviour if you wanted to?*
- *In what way do you think your symptoms will change if you continue your present diet?*
- *What is the worst thing that can happen to you if you were to stop dieting?*
- *What is the worst thing that can happen to you if you keep dieting the way you are now?"*
- *Why is it so important for you to lose weight?*

Theories of weight regulation

Maintenance of body weight depends on the equilibrium or balance that is achieved by the regulation of a number of factors. These factors include dietary intake (quantity and quality), energy balance (intake versus expenditure), and the physical aspects of adipose tissue (number and size of fat cells in the body). In other words, we could view weight regulation as being dependent on: a behavioural component (i.e., eating behaviours); a physiological component (i.e., amount of energy expenditure - which is dependent on our natural rate of metabolism and on our level of activity); and a genetic component (i.e., our body shape and fat distribution - which are inherited from our parents and dependent on our biological sex).

For some people, physiological and genetic factors may be such that the individual can eat as much as he or she likes while maintaining an average weight or even being underweight. Other people, however, may weigh more than average despite the fact that they diet or eat only healthy, normal-sized meals. Attempting to dramatically reduce body weight by excessive dieting is like rebelling against nature since our bodies seem to have a natural set-point. Although our weight may fluctuate slightly depending on our food intake and activity levels, our weight usually hovers around a genetically predetermined set-point. This set-point is different for each person.

What happens when you starve?

Psychological symptoms of starvation	Physical symptoms of starvation
Depression	Amenorrhoea (cessation of menstruation)
Loss of concentration	Dry skin
Preoccupation with thoughts of food	Lanugo hair growth (fine downy hair)
Anxiety	Polyuria (excessive urine secretion)
Social withdrawal	Fatigue
Labile (fluctuating) mood	Hypothermia (low body temperature)
Irritability	Hypotension (low blood pressure)
Feelings of inadequacy	Reduced gastric motility
Hypersensitivity to noise	Disturbed blood chemistry
Obsessional thinking	Bradycardia (pulse rate < 60)
Increasing perfectionism	Paresthesias (abnormal sensations of burning, prickling)

Physical aspects of starvation

Tissue breakdown. During fasting, the various body tissues break down in different proportions depending on whether the individual is lean or obese. Loss of muscle tissue may lead to disturbances of electrolytes, liver damage, stress fractures of the bones, and cardiac problems.

Electrolyte disturbance. Electrolytes are substances that dissolve in solution to become ions (positively and negatively charged particles). These ions conduct the electric currents that are necessary for cellular functioning to occur. One of the important electrolytes affected by anorexia nervosa and bulimia nervosa is potassium.

As weight loss progresses, protein tissue begins to break down, the loss of intracellular water content from these cells leads to a reduction in the amount of total body potassium (hypokalemia). Hypokalemia may lead to cardiac arrhythmias (irregular heartbeats), muscle weakness, failure of nerve conduction, and kidney disorders. In severe cases the heart may simply stop beating. Epileptic attacks may also occur as a result of electrolytic disturbance.

The use of diuretics, laxatives, and vomiting further exacerbates intracellular water loss and hence loss of potassium. Chloride levels and sodium levels may also be diminished. If the individual drinks excessive amounts of fluid to alleviate hunger pangs, sodium levels increase disproportionately and the electrolytic balance is further disturbed.

Endocrine disorder. Behaviours associated with anorexia nervosa lead to a widespread disorder of the endocrine system involving amenorrhoea or menstrual irregularities. Women with bulimia nervosa may also experience menstrual irregularities. Extensive medical investigations are not usually necessary since evidence of endocrine disorder is generally a *consequence* of the dieting disorder rather than an indicator of endocrine disease.

Weight. During a prolonged crash-diet, the metabolism alters so that the body utilises energy more efficiently. The basal metabolic rate (i.e., the energy expenditure required for the maintenance of basic bodily functioning such as respiration and circulation) is reduced so that fewer calories are expended for basic survival. Thus, when normal eating patterns are resumed, weight gain is more rapid. Crash-diets are therefore an ineffective way of regulating weight. One of the treatment strategies for dieting disorders involves encouraging individuals to learn to accept their *natural* body weight and to focus their time and energy on other more important and productive aspects of their lives.

Psychological aspects of starvation

Preoccupation with food. One of the direct side effects of starvation is a preoccupation with thoughts of food. Such obsessional thoughts are especially frightening for the individual who has the dieting disorder due to a fear of losing control on resumption of eating. A vicious cycle develops in which starvation leads to preoccupation with thoughts of food, which in turn leads to further efforts at starvation. In most cases, however, once a controlled and well-balanced eating plan is commenced, preoccupation with thoughts of food tends to diminish somewhat, as do the episodes of binge-eating.

What happens when you binge?

Binge-eating is thought to be precipitated by restricted eating behaviour. When fasting can no longer be continued, it is usually the foods they denied themselves which form the content of the binge. Binge-eating is often used as a coping strategy during times of stress and tension. After binge-eating the individual may feel more able to face a difficult situation. However, the opposite can also be true whereby the individual comes to feel guilty or ashamed and may consequently develop suicidal thoughts. Often after a binge, because of the fear of weight gain, dieting may be recommended in order to lose the weight. Binge-eating may also result in nausea, headache, exhaustion and abdominal pain from a stretched stomach. It can also cause financial hardship if binge-eating episodes are frequent. Some people resort to shoplifting to obtain food for their next binge.

What happens when you vomit, purge, or use diuretics?

Vomiting

Vomiting initially begins as a means of eliminating food from the body before calories have been absorbed. Some people, particularly those with bulimia nervosa, vomit so that they can overeat without gaining weight. In other instances, vomiting is used to prevent weight gain after the individual has failed to avoid eating a particular meal. Others, especially those with anorexia nervosa, repeatedly regurgitate their food after meals, chew the regurgitated food for lengthy periods of time, then swallow the food again. Such behaviour acts to prolong the eating experience.

The number of calories absorbed during binge-eating episodes depends on the type of food eaten and the duration of time the food has been in the body before vomiting occurs. The longer the food has been in the body before vomiting occurs, the less effective vomiting will be for preventing weight gain. Some foods, such as simple carbohydrates, begin to be absorbed as soon as they come into contact with saliva. Hence, calories may be absorbed from the moment food enters the mouth.

It is extremely important that the individual understands the dangers associated with vomiting and why vomiting is discouraged. Vomiting causes a severe loss of body fluid and electrolytes, especially potassium. Decreased potassium (hypokalemia) can lead to cardiac problems and possibly death. Furthermore, vomiting can cause vitamin deficiencies, erode the enamel on the teeth, irritate the salivary glands, and burn the lining of the throat, not to mention causing bad breath, an unpleasant tasting mouth, and a messy bathroom.

Purging

Even with large doses of laxatives, purging has little or no effect on calorie absorption. Laxatives work by irritating the colon, which then contracts to push the food into the rectum and out of the body. However, by the time food reaches the colon, most of the calories have already been absorbed by the small intestine. Like vomiting and fasting, purging can also cause hypokalemia and cardiac problems due to the severe loss of body fluid and electrolytes. Regular purging may cause chronic diarrhoea and also interferes with the natural functioning of the bowel such that, in the absence of laxatives, the bowel becomes unable to efficiently eliminate faecal waste. The bowel usually returns to normal functioning, although this recovery may take time.

It is important that people who are contemplating cessation of laxative use are advised in advance that fluid retention and apparent weight gain may occur and will disappear within a few days. It is also advisable for people who are regularly taking large quantities of laxatives to taper off laxative use gradually. Sudden cessation of laxatives places greater stress on the body than a gradual decrease.

Diuretics

A diuretic is a chemical that acts on the kidney to increase urine output. When a diuretic is used, the concentration of electrolytes in the kidneys is increased. In order to prevent the urine from becoming too concentrated, extra water is absorbed into the kidneys to dilute the urine. Hence, dehydration may occur as large quantities of body fluid are lost during urination. Electrolyte imbalances may also occur due to the increased loss of important ions and may lead to cardiac problems. If diuretics are used in conjunction with laxatives (which also enhance water loss), the individual can become severely dehydrated. Like laxatives, diuretics are an ineffective way of controlling body weight.

Exercise

Anorexics are more likely than other people with dieting disorders to engage regularly in excessive exercise as a means of reducing weight. Bulimic individuals may occasionally engage in excessive exercise as punishment or as compensation for recent episodes of binge-eating. Alternatively, bulimic individuals may have periods of 'good' behaviour which are characterised by strict dieting and strenuous exercise and periods of 'bad' behaviour which are characterised by binge-eating and a complete absence of exercise. Exercise often assumes a compulsive and rigid pattern with distress, anxiety, and self-recrimination developing if the person is prevented from exercising or does not satisfy the self-imposed exercise requirements.

Excessive exercise can be extremely dangerous for people who have dieting disorders, especially those with anorexia nervosa. Anorexics typically experience a reduction in bone mass (osteoporosis) probably as a result of decreased levels of circulating oestrogen. Stress fractures and joint injury are common following excessive exercise, and pain sensation may be decreased due to pathology of peripheral nerves. Anorexia nervosa and bulimia nervosa both involve cardiovascular complications such as decreased heart size, slow heart rate, and arrhythmias, probably as a result of electrolyte disturbances, thus increasing the risk of heart failure during or following excessive exercise. It is important to educate people about the dangers of excessive exercise, to provide information about how much and what kind of exercise is healthy, and to assist with establishing an appropriate exercise programme.

Common dieting myths

People who have dieting disorders generally believe numerous myths about dieting strategies, weight control, food, and so forth. It is important to explore these myths so that false beliefs may be corrected where appropriate. Common myths include:

Being slim will make me happy

Thinness at any cost will NOT lead to happiness. Admittedly, we live in a society in which being thin is valued and being obese is less desirable. However, there are many naturally thin people who are *unhappy* and many obese people who are *happy*. Even when an individual becomes very thin and reaches the 'ideal' weight, he or she is usually still unhappy and dissatisfied and hence strives to become even thinner! Happiness can only be achieved by accepting oneself as is and by working towards greater independence and personal achievements in other areas such as in one's career, home, or leisure pursuits.

Carbohydrates, sugars, and fats are bad for you

Many people believe that carbohydrates are fattening (e.g., potato, pasta, bread). Generally, however, it is not the carbohydrate that is fattening but the huge quantities of butter and other potentially fattening foods that are added to the carbohydrates. Carbohydrates, as well as sugars and fats, are very important parts of a well-balanced diet. Carbohydrates and sugars break down in the body to form glucose. Glucose is an important source of energy and is normally the only source of energy used by the brain. Fats are also an important and efficient energy source. Energy release from this food is enhanced by the presence of carbohydrates. These foods also reduce hunger because they take longer to break down and hence leave you feeling full for longer. The problem with fats and sugars is that many people mistakenly assume that if a little bit of something is good then a lot must be better. Alternatively, they may assume that if eating too much of a particular food is bad for you then a complete *absence* of that food must be better. The secret is to eat *all foods in moderation*.

Once I start eating I won't be able to stop

With a carefully regulated diet, the individual will be assisted to return to normal weight and will be encouraged to avoid maladaptive eating or dieting behaviours such as binge-eating, vomiting, purging, and so forth. A good diet plan will include eating moderate and limited amounts of 'forbidden' foods such as cake and sweets so that the individual learns to eat these foods without overindulging.

Exercise will help me to lose weight

While it is true that exercise does accelerate weight loss by increasing energy expenditure, the amount of calories consumed during exercise is not large in comparison to those consumed from just being alive. It takes a lot of exercise to make even a small difference to your weight. Even then one may not lose weight because exercise develops muscle tissue and muscle tissue is heavier than fat tissue. Stress on the heart muscle when one has an indequate diet may lead to heart failure and possible death.

'Normal' people only eat when they're hungry

People who have dieting disorders usually try to avoid eating, even when they are very hungry. Individuals with anorexia nervosa who continue to resist the urge to eat develop very strong and uncomfortable cravings which strengthens their resolve to resist eating, while individuals with bulimia nervosa eventually give in to the cravings and engage in binge-eating. While it is important to eat three regular meals per day, it is also important to be able to eat the occasional snack or dessert every now and again.

Recommended reading for clients and their families

One or other of the following books may be helpful.

Ball, J. & Ball, R. (1995) *Eating Disorders: A Survival Guide for Family and Friends.* Sydney: Astam Books.

Ball, J., Butow, P., & Place, F. (1991). *When Eating is Everything.* Sydney: Astam Books.

Boone O'Neill, C. (1982). *Starving for Attention.* Melbourne: Dove Communications.

Bruch, H. (1978). *The Golden Cage: The Enigma of Anorexia Nervosa.* Cambridge, Massachusetts: Harvard University Press.

Cooke, K. (1994). *Real Gorgeous: The Truth About Body and Beauty.* St Leonards, Sydney: Allen & Unwin.

Crisp, A.H. (1980). *Anorexia Nervosa: Let Me Be.* London: Academic Press.

Dana, M. & Lawrence, M. (1988). *Women's Secret Disorder: A New Understanding of Bulimia.* London: Grafton Books.

Huon, G.F. & Brown, L.B. (1988). *Fighting With Food.* Kensington: New South Wales University Press.

Meltsner, S. (1993). *Body & Soul: A Guide to Lasting Recovery from Compulsive Eating and Bulimia.* Minnesota: Hazelden Educational Materials.

Palmer, R.L. (1989). *Anorexia Nervosa: A Guide for Sufferers and Their Families.* London: Penguin Books.

Schmidt, U. & Treasure, J. (1993). *Getting Better Bit(e) by Bit(e): A Survival Kit for Sufferers of Bulimia Nervosa and Binge-Eating Disorders.* United Kingdom: Lawrence Erlbaum Associates.

6.1.8 GOAL PLANNING

Goal planning is an extremely important and useful technique for the management of dieting disorders. Firstly, during the early phase of management, goal planning will be important for securing co-operation. By identifying specific areas of need, it will be possible to develop broad treatment goals. These are simple to do in bulimia nervosa, but may have to be delayed in anorexia nervosa. During the engagement phase it will not be necessary to plan goals in great detail, however, it will be helpful to agree on basic goals that need to be, and can be, achieved during treatment. More detailed goal planning can be used after the individual has decided to participate in treatment and has had the opportunity (through education and discussion) to understand more fully his or her most important problems, strengths, and needs.

Secondly, once the individual accepts the need for treatment, goals can be very motivating because there is a clear target for which to aim. Such motivation is enhanced if rewards are made available when the goal is achieved (see Section 6.1.11).

Thirdly, the individual's life is likely to be consumed with thoughts of weight control, food and food-related rituals. By removing such food-related activities and thoughts, a great sense of loss may be experienced. The individual may be fearful about who he or she is, and what will occupy his or her life once food and body weight cease to be the main focus in life. Goal planning will be vital for reassuring the individual that adequate attention will be given to enhancing other aspects of his or her life (e.g., self-esteem, career and recreational goals, coping strategies).

ENGAGEMENT

Offer *rationales* for behaviour change, such as encouraging the individual to increase enjoyment of life, or increase harmony within the household setting. Encourage detailed *discussion of pros and cons* of behaviour change letting the individual talk about his or her thoughts, fears, and hopes. Make sure that the individual *understands* what has been said and accepts the need for change.

IDENTIFYING PROBLEM AREAS, NEEDS, STRENGTHS AND RESOURCES

Ask the individual to *list problem areas* that need attention. For example, problem areas may include low self esteem, binge-eating, thinking about food all the time, depression, or not having many friends. It is important that personal goals are set *by* the individual, rather than having the clinician set goals *for* the individual. Once the main problem areas have been gathered it is important to *rephrase the problems in positive terms and define the needs*. For example, the problem "thinking about food all the time" could be rephrased as "spend more time doing things other than thinking about food". Ask the individual to identify interests, abilities or resources, including activities and skills that the individual used to enjoy or do well at before the onset of the illness.

GOAL SETTING EXAMPLE

Problems
- Low self esteem
- Don't have many friends
- Think about food all the time
- Binge-eating
- Vomiting
- Fear of becoming fat
- Depression

Strengths/resources
- Watercolour painting
- Competition netball
- Still friends with Jacqui and Pat
- I get on well with my sister, Sue
- Enjoy my uni course
- Good cook
- I recognise that I have a dieting problem

Most important needs
- To eat healthy and regular meals
- To learn to control my binge-eating
- To find better ways than binge-eating to cope with my problems
- To learn to like myself
- To increase my social circle
- To stop vomiting

TIPS FOR SETTING SPECIFIC GOALS

The next step in goal planning is to decide upon appropriate goals. Goals must be realistic, achievable, specific, broken down into small steps, and 'owned'. Use the individual's strengths and resources listed earlier.

Developing realistic and achievable goals

Sometimes individuals may be inclined to set goals for themselves that are extremely high and practically impossible to achieve. Naturally, when they fail to achieve these goals they feel depressed and very disappointed. If they *do* achieve these goals they feel extremely delighted and proud, however, their chances of succeeding are not high. Alternatively, sometimes individuals set no goals at all or set goals that are too easy. Achieving easy goals is not going to be very rewarding because success does not require much effort.

Developing specific goals

The goal that is set needs to be very specific so that you can identify when that goal has been achieved. For instance, setting the goal *to eat healthy and regular meals* will mean having clear guidelines from a dietician as to what constitutes healthy and regular meals. Or, if the goal was to engage in more social and recreational activities, it will be helpful to specify how frequently the individual may be expected to engage in specific activities (e.g., attend an evening painting class once a week and join a Saturday morning social sport team).

Break long-term goals down into smaller steps

While it is important to develop long-term goals to give direction for the future, long-term goals by themselves are less rewarding than more imminent goals as it is difficult to feel motivated when the goal does not have to be reached for a long period of time. It is, therefore, a good idea for the individual to break the long-term goal into a series of short-term or stepwise goals. For example, if the individual expresses an interest in travelling overseas in a year's time, he or she can make short-term goals such as: reading about where he or she would like to go, completing a brief foreign language class, working out a savings plan, and so forth. These short-term goals provide rewards along the way and are evidence that the long-term goal is ultimately achievable.

Goal planning example

Long-term goal: To restore normal eating patterns (bulimia nervosa)

Short term goals for stage 1 (to be reviewed in one week):
1. Eat three regularly-spaced meals per day as per the diet plan
2. Keep a food diary of all other foods eaten
3. Eat in the company of others whenever possible
4. Remain in the company of others for at least one hour after meals to control vomiting
5. Ask Tom to do the grocery shopping

Short term goals for stage 2 (review date to be set)
1. Use activity planning for high risk situations
2. Use distraction, thought stopping, or relaxation when the desire to binge is first noted
3. Use delay tactics if the binge seems unavoidable
4. Remind myself that it is never too late to stop a binge

PUTTING GOAL PLANNING INTO PRACTICE

Once goals have been decided upon it may be useful to employ a structured problem solving approach for planning complicated goals (see Chapter 1: Core Management Skills). It will be necessary to determine the time frame and order of each phase of the goal.

In the planning stage, it is also important to consider issues such as:
- Who will remind the individual about the goal (if necessary)
- Planning what to do if something goes wrong
- Deciding on possible rewards for when the goal is reached

REVIEWING PROGRESS

It is always important to monitor progress and to praise the individual for success or for attempts at achieving the goal.

Gaining reward from 'failure'

Sometimes the individual may not attain the goal he or she has set, perhaps because the goal was too difficult, or because success was not entirely in his or her hands. For example, the failure to completely cease binge-eating within two weeks of the commencement of treatment could be due to unrealistic expectations, situational events such as the occurrence of special occasions during that time such as birthdays that involved the presence of large quantities of tempting food, and so on. It is important that the individual does not focus on the failures but instead focuses on what *has* been learned. The individual can then be encouraged to set some new goals based on what has already been achieved. Repeated failure or high expectations may result in *feelings of helplessness, anxiety or pressure*. It is better to persevere at a slightly easier task than to give up on a harder task.

Monitoring progress

There is no point in setting goals unless the individual keeps track of whether or not the goals have been achieved. Monitoring provides a chance for the people involved to receive praise and rewards from themselves or others which will also help to maintain the new behaviours. If the goal has *not* been achieved, monitoring enables revision of goals and praise for partial success or for any *attempts* to achieve the goal. (See "Rewarding and Encouraging Adaptive Behaviours" - Section 6.1.11).

PROBLEMS ENCOUNTERED IN GOAL PLANNING

Some people seem *unable to set realistic goals*. This inability may be due to personal or family pressure to excel, or perhaps due to denial that the individual is actually unwell (physically or psychologically). In these situations it is important to remind the individual that:
- Recovery may be slow and should not be rushed
- Excessive pressure by family members for the individual to 'perform' may increase stress and lead to frustration and lack of co-operation
- Goals need to be flexible
- More difficult goals can be set once previous goals have been achieved

Cultural expectations also need to be considered. For example, in some cultures, food and feasting play a central role in social gatherings. While it is important to respect and empathise with different cultural ideas and expectations, the clinician can help the individual and family realise that their expectations may need to be reconsidered at times. Encourage everyone to work towards what is best for the individual, and what will be most effective for improving his or her physical and psychological well-being.

6.1.9 RESTORING NORMAL EATING PATTERNS

Planning an appropriate diet and providing accurate knowledge about nutrition and weight control will help dispel the many food myths held by these individuals and will assist with the return to more normal and relaxed eating patterns. Initially, expect people who have anorexia nervosa to refuse to accept the need for weight gain. Similarly, expect people who have bulimia nervosa to be reluctant to resume normal eating behaviours for fear of gaining weight. Reassure individuals with bulimia nervosa that weight gain usually does not occur or only occurs slightly after restoration of normal eating. At the commencement of treatment, it will be helpful to reassure the individual that an extreme fear of weight gain is *part of the illness* and that treatment does not simply require an increased calorie intake. Helping the individual learn to feel more comfortable about being at a normal and healthy weight is just as important as encouraging weight gain and appropriate eating patterns.

GOALS AND OBJECTIVES OF DIETARY MANAGEMENT

1. To attain normal nutritional status in adults and normal growth in adolescents, and to maintain this status over time.
    *   For adults, the objective is steady weight gain, or weight maintenance at a weight where the individual is physically healthy and can eat a normal diet to maintain that weight. The ideal weight is such that the BMI is in the range of 20-25.
    *   For adolescents, the objective is steady weight gain or weight stability so that the individual is physically healthy and continues to grow at a normal rate. The ideal weight is such that the BMI is around 18.5-25 although premorbid weight may also be used as a guide. For very young people (<14 years), height and weight charts should be used to recommend the appropriate age related weight for height. Consultation with the child's family doctor may be helpful here.
    *   Weight loss behaviours such as vomiting, purging, diuretic abuse, and excessive exercise need to be eliminated.
2. To establish normal eating behaviours.
    *   The diet should be varied with no food groups avoided simply because they are fattening. Furthermore, special low-calorie foods should be avoided.
    *   The meal pattern should be regular so that the individual eats three main meals per day, plus some snacks.
    *   Binge-eating and other abnormal eating behaviours need to be ceased.
    *   The individual needs to learn to eat adequately and comfortably in the company of others.
3. To establish a normal attitude to food.
4. To establish a normal response to hunger cues and to satiety cues.

DIETARY ADVICE

What is the appropriate target weight?
*   Ideally, the target weight will be determined and agreed upon at the beginning of treatment.
*   The target weight if measured in kilograms should actually be a weight *range* (e.g., 63-65 kg). It is normal for weight to fluctuate slightly from one day to the next and the target weight should reflect this natural fluctuation.
*   The weight range should be such that the individual can maintain the appropriate weight in the long-term without the need for continued dieting and calorie counting. Fine tuning of the diet or of the individual's target weight may be needed.

What sort of food should the individual eat?

It is important that individuals learn to eat normal everyday food. This includes red meat if it was eaten before the dieting disorder developed. Individuals need to learn to manage their weight without reliance on dietary products since dieting has been one of the major causes of their problem. High cholesterol levels sometimes associated with anorexia nervosa usually return to normal once individuals return to a healthy weight range, hence, low-fat or fat-modified foods are not needed. Dietary supplements such as vitamins and minerals are not usually required.

Individuals with bulimia nervosa generally try to avoid eating sweet and fatty foods as part of their daily diet. These foods usually produce strong cravings and are generally eaten in large amounts during episodes of binge-eating. By introducing these foods into the diet, their significance will diminish. If consumption of these foods no longer indicates failure, the individual may find it easier to maintain control of his or her eating behaviour.

Many people with dieting disorders claim to be vegetarian, however, it is usually the case that their vegetarian status has developed *after* the onset of their dieting disorder. Unless individuals are true vegetarian (for religious or other reasons), they are to be strongly encouraged to eat red meat in moderation. However, a great deal of care and persuasion may be required from the clinician to convince individuals to do so.

How much food should the individual eat?

For people who are very underweight, food intake should be enough to produce a weekly weight gain of about 1.5 kg. For emaciated people who have eaten only very small amounts prior to treatment, the daily intake at the beginning of treatment should deliberately be lower than ideal for several reasons. Firstly, individuals are likely to be scared away from treatment if they are required to eat too much too soon. Secondly, low initial food intake allows the stomach to expand gradually, thus avoiding excessive abdominal pain.

During the early stages of treatment for anorexia nervosa, the focus should be on *weight gain* rather than on *eating* per se. The reason for this focus is because individuals may be eating appropriately but if they continue to engage in weight loss tactics such as vomiting, may continue to avoid gaining weight. Once the target weight has been reached, the daily intake may be slowly reduced to a level at which a healthy weight can be maintained with normal eating behaviour. A dietician can provide advice about the recommended daily food intake at various stages of the weight gain programme.

Individuals with bulimia nervosa are usually at, or close to, a normal weight. These people will require a nutritious diet aimed at maintaining a healthy weight. Once eating is regulated, vomiting and purging tend to diminish on their own since these behaviours are usually a consequence of overeating.

Encourage normal eating patterns

Individuals with both anorexia nervosa and bulimia nervosa will be required to eat three meals per day with snacks between meals. Regularly-spaced meals will make it easier for individuals to eat the quantities of food that are recommended and will reduce hunger and cravings.

What if the individual does not finish his or her meals?

If individuals with anorexia nervosa dispose of, or do not finish, their meals, any increases in dietary intake should not continue until the individual is able to eat all the food prescribed at the present level. People who simply refuse to eat, or who are not motivated to change their present behaviours, may need to be referred to someone who has more experience in this area.

Warn the individual about fluid build-up and increased hunger

If the individual is underweight and commencing a weight gaining diet, it is important that he or she is warned that rehydration is likely to occur. Fluid retention may also occur resulting in oedema (swelling) of the ankles, and dramatically increased weight gain. It will be necessary to inform the individual *in advance* that this weight gain may occur. As the body's fluid balance becomes normal and urine output increases, excess fluid will be reduced and weight will stabilise. Furthermore, it is important to provide reassurance that as weight increases and body tissue is regained, the sensation of constant hunger will decrease.

Overcoming constipation

Individuals with bulimia nervosa usually experience severe diarrhoea if they are abusing laxatives and experience constipation when they cease laxative use. Individuals with anorexia nervosa are also usually constipated as a result of the low quantities of food residue passing through the digestive system. A well balanced diet that contains plenty of fluids and sufficient quantities of fibrous foods such as fruit, vegetables, and wholegrain cereals should reduce constipation. If laxatives have been used regularly as a form of weight control it may take many days or even weeks for the previously over-stimulated bowel to respond to normal quantities of dietary fibre.

Altering abnormal eating-related behaviours

There are a number of unusual eating behaviours that are common among people with dieting disorders (e.g., refusing to eat, obsessional calorie counting, playing with food, eating very slowly). Such behaviours may stem from high anxiety levels during meals, attempts to minimise weight gain, and preoccupation with food itself rather than with simply enjoying the social aspects of eating a meal with other people. A system of rewards and reinforcements may help to encourage and motivate individuals to abstain from these unusual eating behaviours.

Maintaining a healthy weight after weight gain

Once the desired healthy weight range has been attained, food intake will need to be adjusted to a more appropriate level. In the case of bulimia nervosa, individuals need to be strongly advised against dieting in the future, since dieting is likely to encourage a return of binge-eating. Rather, sensible yet flexible meal plans are to be encouraged.

6.1.10 MODIFYING BULIMIC BEHAVIOURS

SELF-MONITORING

Before attempting to modify bulimic behaviours, it will be helpful to obtain detailed information about the person's behavioural pattern.

RESTORATION OF NORMAL EATING PATTERNS

A return to normal eating patterns is the first step towards the cessation of bulimic episodes (see Section 6.1.9). Normal eating patterns involve the consumption of normal quantities and types of food at appropriate times of the day. In the early stages of management, it may be helpful if the dietary plan is rigid such that the individual eats *only* what is written on the dietary plan, in accordance with the dietician's instructions. The meal plan eventually becomes more flexible with the individual gradually exercising more choice and control about what and when to eat.

EDUCATION ABOUT BINGE-EATING AND COMPENSATORY WEIGHT LOSS BEHAVIOURS

It will be important to discuss the causes and consequences of binge-eating, and to provide education about the effectiveness and consequences of using compensatory weight loss behaviours for weight control.

DEVELOPING ALTERNATIVE COPING STRATEGIES

For most people with dieting disorders, maladaptive eating and dieting behaviours are a way of coping with stressful, anxiety-provoking, or unpleasant life circumstances or events. For example, an individual may binge-eat when depressed, when bored, or after a stressful event such as an argument with a friend or relative. Starvation may be a way of asserting oneself and taking control of life situations that are perceived to be intolerable or distressing. The Binge Monitoring Form or food diary are useful ways of identifying events or feelings that trigger bulimic episodes or perpetuate disturbed eating and dieting behaviours.

Thought stopping

It is important to encourage the individual to think about things other than food. The thought stopping technique may be useful. This technique simply involves shouting or thinking the word "STOP!" every time a food-related thought enters the mind and then finding a distraction that will *keep* him or her from thinking about food.

Distraction

Distraction involves finding an alternative activity or thought that will prevent the individual from thinking about food or acting upon an urge to binge. Distractions may be unplanned and impromptu, such as ringing a friend, picking up a good book, turning on the television, seeking out a family member, or going for a walk.

Activity Planning

Activity planning is very similar to the distraction technique except that activities are planned in advance. In this way, the individual is kept occupied throughout the day or during high-risk periods so as to minimise the opportunity of thinking about food or engaging in food-related rituals. Additionally, goal planning techniques (see Section 6.1.8) can be used in conjunction with activity planning so that the planned activities can be chosen to also enhance the individual's short and long-term goal achievement.

Using delay tactics

During the early stages of the management, delaying binges may be helpful. Quite often binge-eating is planned in advance and careful preparations are made. Alternatively, binge-eating may occur regularly at a certain time each week. These habitual or planned binges may be a good starting point for practising the technique of postponement. As self-control builds, the individual can try to postpone the binge for longer periods each time. (See Section 6.3.5).

Avoiding 'all-or-none' thinking

For many people, once a snack has turned into a meal, they feel like failures and decide they may as well continue on to have a binge. Such all-or-none thinking is not helpful for people who are trying to control their bulimic behaviours. Encourage individuals to adopt the view that there is no time during a snack or binge at which it is too late to stop. Partial control of a binge is better than no control. Individuals are to be praised and encouraged if they report early termination of binge-eating sessions. Explore the strategies that have been successful for stopping a binge-eating episode so that they may be applied effectively during future binges.

Structure the environment

Environmental cues may play an important part in triggering episodes of binge-eating. For example, the individual may go to the cupboard, find packets of junk food inside, and be unable to resist the temptation to binge. Having identified such stimuli the individual can try to minimise temptations where appropriate. For example, the individual could agree to shop only once per week and buy only what is on the shopping list (no impulse buys in the confectionery aisle!).

Structured problem solving

Structured problem solving can be effective for helping individuals with both anorexia and bulimia nervosa cope with stress. Instead of turning to food whenever problems arise, problems can be managed more effectively with the use of structured problem solving.

Relaxation

Relaxation training can be extremely beneficial for people who have dieting disorders. Relaxation is useful for:
- Decreasing anxiety
- Enhancing the individual's ability to cope with stress
- Avoiding maladaptive behaviours that often occur when the individual is stressed (e.g., binge-eating)
- Enhancing self-esteem through increased control in stressful situations
- Improving personal relationships

Assertiveness training

Many individuals with dieting disorders choose to express their anger and other emotions through their eating behaviours. Instead of taking control of difficult situations by calmly expressing their thoughts, feelings, and intentions, these individuals may exert their strength and willpower inappropriately by refusing to eat or by binge-eating. Individuals may be unassertive because of poor self-confidence or because of a lack of practice or knowledge about *how* to be assertive. Information about assertiveness training is provided in the Chapter on Affective Disorders.

6.1.11 REWARDING AND ENCOURAGING ADAPTIVE BEHAVIOURS

Unfortunately, there is no fail-proof method for ensuring that individuals adhere to the recommended treatment programmes. The decision to eat, overeat, or engage in treatment rests solely with the individual. However, the suggestions below may be useful for fostering adherence, progress, and increased self-esteem.

BE GENEROUS WITH PRAISE AND ENCOURAGEMENT

Words of encouragement and understanding from the clinician, family, and friends can contribute greatly to the individual's progress. It needs to be acknowledged that the individual's task is a difficult one and that all progress is good, even if small.

PROVIDE FEEDBACK ABOUT PROGRESS

Feedback about progress can be very motivating. This feedback may include such things as:

- Weekly weight measurements with results graphed for visual feedback. Depending on the treatment programme, a positive outcome would be: weight gain (anorexics and underweight bulimics); weight loss (overweight bulimics); or no change in weight (normal weight bulimics).

- The use of graphs to illustrate daily and weekly episodes of vomiting, purging, or binge-eating (see Section 6.3.6). Alternatively, it may be helpful to graph the number of days each week during which the individual did *not* engage in these behaviours.

- A record of physical and psychological symptoms and their levels of improvement. Where possible it may be helpful to provide feedback in terms of *improvement* in mental and physical health rather than in terms of *reduction* of illness. For example, decreased fatigue could be viewed as increased energy.

- Results of physical examinations and laboratory tests such as electrolyte levels, blood pressure, and heart rate. These results will be rewarding if improvement is evident and may motivate increased efforts if the individual's health has deteriorated or remains poor or unchanged.

- Provide advice to family members about how to manage eating behaviours, mood swings and non-compliance at meal times (see Section 6.3.7).

6.1.12 FOSTERING HEALTHY BELIEFS ABOUT BODY WEIGHT & SHAPE

One of the key features of both anorexia nervosa and bulimia nervosa is the excessive concern about controlling body weight and shape. These individuals maintain the belief that their body is not acceptable, either to themselves or others, unless it is thin. To these individuals, a thin body is a statement of strength, beauty, and power. Cognitive techniques that lead to a change in an individual's beliefs and values about his or her weight are extremely important for maintaining normal eating behaviour, even when normal weight has been restored. Many of the individual's beliefs about food, diet, and weight will be strongly held (or are overvalued ideas) and thus may be resistant to change. If dietary management is provided in the absence of cognitive change, treatment is bound to result in relapse once individuals leave supervised treatment and return to their old habits and beliefs.

CHALLENGING UNREALISTIC BELIEFS AND VALUES

Introduce doubt about the belief

Without being critical or punitive, it is helpful to encourage the individual to re-examine the basis of his or her belief. For example, if the individual believes that losing more weight will make him or her more popular you may say something like:

"If losing weight makes you more popular, do you feel that you are closer to your friends now at 50 kg than you were at 53 kg?".

Point out generalisations

Sometimes individuals will recall what has happened in one particular situation and will assume that the same thing will happen in all situations. For example, an individual may state that when she was fat last time she was unhappy, therefore, she can *never* be happy if she is fat. By encouraging the individual to recognise and challenge generalisations, the individual may to learn to challenge his or her generalisations in the future.

Discourage exaggerations or catastrophising

The individual may have a habit of looking at a particular problem or concern and blowing the problem out of proportion. For example, the individual may believe that if he or she eats the recommended daily meal plan then he or she will "double in size overnight". In such instances, it will be necessary to point out the lack of plausibility of such statements.

Challenge excessive self-consciousness and overinterpretation of personal events

Individuals may be extremely self-conscious such that they believe people are always looking at them or evaluating them (especially their appearance). For example, an individual may report feeling embarrassed if other people watch him or her eat. Alternatively, individuals may incorrectly perceive specific events to be directly related to them or their weight. In such cases, it may be helpful to ask the individual what evidence he or she has that such a belief is accurate. Ask whether there are other possible explanations for the situation.

6.1.13 ENHANCING PSYCHOLOGICAL AND PHYSICAL WELL-BEING

While a return to normal eating behaviour is imperative for recovery from a dieting disorder, normal eating behaviour alone is not sufficient. It is important that treatment takes a holistic approach to the individual's well-being and addresses a range of important issues such as self-esteem, career, social relationships, and personality development. Such areas of the individual's life are often disrupted because of the dieting disorder. Alternatively, it is possible that disruption in such areas may have contributed to the onset of the dieting disturbance. The strategies outlined on the following pages are a useful but by no means comprehensive guide to enhancing an individual's psychological and physical well-being.

INDIVIDUAL THERAPY

People who have dieting disorders may experience numerous psychological and social difficulties such as low self-esteem, guilt and shame about dieting behaviours, poor interpersonal relationships, or disturbances associated with personality and self-concept. Furthermore, some people are victims of sexual abuse while others may abuse alcohol or other drugs. While the strategies outlined in this chapter are able to address some of these issues, many people will require more intensive therapy.

Individuals with anoerxia nervosa often fear losing control. They may strive for perfection and perceive their behaviours as never being good enough. Obsessionality, rigidity and avoidance are common attempted solutions to stay in control when they lack alternative strategies. Other individuals with anorexia nervosa have difficulty identifying and expressing feelings (alexythymia), trusting their bodily sensations (e.g., identifying hunger cues) and communicating effectively. Therapy focuses on developing startegies to deal with these issues.

Individuals with bulimia nervosa are often more erratic and disorganised in their personality styles than those with anorexia nervosa and experience extreme moods and behaviour, reflected in their bingeing and fasting episodes. Therapy focuses on strategies for controlling moods and improving interpersonal relationships.

FAMILY INVOLVEMENT

The majority of people with dieting disorders will be living in a family situation; either at home with their parents or in an ongoing relationship. Ideally, family members will be included in the management of the disorder so that family support can be enlisted and family behaviours or attitudes that contribute to the disorder can be examined and altered. Family involvement will include education about the nature of the disorder and about the treatment the individual is receiving for the disorder. Particularly important is an understanding of how family behaviours and attitudes (e.g., overprotectiveness, rigidity, pressure, dietary habits) may contribute to the disorder. However, it is important to emphasise that families do not *cause* dieting disorders and that it is unproductive for the family to expend energy dwelling on feelings of guilt. The family can play an important role by providing encouragement and acceptance of new behaviours (particularly of appropriately assertive and independent behaviours), as well as providing rewards and reinforcements to enhance and foster continued progress.

6.1.14 MEDICATION

ANOREXIA NERVOSA

Individuals with anorexia nervosa who are malnourished and depressed gain at least some relief from depression following weight gain. Therefore, it is recommended that antidepressant medication be avoided where possible among people with anorexia because of the risk of cardiac arrhythmias and hypotension. The risk of these side effects is enhanced if the person also engages in vomiting and purging behaviours. However, antidepressant medication should always be considered for persistent or severe cases of depression. Benzodiazepines should be avoided in favour of behavioural methods of anxiety control. If mild tranquillisation is necessary, a very low dose of chlorpromazine may be preferable.

Women with anorexia nervosa do not menstruate regularly and are likely to experience a reduction of oestrogen. Low oestrogen contributes to reduced calcium mass in the bones and subsequent osteoporosis, as evident among post-menopausal women. Hormone replacement therapy is used in appropriate cases to minimise calcium loss, thereby reducing the risk of osteoporosis.

BULIMIA NERVOSA

Many studies have shown the tricyclic antidepressants and fluoxetine (a selective serotonergic reuptake inhibitor, or SSRI antidepressant) to be effective for the treatment of bulimia nervosa. These antidepressants have been shown to be superior to placebo in the treatment of bulimia nervosa but appear to confer no additional benefit if appropriate counselling treatment is available. In the absence of appropriate psychological strategies, the maintenance of change with these drugs has been disappointing, and relapse is prompt when the medication is discontinued.

6.1.15 RELAPSE PREVENTION AND MANAGEMENT

EDUCATION ABOUT RELAPSE

The subject of relapse is best broached early in management so that individuals can rehearse how they will react if it occurs. It will be important to encourage the view that relapse is a setback rather than an indication of failure. Behavioural change is often difficult, especially if the behaviours have been present for a long period of time. Some degree of relapse is almost inevitable. By focusing on positive changes, and on the individual's particular strengths and coping abilities that have helped maintain progress prior to relapse, the clinician will be in a better position to encourage and motivate the individual to try again.

TRY TO IDENTIFY CAUSES OF RELAPSE

Sometimes relapse occurs following a clearly identifiable event. For example, the individual may have started a new job, been under considerable stress, or may have experienced a relationship break-up. In such cases it may be helpful for the individual to talk to someone, a professional, family member or friend, about how he or she is feeling following the stressful situation and the relapse of the dieting disorder.

Occasionally there will be no clear cause of relapse, or at least no cause that is immediately identifiable. A clinician may help the individual examine the events and emotions that preceded the relapse. Perhaps the individual never accepted the need for weight gain, or never appreciated the harm that could be caused by repeated vomiting. Or maybe the individual did not quite master some of the alternative coping strategies or stress management techniques such that he or she had difficulty applying these strategies when they were required. By identifying possible causes of relapse, the clinician can address appropriate areas that require further assistance.

REINTRODUCTION OF USEFUL STRATEGIES

During relapse or vulnerable times, it will be useful for individuals to return to using the strategies that have been successful in the past. For example, starting a food diary again may help individuals reassess their behaviour patterns and dysfunctional thoughts; family and friends can be encouraged to increase their levels of support; delay tactics can be reintroduced for those who have returned to binge-eating; and so on. A list of useful strategies for the prevention or minimisation of relapse is provided in Section 6.3.8.

FOLLOW-UP

Ongoing follow-up will be helpful for encouraging adherence to treatment. Follow-up sessions will also allow the individual to discuss particular problems that may have arisen during the intervening period.

6.2 BIBLIOGRAPHY

Abraham, S.F. & Beumont, P.J.V. (1982). How patients describe bulimia and binge-eating. *Psychological Medicine, 12*, 625-635.

American Psychiatric Association (1994). *Diagnostic and Statistical Manual of Mental Disorders (4th ed.)*. Washington: American Psychiatric Press.

American Psychiatric Association (1993). Practice Guideline for Eating Disorders. *American Journal of Psychiatry, 150*, 207-228.

Beumont, P.J.V. (1988). Bulimia: is it an illness entity? *International Journal of Eating Disorders, 7*, 167-176.

Beumont, P.J.V. (1995). The clinical presentation of anorexia and bulimia nervosa. In K.D. Brownell & C.G. Fairburn (Eds.), *Eating Disorders and Obesity: A Comprehensive Handbook* (pp. 151-158). New York: Guildford Press.

Beumont, P.J.V. & Touyz, S.W. (1995). The nutritional management of patients with anorexia and bulimia nervosa. In K.D. Brownell & C.G. Fairburn (Eds.), *Eating Disorders and Obesity: A Comprehensive Handbook* (pp. 306-312). New York: Guildford Press.

Beumont, P.J.V., Arthur, B., Russell, J.D. & Touyz, S.W. (1994). Excessive physical activity in dieting disorder patients: proposals for a supervised exercise program. *International Journal of Eating Disorders, 15*, 21-36.

Beumont, P.J.V., Garner, D.M. & Touyz, S.W. (1994). Diagnoses of eating or dieting disorders: What may we learn from past mistakes? *International Journal of Eating Disorders, 16*, 349-362.

Beumont, P.J.V., George, G.C.W. & Smart, D.E. (1976). "Dieters" and "vomiters and purgers" in anorexia nervosa. *Psychological Medicine, 6*, 617-622.

Beumont, P.J.V., O'Connor, M., Touyz, S.W. & Williams, H. (1987). Nutritional counselling: the treatment of anorexia and bulimia nervosa. In P.J.V. Beumont, G.D. Burrows & R.C. Casper (Eds.), *Handbook of Eating Disorders, Part 1, Anorexia and Bulimia Nervosa* (pp. 201-232). Amsterdam: Elsevier.

Beumont, P.J.V., Russell, J.D. & Touyz, S.W. (1993). Treatment of anorexia nervosa. *The Lancet, 341*, June 26.

Channon, S. & Wardle, J. (1989). Eating Disorders. In J. Scott, J.M.G. Williams & A.T. Beck (Eds.), *Cognitive Therapy in Clinical Practice: An Illustrative Case Book*. London: Routledge.

Cooke, K. (1994). *Real Gorgeous: The Truth About Body and Beauty*. St Leonards, Sydney: Allen & Unwin Pty Ltd.

Dieting Association of Australia (1990). *Principles in the Nutritional Management of Clinical Disorders: Handbook No. 6*. Dieting Association of Australia (D.A.A.).

Fairburn, C. (1981). A cognitive-behavioural approach to the treatment of bulimia. *Psychological Medicine, 11*, 707-11.

Garner, D.M. (1990). *The Eating Disorders Inventory - 2*. Odessa, Florida: Psychological Assessment Resources.

Garner, D.M. & Bemis, K.M. (1982). A cognitive-behavioral approach to anorexia nervosa. *Cognitive Therapy and Research, 6*, 123-150.

Garner, D.M. & Garfinkel, P.E. (1979). The eating attitudes test: an index of symptoms of anorexia nervosa. *Psychological Medicine, 9*, 273-9.

Garner, D.M., Rockert, W., Olmsted, M.P., Johnson, C. & Coscina, D.V. (1985). Psychoeducational principles in the treatment of bulimia and anorexia nervosa. In D.M. Garner & P.E. Garfinkel, *Handbook of Psychotherapy for Anorexia Nervosa and Bulimia.* New York: Guilford Press.

Laessle, R.G., Beumont, P.J.V., Butow, P., Lennerts, W., O'Connor, M., Pirke, K.M., Touyz, S.W. & Waadt, S. (1991). A comparison of nutritional management with stress management in the treatment of bulimia nervosa. *British Journal of Psychiatry, 159,* 250-261.

Lucas, A.R., Beard, C.M., O'Fallon, W.M. & Kurran, L.T. (1991). 50-year trends in the incidence of anorexia nervosa in Rochester: a population-based study. *American Journal of Psychiatry, 148,* 917-922.

Mental Health Act: A Guide Book (1990). Rozelle: NSW Institute of Psychiatry.

Mitchell, P. B. & Truswell, A.S. (1987). Body composition in anorexia nervosa and starvation. In P.J.V. Beumont, G.D. Burrows & R.C. Casper (Eds.), *Handbook of Eating Disorders, Part 1, Anorexia and Bulimia Nervosa* (pp. 201-232). Amsterdam: Elsevier.

Pope, H.G. & Hudson, J.I. (1988). Is bulimia nervosa a heterogenous disorder? Lessons for the history of medicine. *International Journal of Eating Disorders, 7,* 155-166.

Ratnasuriya, R.H., Eisler, I., Szmukler, G.I. & Russell, G.F.M. (1991). Anorexia nervosa: outcome and prognostic factors after 20 years. *British Journal of Psychiatry, 158,* 495-502.

Russell, G.F.M. (1989). Bulimia nervosa: an ominous variant of anorexia nervosa. *Psychological Medicine, 9,* 429-448.

Russell, G.F.M. (1983). Anorexia nervosa and bulimia nervosa. In *Handbook of Psychiatry 4: The Neuroses and Personality Disorders.* Cambridge: Cambridge University Press.

Russell, J. & Beumont, P.J.V. (1987). The endocrinology of anorexia nervosa. In P.J.V. Beumont, G.D. Burrows & R.C. Casper (Eds.), *Handbook of Eating Disorders, Part 1, Anorexia and Bulimia Nervosa* (pp. 201-232). Amsterdam: Elsevier.

Scott, D. (1988). *Anorexia and Bulimia Nervosa: Practical Approaches.* NY: New York University Press.

Touyz, S.W. & Beumont, P.J.V. (1985). *Eating Disorders: Their Prevalence and Treatment.* Sydney: Adis Press, Williams & Wilkins.

Touyz, S.W. & Beumont, P.J.V. (1989). Anorexia and bulimia nervosa, the dieting disorders. In P.J.V. Beumont & R.B. Hampshire (Eds.), *Textbook of Psychiatry* (pp. 119-128). Melbourne: Blackwell Scientific Publications.

Touyz, S.W. & Beumont, P.J.V. (1991). The management of anorexia nervosa in adolescence. *Modern Medicine, 34,* 86-97.

Treasure, J. (1991). Long-term management of eating disorders. *International Review of Psychiatry, 3,* 43-58.

Vandereycken, W. (1987). The management of patients with anorexia nervosa and bulimia - basic principles and general guidelines. In, P.J.V. Beumont, G.D. Burrows & R.C. Casper (Eds.), *Handbook of Eating Disorders, Part 1: Anorexia & Bulimia Nervosa.* Amsterdam: Elsevier.

World Health Organisation (1992). *ICD-10 Classification of Mental and Behavioural Disorders: clinical descriptions and diagnostic guidelines.* Geneva: World Health Organisation.

6.3 RESOURCE MATERIALS

6.3.1 EATING BEHAVIOUR ASSESSMENT INTERVIEW

To be completed by the clinician.

General Questions

What is your ideal weight? _____

Why is this weight ideal for you? _____

What is the most you have ever weighed? _____

What is the least you have ever weighed? _____

Can you tell me which method you plan to use to reach your ideal weight? _____
_____

How much time would you spend each day thinking about such things as food, losing weight, your appearance, and so on? _____
_____

Do you think you are fat now? _____

What are your feelings about being fat? _____

Have people commented on your being fat in the past? _____

Who? _____

What did they say? _____

Does anyone comment on your being fat now? _____

Who? _____

What do they say? _____

Do you have a regular menstrual period each month? _____

If not, when did your periods stop? _____

What food or dieting-related problems do you have at the moment? _____
_____

Which of these problems is the most difficult for you? _____

Can you tell me how your eating problems affect:

The way you feel about yourself: _____

Your personal relationships: _____

Your work: _____

Your social activities: _____

Your life in general: _____

Binge Eating

Do you ever binge-eat? (i.e., eat, during a short space of time, quantities of food that are definitely larger than most people would eat during a similar time frame and in similar circumstances). _____

_____

How often do you binge-eat? _____

Why do you binge-eat? _____

Is binge-eating a problem for you? _____

Tell me about a typical binge? (Obtain information about type of foods eaten, the pace of eating, quantity of food, duration of the binge, vomiting or purging after the binge.) _____

_____

When did you first start binge eating? _____

How do you feel just before you binge? _____

Can you identify anything (e.g., feelings, social situations, etc.) that may trigger the binge? __

_____

How do you feel while you are binge eating? _____

How do you feel after a binge? _____

Do you try to avoid binge eating? _____

What do you do? _____

_____

Do you try to stop the binge once you have started? _____

How? _____

_____

Laxatives

Do you ever use laxatives? _____

  What kind? _____

How many? _____

  How often? _____

For what reason do you use laxatives? _____

Do you believe the laxatives are useful for this purpose? _____

Why? _____

When did you first start using laxatives? _____

What prompts you to take a laxative? _____

How do you feel after taking laxatives? _____

Do you experience any unpleasant side effects that you feel may be caused by the laxatives? _

_____

_____

Have you ever tried to stop using laxatives? _____

What happened? _____

Diuretics

Do you ever use diuretics? _____

What kind? _____

How many? _____

How often? _____

Where do you get the diuretics from? _____

For what reason do you use diuretics? _____

Do you believe diuretics are useful for this purpose? _____

When did you first start using diuretics? _____

How do you feel after taking a diuretic? _____

Do you experience any unpleasant side effects that you feel may be caused by the diuretic? _

_____

_____

Have you ever tried to stop using diuretics? _____

What happened? _____

Vomiting

Have you ever made yourself vomit on purpose? _____

When was this? _____

How often do you do this? _____

Can you tell me what you do to make yourself vomit? (N.B.: Ask about the use of drugs and note the name of the drug, dose, frequency, where the drug is obtained, side effects of the drug, etc.)

_____

_____

Can you tell me why you make yourself vomit? _____

Do you believe vomiting is effective for this purpose? _____

Do you vomit:

After a binge? _____

After eating specific kinds of food? _____

After a normal meal? _____

When you have not eaten recently? _____

How do you feel just before you vomit? _____

How do you feel just after you vomit? _____

Do you try to stop yourself from vomiting? _____

How? _____

Why? _____

Exercise

Do you use exercise as a means of controlling your weight? _____

Do you find exercise useful for this purpose? _____

How often do you exercise? _____

How long each day / week do you spend exercising? _____

What kind of exercise do you do? _____

How do you feel before exercising? _____

How do you feel after exercising? _____

How are your energy levels in general? _____

Other notes

_____

_____

_____

_____

_____

_____

6.3.2 FOOD AND BEHAVIOUR DIARY

Day and Date: _____

*B = Binge   V/P = Vomiting or Purging

Time	Food and liquid consumed	Place	*B	*V/P	Context	Exercise	
						Type	Duration

6.3.3 BINGE MONITORING FORM

Date: _____   Day of week: _____   Time: _____

What were you *doing* immediately before the binge? _____
_____
_____
_____

How did you *feel* immediately before binge-eating? _____
_____
_____
_____

What did you *eat* during the binge? _____
_____
_____
_____

What did you *think or feel* during the binge? _____
_____
_____
_____

Why did you end the binge? _____
_____
_____
_____

How did you *feel* by the end of the binge? _____
_____
_____
_____

Did you *vomit, take laxatives or diuretics, or exercise* before, during, or after the binge?
(If yes, please give details.) _____
_____
_____

If yes to the previous question, how did you *feel* afterwards (i.e., after vomiting, going to the
toilet, etc.)? _____
_____
_____

What do you feel *caused* you to binge on this occasion? _____
_____
_____

Other relevant comments you wish to record: _____
_____
_____

6.3.4 LETTER AND INFORMATION FOR DOCTORS

Date:

Dear Doctor,

Your patient _____ has been attending our centre. Our assessment to date suggests that he/she may have _____ a dieting disorder. To aid our assessment, it is important that your patient receives a medical check-up including the following investigations:

- Full blood biochemistry
- Blood count
- Liver function
- Renal function
- ECG

We would appreciate it if you could conduct these investigations and assess for any other health problems that may be related to your patient's dieting behaviours.

I have enclosed an information sheet about dieting disorders.

Please feel free to contact me on the number below if you would like to discuss his/her management further.

Thank you.

Treating clinician: _____

Mental health centre: _____

_____

_____

_____

Phone no.:   _____

INFORMATION SHEET ABOUT DIETING DISORDERS

Anorexia Nervosa
- Deliberate loss of weight (BMI < 17.5)
- Excessive fear of obesity and weight gain
- Associated physical dysfunctions, especially of the endocrine system (see symptoms listed below)
- Bulimic behaviours, such as binge-eating with compensatory weight loss behaviours, may also be present

Individuals who have anorexia nervosa may engage in weight loss behaviours such as:
- Self-induced vomiting (sometimes with the assistance of emetics such as Ipecac)
- Self-induced purging (abuse of laxatives or high quantities of fibrous foods such as unprocessed bran or prunes)
- Excessive exercise
- Use of appetite suppressants
- Use of diuretics (tablets that assist with the loss of body fluid)

Physical symptoms include:
- Amenorrhoea and other manifestations of endocrine disorder
- Hypothermia
- Hypotension
- Bradycardia
- Disturbed blood chemistry
- Lanugo hair growth, brittle hair, or hair loss
- Constipation and abdominal discomfort
- Headaches, dizziness, and ringing in the ears
- Dry skin
- Stunting of growth in younger people
- Reduced gastric motility
- Hyperactivity
- Brittle bones and osteoporosis (leading to stress fractures among those who overexercise)
- Dental decay and swollen salivary glands from excessive vomiting
- Polyuria
- Paresthesias

Psychological symptoms include:
- Depression / suicidal ideation
- Loss of concentration
- Preoccupation with thoughts of food and body image
- Anxiety
- Irritability
- Labile mood
- Low self-esteem
- Perfectionism and obsessional thinking
- Hypersensitivity to noise

Bulimia nervosa
- Recurrent and uncontrolled bouts of binge-eating (i.e., eating during a short period of time, quantities of food that are definitely larger than most people would eat during a similar time frame and in similar circumstances)
- A feeling of loss of control over eating behaviour during eating episodes
- Excessive preoccupation with body weight, body shape, and food
- The use of inappropriate compensatory weight loss behaviours to prevent weight gain after binge-eating (see below)

Compensatory weight loss behaviours include:
- Self-induced vomiting (sometimes with the assistance of emetics such as Ipecac, bran or prunes)
- Excessive exercise
- Use of appetite suppressants
- Use of diuretics (tablets that assist with the loss of body fluid)

Physical symptoms include:
- Swollen salivary glands from excessive vomiting
- Amenorrhoea and / or other manifestations of endocrine disorder
- Dental decay
- Acute stretching or dilatation of the stomach, often associated with abdominal pain
- Irritable bowel, melanosis coli, and disturbed bowel motions from chronic laxative abuse
- Electrolyte imbalances from purging, possibly leading to heart arrhythmias, brain seizures, abnormal EEGs, muscle cramps and stiffness, liver disease, and kidney failure
- Swollen hands and feet
- Fatigue
- Nausea
- Headaches
- Hair loss
- Bruising
- Insomnia
- Chronic hoarseness of the voice
- UTIs

6.3.5 DELAYING A BINGE

When you feel like binge eating, it may be helpful to ask yourself the following questions:

Am I hungry at the moment?

If you are hungry, it is important that you have something to eat. However, select only a small portion of appetising food and return the excess food to the cupboard or fridge. Take small bites and chew each mouthful slowly and carefully. Do not put more food into your mouth until you have finished your current mouthful. While you are eating, think about whether the food has managed to stop you from feeling hungry. If you are still hungry, select another small portion of food (returning the excess food to the fridge or cupboard), and chew each mouthful slowly and carefully. Once again, think about whether you are still hungry. Continue eating small portions of food (returning the food to the cupboard or fridge each time) until you no longer feel hungry. If you stop feeling hungry but want to keep eating, ask yourself the following questions.

If I am not hungry, what am I trying to achieve by eating?

Write your thoughts into your food diary.

Will binge-eating make me feel better?

Write your thoughts into your food diary.

Why will binge-eating make me feel better?

Write your thoughts into your food diary.

Is there any other way to feel better apart from binge-eating?

Options you may consider are:

- Calling a friend for a chat or to talk about how you are feeling
- Going for a walk
- Doing something else enjoyable
- 15 minutes of progressive muscle relaxation
- Structured problem solving (if your urge to binge-eat has resulted from something unpleasant that may have just happened)
- Talking and communicating about your feelings in a clear and assertive manner (if your urge to binge-eat has resulted from a disagreement with someone)

N.B.: Delay tactics can also be used to reduce the likelihood of vomiting or purging after a snack, meal, or binge. After eating, gradually try to increase the delay before vomiting or taking laxatives by engaging in distracting activities. Try to get used to the feeling of having food in your stomach. Given time, the food will be digested and your stomach will no longer feel full or bloated.

6.3.6 FREQUENCY OF BINGE-EATING, VOMITING AND PURGING

**Number of binges,
vomits, and
purges**

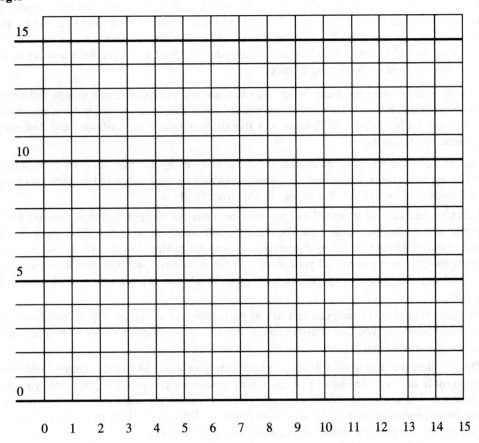

Weeks

Use a **red** pen to record the number of binge eating sessions each week.
Use a **blue** pen to record the number of times you vomit each week.
Use a **black** pen to record the number of times you purge (take laxatives) each week.

6.3.7 A NOTE TO FAMILIES AND FRIENDS

Anorexia and bulimia nervosa can occur as brief and temporary episodes, or they can be long term, life-threatening crises that disrupt families and destroy relationships. When attention is focused exclusively on the person with the dieting disorder, family members and friends often become the forgotten victims of anorexia and bulimia nervosa. They are left with no resources, feeling guilty, frustrated, frightened, and angry.

Living with someone who has a dieting disorder is very difficult. The individual's demands for attention, together with his or her rejection of other people's attempts to help, can leave friends and family feeling inadequate and impotent. They need to learn to balance their lives so as not to spend all their energy worrying about the disorder. Family and friends need to devote a significant portion of their time to self restoring activities and relationships so they will have the resources to deal with problems caused by the dieting disorder.

Individuals with anorexia and bulimia nervosa can seem sad and pathetic one minute and fiercely stubborn and hostile the next. They have great power in their families and relationships, even though they may not realise it. To help families and friends overcome their confusion and distress we recommend the following:

- Accept that there are no quick or easy solutions to a dieting disorder; and that clinicians and other 'experts' have no magic cures. If people are to recover, they will have to make vital changes in attitudes and behaviours. You cannot do this work for them.

- Learn to take care of yourself! Do not become a martyr. Do not sacrifice yourself for the person who has the dieting disorder. You will accomplish nothing, and you will become exhausted and resentful. Do not let family life revolve around the dieting disorder. Do not neglect other relationships. Do not spend all your time with the individual; you will only encourage more dependency. Encourage the person to make new friends and explore new activities out in the world.

- You have control over how much you will let the person take advantage of you. You do not have to accept behaviour you find abusive. You do not have to provide him or her with opportunities to abuse your love and generosity.

- Do not allow the dieting disorder to run your family or group of friends. They should not be responsible for what the rest of you eat, which restaurants you patronise, or where you go on outings and holidays. Individuals with anorexia and bulimia nervosa need to learn to deal with the consequences of their decisions. Do not make it difficult for them to learn this lesson by giving them the power to avoid all situations they find distressing.

- Express honest love and affection verbally and physically. Do not tie your caring to sermons about eating or demands to gain weight.

- Develop dialogues with the person about issues other than food, weight and diets. Discuss current affairs, sports, or any other good topic.

- Be a good listener. Listening to hour after hour of moody brooding about food, body weight and dieting is a waste of time, but listening to feelings, opinions and original thinking can be a great service to an individual with anorexia or bulimia nervosa.

- Avoid power struggles over eating or weight gain; the person with the dieting disorder will always win.

- Do not use manipulative comments like *"You are ruining the whole family"* or *"Why are you doing this to me?"*. The person will feel guilty but will not change the problem behaviours. You need to take care of yourself. Do not make the individual responsible for your happiness; that is too much to ask.

- Once therapy begins, avoid getting hooked into discussions or arguments about food and weight. Feeding oneself properly is an adult activity, and learning to do so is one of the goals of therapy.

- Do not allow the anorexic or bulimic person's peculiar eating habits and food choices to dominate your kitchen, your own meals, or your schedule.

- If the individual is food shopping or cooking for the family, realise he or she may be using this nurturing role to deny a personal need for food; feeding others may have become a substitute for feeding oneself.

- Co-operate with the clinician in devising and sticking to a plan that will encourage the individual to become mature, self-loving, and responsible.

- Realise that at best individuals with anorexia and bulimia nervosa are usually ambivalent about wanting to get well. At times they really do want to be normal, at other times they will retreat into what they experience as the relative safety and security of rituals and other food behaviours.

- Be kind to yourself; avoid wasting time blaming yourself for the dieting disorder. Blame will accomplish nothing; you will only make yourself miserable. Gather information and review your options, then decide what to do next. Find new ways of strengthening your inner resources to sustain you through whatever happens.

THE PREVENTION OF DIETING DISORDERS: INFORMATION FOR FAMILY & FRIENDS

Dieting disorders seem to be much easier to prevent than to cure. Families, teachers and counsellors can help.

- Educate those you care for about the dangers of prolonged, excessive dieting.

- Educate young people about advertising strategies that first make them feel inferior, and then promise magic results if only a certain 'look' is achieved.

- Do not push children or friends to excel in school, sport, or other areas. Let them grow and develop at their own pace. If you consistently suggest they could do better if only they tried harder, you may want to examine your own situation to see if you are living your life through them.

- Adolescents need a balance between rules and limits on the one hand and freedom and responsibilities on the other. Give them appropriate choices, and let them experience the consequences of their own decisions. Be neither too protective nor too abandoning.

- Be aware of stress and pain in the lives of friends and young people. Don't try to 'fix' someone else's problems; let that person work through the issues and grow from the experience.

- Your primary role is one of love, support, and encouragement.

- Teach good nutrition at home and in school. Distinguish between dieting and a good diet; many young people think they are synonymous.

- Avoid encouraging young people to lose weight. Express your love and caring regardless of how they look, and encourage them to be healthy; not clones of fashion models.

- If you are a woman, be a good role model for younger women. Avoid criticising your own body. Stop spending so much time talking about diets and physical appearance. Express admiration for healthy bodies, even your own, and even if the bodies do not conform to society's idea of pencil thinness.

- If you are a man, avoid criticising women who do not meet your standards of physical beauty. Women are people, not just bodies. Realise that not all women can be model thin and still healthy. Do not encourage your wife, girlfriend or daughter to lose weight just because this would make *you* feel better.

- If a friend or young person wants to lose weight, find out what he or she wants to *achieve* by dieting. If the goals are unrealistic, or if the individual is feeling inadequate and unacceptable, deal with those issues directly. If the feelings persist, seek help from a counsellor or therapist who is trained to work with dieting disorders.

- If you are concerned about an individual's behaviour, discuss your concerns with the individual in a warm, understanding, and non-judgmental manner. Encourage the individual to clarify the main problems he or she is facing. Reassure the individual that it is all right to ask for help and then actively assist the individual to find appropriate help if that is what he or she desires.

A useful book for guidelines on management strategies is J. Ball and R. Ball *Eating Disorders: A Survival Guide for Familes and Friends*

6.3.8 HOW TO HANDLE OR PREVENT RELAPSE

1. Take *time out* to think about what is happening and to make a plan of action.

2. Start keeping a food and behaviour *diary* again.

3. Make sure you *eat three meals a day plus snacks*. Do not let more than three hours pass without eating something.

4. *Talk to a close friend* or relative about your concerns. They will probably be pleased that you confided in them.

5. *Avoid weighing yourself* more than once a week. If necessary, stop weighing yourself altogether.

6. If you are feeling anxious, depressed, or stressed, *try using the problem solving technique* to work out a positive solution to your problem.

7. Make sure your goals are realistic. If you are aiming for something that is too difficult, set yourself an easier goal. Relapse is very common, and does NOT mean that you are a failure. Progress takes time and effort. *DON'T GIVE UP!!*

8. Make an appointment to *see your usual clinician* or doctor. He or she will assist you to get back on track.

For those who have trouble with overeating:

9. *Plan (in advance) how you are going to spend your time*. If necessary, try to avoid being alone. Have a list of interesting activities you can become involved in during 'difficult' moments.

10. *Identify 'high-risk' activities* or times of day when you think you may be most likely to overeat. Try to avoid these activities or situations.

11. Try to *avoid entering the kitchen between meals*, and avoid going to the supermarket. If necessary, ask someone else to do your shopping for you.

12. *Avoid carrying money* if you think you may be tempted to buy food. If you must carry money, carry as little as possible.

7

SUBSTANCE USE DISORDERS

7.1 SUBSTANCE USE DISORDERS

ABOUT THIS CHAPTER

This chapter concerns the assessment and treatment of individuals who have substance use disorders. Frequently, individuals seeking treatment have a problem with several substances. Most of the techniques described in this chapter are applicable across all psychoactive drugs, including alcohol, and prescribed and illicit drugs. These techniques can also be helpful to the many individuals who experience problems with alcohol and drug use, yet do not meet criteria for a formal diagnosis of a substance use disorder.

7.1.1 DESCRIPTION AND DIAGNOSIS

DESCRIPTION

There is a wide spectrum of use and misuse of psychoactive substances. When it becomes a problem to the individual, substance use is generally characterised by:

- a strong, and sometimes overpowering desire to take alcohol, drugs or prescribed medication;
- difficulty in controlling use;
- problems associated with drug and alcohol use.

DIAGNOSIS

Harmful Use

The diagnosis of harmful use (as defined in the World Health Organization's ICD-10) is made when an individual has a pattern of substance use that is causing damage to their health. The damage may be physical (e.g., liver damage or hepatitis) or mental (e.g., episodes of depression secondary to heavy consumption). This condition is diagnosed only when the individual does not fulfil the criteria for dependence.

Dependence

Dependence is a psychological syndrome which occurs after repetitive use of a psychoactive substance, typically for months or years. According to ICD-10, the diagnosis of dependence should only be made if three or more of the following have been experienced at some time during the previous year:

1. a strong desire to take the substance;
2. difficulties in controlling the use of the substance;
3. a withdrawal syndrome when substance use has ceased or been reduced. The physical symptoms of withdrawal vary across drugs, but psychological symptoms include anxiety, depression and sleep disturbance. The individual may also report the use of substances to relieve the withdrawal symptoms;
4. evidence of tolerance such that higher doses are required to achieve the same effect;
5. neglect of interests and an increased amount of time taken to obtain the substance or recover from its effects;
6. persistence with the substance use despite evidence of its harmful consequences.

DIFFERENTIAL DIAGNOSIS

Individuals who are experiencing substance use disorders may present with physical or psychological complaints that they do not attribute to their substance use. A full alcohol and drug assessment is necessary to ascertain the role of a substance in the presenting problems. For some mental disorders, individuals may not need to be drug free before treatment is begun. Comorbidity between substance use and other mental disorders is substantial. One in five who seek treatment for a mental disorder have a comorbid substance use disorder. Conversely, a third of persons seeking treatment with a substance use disorder have a comorbid mental disorder.

EPIDEMIOLOGY

Alcohol use disorders are frequent. One in 16 adults will meet criteria for an alcohol use disorder in the past 12 months, whereas one in 50 will have a drug use disorder. Men are more likely than women to have an alcohol use disorder and the highest rates are in the young (before the age of 30 years). Illicit drug use and drug use disorders in the population vary widely but as with alcohol, the majority will be young males.

COURSE AND PROGNOSIS

As the prevalence drops with age, remission in both men and women is high and most of those who stop or moderate their drinking or drug use do so without professional help.

TERMINOLOGY

Standard drinks

Different alcoholic drinks vary markedly in strength. A *standard drink* contains about 10 grams of alcohol. The following are equivalent to one standard drink:

- 2 x 285ml of low alcohol beer
- 285ml of ordinary 5% beer
- 100ml of table wine
- 60ml of port or sherry
- 30ml (nip) of spirits or liqueur

Most people at home pour larger than standard drinks and on social occasions, the habit of topping up drinks can make it difficult to work out how much is actually being consumed. The quantities listed above show that two double scotches and an ordinary beer are equivalent to five standard drinks.

7.1.2 ASSESSMENT

The aim of assessment is to:
1. Identify the main diagnoses and any other comorbid disorders or problems;
2. Highlight the areas that require intervention so that goals can be set and a management plan devised.
3. Identify why the individual continues to take a drug which is causing them harm (but recognising that rationalisation and attribution of use may be inaccurate);
4. Identify a baseline against which improvement or deterioration can be measured.

The assessment of an individual with a substance use disorder therefore involves many tasks. The tasks include a review of the quantity of substance consumed, whether there are features of dependence, and the consequences of that consumption. In addition, the assessment of an individual's commitment to treatment or "readiness to change" is valuable. A psychiatric history and mental state examination are also standard components (see Chapter 1: Core Management Skills). Throughout the assessment process the clinician can work to develop rapport with the individual and thus enhance motivation for change. Assessment should be an ongoing process throughout treatment as well as at the conclusion of treatment, allowing progress to be assessed and the management plan adjusted where necessary. Interventions that do not bring about change will need to be reviewed.

Clinicians need to assess the following:
- Severity of dependence
- Signs and symptoms of withdrawal syndromes
- Physical health consequences of substance use
- Risk taking behaviour which may be associated with substance use
- Stages of change that an individual may be in with regard to their level of commitment to change their substance use behaviour
- The pattern and context of substance use
- Previous attempts to reduce or stop substance use

SEVERITY OF DEPENDENCE

The level or severity of substance dependence is an important factor in planning the intervention. Physical dependence may suggest the need for managed detoxification, a process which aims to achieve a safe withdrawal from a drug of dependence. Abrupt alcohol withdrawal can be life threatening (see Alcohol Withdrawal Syndrome below).

The following are signs of the level of dependence:
- Narrowing of the behavioural repertoire: An individual who is dependent may only drink one or two types of alcoholic drinks in the same way on weekdays and weekends.
- Salience of drinking or drug use: With increasing dependence the individual gives greater priority to substance use
- Subjective awareness of compulsion: The individual experiences loss of control over the substance use or an inability to stop using the substance
- Increased tolerance: The individual uses more of the substance to get the same effects or the same amount of the substance has less effect.
- Repeated withdrawal symptoms: The frequency and severity of withdrawal symptoms increases with increasing dependence. A wide range of symptoms can occur in withdrawal and include fatigue or exhaustion, sweating, diarrhoea, anxiety, depression, irritability, restlessness, trouble sleeping, tremors (hands tremble), stomach aches, headaches, weakness, nausea or vomiting, fits or seizures, muscle aches or cramps, runny eyes or nose, yawning, intense craving, seeing things that aren't really there, heart beating fast, change in appetite, fever.
- Relief from or avoidance of withdrawal symptoms: The individual uses substances in order to stop withdrawal symptoms (e.g., morning drinking)
- Post-abstinence reinstatement: A rapid return to dependence after a period of abstinence.

Standardized questionnaires to assess severity of dependence

Severity of Alcohol Dependence Questionnaire (SADQ-C)

This questionnaire is designed to measure the severity of dependence on alcohol. It covers five areas: physical withdrawal symptoms, affective withdrawal symptoms, craving and withdrawal relief drinking, consumption and reinstatement. It is quick and easy to score. Answers to each question are rated on a four-point scale 0=almost never, 1= sometimes, 2=often, 3=nearly always. Scores lower than or equal to 20 indicate low dependence, scores between 21 and 30 indicate moderate dependence and scores higher than 30 indicate a high level of dependence. It is reproduced in Section 7.3.1.

Severity of Opiate Dependence Questionnaire (SODQ)

The SODQ assesses severity of opiate dependence. It contains items addressing the demographics of drug consumption, as well as items related to four aspects of dependence; withdrawal, affective withdrawal, withdrawal relief drug-taking and rapidity of reinstatement after abstinence. A score indicative of dependence has not yet been developed. It is reproduced in Section 7.3.2 and is scored the same way as the SADQ-C.

The Severity of Dependence Scale (SDS)

The SDS is a brief (5 item) scale which assesses severity of dependence. Cut off scores indicating dependence have been developed for alcohol and amphetamines. It is reproduced in Section 7.3.3.

WITHDRAWAL SYNDROMES

Alcohol withdrawal syndrome

Alcohol withdrawal syndrome can develop in individuals who are dependent on alcohol within 6-24 hours of their last drink. This syndrome is important to recognise as it is potentially fatal. Severe cases will require medical attention. There are three subsets of signs and symptoms on a continuum of increasing severity.

1. autonomic nervous system hyperactivity: restlessness, sweating, tachycardia, systolic hypertension, tremors, nausea, vomiting and anxiety;
2. neuronal excitation: epileptiform seizures (usually grand mal) which are rare in the population, but are frequently seen in individuals with alcohol withdrawal syndrome brought into hospital by ambulance;
3. delirium tremens: loss of insight, severe distortion of perception, sensation and arousal (including auditory and visual hallucinations) and severe disorientation, confusion, clouded consciousness, impaired attention, and disturbed sleep. If untreated death may occur from respiratory and cardiovacular collapse.

The following rating scale is useful in assessing the need for supervised detoxification and the severity of Alcohol Withdrawal Symptoms.

Addiction Research Foundation Clinical Institute Withdrawal Assessment-Alcohol (CIWA-Ar)

The scale is a brief, valid and reliable ten-item rating scale on which an individual's withdrawal symptoms are rated. Scores on the scale can be used to guide clinical interventions. For example a score of over 10 indicates moderate to severe withdrawal symptoms for which medication is required. Care needs to be taken in the interpretation of results of the scale when used with polydrug users. The scale is reproduced in Section 7.3.4.

Opioid withdrawal syndrome

Opioid withdrawal states are characterised by craving, rhinorrhoea or sneezing, lacrimation, muscle aches or cramps, abdominal cramps, nausea or vomiting, diarrhoea, pupillary dilation, recurrent chills, tachycardia or hypotension, yawning, and restless sleep.

Sedative or hypnotic withdrawal syndrome

Sedative or hypnotic withdrawal states are characterised by tremor of the tongue, eyelids or outstretched hands, nausea or vomiting, tachycardia, postural hypotension, psychomotor agitation, headache, insomnia, malaise or weakness, transient visual, tactile, or auditory hallicinations or illusions, paranoid ideation, and grand mal convulsions.

Stimulant withdrawal syndrome

The withdrawal state that results from either stopping or reducing the use of cocaine or other stimulants includes lethargy and fatigue, psychomotor retardation or agitation, craving, increased appetite, insomnia or hypersomnia, and bizarre or unpleasant dreams.

PHYSICAL HEALTH PROBLEMS

Individuals with harmful or dependent alcohol use are liable to develop a range of physical disorders, including liver disease, pancreatitis, peptic ulcers, heart problems, hypertension, poor nutrition, alcohol related brain damage, psychological problems such as depression and anxiety, and neurological disorders such as brain damage.

A liver function test measures the levels of certain enzymes in the blood. Any elevated levels of these enzymes indicate risk of damage to the liver. The enzymes are aspartate aminotransferase (AST), alanine aminotransferase (ALT), gamma glutamyltransferase (GGT), and alkaline phosphate. Another common test is a measure of mean corpuscular volume (MCV). This measures the level of red blood cells and a low level may indicate bone marrow toxicity.

Those who inject drugs are at risk of overdose, HIV, Hepatitis B and C, infection, poor nutrition, dental caries, respiratory illnesses and skin disease.

RISK-TAKING BEHAVIOUR

Assessment of the risk (and presence) of HIV, Hepatitis C and B infection is important in those individuals who are injecting drugs. For example, injecting practices that increase the risk of infection include sharing needles, particularly if not cleaned and sterilised before use. Practices that increase the risk of overdose include mixing opiates, alcohol and benzodiazepines, injecting alone, and not being prepared to call an ambulance if someone overdoses.

STAGES OF CHANGE

The treatment outcome in substance dependence may depend on how ready the individual is to change their drinking or drug-taking behaviour. The following 'stages of change' provide a framework for assessing an individuals willingness to change their behaviour (see Prochaska & DiClemente, 1996).

Pre-contemplative stage

Individuals at this stage do not usually attend for treatment unless they are coerced (for example, by a friend or relative). At this stage the individual is not considering changing. This is often expressed as *"I enjoy drinking"*, *"I do not want to stop taking drugs"*. Motivational interviewing techniques (see Section 1.1.7) may be useful and in some instances, will precede a formal assessment and engagement.

Contemplative Stage

Individuals at this stage are aware of the costs of substance use and the benefits of changing but are still ambivalent about changing. This is often expressed as *"I don't like spending so much money on drugs but I really enjoy the highs I get"*. Again, motivational interviewing techniques may be useful.

Preparation Stage

Individuals at this stage are preparing to take action and may have sought treatment in the past. This is often expressed as *"I want to know how to give up"*, *"I'm ready to try cutting down on alcohol"*. Goal setting strategies may be useful with an individual at this stage.

Action Stage

Individuals at this stage are currently engaged in attempts to reduce or stop their drinking or drug taking and need a treatment plan.

Maintenance Stage

Individuals at this stage have successfully changed their drinking or drug taking behaviour and are continuing to maintain that change. Relapse can occur and relapse prevention strategies may be necessary.

ASSESSMENT OF THE PATTERN AND CONTEXT OF DRINKING OR DRUG USE

It is important to get a detailed description of an individuals current substance use before attempting to modify drinking or drug-taking.

Alcohol Use

Ask the individual when was their last drink and how much they drank on this occasion, then ask about the time before that, and then ask if this is a typical pattern. If you simply ask someone how much they drink, they may say that they drink every week or so and have a glass of wine with dinner, but when asked specifically you may discover they drank a bottle of wine yesterday and the same the day before that. Also ask about the sequence of events on a typical drinking day; time when the individual starts to drink, where and with whom they usually drink, the period of time spent drinking, the amount and type of alcohol consumed, and when and why they stop drinking.

Drug Use

Similarly to alcohol use, ask the individual when they last used drugs, how much they used on this occasion, and the time before that, and if this is a typical pattern. For injecting drug use it may also be useful to ask the individual how often and how much they typically inject. Determining the amount spent on drug use provides a useful indication of the extent of use.

Standardized questionnaires to assess amount of substance consumed

Alcohol Use Disorders Identification Test (AUDIT)

The AUDIT is a 10 item screening instrument designed to screen for a range of drinking problems and in particular for hazardous and harmful consumption. A score of 8 or more is associated with harmful or hazardous drinking, a score of 13 or more in women, and 15 or more in men, is likely to indicate alcohol dependence. The instrument is reproduced in Section 7.3.5.

Opiate Treatment Index (OTI)

This instrument is a structured interview covering six independent outcome areas; drug use, HIV risk-taking behaviour, social functioning, criminality, health status and psychological adjustment. It takes between 20-30 minutes to administer and is available from the National Drug and Alcohol Research Centre, University of New South Wales, Sydney, NSW, 2052.

PREVIOUS ATTEMPTS TO REDUCE OR STOP SUBSTANCE USE

The clinician will need to ask about any strategies that have worked in previous attempts to manage substance use, any strategies that have not worked previously, and what might have gone wrong. With the exception of brief interventions, a clinician will rarely see anyone who hasn't tried to cut down or stop their substance use before.

Individuals may have observed that relapse occurred following a clearly identifiable event or in particular situations. For example, when the individual is anxious or depressed, has experienced a relationship break-up or been under considerable social pressure to drink or take drugs.

Identifying high-risk situations involves attaining the following information:
- where?
- when?
- with whom?
- doing what?
- feeling what?

This information is important as it may be difficult to identify a clear cause of relapse. The individual may never have accepted the reasons for reduced drinking, or perhaps did not master coping strategies and had difficulty applying them across all situations.

Information about previous relapse will also provide an idea of the skills that might need to be targeted in the intervention. For example, if relapse occurred in the context of difficulty in drink refusal skills, skills training may address this deficit. Monitoring of situations that might be associated with a high risk of relapse should start as early as possible.

The following questionnaire is useful in identifying high-risk situations for relapse.

Situational Confidence Questionnaire (SCQ)

This scale assesses the individual's confidence in maintaining moderation across a range of situations. The instrument is available from Marketing Services, Addiction Research Foundation, 33 Russell St., Toronto, Canada, M5S 2S1.

SUMMARY OF ASSESSMENT PROCEDURES

- Adopt a non-judgemental attitude
- Assume a tactfully persistent approach
- Do not be diverted from the interview
- Avoid labels such as *alcoholic*, *addict*, *problem* unless the individual uses them
- Include questions about substance use as normal everyday behaviour along with questions about diet, exercise and other lifestyle issues
- Record the substance intake in standard measurements e.g., for alcohol in grams or standard drinks (10g alcohol)
- Use direct and specific questions (ask for specific amounts on specific times), e.g., *"How many drinks did you have yesterday? And the day before that? Is that typical?"*
- Use leading questions, e.g., *"Many people like a drink with lunch, how many drinks do you have with lunch?"*
- Use collateral information (e.g., partner, family, friend with individuals' permission preferably in their presence).

7.1.3 MANAGEMENT PLAN

The management plans outlined below are relevant for hazardous or harmful use and mild dependence in all substance use disorders. Where there are differences, separate sections are written. The clinician should adapt the management plan depending on the specific problems with which the individual presents. People with severe dependence should be referred to a specialised agency.

1. To conduct a thorough assessment (Section 7.1.2)
   - assess immediate risk – overdose, delirium tremens, suicide
   - identify signs of withdrawal
   - identify severity of dependence
   - include a physical assessment
   - identify risk taking behaviour
   - identify the stage of change (pre-contemplative, contemplative, preparation, action, or maintenance)
   - identify patterns and context of drinking or drug use
   - identify previous attempts to reduce or stop substance use

2. To gain the co-operation of the individual
   - use motivational interviewing (Section 1.1.7)
   - educate about the disorder and the process of recovery (Section 7.1.5)

3. To assist the individual to plan appropriate and desirable goals (Section 7.1.6)

4. To change substance use (Section 7.1.7)
   - enhance drink-drug refusal skills
   - use structured problem solving
   - provide assertiveness training (see Section 1.1.11)
   - improve communication skills (see Section 1.1.10)
   - assist with challenging thoughts
   - teach relaxation training (see Section 4.1.3)
   - encourage self-management, emphasise the impact of social and environmental cues
   - use pharmacotherapy as appropriate
   - refer to Alcoholics Anonymous or Narcotics Anonymous if appropriate

5. To maintain change in substance use through relapse prevention strategies
   - educate about relapse
   - identify high risk situations
   - maintain monitoring of substance use
   - use motivational interviewing to maintain change

The general principles of management are that a plan should:
- Follow a thorough analysis of all relevant problems.
- Target both the relevant symptoms (e.g., quantity of alcohol and drug use) and the psychosocial consequences (social relationships, work).
- Be based upon specific strategies while remaining sufficiently flexible to suit each person's changing needs.
- Be understood by individuals and their families.
- Involve the family as much as is appropriate.
- Guarantee continuity of care over an extended period of time.
- Be evaluated regularly for both positive and negative outcomes.

7.1.4 BRIEF INTERVENTIONS

Brief Interventions are primarily educational interventions that can be delivered in sessions of 5 minutes up to 30 minutes in time. They are typically single session interventions but a follow-up session is strongly recommended to ensure that behaviour change has occurred. A brief intervention is appropriate for individuals with excessive substance use but who have few medical problems associated with that use. Brief intervention programs usually include a self-help manual with brief support and guidance from the clinician. They aim to provide only enough assistance to ensure the individual achieves the desired behaviour change.

Procedure

- Screen to detect excessive alcohol or drug use (see AUDIT Section 7.3.5).
- Advise individuals to reduce consumption of alcohol and drug taking to safe and responsible levels (see Section 7.3.6 for responsible drinking guidelines and Section 7.3.7 for brief self-help information).
- Make a personal link to the risk information, that is, relate the individual's particular symptoms to drug or alcohol use.

Drink-less Program

The Drink-less Program is a practical package designed to enable primary care workers to screen for alcohol related problems and offer advice to their patients on how to reduce their drinking. The program involves (i) screening patients using the World Health Organization's AUDIT Questionnaire; (ii) scoring the questionnaire with a template; (iii) providing brief advice to 'at risk' patients using an advice card specifically for this use; and (iv) giving patients a pocket sized self-help booklet that reinforces the advice provided. The materials used in the Drink-less Program are based on the a protocol devised during a successful WHO trial of early intervention techniques. The Drink-less Program is available from Drug and Alcohol Services, Building 82, Royal Prince Alfred Hospital, Camperdown, NSW, 2050, Australia.

Flowchart of management plan

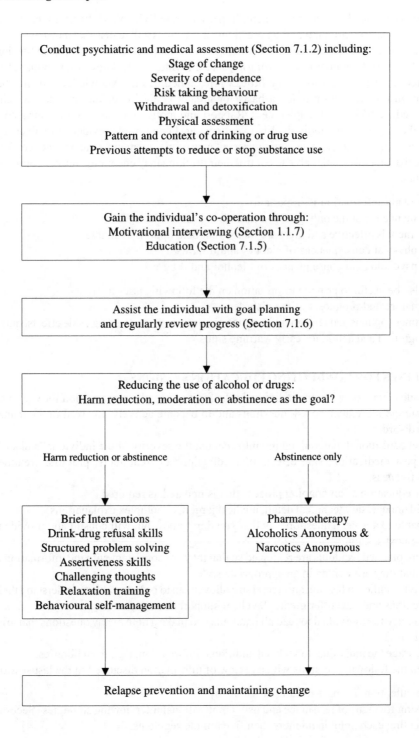

Conduct psychiatric and medical assessment (Section 7.1.2) including:
Stage of change
Severity of dependence
Risk taking behaviour
Withdrawal and detoxification
Physical assessment
Pattern and context of drinking or drug use
Previous attempts to reduce or stop substance use

Gain the individual's co-operation through:
Motivational interviewing (Section 1.1.7)
Education (Section 7.1.5)

Assist the individual with goal planning
and regularly review progress (Section 7.1.6)

Reducing the use of alcohol or drugs:
Harm reduction, moderation or abstinence as the goal?

Harm reduction or abstinence

Abstinence only

Brief Interventions
Drink-drug refusal skills
Structured problem solving
Assertiveness skills
Challenging thoughts
Relaxation training
Behavioural self-management

Pharmacotherapy
Alcoholics Anonymous &
Narcotics Anonymous

Relapse prevention and maintaining change

7.1.5 EDUCATION

Education is a crucial aspect of treatment. In particular, individuals will vary in their extent of their knowledge about safe drinking or drug use. Some individuals will realise that they have a problem with alcohol or drugs while others will not, or will deny the fact (see stages of change in Section 7.1.2 and Section 1.1.7: Motivational interviewing). Some individuals will know a lot about substances and their effects, others will know very little, while sometimes the knowledge will not be accurate. Accurate information can provide a basis for greater control over the disorder, which in turn is likely to reduce feelings of helplessness. Rapport and motivation can also be improved by making explicit the problems the individual is experiencing. For example, evidence of liver damage as a consequence of drinking may encourage acceptance of treatment aimed at abstinence. Alternatively, evidence that an individual is able to control their drinking may encourage further control of drinking behaviours.

The following information is important:
- Abstinence is not the only goal for all individuals
- Treatment is effective and there are many treatment options available
- The physical consequences of alcohol and drug use
- The psychological consequences of alcohol and drug use

It may also be useful to provide information on the following issues:
- The nature and prognosis of the disorder
- Treatment options and relevant information about each alternative (e.g., side effects, duration, costs)
- Recognition and action for early warning signs

GUIDELINES FOR CONDUCTING EDUCATION SESSIONS

- Provide education when the individual asks for it or has given permission for you to provide it.
- Encourage individuals to ask questions and to become actively involved in the management of their disorder.
- Target educational material, taking into account the severity of the individual's disorder, current and past medication, side effects of medications or treatments; previous treatment and its effectiveness.
- View education as an ongoing process that is updated as required.
- Avoid unnecessary technical detail, medical jargon, or complex explanations.
- If unable to answer a question, say that you don't know but will consult and provide the answer in the next session.
- Ensure planned handouts are reviewed so that they are consistent with the information to be given and that they are written in an appropriate style.
- Involve families in the education sessions; allow them to be better able to understand their relative's difficulties and thus offer greater levels of support and assistance.
- Encourage the individual to read all handouts and make a note of any questions that arise between sessions.
- Encourage the individual to seek out additional information, e.g., from libraries.
- Begin the following sessions with a review of information discussed in the last session.

Maintain attention during education sessions by:
- Looking for signs of resistance and using motivational interviewing strategies (Section 1.1.7)
- Presenting each point in no more than five minute segments.
- Encouraging participation to describe their own experiences, voice concerns and ask questions.
- At the end of each segment, encouraging participants to summarise the key points they have understood.
- Repeating important points throughout the session.

EDUCATION ABOUT RELAPSE

Relapse prevention should be broached early in management. It is important to encourage the view from the very start that lapses (periods of inappropriate use) are opportunities to learn rather than indications of failure. Behavioural change is often challenging, especially when the behaviours have been present for a considerable time, and some degree of relapse is likely in such circumstances.

The general aims of relapse prevention training are to:
- provide the individual with skills to avoid lapses;
- prevent lapses from becoming relapses to alcohol or drug use;
- reduce the negative consequence of relapse.

When relapses occur, individuals can remind themselves of positive changes they had achieved prior to relapse and hence be more motivated to continue attempts to change.

7.1.6 GOAL PLANNING

The importance of goal setting is to link assessment to intervention for the individual. Goal setting requires that the problems and concerns of the individual have been summarised during assessment. These goals will depend on the stage of change of the individual. The motivational interviewing strategies are useful for negotiating concerns with individuals who might remain ambivalent about change. Once concerns are agreed upon, specific goals and treatment options can be developed and negotiated between the individual and the clinician. The negotiation requires that goals must be realistic, achievable, specific, broken down into small steps and owned by the individual.

Identify problem areas

The process of identifying good and not so good things about substance use (See Section 1.1.7 – Motivational Interviewing) should provide a list of concerns. For example:
- I spend too much time drinking
- I think of myself as worthless
- I get depressed a lot
- I am more likely to get into physical fights
- I fight with my family
- I risk losing my job

Identify strengths and resources

Ask the individual to identify things that they do well, or any abilities, resources (e.g., names of people) or interests. Include activities or skills that the individual enjoyed in the past or did well before the onset of the substance use disorder. For example:
- I used to play cricket
- My wife wants to help
- I enjoy reading
- Paul and Sophie are happy to help
- I recognise drinking causes some problems

Identify needs

Having identified problems areas it will be easy to identify needs. Ensure that personal goals are set by the individual, rather than have the clinician set the goals for the individual. For example:

- to spend more time having fun
- to feel secure in my job
- to stop drinking as much
- to not fight with my family
- to find better ways of coping than drinking

TIPS FOR SETTING SPECIFIC GOALS

Once needs have been defined, the next step in goal planning is to decide upon appropriate goals that are realistic, achievable, specific, broken down into small steps and owned. Use the individual's strengths and resources list as a means of guiding appropriate goals.

Developing realistic and achievable goals

Strategies and goals do not always succeed as they have been planned. This problem can be made worse if an individual sets unrealistic goals, for example *I will stop drinking tomorrow*. Understandably, when such goals are not achieved the individual may feel like there is no point continuing. Alternatively, individuals may set goals which are not challenging at all, and in the long term such goals will result in little change.

The most appropriate goals are those which are high enough to be challenging but not so high as to be impossible. An indicator which can be useful in setting appropriate goals is the individuals current level of substance use. Once the initial goal has been achieved, another slightly more challenging goal can be set. Such step by step goal setting creates a situation where success is more likely, even though it is a slower process.

Developing specific goals

Goals should be refined to reflect an individual's particular concerns and consequences. A question which may be used to explore this area is *"How would your life be different if you followed this goal?"*

Another aspect of developing specific goals is to clearly identify in behavioural and observable terms when the goal has been achieved. For example a goal of *cutting down gradually* is very difficult to measure, whereas a goal of *cutting down by 2 standard drinks a week* can be much more easily measured. Regular monitoring of substance use will help to identify progress towards a goal.

Break long-term goals down into smaller steps

While it is important to develop long term goals to give direction for the future, long-term goals don't provide the immediate rewards that are so useful in maintaining behaviour. Short term goals can provide rewards along the way and also provide evidence that the long-term goal is ultimately achievable.

Owning the goal

It is important that the individual continues to own the decision to change their behaviour and agree that the goals are important to them. One way to achieve this is to offer the individual a range of goals rather than insisting that certain goals be achieved, hence reinforcing personal choice and control. Emphasise that the clinician's role is to provide guidance.

Goal Planning Example

Long-term goal
To reduce consumption of alcohol to 2 standard drinks a day with two alcohol free days

Short term goals (with one week review)
1. Keep a diary of all alcohol consumed
2. Only drink in the company of others

PUTTING GOAL PLANNING INTO PRACTICE

Once goals have been decided upon it may be helpful to use both motivational interviewing and problems solving approaches for planning the response to complicated goals (see Chapter 1: Core Management Skills).

In the planning stage it is also important to consider issues such as :
- Who will remind the individual about the goal (if necessary)
- Planning what to do if something goes wrong
- Deciding on possible rewards for when the goal is reached

It is always important to monitor progress and to praise the individual for success or for attempts at achieving the goal.

Gaining reward from 'failure'

Sometimes the individual may fail to attain the goal they set, perhaps because the. goal was too difficult or not in the individuals hands. For example, the failure to reduce alcohol use to 2 standard drinks a day within one week of treatment may be due to this being an unrealistic goal or the occurrence of a week of special social occasions which involved the presence of large quantities of alcohol. It is important that the individual does not focus on failures but instead focuses on what has been achieved or learned. During the course of the goal the individual may have cut down on the number of standard drinks, even if not by the level set. This positive aspect needs to be emphasised and praised and the individual can then be encouraged to set some new goals based on what has already been achieved.

Monitoring progress

There is no point in setting goals unless the individual keeps track of whether or not the goals have been achieved. If a goal has been achieved, monitoring provides the opportunity for reward. This feedback will also help to maintain the new behaviours. If the goal has not been achieved, monitoring enables revision of goals and praise for attempts to change. It may be useful for the individual to keep a progress chart of the goals that have been set and their completion dates. Encourage individuals to monitor their progress from early in their treatment and to persist with it for as long as they can to maintain their motivation for change and reduce the risk of relapse (see also Rewarding and Encouraging Adaptive Behaviours in Section 6.1.11).

Some individuals will have difficulty in setting realistic goals. In these situations it is important to remind the individual that:
- Change may be slow and should not be rushed
- Excessive pressure by family members for the individual to *perform* may increase stress and lead to frustration.
- Goals need to be flexible
- More difficult goals can be set once initial goals have been achieved.

GOALS FOR ALCOHOL USE

The ultimate goal in terms of harm-reduction in drug use is *abstinence*. In many instances total abstinence will be unacceptable to the individual and other goals linked to reducing alcohol use and associated harm must be considered.

In *moderated drinking*, the individual moderates their drinking to harm-free levels that reduce the risk of physical and psychological problems from drinking.

In *attenuated drinking*, the individual moderates their drinking so as to reduce the harm to self or others. This is obviously not an ideal goal but may be the only goal some individuals will accept.

Deciding on abstinence or moderation

The following complicating factors all indicate that consideration should be given to a goal of abstinence:

- Physical Health: When the individual has already developed physical illnesses as a consequence of alcohol use and these are likely to be aggravated by further use. An individual with significant health problems should be directed towards abstinence.
- Brain damage: Individuals with impaired cognitive functioning may experience difficulty in learning the skills required for a goal of moderated drinking.
- Physical withdrawal: Individuals who have experienced frequent and severe withdrawal (for example, delirium tremens) should be directed towards a goal of abstinence.
- Severity of dependence: Highly dependent individuals are less likely to be able to moderate their drinking successfully.
- History of treatment: If the individual has had repeated failed attempts at moderating their drinking then abstinence may be a more realistic goal.
- Partner's preference and social support.

Trouble-shooting

It is possible that an individual may wish to pursue a goal which you consider unsuitable. It may be helpful to accept the individual's chosen goal on a provisional basis or make a compromise including:

- a negotiated trial of abstinence (holiday away from drinking). For example, if the individual has serious physical health consequences of alcohol use and yet wishes to set a goal of moderation then suggest a six month period of abstinence before a goal of moderation. This has the benefit of giving the individual time to recover from some of the consequences of heavy drinking.
- a gradual reduction in consumption of alcohol towards abstinence.
- a trial period of moderation. This provides the opportunity for the individual to test out whether they are able to sustain moderate drinking.

The final option may be to decline to assist the individual to reach their chosen goal.

GOALS FOR OPIATE/POLYDRUG USE

Abstinence is an ideal goal from a harm reduction perspective. From a public health point of view, changes in behaviour which place individuals at risk of acquiring/transmitting blood-borne viruses are the most urgent, and hence the focus is on reducing unsafe injecting practices and unsafe sexual practices. As with alcohol use disorders, abstinence may be unacceptable as a goal for the individual and in such cases treatment will focus on moderation in use and reducing drug related harm (e.g. crime, needle sharing, overdose).

Reducing unsafe injecting practices

Goal planning in reducing unsafe injecting practices should focus on achievable goals, for many abstinence from illicit drug use may not be an appropriate first goal. The following goals may be considered in this instance:

- cleaning and sterilising shared needles before use
- only using new needles for injection
- taking illicit drugs without injecting
- not mixing alcohol, benzodiazepines and opiates
- not injecting alone
- being prepared to call an ambulance

Further information on this intervention is available in a thorough review by Baker, Heather, Stalwart, O'Neill & Wodak (1996). A manual of cognitive behavioural techniques aimed at reducing HIV risk-taking behaviour in injecting drug users is available from the National Drug and Alcohol Research Centre, University of New South Wales, Sydney, NSW, 2052, Australia.

Reducing unsafe sexual practices

The focus is to reduce the risk of transfer of HIV and other infectious diseases (e.g., hepatitis) through unsafe sexual practice. Safe sex is sex where semen, vaginal fluid or blood does not have the chance to pass into the blood stream of the other person. There are some sexual practices which carry a high risk of infection (e.g. unprotected anal intercourse) and those that carry only a small risk (e.g., masturbation). An information resource on safe sex strategies is referenced in the resource series.

7.1.7 REDUCING THE USE OF ALCOHOL OR DRUGS

The following strategies can be used with goals of harm minimisation or abstinence. Action strategies should be fully discussed with the individual and a menu of options developed to enhance optimism.

DRINK AND DRUG REFUSAL SKILLS

Individuals with alcohol and drug problems will inevitably be faced with situations where they experience social pressure to drink or use drugs. Drink- and drug-refusal training teaches individuals how to refuse offers of alcohol or drugs with confidence. The training can assist individuals with a goal of abstinence to avoid relapse or to assist individuals with a goal of moderated substance use to keep to predetermined levels of use. The skills can also be useful in reducing harmful behaviours such as needle sharing and unsafe sexual practices.

The basis of drink and drug refusal skills

- Almost everyone is placed, at some time, in a situation where they will be offered drinks or drugs
- There are strategies which make it easier to refuse alcohol or drugs. These strategies include the use of appropriate body language and tone of voice, and using direct statements to refuse the offer of alcohol or drugs.
- A confident refusal is more likely to be accepted. Confidence includes speaking in a firm and unhesitating manner, making direct eye contact, standing or sitting straight.

It may be helpful to choose a potential situation where the individual may be offered drugs or a drink and model an inappropriate response. The individual can provide feedback on the response in terms of body language and tone.

Review the last time the individual was offered alcohol or drugs. It may be the case that the individual set themselves up for failure, such as agreeing to meet their friend in the pub rather than a coffee shop – refusal skills can be much harder in the pub!

It will also be important to ask the individual to practice a response in a role-play before they need to apply it in the real world. Get them to practice the response and then you, the therapist, can provide feedback in terms of body language and tone. If necessary, brainstorm more appropriate responses and again get the individual to practice until they are confident in using the most effective response.

STRUCTURED PROBLEM SOLVING

Individuals will be faced with situations and life problems that may threaten their commitment to change their drinking and drug use. Structured problem solving provides a technique for the individual to deal with these issues rather than turning to alcohol or drugs.

Structured problems solving is appropriate whether the individual has a goal of abstinence or moderation and is appropriate for any type of drug problem.

The problem solving process includes the following features:
- Defining problems and goals in an everyday manner
- Encouraging people to seek a wide range of ideas and solutions
- Defining solutions in terms of current needs and resources
- Careful consideration of the practical constraints that are involved in successfully applying a solution.

The application and training of the structured problem solving method is discussed in detail in Chapter 1: Core Management Skills.

ASSERTIVENESS TRAINING AND COMMUNICATION SKILLS

Assertiveness training is recommended for individuals who have difficulty in expressing their emotions. Instead of taking control of difficult situations by expressing their thoughts, individuals may become frustrated, angry and distressed and this may in turn contribute to excessive drinking and drug use. Since being assertive also involves communicating effectively, individuals may also benefit from training or discussion about clear communication and drink or drug refusal skills training. The three skills can be taught effectively together. Although not everyone will need communication skills training, effective communication skills can reduce feelings of embarrassment and social tensions which can lead to excessive drinking and drug use.

Assertiveness and communication skills are equally important for those individuals with goals of abstinence and those with goals of moderated drinking. Information about assertiveness training and clear communication is contained within Chapter 1.

CHALLENGING THOUGHTS

While reducing the amount of alcohol or drugs consumed is a key goal in the treatment of substance use disorders, individuals are often find it difficult to maintain control over the negative thoughts and urges which lead them to drinking and drug taking. Furthermore, if drink and drug taking is reduced in the absence of cognitive change, treatment is likely to result in relapse. The aim of challenging thoughts is firstly to help the individual to recognise when they are thinking in a way that could lead to drinking or drug use. The individual is then taught to interrupt such a train of thought, to challenge the negative or unproductive thoughts and replace them with more helpful thoughts. This intervention is best provided by clinicians with training and experience in cognitive therapy.

A number of typical unhelpful thinking patterns are outlined in the following section:

Generalisations

Some individuals will recall what has happened in one situation and assume it will happen in all such situations. For example, an individual might state that they relapsed after they stopped last year and therefore they will never be able to stop. Or, they may believe that because one of their friends said they were a loser for not smoking marijuana that all their friends think they are a loser. In such cases it can be helpful to point out the generalisation and to encourage the individual to think about the belief. For example:

"I understand that one of your friends said that you were a loser for not taking drugs. But how can you be sure that all your friends think the same way?"

Catastrophic thoughts

The individual may respond to problems by exaggerating their consequences. For example, the individual may believe that if they get a craving to drink or take drugs it will be unbearable and they will have to give in to it. In such instances it may be helpful to point out the lack of plausibility of such thinking.

"When people are in stressful situations it is easy to blow things out of proportion. Because of some of your past experiences, its easy for you to worry that you couldn't cope if you had a craving. But you know people who have had a craving and not given into it. You've also had cravings in the past and have survived them. I wonder what effect thinking the way you do now has on you? How might things be different if you could tell yourself that craving may be unpleasant but that you are likely to cope?"

Should statements

Individuals using *"should"*, *"ought"* and *"must"* can lead to guilt and sets the individual up to be disappointed. For example, *"I should stop drinking"*. Encourage the individual to avoid unrealistic demands on themselves and others and to remind themselves why they want to change.

Overinterpretation of personal events

Individuals may believe that all personal problems they experience are due to their urge for drinking. For example, after fighting with their partner after getting home late from work, the individual may believe *"my partner mistrusts me because I drink; things will never change, there's no point in trying any more; I need a drink."* Ask the individual if there are any other explanations as to why they had a fight with their partner? For example *"We were both tired, my partner was worried about me."* Ask the individual what evidence they have that their partner mistrusts them and trusts them.

Other strategies to deal with unhelpful thinking

Blame your reaction to the event, not your personality: Everyone makes mistakes sometimes, mistakes made in a particular situation are not permanent reflections of you as a person

Recall good things: Focus on the positive, for example, what has gone well lately?

Re-label distress: Negative thoughts do not necessarily mean that you will end up taking drugs or drinking. They can be seen as signals for you to use coping strategies to help you not drink.

RELAXATION TRAINING

Stress and tension may contribute to the onset of drinking or drug taking. Relaxation training enables the individual to:

- recognise tension and stress
- learn to relax muscles in the body
- learn to actively release tension in day-to-day situations
- learn to cope with tension which may have lead to drinking or drug taking

Relaxation techniques are useful for individuals with goals of abstinence and moderated drinking or drug taking. The relaxation strategies are discussed in detail in Chapter 4.

ENCOURAGING SELF MANAGEMENT

Behavioural self-management is recommended for those individuals who wish to cut down on drinking or drug taking (rather than abstain) and who do not have severe problems with or dependence on alcohol or drugs. The aim is to help the individual to minimise both physical health and social problems by things such as *low-risk* drinking (see guidelines in Section 7.3.6).

Behavioural self-management involves the following strategies:

- self-monitoring
- setting drinking/drug taking limits and controlling rates of drinking/drug taking
- identifying at risk situations
- drink/drug refusal skills
- problem solving
- self-reward

Self monitoring

The aim of self-monitoring is to make the individual aware of how much, when, where and why they drink and to encourage strategies for coping with situations where they are likely to drink more than their agreed limit. The rationale is that eventually the individual will learn skills to help them cut down and maintain their drinking or drug taking at a low-risk level.

The use of diary can also be an important component of treatment. The monitoring of intake can be reactive, such that the individual decreases their intake purely because they are recording it. Section 7.3.8 contains a sample day diary.

Ask the individual to record:

- Day, date and times of drinking or drug taking.
- The amount and type of drink or drugs taken. The context of drinking or drug taking (e.g., where, with whom, doing what).
- Number of standard drinks or drugs taken.
- Thoughts before drinking or drug taking.
- Behaviours, thoughts, or feelings following drinking or drug taking.

It is important to be aware that not everyone will agree to keep a diary or be accurate with their diary. Individuals may initially resent the diary or will not appreciate its usefulness but may come to recognise the benefit. Motivational interviewing strategies can be used to keep the individual engaged in diary keeping.

RELAPSE PREVENTION TRAINING

Successful relapse prevention is influenced to a large extent by lifestyle issues. Therefore relapse prevention training also involves examining lifestyle factors that can either hinder or support behaviour change.

Relapse prevention training can be divided into the following areas:
- Enhance commitment to change
- Identify causes of relapse (see Section 7.1.2)
- Reintroduce useful strategies
- Prepare for relapse
- Deal with lifestyle issues important to maintaining initial change

Commitment to maintaining behavioural change is an essential component in relapse prevention training. The individual may benefit from reviewing the negative aspects of drug or alcohol use and the reasons for changing their patterns.

Following relapse, or when the individual is at risk of relapse, it will be useful for the individual to return to the strategies that had been successful in the past. Starting a diary again may help individuals reassess their behaviour patterns and unhelpful thoughts. Drink-drug refusal skills, relaxation skills and cognitive restructuring may be useful for coping with social pressure, anxiety, depression and anger.

Individuals should be reassured that feelings of craving or urges are a warning sign that they may be in a high risk situation and a sign to use specific coping skills. Some individuals will fear being overwhelmed by craving and expect that the craving will become so unbearable that they will not be able to resist drinking or taking drugs. *Urge surfing* is a useful technique in such circumstances. The individual is encouraged to *ride out* an urge, waiting until the craving peaks and then subsides. The more often an individual copes with urges and cravings, the less frequent they will become.

Ongoing follow-up will encourage adherence to treatment achievements. Follow-up sessions will allow the individual to discuss problems or relapses that may have occurred and to discuss strategies for coping with these. The time and length of follow-up is best determined by the individual and the clinician and depends on the initial severity of the problem and the level of functioning achieved after treatment. Sessions should be arranged in advance. When individuals do not attend, chase them up with a hand-written letter or where appropriate telephone contact.

7.2 BIBLIOGRAPHY

Barber, J.G. & Cooper, B.K. (1991). The Situational Confidence Questionnaire (Heroin). *International Journal of the Addictions, 26*, 565-575.

Darke, S., Ward, J., Hall, W., Heather, N. & Wodak, A. (1991). *The Opiate Treatment Index (OTI) Manual.* Technical Report Number 11. National Drug and Alcohol Research Centre, Sydney, Australia.

Gossop, M., Darke, S., Griffiths, P., Hando, J., Powis, B., Hall, W. & Strang, J. (1995). The Severity of Dependence Scale (SDS): Psychometric properties of the SDS in English and Australian samples of heroin, cocaine and amphetamine users. *Addiction, 90*, 607-614.

Hall, W. & Zador, D. (1997). The alcohol withdrawal syndrome. *The Lancet, 349*, 1897-1900.

Hester, R.K. & Miller, W.R. (1995). *Handbook of alcoholism treatment approaches: Effective alternatives* 2nd Edition. NY: Pergamon Press.

Marlatt, G.A. & Gordon J. (Eds) (1985). *Relapse prevention: Maintenance strategies the treatment of addictive behaviours.* NY: Guilford Press.

Mattick, R.P. & Baillie, A.J. (1992). *An outline for approaches to smoking cessation: Quality assurance in the treatment of drug dependence project,* National Campaign Against Drug Abuse Monograph Series No. 19. Canberra, Australia: Australian Government Publishing Service.

Mattick, R.P. & Hall, W. (1993). *An outline for the management of opioid dependence: Quality assurance in the treatment of drug dependence project*, National Campaign Against Drug Abuse Monograph Series No. 21. Canberra, Australia: Australian Government Publishing Service.

Mattick, R.P. & Jarvis, T.J. (1993). *An outline for the management of alcohol problems: Quality assurance in the treatment of drug dependence project*, National Campaign Against Drug Abuse Monograph Series No. 20. Canberra, Australia: Australian Government Publishing Service.

Mattick, R.P., Baillie, A.J., Digiusto, E., Gourlay, S., Richmond, R. & Stanton, H.J. (1994). A summary of the recommendations for smoking cessation interventions: The quality assurance in the treatment of drug dependence project. *Drug and Alcohol Review, 13*, 171-177.

Mattick, R.P. & Hall, W. (1994). A summary of the recommendations for the management of opioid dependence: The quality assurance in the treatment of drug dependence project. *Drug and Alcohol Review, 13*, 319-326.

Mattick, R.P. & Jarvis, T.J. (1994). A summary of the recommendations for the management of alcohol problems: The quality assurance in the treatment of drug dependence project. *Drug and Alcohol Review, 13*, 145-155.

Mattick, R.P. & Hall, W. (1996). Are detoxification programmes effective? *The Lancet, 347*, 97-100.

Miller, W.R. & Marlatt, A. (1984). *Manual for the Comprehensive Drinker Profile, Brief Drinker Profile and Follow-up Drinker Profile.* Psychological Assessment Resources, Inc. P.O.Box 98, Odessa, Florida, 33556.

Miller, W.R. & Rollnick, S. (1991). *Motivational Interviewing: Preparing people to change addictive behaviour.* New York: Guildford Press.

Saunders, J.B. & Allsop, S. (1991). Helping those who relapse. In: R. Davidson, J. Rollnick and I. MacEwan (eds). *Counselling Problem Drinkers.* London: Tavistock/Routledge.

Saunders, J.B., Aasland, O.G., Babor, T.F., de le Fuente, J.R. & Grant, M. (1993). Development of the alcohol use disorders identification test (AUDIT). WHO Collaborative project on early detection of persons with harmful alcohol consumption - II, *Addiction*, *88*, 791-804.

Sitarthan, T. & Kavanagh, D.J. (1990). Role of self-efficacy in predicting outcomes from a programme of controlled drinking. *Drug and Alcohol Dependence*, *27*, 87-94.

Stockwell, T., Sitharthan, T., McGrath, D. & Lang, E. (1994). The measurement of alcohol dependence and impaired control in community samples. *Addiction*, *89*, 167-174.

Sutherland, G., Edwards, G., Taylor, C., Phillips, G., Gossop, M. & Brady, R. (1986). The measurement of opiate dependence. *British Journal of Addiction*, *81*, 479-484.

Treatment Manuals

Baker, A., Heather, N., Stallard, A., O'Neill, K. & Wodak, A. (1996). *A manual of cognitive behavioural techniques aimed at reducing HIV risk-taking behaviour in injecting drug users.* NDARC Monograph No. 28, Sydney: National Drug and Alcohol Research Centre.

Jarvis, T, Tebbutt, J. & Mattick, R.P. (1995). *Treatment approaches for alcohol and drug dependence: An introductory guide.* Sydney: Wiley & Sons.

Monti, P.M., Abrams, D.B., Kadden, R.M. & Cooney, N.L. (1989). *Treating alcohol dependence: A coping skills training guide.* New York: Guilford Press.

Ward, J., Mattick, R.P. & Hall, W. (1998). *Methadone maintenance treatment and other opioid replacement therapies.* Sydney: Harwood Academic Publishers.

7.3 RESOURCE MATERIALS

7.3.1 SEVERITY OF ALCOHOL DEPENDENCE QUESTIONNAIRE (SADQ-C) [1]

NAME_____AGE _____SEX_____

Have you drunk any alcohol in the past six months?   YES / NO

If YES, please answer all the following questions about your drinking by circling your most appropriate response.

During the past six months

1. The day after drinking alcohol, I woke up feeling sweaty.
    ALMOST NEVER   SOMETIMES   OFTEN   NEARLY ALWAYS

2. The day after drinking alcohol, my hands shook first thing in the morning.
    ALMOST NEVER   SOMETIMES   OFTEN   NEARLY ALWAYS

3. The day after drinking alcohol, my whole body shook violently first thing in the morning if I didn't have a drink.
    ALMOST NEVER   SOMETIMES   OFTEN   NEARLY ALWAYS

4. The day after drinking alcohol, I woke up absolutely drenched in sweat.
    ALMOST NEVER   SOMETIMES   OFTEN   NEARLY ALWAYS

5. The day after drinking alcohol, I dread waking up in the morning.
    ALMOST NEVER   SOMETIMES   OFTEN   NEARLY ALWAYS

6. The day after drinking alcohol, I was frightened of meeting people first thing in the morning.
    ALMOST NEVER   SOMETIMES   OFTEN   NEARLY ALWAYS

7. The day after drinking alcohol, I felt at the edge of despair when I awoke.
    ALMOST NEVER   SOMETIMES   OFTEN   NEARLY ALWAYS

8. The day after drinking alcohol, I felt very frightened when I awoke.
    ALMOST NEVER   SOMETIMES   OFTEN   NEARLY ALWAYS

9. The day after drinking alcohol, I liked to have an alcoholic drink in the morning.
    ALMOST NEVER   SOMETIMES   OFTEN   NEARLY ALWAYS

---

[1] Stockwell, T., Sitharthan, T., McGrath, D. & Lang, E. (1994). The measurement of alcohol dependence and imparied control in community samples. *Addiction*, *89*, 167-174.

10. The day after drinking alcohol, I always gulped my first few alcoholic drinks down as quickly as possible.

ALMOST NEVER   SOMETIMES   OFTEN   NEARLY ALWAYS

11. The day after drinking alcohol, I drank more alcohol in the morning to get rid of the shakes.

ALMOST NEVER   SOMETIMES   OFTEN   NEARLY ALWAYS

12. The day after drinking alcohol, I had a very strong craving for a drink when I awoke.

ALMOST NEVER   SOMETIMES   OFTEN   NEARLY ALWAYS

13. I drank more than a quarter of a bottle of spirits in a day (OR 1 bottle of wine OR 7 beers).

ALMOST NEVER   SOMETIMES   OFTEN   NEARLY ALWAYS

14. I drank more than half a bottle of spirits per day (OR 2 bottles of wine OR 15 beers).

ALMOST NEVER   SOMETIMES   OFTEN   NEARLY ALWAYS

15. I drank more than one bottle of spirits per day (OR 4 bottles of wine OR 30 beers).

ALMOST NEVER   SOMETIMES   OFTEN   NEARLY ALWAYS

16. I drank more than two bottles of spirits per day (OR 8 bottles of wine OR 60 beers).

ALMOST NEVER   SOMETIMES   OFTEN   NEARLY ALWAYS

Imagine the following situation:

1. You have **hardly drunk any alcohol for a few weeks**
2. You then drink **very heavily** for **two days**

How would you feel the **morning after** those two days of heavy drinking?

17. I would start to sweat.

NOT AT ALL   SLIGHTLY   MODERATELY   QUITE A LOT

18. My hands would shake.

NOT AT ALL   SLIGHTLY   MODERATELY   QUITE A LOT

19. My body would shake.

NOT AT ALL   SLIGHTLY   MODERATELY   QUITE A LOT

20. I would be craving for a drink.

NOT AT ALL   SLIGHTLY   MODERATELY   QUITE A LOT

7.3.2 SEVERITY OF OPIATE DEPENDENCE QUESTIONNAIRE (SODQ)[1]

NAME_____ AGE _____ SEX_____

First of all we would like you to recall a recent month when you were using opiates heavily in a way that for you, was fairly typical of a heavy use period. Please fill in the month and the year.

MONTH_____ YEAR_____

Answer every question by circling one response only

1. **On waking, and before my first dose of opiates:**

    a. My body aches or feels stiff:

    NEVER OR   SOMETIMES   OFTEN   ALWAYS OR
    ALMOST NEVER   NEARLY ALWAYS

    b. I get stomach cramps:

    NEVER OR   SOMETIMES   OFTEN   ALWAYS OR
    ALMOST NEVER   NEARLY ALWAYS

    c. I feel sick:

    NEVER OR   SOMETIMES   OFTEN   ALWAYS OR
    ALMOST NEVER   NEARLY ALWAYS

    d. I notice my heart pounding:

    NEVER OR   SOMETIMES   OFTEN   ALWAYS OR
    ALMOST NEVER   NEARLY ALWAYS

    e. I have hot and cold flushes:

    NEVER OR   SOMETIMES   OFTEN   ALWAYS OR
    ALMOST NEVER   NEARLY ALWAYS

    f. I feel miserable or depressed:

    NEVER OR   SOMETIMES   OFTEN   ALWAYS OR
    ALMOST NEVER   NEARLY ALWAYS

    g. I feel tense or panicky:

    NEVER OR   SOMETIMES   OFTEN   ALWAYS OR
    ALMOST NEVER   NEARLY ALWAYS

[1] Sutherland, G., Edwards, G., Taylor, C., Phillips, G., Gossop, M. & Brady, R. (1986). The measurement of opiate dependence. *British Journal of Addiction*, *81*, 479-484.

1.   On waking, and before my first dose of opiates:

h.   I feel irritable or angry:

NEVER OR   SOMETIMES   OFTEN   ALWAYS OR
ALMOST NEVER   NEARLY ALWAYS

i.   I feel restless or unable to relax:

NEVER OR   SOMETIMES   OFTEN   ALWAYS OR
ALMOST NEVER   NEARLY ALWAYS

j.   I have a strong craving:

NEVER OR   SOMETIMES   OFTEN   ALWAYS OR
ALMOST NEVER   NEARLY ALWAYS

2.   Please complete all sections (a-f) of this question

a.   I try to save some opiates to use on waking:

NEVER OR   SOMETIMES   OFTEN   ALWAYS OR
ALMOST NEVER   NEARLY ALWAYS

b.   I like to take my first dose of opiates within two hours of waking up:

NEVER OR   SOMETIMES   OFTEN   ALWAYS OR
ALMOST NEVER   NEARLY ALWAYS

c.   In the morning, I use opiates to stop myself feeling sick:

NEVER OR   SOMETIMES   OFTEN   ALWAYS OR
ALMOST NEVER   NEARLY ALWAYS

d.   The first think I think of doing when I wake up is to take some opiates:

NEVER OR   SOMETIMES   OFTEN   ALWAYS OR
ALMOST NEVER   NEARLY ALWAYS

e.   When I wake up I take opiates to stop myself aching or feeling stiff:

NEVER OR   SOMETIMES   OFTEN   ALWAYS OR
ALMOST NEVER   NEARLY ALWAYS

f.   The first thing I do after I wake up is to take some opiates:

NEVER OR   SOMETIMES   OFTEN   ALWAYS OR
ALMOST NEVER   NEARLY ALWAYS

3. **Please think of your opiate use during a typical period of drug taking for these questions**

    a.   Did you think your opiate use was out of control?

NEVER OR ALMOST NEVER	SOMETIMES	OFTEN	ALWAYS OR NEARLY ALWAYS

    b.   Did the prospect of missing a fix (or dose) make you very anxious or worried?

NEVER OR ALMOST NEVER	SOMETIMES	OFTEN	ALWAYS OR NEARLY ALWAYS

    c.   Did you worry about our opiate use?

NEVER OR ALMOST NEVER	SOMETIMES	OFTEN	ALWAYS OR NEARLY ALWAYS

    d.   Did you wish you could stop:

NEVER OR ALMOST NEVER	SOMETIMES	OFTEN	ALWAYS OR NEARLY ALWAYS

    e.   How difficult would you find it to stop or go without?

IMPOSSIBLE	VERY DIFFICULT	QUITE DIFFICULT	NOT DIFFICULT

7.3.3 SEVERITY OF DEPENDENCE SCALE (SDS)[1]

Please answer each question by circling one response only

These questions are about how you felt about your [named drug] use in the last year.

1. Did you ever think your [named drug] use was out of control?

   Never or almost never 0
   Sometimes 1
   Often 2
   Always 3

2. Did the prospect of missing a [fix or shot or drink] make you very anxious or worried?

   Never or almost never 0
   Sometimes 1
   Often 2
   Always 3

3. Did you worry about your [named drug] use?

   Not at all 0
   A little 1
   Often 2
   Always or nearly always 3

4. Did you wish you could stop?

   Never or almost never 0
   Sometimes 1
   Often 2
   Always 3

5. How difficult would you find it to stop or go without?

   Not difficult at all 0
   Quite difficult 1
   Very difficult 2
   Impossible 3

[1] Gossop, M., Darke, S., Griffiths, P., Hando, J., Powis, B., Hall, W. & Strang, J. (1995). The Severity of Dependence Scale (SDS): Psychometric properties of the SDS in English and Australian samples of heroin, cocaine and amphetamine users. *Addiction, 90*, 607-614.

7.3.4 ADDICTION RESEARCH FOUNDATION CLINICAL INSTITUTE WITHDRAWAL ASSESSMENT-ALCOHOL (CIWA-Ar)

Patient: _____   Date: ___ / ___ / ___   Time: ____ : _____

                                                     y   m   d   (24 hr clock, midnight = 00:00)

Pulse or heart rate, taken for one minute: _____   Blood pressure: _____ / _____

NAUSEA AND VOMITING - Ask "Do you feel sick to your stomach? Have you vomited? Observation.

0   no nausea and no vomiting
1   mild nausea with no vomiting
2
3
4   intermittent nausea with dry heaves
5
6
7   constant nausea, frequent dry heaves and vomiting

TREMOR - Arms extended and fingers spread apart. Observation.

0   no tremor
1   not visible, but can be felt fingertip to fingertip
2
3
4   moderate, with patient's arms extended
5
6
7   severe, even with arms not extended

PAROXYSMAL SWEATS - Observation.

0   no sweat visible
1   barely perceptible sweating, palms moist
2
3
4   beads of sweat obvious on forehead
5
6
7   drenching sweats

ANXIETY - Ask "Do you feel nervous?" Observation.

0   no anxiety, at ease
1   mildly anxious
2
3
4   moderately anxious, or guarded, so anxiety is inferred
5
6
7   equivalent to acute panic states as seen in severe delirium or acute schizophrenic reactions.

AGITATION - Observation.

0   normal activity
1   somewhat more than normal activity
2
3
4   moderately fidgety and restless
5
6
7   paces back and forth during most of the interview, or constantly thrashes about

TACTILE DISTURBANCES - Ask "Have you any itching, pins and needles sensations, any burning, any numbness, or do you feel bugs crawling on or under your skin? Observation.

0   none
1   mild itching, pins and needles, burning or numbness
2   mild itching, pins and needles, burning or numbness
3   moderate itching, pins and needles, burning or numbness
4   moderately severe hallucinations
5   severe hallucinations
6   extremely severe hallucinations
7   continuous hallucinations

AUDITORY DISTURBANCES - Ask "Are you more aware of sounds around you? Are they harsh? Do they frighten you? Are you hearing anything that is disturbing to you? Are you hearing things you know are not there? Observation.

0   not present
1   very mild harshness or ability to frighten
2   mild harshness or ability to frighten
3   moderate harshness or ability to frighten
4   moderately severe hallucinations
5   severe hallucinations
6   extremely severe hallucinations
7   continuous hallucinations

VISUAL DISTURBANCES - Ask "Does the light appear to be too bright? Is its colour different? Does it hurt your eyes? Are you seeing anything that is disturbing to you? Are you seeing things you know are not there?" Observation

0   not present
1   very mild sensitivity
2   mild sensitivity
3   moderate sensitivity
4   moderately severe hallucinations
5   severe hallucinations
6   extremely severe hallucinations
7   continuous hallucinations

HEADACHE, FULLNESS IN HEAD - Ask "Does your head feel different? Does it feel like there is a band around your head?" Do not rate for dizziness or lightheadedness. Otherwise, rate severity.

0   not present
1   very mild
2   mild
3   moderate
4   moderately severe
5   severe
6   very severe
7   extremely severe

ORIENTATION AND CLOUDING OF SENSORIUM - Ask "What day is this? Where are you? Who am I?

0   oriented and can do serial additions
1   cannot do serial additions or is uncertain about the date
2   disoriented for date by no more than 2 calendar days
3   disoriented for date by more than 2 calendar days
4   disoriented for place and/or person

Total CIWA-A Score   _____

Rater's initials   _____

Maximum Possible Score   67

7.3.5 ALCOHOL USE DISORDERS IDENTIFICATION TEST (AUDIT) [1]

Please circle the answer that is correct for you

1. How often do you have a drink containing alcohol?

    | never | monthly or less | 2-4 times a month | 2-3 times a week | 4 or more times a week |

2. How many standard drinks containing alcohol do you have on a typical day when drinking?

    | 1 or 2 | 3 or 4 | 5 or 6 | 7 to 9 | 10 or more |

3. How often do you have six or more drinks on one occasion?

    | never | less than monthly | monthly | weekly | daily or almost daily |

4. How often during the last year have you found that you were not able to stop drinking once you had started?

    | never | less than monthly | monthly | weekly | daily or almost daily |

5. How often during the last year have you failed to do what was normally expected from you because of your drinking?

    | never | less than monthly | monthly | weekly | daily or almost daily |

6. How often during the last year have you needed a drink in the morning to get yourself going after a heavy drinking session?

    | never | less than monthly | monthly | weekly | daily or almost daily |

7. How often during the last year have you had a feeling of guilt or remorse after drinking?

    | never | less than monthly | monthly | weekly | daily or almost daily |

8. How often during the last year have you been unable to remember what happened the night before because you had been drinking?

    | never | less than monthly | monthly | weekly | daily or almost daily |

9. Have you or someone else been injured as a result of your drinking?

    | no | yes, but not in the last year | yes, during the last year |

10. Has a relative or friend or a doctor or other health worker been concerned about your drinking or suggested you cut down?

    | no | yes, but not in the last year | yes, during the last year |

[1] Saunders, J.B., Aasland, O.G., Babor, T.F., de le Fuente, J.R. & Grant, M. (1993). Development of the alcohol use disorders identification test (AUDIT): WHO collaborative project on early detection of persons with harmful alcohol consumption – II. *Addiction, 88*, 791-803.

Scoring the AUDIT

Scores for each question range from 0 to 4, with the first response for each question (e.g. never) scoring 0, the second (e.g. less than monthly) scoring 1, the third (e.g. monthly) scoring 2, the fourth (e.g. weekly) scoring 3, and the last response (e.g. daily or almost daily) scoring 4. For questions 9 and 10, which only have 3 responses, the scoring is 0, 2, and 4 (from left to right).

A score of 8 or more is associated with harmful or hazardous drinking, a score of 13 or more in women, and 15 or more in men, is likely to indicate alcohol dependence.

7.3.6 RESPONSIBLE DRINKING GUIDELINES

Responsible or low risk: Level at which drinking is unlikely to cause health problems	**MEN** 4 standard drinks per day, with a maximum of 28 drinks per week (including at least 2 alcohol free days per week) **WOMEN** 2 standard drinks with a maximum of 14 drinks per week (including at least 2 alcohol free days per week)
Hazardous or increased risk: Level at which there is an increasing risk of problems such as raised blood pressure, stroke, liver cirrhosis	**MEN** 4-6 standard drinks per day, or 28-42 drinks per week **WOMEN** 2-4 standard drinks per day, or from 14-28 drinks per week
Harmful or definitely dangerous: Sustained drinking at this level is likely to cause physical, mental, social problems	**MEN** 6+ standard drinks per day, or 42 drinks per week **WOMEN** 4+ standard drinks per day, or 28 drinks per week

7.3.7 HOW TO CUT DOWN ON YOUR DRINKING [1]

How to cut down on your drinking

If you are drinking too much, you can improve your life and health by cutting down. How do you know if you drink too much? Read these questions and answer "yes" or "no":

- Do you drink alone when you feel angry or sad?
- Does your drinking ever make you late for work?
- Does your drinking worry your family?
- Do you ever drink after telling yourself you won't?
- Do you ever forget what you did while you were drinking?
- Do you ever get headaches or have a hang-over after you have been drinking?

If you answered "yes" to any of these questions, you may have a drinking problem. Check with your doctor to be sure. Your doctor will be able to tell you whether you should cut down or abstain. *If you are alcoholic or have other medical problems, you should not just cut down on your drinking - you should stop drinking completely. Your doctor will advise you about what is right for you.*

If your doctor tells you to cut down on your drinking, these steps can help you:

1. Write your reasons for cutting down or stopping

Why do you want to drink less? There are many reasons why you may want to cut down or stop drinking. You may want to improve your health, sleep better, or get along better with your family or friends. Make a list of the reasons you want to drink less.

2. Set a drinking goal

Choose a limit for how much you will drink. You may choose to cut down or not to drink at all. If you are cutting down, keep below these limits:

Women: No more than one drink a day
Men: No more than two drinks a day

A drink is:
- 285ml bottle of beer
- 120ml glass of wine
- 30ml (nip) of spirits

These limits may be too high for some people who have certain medical problems or who are older. Talk with your doctor about the limit that is right for you.

---

[1] Pamplet produced by the National Institute on Alcohol Abuse and Alcoholism, National Institutes of Health (NIH Publication No. 96-3770).

Now - write your drinking goal on a piece of paper. Put it where you can see it, such as on your refrigerator or bathroom mirror. Your paper might look like this:

DRINKING GOAL

- I will start on this day _____

- I will not drink more than _____ drinks in 1 day.

- I will not drink more than _____ drinks in 1 week.

  or

- I will stop drinking alcohol.

---

3. Keep a "diary" of your drinking

To help you reach your goal, keep a "diary" of your drinking. For example, write down every time you have a drink for 1 week. Try to keep your diary for 3 or 4 weeks. This will show you how much you drink and when. You may be surprised. How different is your goal from the amount you drink now? Use the "drinking diary" below to write down when you drink.

Week:	number of drinks	type of drinks	place consumed
Monday			
Tuesday			
Wednesday			
Thursday			
Friday			
Saturday			
Sunday			

Week:	number of drinks	type of drinks	place consumed
Monday			
Tuesday			
Wednesday			
Thursday			
Friday			
Saturday			
Sunday			

Now you know why you want to drink less and you have a goal. There are many ways you can help yourself to cut down. Try these tips:

Watch it at home

Keep a small amount or no alcohol at home. Don't keep temptations around.

Drink slowly

When you drink, sip your drink slowly. Take a break of 1 hour between drinks. Drink soft drinks, water, or juice after a drink with alcohol. Do not drink on an empty stomach! Eat food when you are drinking.

Take a break from alcohol

Pick a day or two each week when you will not drink at all. Then, try to stop drinking for 1 week. Think about how you feel physically and emotionally on these days. When you succeed and feel better, you may find it easier to cut down for good.

Learn how to say NO

You do not have to drink when other people drink. You do not have to take a drink that is given to you. Practice ways to say no politely. For example, you can tell people you feel better when you drink less. Stay away from people who give you a hard time about not drinking.

Stay active

What would you like to do instead of drinking? Use the time and money spent on drinking to do something fun with your family or friends. Go out to eat, see a movie, or play sports or a game.

Get support

Cutting down on your drinking may be difficult at times. Ask your family and friends for support to help you reach your goal. Talk to your doctor if you are having trouble cutting down. Get the help you need to reach your goal.

Watch out for temptations

Watch out for people, places, or times that make you drink, even if you do not want to. Stay away from people who drink a lot or bars where you used to go. Plan ahead of time what you will do to avoid drinking when you are tempted.

Do not drink when you are angry or upset or have a bad day. These are habits you need to break if you want to drink less.

DO NOT GIVE UP!

Most people do not cut down or give up drinking all at once. Just like a diet, it is not easy to change. That is okay. If you do not reach your goal the first time, try again. Remember, get support from people who care about you and want to help. Do not give up!

7.3.8 SAMPLE DIARY

Day, date, times	Where, with, when, what	Thoughts before drinking/drug taking	What did you do?	Behaviours, feelings, consequences	What did you drink/take?	No. of standard drinks/ drugs

8

CHILD & ADOLESCENT DISORDERS

8.1 CHILD AND ADOLESCENT DISORDERS

8.1.1 EPIDEMIOLOGY

There has been a considerable rise in the incidence of mental disorders in young people, particularly in the decades since World War II. The rates of behavioural disorders, substance abuse, eating disorders, depression, and suicidal behaviour have all increased substantially.

Epidemiological studies in a number of countries have shown rates of illness similar or higher than those in adults. Between 10% and 20% of young people at any one time have mental disorders that are severe enough to cause significant impairment in functioning and to warrant treatment. A comprehensive epidemiological study conducted in Australia in 1995 showed that 19% of children aged 4-16 years had experienced significant mental health problems in the past six months. Other studies have indicated that many psychiatric disorders have an onset during childhood or adolescence, and so impair education and vocational choice.

There is a strong argument for increased resources being directed towards child, adolescent, and family psychiatric services. Services should be aimed at:
1. prevention;
2. delaying onset (later onset is associated with greater rates of recovery); and
3. early identification and treatment.

8.1.2 INFLUENCES ON DEVELOPMENT

Development is affected by both biological and environmental factors. Some influences are protective and enhance resilience, while others increase the risk of mental disorder. The multitude and complexity of interactions among individual, family, and social factors makes empirical research difficult. For example, the effects on a child of an ostensibly straightforward event such as parental divorce can vary greatly according to the context in which it occurs, the child's perception of the event, and the outcomes of the event. The field of developmental psychopathology has substantial implications for the prevention of mental health problems via the identification and targeting of protective and risk factors.

What are some of the factors affecting the onset or outcome of psychiatric disorders?

*   **Intelligence**. Higher intelligence is usually associated with a decreased risk and a better prognosis.
*   **Temperament**. This terms refers to the pattern or 'style' of the child's behaviour. Such style is fairly stable during infancy and early childhood. 'Easy' children tend to be happy, regular in feeding and sleeping patterns, and adapt well to new situations. 'Difficult' children tend to be irritable, unhappy, intense, irregular, and have difficulty adjusting to change. Children with a difficult temperament are at a higher risk for emotional and behavioural problems.
*   **Family environment**. Development is influenced by the quality of the family environment in which the child is reared. Good family environments which foster adaptive psychological development are characterised by the family's ability to provide physical and emotional care, secure attachment relationships, consistency, and appropriate, non-punitive limit-setting. Secure attachment relationships are those that reduce anxiety and provide emotional protection in stressful situations. Poor family environments that have a negative effect on psychological development tend to be characterised by lack of affection, parental conflict, overprotection, and inconsistent rules and discipline.
*   **Maltreatment**. Maltreatment (physical or sexual abuse, harsh discipline, neglect) has a marked influence on development, and often results in significant psychopathology.

- **Parental ill-health**. Mental illness (including maternal depression) and drug and alcohol abuse in parents are risk factors for the emotional well-being of the child.
- **Chronic and severe physical illness**. This increases the likelihood of psychiatric problems, particularly if the central nervous system is involved.

The above factors have practical implementations for the prevention and treatment of mental disorders in children. Clinicians should bear these factors in mind during their assessment and treatment of children and families.

It is important to remember that good parenting is not an innate skill. Most parents bring up children largely based on how they themselves were brought up. Efforts by primary health care practitioners to enhance parenting skills in at-risk families through education and counselling will be very effective in the long-term, and represent a good use of resources. It is important to target both the physical (nutrition, vaccination) and emotional domains (affection, consistency, positive reinforcement).

8.1.3 SPECIFIC ISSUES IN THE ASSESSMENT OF CHILDREN AND ADOLESCENTS

There are a number of specific issues in the assessment of childhood problems which need to be considered in addition to the general approach to history taking and assessment of mental status in adults described earlier (see Section 1.1.2).

- **Obtain information from several informants**. As children are less able to verbalise feelings and have limited insight, in order to gain a clear picture of the problems you will need to interview the child, a parental figure, and obtain information from teachers. Discrepancies in reports from different informants are common and these differing perspectives can contribute important clinical information.
- **Systematically assess all potential areas of psychopathology**. Comorbidity is extremely frequent in this age group, and emotional problems are often overlooked in the presence of aggressive and disruptive behaviour. During assessment you will need to ask about:
  - achievement of developmental milestones (e.g. speech development, toilet training)
  - fears, phobias, obsessions
  - depressive symptoms
  - inattention, impulsivity, excessive activity
  - aggressive, delinquent, and rule-breaking conduct
  - problems with learning
  - bizarre or strange ideas and behaviour
  - use of alcohol and drugs
  - relationships with parents, siblings, and peers
- **Ask about abuse and suicidal behaviour**. These issues need to be explored in almost every case. Questions must be sensitive and tailored to the child's age.
- **Determine the significance of symptoms given the child's age**. Many behaviours that are normal at one age are abnormal at other times (e.g. bed-wetting). The child's intelligence should also be taken into account when assessing behaviour (see Section 1.1.13).
- **Assess impairment in functioning**. Impaired psychosocial functioning is an important marker of disorder.
- **Identify strengths and resources in the child and family**. This is essential in planning treatment (see Section 1.1.8).
- **Determine the quality of the family environment**. The family's ability to provide adequate affection, care, consistent limits, and supervision must be evaluated.

- **Conduct a mental state examination (MSE).** Younger children in particular are less able to verbalise their thoughts and feelings. Clinicians have to rely largely on observations of the child's interactions with others in the room and their behaviour in play. With adolescents, the MSE is similar to that of an adult.

DIAGNOSTIC INTERVIEWS, QUESTIONNAIRES, AND CHECKLISTS

There are many instruments available to help clinicians gather information systematically from a variety of sources, to aid in diagnosis and determining the severity of a condition. Some tools can be used a number of times and used to measure outcome. Computer administration and/or scoring are often available. Some of the better known are:

Instrument [1]	Administered by	Source of information	Areas covered
Diagnostic Interview Schedule for Children (DISC)	Lay interviewer, computer self-administration	Parent, Child (>11 yrs)	Most diagnoses
KIDDIE-SADS	Clinician [2]	Parent, Child (>11 yrs)	Most diagnoses
Child Behaviour Checklist (CBCL)	Self-report	Parent, Teacher, Child (>11 yrs)	Several emotional and behavioural syndromes
CES-DC	Self-report	Child (>11 yrs)	Depression
The Children's Yale-Brown Obsessive Compulsive Scale (CYBOCS)	Clinician [2]	Parent, Child	OCD
Conners Rating Scale	Self-report	Parent, Teacher	Hyperactivity
CGAS or GAF	Clinician [2]	All sources	Global functioning
Family Assessment Device (FAD)	Self-report	Parents	Family functioning

INVESTIGATIONS

Psychometric testing is used widely in paediatric psychiatry to determine a child's level of cognitive functioning and academic achievement. These tests are administered and interpreted by psychologists or school counsellors who have specialist skills in this area. Assessment of cognitive functioning is usually conducted using the Weschler Intelligence Scale for Children (WISC-III). Assessment of academic achievement seeks to establish whether a child's performance in the areas of reading, spelling, and arithmetic is comparable to that of his or her peers and consistent with his or her own cognitive ability. *Every child who has problems at school should have these investigations.* The main types of learning problems are discussed in the table on the following page.

It should be noted that there are various types of intelligence (e.g. emotional, musical, motor), and that IQ tests primarily measure aspects of intelligence relevant to academic achievement, such as abstract thinking and verbal ability.

[1] References of published reports about the psychometric properties of these instruments and information on how to obtain them can be found in Rapport & Ismond, 1996.

[2] Health professional (psychiatrist, psychologist, etc.) trained to administer the instrument.

Learning Problem	Description
Developmental Disability	IQ < 70. The child has an intelligence which is below average and finds it difficult to cope with the normal demands of everyday living.
Specific developmental disorders or specific learning disabilities	IQ > 70 and child's performance in tests that measure reading, mathematics or written expression is well below their expected level according to their IQ and schooling.
School under-achievement	IQ > 70 and child's performance in most subjects is below that which would be expected according to their age and intelligence. Low performance in these cases is due to factors other than learning disabilities, such as lack of motivation, poor concentration or depression.

ASSESSMENT REPORT FORMAT

It is suggested that the following information be included in an assessment report.

1. Sources of information
   - Sources of information used (e.g. interview with child, parents, family; school counsellor's report; Child Behaviour Checklist, CES-D).
2. Reasons for referral and presenting problems
3. History of current problems
   - Detail presenting problems
   - Several symptoms need to be listed as present or absent because of their frequency or clinical relevance, namely depressive symptoms, suicidal behaviour, hyperkinetic symptoms, delinquent acts, obsessions or compulsions, hallucinations and delusions.
   - Level of impairment in psychosocial functioning
   - Circumstances and stressors associated with the onset of problems
4. History of previous and current psychological or psychiatric treatment
5. Current medications
   - Effectiveness, unwanted events, and who prescribed them
6. Social and family background
   - Composition of the family
   - Occupational and educational information
   - Financial resources
   - Family psychiatric history
   - Other relevant social and cultural factors
   - Strengths, weaknesses, areas of conflict
7. Developmental history
   - Circumstances of conception, pregnancy, delivery, adoption, and infancy
   - Physical development
   - Medical history
   - School functioning
   - Peer relations
   - Unusual or traumatic circumstances
   - Areas of special talent or interest

8. Family interview
    - Family's relationship style
    - Parental attitudes towards the child
    - Is there excessive criticism, control, or enmeshment, or harsh discipline?
    - Consistency of limit setting, love, and affection
    - Relationship between siblings

9. Individual interview with the child and MSE
    - Mention main positive and negative findings, particularly regarding suicidal ideas and disclosure of abuse.

10. Investigations
    - Results of psychometric testing etc.

11. Diagnostic formulation
    - Summary of child's difficulties and impairment
    - Provisional diagnosis and diagnostic uncertainties
    - Potential aetiological factors
    - Potential exacerbating or mitigating factors
    - Summary of child and family's strengths and weaknesses

12. Management
    - Describe further steps needed to clarify diagnosis (if required)
    - Treatment options offered to family or child
    - Child and family's response to these options and to the explanations of the nature of the child's problems
    - Arrangements for further treatment
    - Feedback to referring agent

8.1.4 SPECIFIC ISSUES IN THE MANAGEMENT OF CHILDREN AND ADOLESCENTS

In contrast to working with adult clients, young people are usually brought to treatment by a parent or other caregiver. Engaging children can be difficult, requiring patience and skill. There are some basic principles in the management of children and adolescents:

- **Form a therapeutic relationship**. Adjust your approach to the age of the child or adolescent while following the guidelines to building a therapeutic relationship (see Section 1.1.5). Treat the young person with respect, not like an object to be talked about. Make the young person feel at ease (e.g. offer toys to play, or pencils and paper to draw; show an interest in the young person's interests).

- **Educate the child**. Young people generally feel confused and bewildered by their symptoms. Reassure them by explaining the disorder and its treatment in simple language.

- **Educate parents** on the nature of their child's disorder, what they can expect, and what they can do to improve the situation. Follow the guidelines regarding education of patients and relatives (see Section 5.3.3) but modify these according to the age of the child and the type of problem.

- **Working with the family is essential**. The younger the child, the more critical family or carer involvement becomes. The only exceptions may be older adolescent, particularly if they no longer live at home.

- **Families are usually an important part of the treatment team**, implementing at home the strategies learnt in the clinic.

- **Offer several treatment alternatives**, where available. Explain the pros and cons of each treatment option. Most conditions will require a multimodal approach to treatment.

- **Keep parents informed** about their child's treatment and progress.
- **Avoid blaming parents**. Parents often feel guilty when their child is having problems. Blaming parents is useless at best and destructive at worst.
- **Liaise with teachers and school**. In addition to obtaining information about the child from his or her teachers, provide them with information about the child's impairments and teach them strategies to reduce impairment.
- **Regularly review the child and the treatment plan**, particularly if progress is not as expected.

MEDICATION

Drug treatment can be used to reduce symptoms in children. Follow the principles described earlier (see Section 2.1.2). Specific issues need to be considered:

- There is generally less information about the efficacy, side effects, and pharmacological properties of drugs in young people than in adults.
- A medication that is effective in adults will not necessarily be effective in children.
- Dosage may need to be modified according to weight.
- Using several medications at the same time (polypharmacy) should be avoided because of the increased cost, the likelihood of reduced adherence, and possible adverse drug interactions.
- Poor adherence and overdosing are common issues with adolescents. Reasons for poor adherence need to be examined, and may include the desire to become independent and fit in with one's peers, peer pressure, teasing, concerns about body image, or side-effects of medication such as acne or weight gain. When overdosing is a risk, drugs need to be kept in a safe place and parental administration or supervision may be required.

ETHICAL CONSIDERATIONS

Informed consent is a complex issue with young people.
- For children under the age of 14 years, a parent or guardian's consent is required in most legislatures.
- Children over the age of 16 years may consent to and seek treatment on their own behalf.
- Between the ages of 14 and 16 years is a grey area, although parents still have the legal ability to consent to treatment.
- Regardless of the young person's age, it is important to gain his or her assent and cooperation for the effective implementation of most treatments.
- In relation to the involuntary admission to hospital of children older than 14 years due to mental illness, follow the same procedures as with adults (see Section 1.1.4).

Confidentiality needs to be maintained, as with adults. Adolescents are often particularly concerned about their privacy. The main exceptions to maintaining confidentiality are:
- When abuse is disclosed. Many Western countries have a legal requirement that this is reported to the relevant government department.
- When the child's behaviour poses a serious risk to themselves (suicidal behaviour) or others (homicidal behaviour). In these cases the child's parents may need to be informed.

8.1.5 MAKING A REFERRAL

Only a very small proportion of young people with psychiatric problems receive specialised treatment. Resources currently do not exist to meet the need, such that referring patients to a specialist or obtaining consultations quickly is often difficult.

It is imperative that more primary health care practitioners acquire enough knowledge, experience, and skills to:
1. Identify and treat milder conditions (e.g. problems with sleep, feeding and eating in preschool children);
2. Implement preventative measures (e.g. basic parenting skills training);
3. Recognise when more specialist services are required (e.g. clinical psychologist, psychiatrist);
4. Provide follow-up services after a specialist's opinion/intervention has been provided, given that mental health problems in children are often persistent.

MENTAL HEALTH SERVICES FOR CHILDREN, ADOLESCENTS, AND FAMILIES

Services are usually grouped in three levels:
1. Community clinics. These typically provide services to a designated catchment area and are staffed by psychologists, social workers, and nurses. Some may have access to a paediatrician or child psychiatrist.
2. Specialist multidisciplinary community-based teams providing outpatient assessment and treatment (e.g. adolescent service, child sexual assault service). These are often located within a hospital department and staff include child psychiatrists, clinical psychologists, and social workers.
3. Specialist tertiary-level units which offer inpatient and day patient services. These are staffed by multidisciplinary teams and deal with the more severe disorders. These units are usually supra-regional.

Other services in child and adolescent mental health include:
- Consultation-liaison psychiatry/clinical psychology services in paediatric hospitals
- School counsellors
- Specialist programmes within the education system
- Mental health professionals employed in the welfare and juvenile justice systems
- Services provided by non-government organisations, including counselling and residential programmes
- Mental health practitioners in private practice

Triaging in child and adolescent mental health is often complex. This can be exacerbated by the scarcity of resources and a blurring of responsibilities for the provision of services. Effective triaging requires a good knowledge of the services available in the local area and matching these to the needs of the child and family. Choose the least restrictive form of treatment for each patient. When there is a conflict of interest, the interests of the child take precedence over those of the family.

WHEN TO REFER

Refer a young person to a specialist service when:
- symptoms do not improve or become worse despite treatment (e.g. a depressed adolescent who does not get better with counselling, a child who continues refusing to attend school);
- psychotic or manic symptoms are present (e.g. hallucinations, delusions);
- the condition requires specialised psychotherapeutic or pharmacological skills (e.g. as for Obsessive-Compulsive Disorder, Tourette's disorder);
- a comprehensive assessment is required to determine the nature of the child's problems;
- the child's functioning is severely impaired.

Where to refer in an emergency?

- Seek emergency treatment when there is a significant risk of self-harm, or harm to others. The safety of the young person is the most important consideration.
- Crisis or extended hours mental health teams, where available, can be useful to deal with these situations, particularly during evenings and weekends.
- An ambulance can be called to transport the child or adolescent to the Emergency Department of the local hospital.
- Emergency treatment may entail admission to an inpatient facility.
- Behavioural crises (e.g. aggressive outbursts, severe temper tantrums in older children, severe loss of control or delinquent acts) are sometimes better handled in the first instance by welfare or law enforcement agencies.

Since many childhood psychiatric problems persist over time, continuity of care is essential. Families often need to be encouraged to engage in ongoing treatment with a practitioner, and it is important that they discuss any misgivings about treatment with that practitioner before seeking another referral. Similarly, practitioners should discuss any concerns they have about the outcome of their referral with the agency involved, before contemplating referring the family elsewhere.

HOW TO REFER

Most services require a telephone call and/or report from the referring professional. You will be expected to provide a brief description of the problems and previous treatment, specify the service required (e.g. assessment, ongoing treatment, advice about a specific issue such as medication, a court report), and forward copies of reports of previous assessments or test results.

An essential aspect of the referral process is preparing the family and child:
- Demystify the referral process. Try to reduce the child and family's anxiety by emphasising that a referral does not mean they are bad parents or that the child is 'crazy'.
- Gain the family and child's consent and cooperation for the referral and for treatment, otherwise it is unlikely to be helpful. Emphasise the collaborative nature of psychological therapy.
- Ensure that parents and children have a realistic expectation of what might be achieved.
- Ensure that all family members requested to attend can actually attend. Older adolescents may wish not to involve the family. This should be respected.
- Give the family an idea of the time they will need to put aside for the consultation.
- Let the family know if there are costs involved.
- Advise the family to take relevant information with them to the appointment (e.g. medical or school reports).

8.1.6 YOUTH SUICIDAL BEHAVIOUR

- Suicide is a leading cause of death in people aged 15-24 years.
- Suicide in children younger than 12 years is very rare. Suicide rates increase steeply during adolescence to reach a peak in the early to mid 20's.
- Suicide attempts, on the other hand, are most frequent during adolescence. For each completed suicide in the young there are about 100 suicide attempts reported.
- Suicidal thoughts are also extremely common in young people. About 16% of females aged 12 to 16 years report having had suicidal thoughts in the previous six months. The figures for males are about half those of females.
- Rates in clinic samples are more than double those in the general population.

Suicide assessment and management has been described earlier and these principles are generally applicable to young people. Specific issues in adolescent suicidal behaviour need to be considered:

- Ask direct questions about suicidal thoughts or behaviours rather than vague or open-ended questions.
- Ask questions about suicidal behaviour in most cases, given how common it is in young people.
- Do not agree to keeping this type of information confidential. Many adolescents want a promise of secrecy. Explain that you will need to inform parents or take other appropriate steps if the young person's safety is at risk.
- Focus on the early recognition and treatment of mental disorders where suicide is a risk, such as depression. Also target those adolescents who abuse substances or who have a history of attempted suicide.

8.1.7 DISORDERS WITH ONSET DURING CHILDHOOD OR ADOLESCENCE

Child and adolescent psychiatric conditions are traditionally divided into two main groups: *emotional disorders* and *behavioural or disruptive disorders*. Children with emotional disorders exhibit disordered emotions, whereas those with behavioural disorders display abnormal conduct. A third group of disorders - *developmental disorders* - have a neuropsychological origin and normal development is impaired. Other groupings include *elimination disorders*, in which toilet training is affected, and the so-called *'adult' disorders* such as anorexia nervosa, schizophrenia, and bipolar disorder, which often have their onset during childhood or adolescence.

Discrete psychiatric conditions are difficult to identify in infants. An exception to this is with respect to some developmental disorders. During infancy extreme behaviour can generally be interpreted as a response to environmental problems (e.g. related to attachment difficulties) or related to variations in temperament. During the preschool and primary school years the characteristics of most psychiatric conditions become increasingly clear, although many of them are rarely seen before adolescence.

COMORBIDITY

Like adults, nearly half of young people with a mental disorder have two or more disorders. Disorders commonly co-occur in two clusters. These are: (1) conduct problems, hyperkinetic syndrome, learning disorders, and drug and alcohol abuse; and (2) depression, anxiety, and behavioural disorders. A comprehensive assessment of a wide range of conditions is therefore essential in young people. As with adult psychiatry, there are significant theoretical and practical implications of comorbidity in child and adolescent psychiatry.

8.1.8 EMOTIONAL DISORDERS

Young people with emotional disorders usually appear unhappy, frightened, or worried. In prepubertal children, the prevalence of emotional disorders is roughly equal amongst boys and girls; after puberty, emotional disorders become more common in females. Youngsters with emotional disorders represent about half of those seen in child and adolescent mental health services.

The *presentation* and *treatment* of affective and anxiety disorders is similar in young people and adults, with the exception of depression and separation anxiety in which specific issues need to be considered.

MAJOR DEPRESSION

The presentation and treatment of major depression is similar to that described for adults (see Chapter 3). A number of specific issues need to be considered in young people:

- Depressed young people often appear cranky, grouchy, and irritable, rather than sad or unhappy.
- 'Atypical' presentations are common (e.g. sleeping more than usual, having an increased appetite).
- Depression in young people often co-occurs with disruptive disorders, drug and alcohol problems, and anxiety disorders.
- Parents, teachers, and health professionals tend to underestimate the degree of depression in young people.
- Depression in young people often goes unrecognised or untreated.
- Unhappiness in young people is often dismissed as a normal part of growing up or as an 'existential crisis'.
- Psychological treatment should be tried in the first instance (e.g. cognitive behaviour therapy, family counselling).
- Use antidepressants if psychological treatment has been ineffective. Antidepressants are less effective in children and adolescents than in adults.
- If medication is used (see Chapter 2), SSRIs and RIMA antidepressants should be prescribed in the first instance (e.g. fluoxetine, paroxetine, sertraline, moclobemide).
- *Avoid tricyclic antidepressants*, at least initially. There is less evidence about their effectiveness and they are cardiotoxic, particularly in overdose.
- ECT may be prescribed in adolescents with severe depression (e.g. psychotic depression) who have not responded to other treatments. There is no evidence that ECT is less effective or more dangerous in adolescents than in adults.
- Without treatment, a depressive episode will last nine months on average. About half of the young people with depression will have further depressive episodes in adulthood, and 20% will develop bipolar disorder. About 15% will commit suicide.

Examples of questions that may be asked to elicit symptoms of major depression

- In the past month (two weeks, six months) were there times when you felt very sad or unhappy?
- (If yes) When you felt this way, did it last for most of the day?
- Was there a time when you felt sad almost every day?
- In the past month, were there times when you were grouchy or irritable, in a bad mood, when even little things would make you mad?
- (If yes) When you felt like this, did it last for most of the day?
- Would you say that you felt cranky and in a bad mood a lot of the time, almost every day?
- In the past month, has there been a time when nothing was fun for you, even things you used to like?
- Has there been a time when you just weren't interested in anything, felt bored or just sat around most of the time?
- In the past month, have there been times when you had much less energy than usual, so that it was a big effort to do anything?
- Have you been more down on yourself than usual, feeling that you couldn't do anything right?
- Were there times when you felt that you were about to cry or were in tears?
- Have you had times when you felt that life was hopeless, that there was nothing good for you in the future?

Modelled on questions from the Diagnostic Interview Schedule for Children (Shaffer et al. 1993).

ANXIETY DISORDERS

Fears are normal and more common during childhood and adolescence. Infants are frightened by loud bangs and falling. Children aged one to two years are scared when separated from their parents. Later on children dread the dark, animals, storms, strange imaginary beasts, and monsters. From the age of seven or eight years, children begin to worry about their performance. Adolescents are concerned about being disliked, rejected, or criticised by their peers. The type of fears experienced at each stage of development is largely a reflection of the intellectual and emotional growth of the child at that point in time. *An anxiety disorder is likely if fears become intense or pervasive and cause substantial impairment in functioning.*

Anxiety disorders are frequent in young people. Their onset is often during childhood or adolescence, and they can follow a chronic, fluctuating course. All the anxiety disorders occur in both children and adults, and have similar although not identical symptoms, with the exception of separation anxiety which is peculiar to children and adolescents. Anxiety disorders are not easy to recognise because young people often know that their fears are groundless and feel ashamed of what they think is a flaw in their character, and so try to conceal them.

SEPARATION ANXIETY DISORDER

Description

Youngsters with separation anxiety disorder become very anxious when they are away from home or from their parents. They can not tolerate the separation. The following are often observed in the young person with separation anxiety disorder:

- Refusal to attend school. What bothers the young person is *not* school itself but being away from parents and home.
- Seeming to become physically ill in the morning when they are due to leave for school (e.g. headaches, vomiting). Monday mornings and the period immediately following school holidays are the worst times for this.
- Reluctance to sleep over at friends' places or to attend school camps.
- Worrying that some harm may come to their parents while they are separated from them (e.g. a car accident, rape, burglary, heart attack), and having vivid fantasies about it.
- Difficulty coping with their parents going out. If their parents do go out, they may require a great deal of reassurance and need to know every single detail about the outing.
- Difficulty going off to sleep, or needing the company and comfort of a parent when they go to bed. Some older children and adolescents with separation anxiety still share a room/bed with their parents.

Examples of questions that may be asked to elicit symptoms of separation anxiety

- Have you worried a lot recently about something bad happening to your mother (or father) like an accident or an illness?
- Do you worry a lot that you mother (father) might actually die?
- Have you worried a lot that your mother (father) might go away and never come back?
- In the last six months, have you been away from home without your parents for several days in a row, like to stay with friends or relatives or to go to a camp?
- In the last six months, have you refused to go to school, just wouldn't go at all?
- Have you had to be forced or dragged to school?
- Has there been a time when you complained of headaches or feeling sick to the stomach nearly every morning before going to school?

Modelled on questions from the Diagnostic Interview Schedule for Children (Shaffer et al. 1993).

Adolescents with separation anxiety eventually become isolated from their friends, lose contact with what is going on at school, and fall behind in their school work. They also feel embarrassed and different. Their self-esteem and confidence slump and they may become depressed. All this makes returning to school increasingly difficult.

Diagnosis

The *key symptom* in making a diagnosis of separation anxiety disorder is the child's irrational fear that some harm may come to his or her parents, or that he or she may be abandoned by them. These fears intensify when parents and child are separated or threatened with separation, resulting in severe distress and in some a refusal to separate (e.g. refusal to attend school). *Suspect the presence of separation anxiety in any child who misses an excessive amount of school.* Bear in mind that non-attendance at school can result from a variety of other problems, as listed below, which need to be considered before making a diagnosis of separation anxiety disorder. Physical symptoms are common (e.g. nausea, vomiting, stomach ache, headache) and often result in unnecessary and repeated physical examinations or investigations. The fact that the physical symptoms are usually triggered by separations should alert the clinician to the likelihood that they are anxiety-based.

Common reasons for school non-attendance

- **Truancy, conduct disorder**
  A teenager leaves home as if to go to school but does not attend (typically spending the day with friends doing things they enjoy, often illicit).
- **Anxiety-based refusal**
  The adolescent complains of feeling ill when the time to go to school approaches or refuses to go to school. This can be due to separation anxiety or to actual fear of school as a result of bullying, social phobias, learning problems, etc.
- **Major depression**
  The teenager lacks motivation or strength to go to school.
- **Non-attendance for other reasons**
  Parents may keep the child at home to help with work, for companionship or for other reasons.

Epidemiology

Separation anxiety disorder is a common condition that affects around 4% of all children and adolescents. It is slightly more common in females. Frequency peaks during early adolescence and decreases thereafter. Minor worries about separation are seen in adults, and some may experience severe discomfort when separated from their spouse or children.

Course and prognosis

The onset of separation anxiety disorder is often triggered by a worrying or traumatic incident, such as an illness or death in the family, a separation or divorce, a change of school, or a minor illness that keeps the young person at home for a few days. The disorder can also emerge out of the blue. There may be a family history of anxiety problems. It is not uncommon for at least one parent of a child with separation anxiety disorder to be highly anxious themselves.

Anxiety disorders tend to run a chronic course when not treated, however they can become less intense or even disappear during adulthood. In separation anxiety disorder, the level of distress associated with separation can vary across time. Prognosis depends on personality factors within the young person, family strengths, and the severity of the condition. Separation anxiety may result in a loss of schooling, a lack of training, and thereby fewer work opportunities in the future. Young people with separation anxiety have an increased risk of developing agoraphobia in adulthood.

Management

- *The guiding treatment principle is the quick return of the young person to school* before the problem becomes entrenched, even if the child manages to attend only a small part of the day.
- It is essential to educate parents and child about the nature and treatment of this condition. They need to understand that exposing the child to the anxiety-provoking situation is necessary to get better, and that encouraging their child to do so is not cruel. Work with the fact that intense anxiety is mainly confined to the time immediately before school and during the first lessons.
- Encouraging the parents to be firm and consistent in their commitment to return the child to school is essential. If one parent is better than the other in doing this, that parent should take control of the situation until attendance is re-established.
- School staff need to be involved in the process of returning the child to school by supporting the parents and by ensuring that the return to school is as smooth as possible.
- Severe or chronic cases may require referral to a specialist paediatric mental health service.
- A short admission to a specialised inpatient unit can be helpful when there has been no response to other treatments.
- Oppositional children or those who come from families with few psychosocial resources are more difficult to treat.
- There is little evidence that medication is helpful in these young people, except when school refusal is the result of another disorder such as major depression.

8.1.9 BEHAVIOURAL OR EXTERNALISING DISORDERS

Young people with behavioural disorders display socially unacceptable conduct and cause disruption or distress to others through behaviours such as restlessness, impulsivity, disobedience, destructiveness, aggression, violence, defiance, stealing, and running away from home. They often upset others more than they upset themselves, and therefore rarely go undetected. These problems may be limited to the home or family environment, or may extend to school and the wider community. Children with behavioural disorders are quickly identified as 'troubled' or labelled as 'trouble-makers'.

Young people with behaviour problems share many characteristics:

- **They are mainly male**. It is well established that aggression, conduct disorders, hyperactivity, and delinquency are much more frequent in males than in females.
- **Disruptive children tend to externalise conflict**. They have great difficulty taking responsibility for the consequences of their actions and blame others such as parents, siblings, and teachers for their problems. As a consequence they seldom feel guilt or remorse.
- **Disruptive symptoms have an early onset**, usually prior to commencing school or during the first years of primary school.
- **Disruptive conduct has a chronic course**. Symptoms tend to persist in one form or another for a number of years. A significant proportion of these children go on to develop a variety of personality problems during adulthood.

- **They find it difficult to learn from experience**. Most children learn that doing something is wrong after being told so, or after being chastised or punished for doing that thing on a number of occasions. Children with behavioural disorders do not seem to learn this, even after going through this process many times.

Behavioural, disruptive or externalising disorders

Hyperkinetic disorder or attention deficit disorder (ADD)	Difficulty concentrating, overactivity, restlessness, and impulsivity, with onset before the age of seven years, that causes significant impairment in functioning.
Oppositional disorder	Markedly defiant, disobedient and provocative behaviour in the absence of more severe antisocial or aggressive acts.
Conduct disorder	Repetitive and persistent pattern of antisocial or aggressive conduct with violations of major social rules or norms.

HYPERKINETIC DISORDER OR ATTENTION DEFICIT DISORDER (ADD)

Description

Children with this condition display significant and developmentally inappropriate *inattention, impulsivity, and overactivity* from an early age (before seven years). These behaviours are typically present across situations (home, school, clinic) and produce substantial impairment in functioning. Children who have this problem are typically rejected by their peers and show a variety of difficulties in social relationships. They are a considerable burden to families and schools.

Common complaints by parents and teachers about children with hyperkinetic disorder

- Can't finish anything he starts doing
- Doesn't seem to listen
- Is completely disorganised
- He forgets to even take his books to school
- Seems to have his head in the clouds most of the time
- Anything distracts him
- Squirms and fidgets all the time
- Can't sit still. Gets up from the table ten times during dinner
- Is very restless
- Is on the go all the time, seems to have an engine inside
- Runs and climbs everywhere
- Talks too much
- Is the class clown
- Is very loud and noisy
- Can't wait for his turn
- Seeks attention all the time
- Does things without thinking
- Always answers when he is not asked and butts into conversations
- Gets injured a lot: broken bones, falls, scratches ... I feel embarrassed when I take him to emergency, they may think that I abuse him

---

Diagnosis

- Inattention and overactivity are the key features of this disorder according to ICD-10. Both are required for a diagnosis plus they should be evident in more than one situation.
- Behaviours should be clearly excessive for the child's age and produce significant impairment.
- This condition is often first identified when the child starts school.
- Information from teachers is always required for diagnosis in school-aged children.
- Diagnosis can be difficult in milder cases because there is a wide range of attention and activity levels in the population.
- Laboratory tests are of little assistance in diagnosing this condition (e.g. EEG, tests of attention).
- Exclude restlessness and impaired concentration that are due to a mood disorder (either depression or mania). In these cases symptoms usually follow an episodic course and lack the early onset and chronicity of the hyperkinetic syndrome.
- Comorbidity with conduct problems and specific learning disabilities is common.

Epidemiology

Rates vary widely according to the criteria used but it is accepted that between 3% and 5% of school-aged children suffer from hyperkinetic disorder. It is several times more frequent in boys than in girls.

Course

The course is chronic but little is known about the natural history of the condition after adolescence. Overactivity often lessens during adolescence and other symptoms gradually become less prominent during early adulthood. Symptoms seem to persist into adulthood in a minority of sufferers. There is little information about hyperactivity in females.

Prognosis

- Around 60-70% grow up to become well functioning adults. These children do much better once they leave school. They often find occupations in which their impairment is not a serious problem. By the age of 18 or 20 years many of these young people are difficult to distinguish from their peers.
- About 20-30% develop antisocial and delinquent behaviours or an antisocial personality disorder. Having an understanding, caring, supportive family and school are protective factors that lessen the risk of these negative outcomes.
- These children are more likely to fail at school. It is not clear whether this is due to the disorder or to the presence of specific learning problems.
- Treatment with stimulant medication does not seem to make much difference to what happens to these children when they grow up, in terms of academic success or behaviour.
- Some studies suggest these children are more likely to abuse alcohol or smoke cigarettes as adults.

Management

A multidisciplinary approach is essential in the management of this disorder. Medication on its own is not a sufficient treatment. Conditions which co-occur need to be separately targeted.

The use of *medication* in this disorder remains controversial:
- While medication is by far the most dramatic, efficient, and quickest way to reduce symptoms, alone it does not seem to result in lasting changes.
- Drug treatment is not always necessary, even in children with severe ADD.
- One of the main benefits of medication is that it can facilitate the implementation of other treatments such as behaviour therapy or academic remediation, thereby increasing their effectiveness.

Treatment of hyperkinetic disorder

1. **Psychological treatments**. Recommended in all instances.
   Behaviour therapy
   Family therapy
   Classroom management

2. **Medication**.
   Stimulants: The most effective drugs to reduce the symptoms of this disorder.
   Dexamphetamine
   Methylphenidate
   Pemoline

   Tricyclic antidepressants: Second line of treatment. Indicated only when stimulants produce significant side effects or can't be used (e.g. comorbid Tourette's disorder). However, tricyclics are quite toxic in children and should be prescribed with caution (e.g. assessing cardiotoxicity through ECG).
   Imipramine

   Other: Second line of treatment. Indicated in children with Tourette's disorder, in those who do not respond to stimulants or experience significant side effects.
   Clonidine (Clonidine should be used with caution because it can have significant cardiotoxicity. Regular monitoring of blood pressure, pulse rate and ECG is advisable)

3. **Diet**. Dietary substances, such as artificial flavours and colours, can produce ADD symptoms in some children. 'Back to basics' diets may be worth trying in young children with ADD. They are impractical and difficult to implement in adolescents. These diets eliminate artificial flavours, preservatives, artificial colourings, monosodium glutamate, chocolate and caffeine (and milk products in children with symptoms of lactose intolerance). This should be done under the supervision of a medical practitioner and dietician.

Drug treatment with stimulants

Special authority to prescribe these medications may be required in some legislatures as they are substances often abused in the community, and prescription may be restricted to some specialist groups such as child psychiatrists and paediatricians.

Stimulant drugs and dosages

Drug	Brand name	Usual daily dose range
dexamphetamine	Dexedrine	2.5-20 mg
methylphenidate	Ritalin	5-40 mg
pemoline	Volital	18.75-112.5 mg

- Stimulant drugs reduce symptoms in 70-80% of children with ADD. Symptoms in 20-30% of cases either do not improve or become worse with these drugs.
- These drugs work by improving concentration and reducing impulsivity and restlessness.
- Stimulants make children more manageable at school and at home, but do not seem to improve academic performance.

- Children who do not benefit from one drug benefit from another.
- Polypharmacy should be avoided to prevent drug interactions.
- Stimulants are given orally two or three times per day: after breakfast, midday, and afternoon. The effects of stimulant medication typically appear less than one hour after ingestion. Duration of effect is 3-4 hours but there is considerable individual variation. Some children's behaviour actually becomes worse when the medication wears off, although this is not a common problem.
- The height and weight of children taking stimulants should be measured at regular intervals.

Side effects

When used as directed and under medical supervision these drugs are safe and have few side effects. Side effects generally diminish after a few weeks of treatment.

- A *mild loss of appetite and insomnia* are most common. *Weight loss* can occur due to diminished appetite. Dose readjustment or changing the time of the day when the medication is taken is often enough to reduce sleep difficulties.
- *Allergic reactions* such as rashes are observed in rare circumstances.
- *Psychotic reactions*, although unusual, can also occur.
- *Tics* can be a worrisome side effect and, if they occur, medication should be ceased. Stimulant medication does not seem to cause Tourette's disorder, but can trigger the onset in predisposed individuals.
- There has been concern in the past that stimulant medications *slow normal growth*. Studies suggest that delayed growth rates are, at worst, a transient problem.
- The risk of *addiction* to these drugs is negligible when prescribed and supervised properly.
- Treatment with Pemoline requires regular monitoring of liver function because of *liver toxicity*.

Psychological management

Psychological treatment is extremely important for improvement in the long-term. The role of parents and teachers is central, as it is they who largely carry out the treatment. In contrast to drug treatment, psychological treatment has little immediate benefit, its results are not dramatic, and it is resource intensive and time-consuming. As a result, parents and teachers often have difficulty persevering with psychological treatment. The clinician should direct his or her efforts towards supporting parents and teachers, and educating them about the appropriate management of their difficult child.

The *main aims* of psychological management are:
1. to help parents and teachers understand the child's difficulties and have realistic expectations of the child;
2. to avoid reinforcing the child's disruptive behaviour;
3. to help the child gradually increase the ability to concentrate;
4. to prevent the development of conduct problems in the longer-term.

Psychological interventions derive primarily from cognitive-behavioural principles. The child's behaviour in all settings must be targeted.

Home:

Assist parents to:
- understand that the child's behaviour is due to a disorder and not to willful misconduct;
- reduce critical comments about the child;
- reward desirable behaviours as soon as possible after they have occurred, as these children have little ability to delay gratification;
- create a routine (e.g. for homework);
- reduce stimulation (e.g. have a quiet area for the child with furniture that is not easily damaged, allow one friend home at a time, limit time spent in shopping centres);

- keep the child busy and encourage sports and other constructive activities;
- reward and praise small achievements and goal-directed behaviour;
- largely ignore disruptive behaviour.

School:

Advise teachers to:
- expect problems with concentration and therefore set short tasks the child can handle;
- reward on-task behaviour immediately;
- avoid critical, negative remarks;
- create a predictable routine;
- reduce stimulation by doing work with the child on a one-to-one basis for short periods or in a small group;
- deal with specific learning problems through remediation;
- supervise and organise the child's breaks and playground activities.

OPPOSITIONAL DISORDER

Description

Young people with oppositional disorder display a persistent pattern of negativistic and hostile conduct towards people in authority, typically parents or teachers. They lose their temper and swear with little provocation, especially when demands are denied. They are stubborn and can not give in, resulting in frequent arguments with authority figures. When asked to do something, they refuse or procrastinate ("I will do it later"; "I forgot"). They are 'touchy', blame others (circumstances, siblings, teachers, parents) for their mistakes, and seem to enjoy provoking and annoying others. Oppositional children justify their behaviour by saying that what they were asked to do is unreasonable or unfair. They hold grudges and can be angry and vindictive. These problems are often confined to the home, where they usually result in tension and disharmony, but may also be observed in the school setting.

A certain degree of oppositional behaviour is normal at different stages of development (e.g. toddlers test the rules by engaging in non-compliant behaviour, adolescents exert their independence by resisting or opposing the will of others'). Oppositional behaviour observed in this disorder differs from age-appropriate oppositional behaviour in that it is *intense, pervasive, and interferes with the child's functioning.*

Diagnosis

It is necessary to establish whether oppositionality is the primary problem or secondary to another condition, as this will guide treatment. For example, depressed young people may appear angry and oppositional, and anxious children may become oppositional when forced to confront feared situations. A diagnosis of conduct disorder should be made if the child also exhibits antisocial or severely aggressive behaviour. Hyperkinetic children often display oppositional behaviours. In these cases, both diagnoses should be made.

Course and prognosis

- Oppositionality may be a response to a problematic family environment (e.g. chaotic, inconsistent, or over-controlling parenting, or inadequate discipline).
- Some children appear to be born with an oppositional temperament. In these cases, oppositional behaviour tends to start early in life and persists over time, and can be exacerbated by environmental factors such as a problematic family environment. In a minority of cases oppositional behaviour can evolve into a full-blown conduct disorder during adolescence and an antisocial personality in adulthood.

- The conduct of oppositional children is often normal in many situations (e.g. at school, in social settings). This is because oppositionality is, by definition, interactional. For example, not all situations are experienced as equally frustrating by the child.
- Oppositional children seldom carry out serious antisocial or delinquent acts (e.g. stealing, truancy).
- Young people with oppositional traits are often difficult to engage and uncooperative. This can make treatment of other mental or physical disorders very difficult.

Management

- The basic intervention required in oppositional disorder is family counselling. Parenting skills training in the family context has been shown to be effective. This involves educating the parents in techniques for handling oppositional and defiant behaviour, and strategies for encouraging desired behaviour. Improvement in this condition is unlikely unless the parents are actively involved in treatment.
- Individual counselling is seldom useful as these youngsters do not believe there is anything wrong with them, and are likely to discontinue treatment. They are generally reluctant to attend individual counselling and resent being taken to counselling. Forcing them to attend can create new problems.
- Medication is not indicated in the treatment of oppositional disorder unless another condition is also present (e.g. ADD) or if the oppositional behaviour is secondary to another condition (e.g. depression, anxiety).

Consider the following when dealing with oppositional children:

- Parents will need to learn to *give children choices about how to behave*, rather than just telling them to do something. *Specify to the child the consequences of their behaviour.* The idea is that parents remain in charge of the choices and consequences, and that the child learns to make choices and deal with the consequences of his or her behaviour. In this way the child feels that he or she has some control over what they do. For example, the parent may say to the child "Please tidy your room. If you tidy your room then your friend may come over to play tomorrow. If you do not tidy your room then your friend can not come over tomorrow".
- Some children become oppositional if they feel that parents are too intrusive or unnecessarily controlling. *Giving children personal space and encouraging them to make their own decisions may avoid some of these problems, even if from the parents' point of view the child is making a poor decision.* Adolescents in particular need privacy and emotional 'elbow room'.
- It is quite healthy for teenagers to test the limits of what they are allowed to do. It is better if parents see this as a process that will prepare their teenager for the adult world rather than ungratefulness or obstinance on the part of the teenager.
- *Teach parents to target only that behaviour which is worth bothering about.* Because these problems have often been present for many years, parents can become unable to distinguish issues in relation to which they need to take a firm stand from matters that are trivial and not worth the fuss. In this situation, parents become afraid that if they give in or ignore something, their child will get out of control and walk all over them. As a result parents end up nagging, saying 'no' all the time, or trying to set ever more limits and controls. Oppositional children react by becoming even more determined to defy and resist. Therapists can help parents to identify what is important from what is not.

- Alternatively, some parents eventually just give in to their child after facing many years of oppositional behaviour. These parents think their child is too strong-willed for them and lose confidence in themselves as parents, and the child takes increasingly more control. This can happen more easily in single-parent families or families in which the parents provide little support to each other in the upbringing of the children. Once this pattern is well established, change is difficult and requires time. Therapists can help by *teaching parents ways of gradually setting boundaries between them and the children and taking charge of the situation.*

- It is useful for parents to understand that adolescence is a preparation for adulthood and that *teenagers need to be given an increasing level of freedom and responsibility if they are to be expected to make responsible decisions later on.* Discussions about good versus bad behaviour are not useful and lead nowhere. *Discussion about limits or rules in terms of safety and danger is more likely to be accepted* (e.g. "I am happy for you to go to the movies with your friends but I need to be sure that you are safe. It is too dangerous for you to travel home on your own at night. I can come and pick you up or you can come home earlier").

- A negative, angry pattern of relating often develops over the years between parents and their child, involving arguments, screaming, and prohibitions. Parents and child bring out the worst in each other. Alternative, more satisfying interactions are excluded by this pattern. *Parents need advice on how to break that cycle by identifying areas of common interest between them and their child* (e.g. a father may invite his son to go fishing with him and discover that his son enjoys it). This can provide positive, warm, and enjoyable experiences shared by both on which change may be built.

CONDUCT DISORDER

Description
Young people with conduct disorder display a pattern of behaviour characterised by breaking rules, deceit, and a lack of respect for the rights of others'. These adolescents are constantly in conflict with parents, teachers, peers, and society as a whole.

Symptoms of conduct disorder

- Bullying, victimisation and intimidation of others
- Cruelty to other people or to animals
- Starting physical fights
- Using weapons in fights (e.g. knife, bat)
- Stealing, shop-lifting or breaking and entering
- Setting fires to cause damage
- Vandalism or destroying the property of others
- Lying or cheating (to con others)
- Running away from home overnight
- Staying out at night without parents' permission
- Repeated truancy
- Forcing others to perform sexual acts against their will

Diagnosis

Any of the previously mentioned symptoms, if severe enough and present for at least six months, justifies a diagnosis of conduct disorder according to ICD-10.

- Take the child's age into account. For example, it is not within the capacity of most 6-year-olds to violate other people's rights for example by violent crime.
- Although a high proportion of juvenile delinquents have conduct disorder, isolated antisocial acts do not warrant this diagnosis.
- A diagnosis should not be made when behaviours can be accounted for by schizophrenia, bipolar disorder, or pervasive developmental disorder.
- Depression, drug and alcohol abuse, and learning problems often co-occur. Separate diagnoses should be made.
- A diagnosis of 'hyperkinetic conduct disorder' is warranted when the child meets criteria for both hyperkinetic and conduct disorders.

Epidemiology

- Around 6% of adolescent boys and 2% of adolescent girls may have this disorder.
- Conduct disorder is one of the conditions often seen in adolescent mental health clinics.
- There is a strong association with social disadvantage, such that frequency varies substantially from suburb to suburb and town to town.
- Conduct disorder is less common in the country than in large cities.
- This problem seems to have increased in recent years, particularly among females.

Course and prognosis

- It is widely accepted that conduct disorder occurs in a poor family environment. Parental neglect, inconsistency, physical or sexual abuse, harsh discipline, poor supervision and the like are all associated with this condition. Genetic factors (e.g. parents with antisocial personality), low intelligence, a difficult temperament in the child, and the presence of hyperkinetic disorder also increase the risk of conduct disorder.
- Some symptoms typically begin during childhood, for example as oppositional behaviour. Many of the children who will develop conduct disorder can already be identified in kindergarten by their aggressive and disruptive behaviour. The disorder usually becomes fully established after puberty. During adolescence, conduct disorder is often associated with school violence, academic failure and drop out, delinquency, drug and alcohol abuse, damage to property, and physical injury to others.
- It is unusual for conduct disorder to begin during adolescence. Onset during adolescence is often associated with affiliation to a group of peers with conduct or delinquent problems.
- About *one-third* of the adolescents with conduct disorder will grow up to have antisocial personality disorder. These are some of the predictors of a better outcome in adulthood:
  - Onset of symptoms during adolescence. Onset prior to age 10 poses a significant risk.
  - Engaging in fewer and less of a variety of antisocial behaviours.
  - Above average intelligence.
  - Absence of learning problems.
  - Having a caring, affectionate relationship with at least one adult.
  - Having friends who don't get into trouble.
  - Experience of achievement in some activity (e.g. sport).
  - Absence of other mental disorders (e.g. ADD, depression).
  - Has remained at school until the age compulsory schooling ends or longer.

Management

- Many treatments produce short-term relief of symptoms, but improvements usually wear off quickly. *None of the available therapies are particularly effective in the longer-term.*

- *Individual counselling is difficult and ineffective in most cases* because these young people lack remorse and typically believe they have done nothing wrong. Once established, the behaviours are very resistant to change. Young people with this condition are often not used to receiving sympathy from adults and often react by refusing it or with anger towards the counsellor. Some may attend therapy to avoid a more unpleasant consequence such as detention.

- The more promising treatments are *problem-solving skills training, parenting skills training, functional family therapy, and multisystemic therapy.*

- A *close and ongoing working relationship between the family and therapist* offers the best chances of success. Unfortunately for many of these children, if they have a family at all, it is often disorganised, neglectful, or abusive.

- Placement in a *residential setting* may be required. Highly structured programmes specifically tailored for young people with conduct disorder are required: treatment should *not* be attempted in units that treat adolescents with emotional problems. Facilities with *a small number of residents at any one time* and which offer *treatment for a substantial period of time* (e.g. more than one year) are likely to produce the best results.

- *Medication is not generally indicated* in the treatment of conduct disorder, other than to treat conditions which often co-occur.

- It is clear that *prevention* is the best way of dealing with conduct disorder. Parents and teachers should be assisted to identify the *early signs* of such behaviour during early childhood and the first years of school, and to *seek and persist with treatment* to address such behaviour. The most useful intervention at that stage is to help parents to improve their parenting.

8.1.10 DEVELOPMENTAL DISORDERS

Developmental disorders are characterised by the following features, according to ICD-10: (1) a steady course that does not involve remissions and relapses; (2) onset during infancy or childhood; (3) impairment or delay in the development of functions associated with the normal maturation of the central nervous system.

- These disorders are more frequent in boys than in girls.
- There is wide variation in impairment, according to the diagnosis. Impairment can be particularly marked in autism.
- Genetic factors may play a causative role in many cases, but not all.
- Treatment is primarily educational. Many of these conditions are difficult to treat and require ongoing intensive work to achieve even small gains. This is particularly the case with the pervasive developmental disorders.
- Overall, the higher the intelligence of the child the better the prognosis.

Developmental disorders

Pervasive developmental disorders Severe and pervasive impairment of several areas of development, particularly social interaction, evident in the first years of life.	**Childhood autism:** Gross impairment in reciprocal social interaction (e.g. lack of response to other people's emotions); qualitative impairments in communication (e.g. lack of, or poorly developed language, stereotyped or idiosyncratic language); restricted, repetitive and stereotyped interests and activities (e.g. obsessive preoccupation with routine, timetables, objects; stereotyped body movements; fascination with spinning or moving objects). Onset is prior to the age of three years and mental retardation is very frequent. **Asperger's syndrome:** Is similar to autism in many features but differs from it in that there is no language delay or mental retardation.
Specific developmental disorders A particular area of functioning is impaired compared with overall intelligence.	**Of speech and language:** Articulation, expressive or receptive language are significantly affected. **Of scholastic skills:** Performance in reading, spelling or arithmetic is substantially lower than expected for IQ. **Of motor function:** Clumsiness.

8.1.11 OTHER DISORDERS OF CHILDREN AND ADOLESCENTS

There are a range of other psychiatric disorders observed in children and adolescents. Some of the more important of these are briefly described in the table on the following page.

EARLY ONSET PSYCHOTIC DISORDERS

Schizophrenia is very rare during childhood (very early onset psychosis) but becomes increasingly frequent during adolescence. There is growing interest in early onset psychosis because of the view that early diagnosis and treatment may result in a better course and outcome. Specific knowledge remains limited. (See also 'first-episode psychosis' in the chapter on schizophrenia.)

Mania can occasionally be observed in pre-pubertal children. In milder cases diagnosis can be difficult as the clinical picture may be similar to that of hyperkinetic disorder (i.e. overactivity, boisterousness, poor concentration) or conduct disorder.

The symptoms and management of mania, psychotic depression, and schizophrenia are similar in young people and adults. A number of specific issues need to be considered in young people:

- The clinical presentation of mood and schizophrenic disorders is often very similar in young people. Diagnosis can be complicated by comorbid conduct problems, drug abuse, or developmental issues related to adolescence. It is important to avoid making a definite diagnosis prematurely. The course of the illness will ultimately distinguish between schizophrenic and mood disorders.

- Abnormal behaviour in young people, particularly adolescents, is more likely to be interpreted or dismissed as a 'normal' response to life events by mental health professionals, parents, teachers, and patients themselves. Adequate consideration is sometimes not given to the symptoms themselves, and this can result in delays in diagnosis and treatment.
- Children and adolescents are more sensitive to or concerned about some of the side effects of antipsychotic medications, such as dystonic reactions, erectile problems, and weight gain. It is important to inform the young person of these side effects and build up very gradually to the appropriate dosage.
- There are fewer facilities for the acute treatment and rehabilitation that meet the specific needs of young people with these conditions. This is because these conditions are uncommon in this age group. After acute treatment, some young people can fail to resume school attendance and become institutionalised at home. Assertive rehabilitation and follow-up is needed.

Other disorders often found in children and adolescents

Elimination disorders	**Nonorganic enuresis**
	When children wet themselves during the day or night in the absence of physical abnormalities. This is not considered a problem requiring treatment until after the age of five years. In primary enuresis, urinary continence is never achieved. When the child was continent for a period of time and starts wetting again it is called secondary enuresis. The most effective treatment is behavioural (bell and pad alarm). Imipramine and desmopressin often produce symptomatic relief.
	Nonorganic encopresis
	Passage of faeces in places not appropriate for that purpose (e.g. soiling of pants). Organic problems ought to be excluded. As with enuresis, it can be primary or secondary. Treatment is usually behavioural.
Eating disorders	**Anorexia nervosa and bulimia** (see chapter 6)
Tourette's disorder	Characterised by multiple motor tics and one or more vocal tics (e.g. grunts, swear words, throat clearing). Location, number, frequency and severity of tics change over time. The onset is often during childhood. Typically, symptoms wax and wane, frequently becoming less prominent after adolescence. Comorbidity, particularly with hyperkinetic syndrome, is common. Mild forms do not require treatment. When impairment is significant, the treatment of choice is medication: haloperidol, pimozide or clonidine.
Early onset psychotic disorders	**Bipolar disorder** (psychotic depression; manic episode) **Schizophrenia spectrum disorders**

8.2 BIBLIOGRAPHY

Achenbach, T.M. (1991). *Manual for the Child Behaviour Checklist/4-18 and 1991 Profile.* Burlington: University of Vermont Department of Psychiatry.

Cantwell, D.P. (1996). Attention deficit disorder: A review of the past 10 years. *Journal of the American Academy of Child and Adolescent Psychiatry, 35,* 978-987.

Conners, C.K. (1969). A teacher rating scale for use in drug studies with children. *American Journal of Psychiatry, 126,* 152-156.

Faulstich, M.E., Carey, M.P., Ruggiero, L., Enyart, P. & Gresham, F. (1986). Assessment of depression in childhood and adolescence: An evaluation of the Center for Epidemiological Studies Depression Scale for Children (CES-DC). *American Journal of Psychiatry, 143,* 1024-1027.

Fergusson, D.M. & Lynskey, M.T. (1996). Adolescent resilience to family adversity. *Journal of Child Psychology and Psychiatry, 37,* 281-292.

Garralda, M.E. (1996). Somatisation in children. *Journal of Child Psychology and Psychiatry, 37,* 13-33.

Goodman, W.K., Price, L.H., Rasmussen, S.A., Mazure, C., Fleischman, R.L., Hill, C.L., Heninger, G.R. & Charney, D.S. (1989). The Yale-Brown Obsessive Compulsive Scale I. Development, use and reliability. *Archives of General Psychiatry, 46,* 1006-1011.

Hazell, P., O'Connell, D., Heathcote, D., Robertson, J. & Henry, D. (1995). Efficacy of tricyclic drugs in treating child and adolescent depression: a meta-analysis. *British Medical Journal, 310,* 897-890.

Kazdin, A.E. (1997). Practitioner review: Psychosocial treatment for conduct disorder children. *Journal of Child Psychology and Psychiatry, 38,* 161-178.

Kovacs, M. (1996). Presentation and course of major depressive disorder during childhood and later years of the life span. *Journal of the American Academy of Child and Adolescent Psychiatry, 35,* 705-715.

National Health and Medical Research Council (1997). *Clinical Practice Guidelines: Depression in Young People.* Canberra: Australian Government Publishing Service.

Rapoport, J.L. & Ismond, I.R. (1996). *DSM-IV Training Guide for Diagnosis of Childhood Disorders.* New York: Brunner Mazel.

Rey, J.M. & Bird, K.D. (1991). Sex differences in suicidal behaviour in referred adolescents. *British Journal of Psychiatry, 158,* 776-781.

Rey, J.M. & Hutchins, P. (1993). Childhood hyperactivity. *Medical Journal of Australia, 159,* 289-291.

Rey, J.M. & Walter, G. (in press). Oppositional defiant disorder. In J.M. Oldman & M.B. Riba (Eds.), *Review of Psychiatry 1999.* Washington: American Psychiatric Press.

Rey, J.M., Singh, M., Hung, S.F., Dossetor, D.R., Newman, L., Plapp, J.M. & Bird, K.D. (1997). A global scale to measure the quality of the family environment. *Archives of General Psychiatry, 54,* 817-822.

Rutter, M. & Guiller, H. (1983). *Juvenile Delinquency.* Harmondsworth, Middlesex: Penguin Books.

Rutter M. & Rutter M. (1992). *Developing Minds.* Harmondsworth, Middlesex: Penguin Books.

Rutter, M. & Smith, D.J. (1995). *Psychosocial Disorders in Young People. Time Trends and Their Causes.* Chichester: John Wiley.

Shaffer, D., Schwab-Stone, M., Fisher, P. et al. (1993). The diagnostic Interview Schedule for Children -Revised Version (DISC-R): I Preparation, field testing, inter-rater reliability, and acceptability. *Journal of the American Academy of Child and Adolescent Psychiatry, 32,* 643-650.

Silburn, S.R., Zubrick, S.R., Garton, A., Gurrin, L., Burton, P., Dalby, R., Carlton, J., Shepherd, C. & Lawrence, D. (1996). *Western Australia Child Health Survey: Family & Community Health.* Perth, WA: Australian Bureau of Statistics and the Institute of Child Health Research

Volkmar, F.R. (1996). Childhood and adolescent psychosis: a review of the past 10 years. *Journal of the American Academy of Child and Adolescent Psychiatry, 35,* 843-851.

Walter, G., Rey, J.M. & Mitchell, P. (in press). Practitioner review: ECT use in adolescents. *Journal of Child Psychology and Psychiatry.*

Werry, J.S. & Aman, M.G. (1993). *Practitioner's Guide to Psychoactive Drugs for Children and Adolescents.* New York: Plenum.

Wever, C. & Rey, J.M. (1997). Juvenile obsessive-compulsive disorder. *Australian and New Zealand Journal of Psychiatry, 31,* 105-113.

Wood, A., Harrington, R. & Moore, A. (1996). Controlled trial of a brief cognitive-behavioural intervention in adolescent patients with depressive disorders. *Journal of Child Psychology and Psychiatry, 37,* 737-746.

Zametkin, A.J., Ernst, M. & Silver, R. (1998). Laboratory and diagnostic testing in child and adolescent psychiatry: a review of the past 10 years. *Journal of the American Academy of Child and Adolescent Psychiatry, 37,* 464-472.

Zubrick, S.R., Silburn, S.R., Garton, A., Burton, P., Dalby, R., Carlton, J., Shepherd, C. & Lawrence, D. (1995). *Western Australia Child Health Survey: Developing Health and Well-being in the Nineties.* Perth, WA: Australian Bureau of Statistics and the Institute of Child Health Research.

9

SLEEP DISORDERS

9.1 SLEEP DISORDERS

9.1.1 ABOUT SLEEP DISORDERS

Sleep problems are one of the most common complaints in both the general health and mental health settings. For example, it has been estimated that over 20% of the adult population suffers from some form of lasting insomnia at some time in their lives.

The descriptions and guidelines for the sleep disorders contained within this textbook include only those disorders for which psychological, environmental, or emotional causes are considered to be primary. Treatment guidelines for sleep disorders with an organic basis are not included here. However, a number of these disorders are mentioned for the purpose of differential diagnosis. If the sleep disorder is found to have an organic basis, referral to a specialist sleep clinic will be required.

Sleep disturbances may occur as a result of other co-existing physical or mental disorders or may occur independently of other disorders. However, if a sleep disturbance is one of the individual's predominant complaints then a sleep disorder should be diagnosed (providing criteria are satisfied) regardless of whether the disturbance is *caused* by a co-existing disorder or is *independent* of other disorders.

All diagnostic guidelines in this text are taken from the World Health Organization's International Classification of Diseases (ICD-10; 1992).

9.1.2 ASSESSMENT

As always, assessment would commence with a psychiatric history and mental state examination (see Chapter 1: Core Management Skills). It is vital that the individual's problem is examined in context, and that other psychological, social, or medical factors are considered for their role in the onset or maintenance of the sleep disorder. In addition, the following assessment strategies will be helpful.

SLEEP HISTORY

Good clinical management is based on an accurate and detailed sleep history. The following questions can be used to obtain important information about the individual's sleeping difficulties. Questions are ideally directed to both the individual and his or her bed partner, since the bed partner can sometimes supply unique and helpful information about the individual's behaviour while asleep.

- What are the main sleep-related complaints?
- When did these symptoms first occur?
- How severe or troublesome are these symptoms? How much do the symptoms affect the individual's life?
- Do the symptoms fluctuate in severity? When are the symptoms most troublesome? (e.g., Which days of the week? What time of the day?). When are the symptoms least troublesome? How do the symptoms compare if sleeping away from home?
- Were there any identifiable stressors present at the time of onset? (e.g., childbirth, moving house, relationship break-up, illness, or pressure at work/home). Are these stressors still present?

- What is the individual's usual daily routine?
  - Waking time
  - Method of waking (e.g., alarm, natural, partner)
  - Usual routine followed after waking (e.g., shower, breakfast, newspaper)
  - Usual daily activities (e.g., description of occupation, usual start and finish times, after work activities)
  - Daily naps (when, where, why, how long, effect on alertness)
  - Usual routine followed when getting ready for bed (e.g., shower, clean teeth)
  - Usual time at which the individual gets into bed
  - Approximate time at which the individual falls asleep
  - Activities performed in bed before sleep (e.g., reading, sex, television).
  - Description of sleep (e.g., restless, nightmares, lengthy periods of wakefulness).
- If individuals complain about feeling tired or sleepy during the day, they should be questioned about their levels of alertness throughout the day, particularly at times when sleep may be more likely, such as during boring or sedentary activities. Individuals should also be asked about sleepiness during activities such as eating, walking, and driving or operating machinery. Finally, ask about any decreases in performance at work, problems with memory, or episodes of confusion.
- Family history of sleep complaints (describe).
- Type and quantity of drugs or alcohol consumed during the day (e.g., caffeine, nicotine, alcohol, marijuana, sedatives, other legal and illegal psychotropic drugs, other medications). Note the and time of day at which these drugs are taken. Review all medications with regard to their possible alerting or sedating effects.
- What treatment has previously been provided for this problem? (description, usefulness, problems or side effects).
- Questions for the bed partner can include:
  - Does your partner stop breathing at any time during the night? Does this happen every night? How often during the night?
  - Does your partner snore, gasp or make choking sounds during the night? Does this happen every night? How often during the night?
  - Do your partner's legs twitch, jerk or kick during the night? Does this happen every night? How often during the night?
  - Have you noticed any recent changes in your partner's mood?
  - Has your partner's consumption of alcohol, caffeine, or other drugs or medication changed recently?
  - What do you think might be causing your partner's sleeping problem?

SLEEP DIARY

A sleep diary, kept over a two week period, can add a lot of useful information to the sleep history and may identify factors or patterns in an individual's sleep of which they are unaware. A typical sleep diary usually covers the following information:

- Time of getting into bed at night
- Time in bed *not* trying to sleep (e.g., reading)
- Estimated time of sleep onset
- Estimated number and duration of awakenings during the night
- Time of final waking in the morning
- Time of getting out of bed in the morning
- Meals

- Activity patterns
- Drug, alcohol, nicotine, and caffeine consumption
- Job-related and social events
- Timing and duration of exercise
- Timing and duration of daytime naps (add to total daily sleep time)

Estimates of the time spent awake during the night and the number of awakenings can provide a good baseline assessment against which improvement can be evaluated during and following intervention. The diary can also help to identify bad sleeping habits (e.g., sleeping in on weekends to make up for lost sleep, lying awake in bed for hours on end tossing and turning) or relationships between certain factors and a bad nights sleep (e.g., caffeine consumption after 5 p.m., a stressful day at work). A blank sleep diary form is provided in Section 9.3.1.

LABORATORY ASSESSMENT

Laboratory assessment usually requires individuals to sleep for one or more nights in a laboratory during which time a number of physiological variables are measured. These measurements can include EEG and EMG (to assess the stages of sleep), ECG (for cardiac rate and rhythm), diaphragm EMG or other measures of respiratory effort, tibia EMG to measure leg movements, nasal and oral airflow, and oxygen saturation.

Laboratory sleep testing is recommended for:
- Complaints of excessive daytime sleepiness, unless a simple and clear-cut cause is apparent e.g., sedative use *and* the sleepiness ceases when the underlying cause is resolved. Possible diagnoses could include narcolepsy or sleep apnoea.
- Insomnia in cases where periodic limb movements in sleep or sleep apnoea are suspected.

Laboratory assessment of sleep disorders can be conducted through many major teaching hospitals and other private centres.

9.1.3 INSOMNIA

DESCRIPTION

Insomnia is characterised by both lack of sleep and excessive worry about sleep disturbance. Insomnia is not defined by the amount of sleep per se.

Common complaints given by individuals with insomnia are:
- Difficulty falling asleep
- Difficulty staying asleep
- Early wakening at the end of the sleep period
- Feeling anxious, worried, depressed, or irritable, especially at bedtime
- Racing thoughts at sleep onset or during night-time wakenings
- Feeling physically or mentally tired during the day

Insomnia commonly begins during periods of increased life stress. The individual may be lying awake at night thinking about personal problems, work, or the death of a loved one. By the time the stress has gone, the individual may be preoccupied with his or her inability to get to sleep. Thus, a vicious cycle may be set up because worrying about not sleeping keeps the individual awake.

DIAGNOSIS

According to ICD-10, the following criteria must be satisfied for a diagnosis of insomnia:

- The individual complains of difficulty falling asleep, difficulty maintaining sleep, or poor quality of sleep.
- The individual's sleep has been disturbed at least 3 days per week for at least a month.
- The individual is preoccupied with his or her lack of sleep and shows excessive concern, day and night, over the consequences of this lack of sleep.
- The sleep disturbance causes marked personal distress or interferes with social and occupational functioning.
- There is no evidence that the disturbance is caused by an organic factor (e.g., a neurological or other medical condition), a psychoactive substance use disorder, or a medication.

DIFFERENTIAL DIAGNOSIS

When considering a diagnosis of insomnia it is important to remember that there is a large degree of individual variation in sleeping patterns. For example, some individuals may sleep for long periods of time without feeling refreshed upon waking while others may sleep for only short periods of time but feel alert upon awakening and suffer no daytime drowsiness. These short-sleepers can function well on four to six hours per night and may simply need reassurance that they do not have a sleep disorder.

Medical disorders associated with insomnia

Symptoms associated with a wide range of medical disorders can disrupt sleep and contribute to the experience of insomnia. These symptoms include pain (from any cause), night sweats, excessive urination at night (nocturia), and nocturnal confusion.

Examples of medical disorders associated with insomnia are:

- Arthritis, peptic ulcers and chronic headaches, where pain may cause frequent arousal from sleep.
- Respiratory disorders such as chronic obstructive airways disease, cystic fibrosis, or asthma.
- Diabetes. Disturbed sleep is often secondary to nocturnal hypoglycaemia, nocturnal diarrhoea, or pain from peripheral neuropathies.
- Parkinson's disease. Sufferers frequently complain of difficulty getting to sleep and increased time awake during the night.
- Endocrine disturbances, such as Addison's disease and Cushing's syndrome.

The number of medical problems accounting for sleep complaints increases with age.

Mental disorders associated with insomnia

The presence of significant anxiety or depression should alert the clinician to the possibility that the insomnia could be related to a mental disorder.

- The great majority of individuals who experience **major depression** will suffer significant sleep problems during a depressive episode. Insomnia is the most frequent complaint and is often associated with early morning wakening (usually around 3 a.m.) with difficulty returning to sleep.
- Manic phases of bipolar disorder are associated with difficulty sleeping and a decreased need for sleep.
- Nocturnal **panic attacks** will frequently cause chronic insomnia and can occur in individuals who do not experience panic attacks during the day. These individuals will awaken at night with autonomic arousal symptoms such as palpitations, rapid breathing and a feeling of fearfulness and anxiety, and will then find it difficult to return to sleep. These attacks are associated with sleep apnoea in some individuals.

- Difficulty with getting to sleep (both at the beginning of the night and following night time awakenings) is a common feature of **generalised anxiety disorder**, due to increased autonomic arousal and worry.

- Insomnia secondary to the hyperarousal experienced with **post traumatic stress disorder** is common. Sleep can also be disrupted by the re-experiencing of the traumatic event in the form of nightmares.

- Individuals with **anorexia nervosa** are often troubled by difficulty getting to sleep, staying asleep, and may also experience early morning wakening. These symptoms may be related to depression which is a common symptom of starvation.

- Disrupted sleep, including an increase in the frequency of nightmares, can occur in individuals with **schizophrenia** prior to a psychotic episode. If sleep problems develop later in the lives of individuals with schizophrenia, it will be worth considering whether the deterioration in sleep is due to the emergence of a depressive episode, or might be due to a sleep-related disorder such as sleep apnoea.

Prescription medications

A number of prescription medications will also cause insomnia.

- The regular use of *sedatives* or *hypnotics* to get to sleep will interfere with sleep patterns and lead to chronic insomnia. Often the dose of these medications will have been increased in the past so as to maintain hypnotic effectiveness after tolerance begins to develop. Individuals who regularly use sedatives often present with sleep problems when they attempt to stop their medications; insomnia is often associated with sudden withdrawal of a benzodiazepine or other sedative-hypnotic medication. In cases of withdrawal, individuals may sleep only 1-4 hours each night ('rebound insomnia') for several weeks and will also experience an increase in REM (rapid eye movement) sleep ('REM rebound'). This REM sleep may be associated with anxious dreams and nightmares, and awakenings during the night.

  Withdrawal of such substances should be undertaken with close medical supervision, should be slow, and individuals should be educated about the rebound insomnia they are likely to experience. Common problems associated with withdrawal during the day include somatic anxiety symptoms (e.g., tremor, palpitations, dizziness) and perceptual distortions of noise and touch (e.g., tinnitus, increased sensitivity to noise, itching or tingling sensations). Management should include education about good sleep habits and use of the strategies outlined for the management of insomnia.

- Stimulating *antidepressants* (e.g., SSRIs such as fluoxetine or sertraline) and monoamine oxidase inhibiting (MAOI) antidepressants may have insomnia as a side effect. In these cases the sleep complaint will usually begin shortly after the onset of medication use or following a dose increase. With increased use of the newer SSRI antidepressants, complaints of insomnia may become more frequent and there is a danger that these complaints may lead to an increased use of benzodiazepine medication. If insomnia is a problem, the following strategies may be useful alternatives to benzodiazepine use:
  1. Taking SSRI antidepressant medication once daily in the morning, or taking MAOI antidepressants in divided doses (in the morning, and in the afternoon before 3 p.m.).
  2. Changing to a different (more sedating) antidepressant.
  3. Maximising good sleep habits.
  4. Using a non-benzodiazepine hypnotic for a short period of time.

Substance abuse

- Regular *alcohol* use can cause many awakenings during the night, which may even be 'treated' by the sufferer with further alcohol use. While the alcohol will have an initial sedating effect it will cause fragmented sleep and awakenings several hours into sleep.
- Chronic *amphetamine* or *cocaine* users will frequently report that they do not sleep much at all for several days, and then 'crash' to get a few hours of sleep (usually over the weekend).
- Most *heavy or chronic users of drugs or alcohol* will complain of severe insomnia for many weeks after they have stopped using the drugs or alcohol.
- *Caffeine* and *nicotine* may also disrupt sleep, and the use of nicotine skin patches for smoking cessation may cause vivid dreams and disturbed sleep in some people.

Insomnia related to substance abuse will require referral to specialist drug and alcohol services who will have the expertise to manage detoxification, withdrawal symptoms and other interventions where necessary.

Sleep disorders of organic origin

- Individuals with **'restless legs'** will complain of uncomfortable ('crawling' or 'prickly') sensations in their legs at sleep onset which significantly interfere with the ability to get to sleep. This problem is usually resolved with movement such as walking. 'Restless legs' often occurs together with periodic limb movements in sleep (PLMS).
- **PLMS** is not usually perceived by the sufferer during the night but can be perceived by the bed partner as kicking movements. PLMS may also occur in the arms, but is much rarer in upper limbs. Tricyclic antidepressants and lithium have been reported to significantly aggravate PLMS. (N.B., PLMS should be differentiated from sudden body jerks occurring at sleep onset which are frequently accompanied by the sensation of 'missing a step'. These are a normal phenomena).
- In suspected cases of **sleep apnoea** (temporary cessation of respiration during sleep), the bed partner can be asked whether the individual has irregular breathing, pauses in his or her breathing, or snores excessively and disruptively when asleep. The apnoea is usually terminated by brief awakenings, thus producing the subjective sensation of not sleeping and the complaint of excessive daytime sleepiness. Some individuals may complain of insomnia. Being overweight and the use of sedative hypnotics and alcohol will aggravate sleep apnoea.

If any of these organic sleep disorders are suspected, individuals should be referred to a sleep laboratory for specialised assessment.

MANAGEMENT GUIDELINES FOR INSOMNIA

Establish management priorities

If there is evidence that a physical or mental disorder, or a drug or alcohol problem, are contributing to insomnia then these conditions should be treated as a priority. If medication appears to be contributing to the insomnia, it would be worth considering whether the type of medication or the dosing schedule could be altered. If the insomnia continues to persist despite these measures, the following guidelines will be useful.

Education about good sleep habits

Good sleep habits are covered in detail in the handout in Section 9.3.2. In summary, it is helpful to:
- Establish a proper sleep environment
- Allow a wind-down time prior to sleep
- Remove from the bedroom all stimuli that are not associated with sleep

- Avoid spending time in bed worrying
- Avoid alcohol, caffeine, and nicotine
- Take a late tryptophan snack (e.g., warm milk, cornflakes with milk, Horlicks, Ovaltine).
- Take regular exercise in the late afternoon or early evening.

Stimulus control

Individuals with insomnia often engage in behaviours in bed that are incompatible with sleep (e.g., eating, studying, watching television, trying to solve problems, tossing and turning when trying to fall asleep). These behaviours will cause individuals to associate being in bed with sleeplessness, worry and arousal rather than drowsiness and sleep. Stimulus control strategies are designed to change these behaviours so that bed is associated only with sleep. The following guidelines may be given to individuals.

Stimulus control instructions

1. Go to bed *only* when you are sleepy.
2. Do not use your bed for anything except sleeping (sexual activity is the only exception to this rule).
3. If you do not fall asleep in about 10 minutes, get up and go to another room. Stay up until you begin to feel sleepy and only then return to your bed to sleep.
4. If you return to bed and still cannot sleep, repeat the preceding instruction. Repeat as often as necessary until you fall asleep.
5. Get up the same time each morning, no matter how long you slept.

Relaxation training

Regular use of relaxation methods (such as progressive muscle relaxation or meditation) will not only help people become less aroused prior to sleep and thus more likely to fall asleep, but will also foster an increased sense of self-control. The tapes are best used during the day to practise the progressive muscle relaxation technique, which is then implemented (without the tape) at bedtime. Information about relaxation training can be found in Anxiety Disorders in Chapter 4.

Sleep restriction

Individuals with chronic insomnia can end up spending more and more time in bed, but less and less of that time actually asleep. Some people may spend 10 hours in bed, but only 6 hours asleep. The sleep tends to become spread across the time in bed and is therefore fragmented. The principle of the sleep restriction strategy is to significantly decrease the amount of time spent in bed and to consolidate sleep into that time. This sleep consolidation helps to improve subjective sleep quality and to increase the sense of control over sleep. The steps of sleep restriction are as follows:

- Ask the individual to keep a sleep diary for *at least* 5 days, although 1-2 weeks is preferable. (A blank sleep diary form is provided in Section 9.3.1). Using the sleep diary, it will be possible to calculate the total sleep time (TST) for each night, and the percentage sleep efficiency across the recording period as follows:

Total sleep time

Count the number of hours from getting into bed until getting out of bed. Subtract the number of hours spent awake during the night. This figure is the TST for one night. To get the *average* TST over a number of nights, add all the TSTs for each night then divide by the number of nights.

$$\text{Average TST} = \frac{\text{Sum of TST scores for each night}}{\text{Number of nights}}$$

Sleep efficiency

This figure is calculated for each night according to the equation below. That is, for each night, calculate the TST, divide by the total time spent in bed, then multiply by 100 to get a percentage figure. To calculate the *average* sleep efficiency across a number of nights, add the sleep efficiency percentage score for each night then divide by the number of nights.

$$\text{Sleep efficiency} = \left\{ \frac{\text{TST}}{\text{Total time in bed}} \right\} \times 100$$

- For the first few nights of the sleep restriction programme, the number of hours to be spent in bed is equal to the average TST for the past week. For example, if the average TST for the past week has been calculated as 5.5 hours, the individual could go to bed at 12.30 a.m. and get up again at 6.00 a.m. The individual will experience some sleepiness across the first few days of a sleep restriction programme.
- Ask the individual to continue to record the sleep diary and, if possible, get the individual to phone each day with the results of the previous night.
- Calculate the TST and percent sleep efficiency for each night. When the mean sleep efficiency for five nights in a row reaches 85% or better, increase the allowed time in bed 15 minutes by allowing the individual to go to bed 15 minutes earlier. Naps outside the prescribed time in bed are not allowed. If the sleep efficiency starts to drop below 85% it may be necessary to decrease the time in bed by 15 minutes until sleep efficiency rises again.
- The procedure is continued until sleep efficiency is maintained at 85% or better and the individual reports that he or she is getting a satisfactory amount of night-time sleep.

As daytime sleepiness is experienced during a sleep restriction programme, the individual will need to be motivated to stick to the programme and may need some encouragement. However, those who can stick to the programme will have a substantial chance of improving their sleep. Normally, improvements begin to be seen at the end of the first week of the programme after there has been some chance of adjustment to the new sleep schedule.

Medication

Sedatives are not recommended for chronic insomnia as they can contribute to sleep problems if used regularly (see handout in Section 9.3.2 for details). Tricyclic antidepressants (especially the sedative tricyclics such as amitriptyline, doxepin, or imipramine) may be beneficial for problems with sleep awakenings or early morning wakening if major depression is also present.

TRANSIENT OR SHORT-TERM INSOMNIA

The majority of individuals will experience at some stage in their lives a period of transient or short-term insomnia (e.g., for three weeks or less) that will not meet diagnostic criteria. Most often, individuals will have difficulty in getting to sleep during a time of high stress, anticipation, or illness, although it is also useful to ask about changes in the use of medication, caffeine, alcohol, or drugs. While these transient problems will rarely come to the attention of a mental health clinician, the following guidelines may be helpful for those who complain of short-term insomnia.

1. Reassure the individual that most people have difficulty sleeping at some time in their lives and that for the majority, this sleep difficulty is only a temporary phenomenon related to important events that may be occurring in their lives.

2. Assist the individual to resolve (if possible) any specific problem or stressor that might be contributing to the insomnia. Structured problem solving may be helpful for the resolution of social stressors (see Chapter 1: Core Management Skills).
3. Provide education about the principles of good sleep habits.
4. Encourage the individual to avoid using sleeping tablets. If the individual insists that he or she needs sleeping tablets to sleep, these tablets should only be used over one or two nights, and only after the individual has tried for 30-60 minutes that night to get to sleep. Taking sleeping tablets for longer time periods can cause 'rebound insomnia' in which, after the tablets are stopped, the insomnia becomes worse than it was originally.

9.1.4 HYPERSOMNIA

DESCRIPTION

This disorder is characterised by excessive daytime sleepiness and sleep attacks (not resulting from an inadequate amount of sleep) or by sleep drunkenness upon awakening (i.e., prolonged transition to a fully aroused state). Presentations can range from complaints of mild sleepiness through to severe sleepiness and sleep attacks. Complaints of excessive sleepiness should be assessed quickly and comprehensively as they can potentially lead to dangerous consequences, such as motor vehicle or industrial accidents.

DIAGNOSIS

According to ICD-10, for a diagnosis of hypersomnia the following criteria must be satisfied:
- The individual complains of excessive daytime sleepiness and sleep attacks, or of sleep drunkenness, neither of which result from an inadequate amount of sleep.
- The sleep disturbance occurs nearly every day for one month or recurrently for shorter periods of time and causes marked personal distress or interferes with social or occupational functioning.
- There are no symptoms of narcolepsy (i.e., a disorder characterised by the recurrent uncontrollable desire for sleep), cataplexy (sudden and intermittent loss of muscle tone often elicited by emotion or surprise), sleep paralysis (a temporary inability to initiate motor movement preceding sleep or upon wakening), or hypnagogic hallucinations (visual images that occur just before drifting off to sleep). There is also no evidence of sleep apnoea (e.g., temporary cessation of breathing during sleep, or intermittent snorting sounds).
- The daytime sleepiness does not result from organic causes such as medication use, psychoactive substance use, or a neurological or other medical condition.

Excessive sleepiness is frequently a symptom of affective illness such as depression or bipolar disorder. In cases where sleepiness is simply one symptom of a pre-existing mental illness the present diagnosis should not be used. However, if hypersomnia is the individual's primary complaint, this disorder should be diagnosed regardless of the presence of other pre-existing mental illnesses.

DIFFERENTIAL DIAGNOSIS

Insufficient night-time sleep resulting either from insomnia or poor sleep habits should be considered first. Many individuals are unaware that they have been depriving themselves of sleep as a result of social, family, educational, or occupational demands. In these cases, management requires education about individual sleep needs and good sleep habits.

True hypersomnia should be differentiated from fatigue, tiredness, and lack of motivation that can be associated with a **depressive disorder** (particularly atypical depression). If the symptoms of daytime sleepiness do not resolve following treatment of the underlying mood disorder, a sleep laboratory assessment may be required.

Most individuals with **sleep apnoea** will complain of excessive daytime sleepiness because of the disruption to their night-time sleep caused by brief awakenings. In fact, sleep apnoea is the most common cause of daytime sleepiness. The bed partner can be asked whether the individual has irregular breathing, pauses in his or her breathing, or snores excessively and disruptively when asleep. Being overweight and the use of sedative hypnotics and alcohol will aggravate sleep apnoea. Referral to a sleep laboratory for assessment is recommended whenever sleep apnoea is suspected.

Narcolepsy is associated with symptoms such as cataplexy, sleep paralysis, and hypnagogic hallucinations that are not present in hypersomnia. Although it is difficult to differentiate the two in the absence of a sleep lab assessment, the following clinical features may be of help. In narcolepsy the sleep attacks are irresistible and refreshing while in hypersomnia the sleep attacks occur less frequently each day, are of longer duration, and are easier to resist. Individuals with narcolepsy will fall asleep in unusual circumstances, such as when standing, during physical activity, or during stimulating activities. Finally, in narcolepsy nocturnal sleep is disturbed and shortened in duration while in hypersomnia nocturnal sleep is prolonged and is associated with marked difficulty in waking the next day. Referral to a sleep laboratory for assessment is recommended whenever narcolepsy is suspected.

Organic causes of hypersomnia should be excluded. Possible causes may include: encephalitis; meningitis; concussion and other brain damage; brain tumours; cerebrovascular lesions; degenerative and other neurologic diseases; metabolic disorders; toxic conditions; endocrine abnormalities; and post-radiation syndrome. A full medical examination with laboratory tests will identify such disorders.

Hypersomnia may also be secondary to the use of *medication, drugs or alcohol*, including:
- Chronic stimulant use where increasing tolerance may lead to a chronic state of withdrawal (e.g., amphetamines, caffeine).
- Chronic use of central nervous system depressants (e.g., opiates, benzodiazepines, tricyclic antidepressants, narcoleptics, alcohol).

MANAGEMENT GUIDELINES FOR HYPERSOMNIA

There does not appear to be any effective treatment for true hypersomnia. Various medications (such as the serotonin agonist methysergide or stimulant medications) as well as scheduled naps, have been tried with minimal success.

Although there does not appear to be any specific treatment for this disorder, there are a number of common-sense strategies:
- Caffeine (in pill format or in coffee) can be used to sustain alertness on important occasions but must be used with caution because of the possible effect on subsequent sleep.
- The individual should avoid driving, working with machinery, or any other activities during which it would be dangerous to fall asleep.
- Family and work colleagues could be informed that falling asleep does not represent laziness, unsociability, or lack of appreciation for their company.

9.1.5 DISORDER OF THE SLEEP-WAKE SCHEDULE

DESCRIPTION

This disorder is characterised by excessive daytime sleepiness, difficulty awakening in the early morning, and difficulty falling asleep at a 'normal' time at night. The disorder results from a lack of synchrony between the individual's natural sleep-wake schedule and the sleep-wake schedule of the cultural environment.

Sleep-wake schedule disorders may result from organic or psychological causes, although the present disorder is reserved for those cases for which psychological causes are predominant. Such cases may include individuals who have an affective disorder or a personality disorder.

The most common presentation of this disorder is where sleep is delayed, with the typical individual having difficulty falling asleep until very late at night or early in the morning. Once asleep, the individual will have normal sleep, which will last a normal time unless interrupted by the alarm clock or another external disturbance. The individual will awake feeling refreshed following sleep of a normal duration, but will be groggy and tired during the day following an 'early' rising. Often the individual will become more alert and energetic as the day progresses, frequently working late into the night when others are ready to go to bed. These individuals may sleep-in unusually late on weekends and holidays in an attempt to catch up on lost sleep from their 'early' rising during the week. Most have no symptoms of anxiety or depression (apart from frustration over their delayed sleep) and some may have adjusted their work and leisure activities around their sleeping pattern. Records of daytime sleepiness (recorded in a sleep diary) will usually show a progressive increase in sleepiness as the week progresses and the hours of lost sleep accumulate. It is thought that these individuals may have difficulty training their sleep rhythms to a period less than 24 hours. Hence, these individuals are unable to advance their sleep onset to an earlier time once it has been delayed.

A rarer disorder of the sleep-wake schedule is an advanced sleep pattern. This pattern is more common in the elderly. Typically individuals will complain of falling asleep at 8 p.m. or earlier in the evening and waking up between 3 a.m. and 5 a.m. in the morning. The origin of this pattern is unclear although it is thought to be related to changes in the circadian physiology with ageing.

DIAGNOSIS

According to ICD-10, the following criteria must be satisfied for a diagnosis of disorder of the sleep-wake schedule:
- The individual's sleep-wake schedule is not in synchrony with the sleep-wake schedule of the individual's cultural environment or society.
- The individual experiences hypersomnia during the waking period and insomnia during the sleep period nearly every day for at least one month or for recurrent shorter periods of time.
- The sleep difficulties cause marked distress or interfere with social or occupational functioning.

DIFFERENTIAL DIAGNOSIS

The most common differential diagnosis of a delayed sleep pattern is **poor sleep habits**. Many people arise earlier during the week when they have to go to work than they do at the weekend. As sleep rhythms are usually quite adaptable, it is easy for most individuals to sleep late on the weekends. As a result they may not feel like going to sleep until 1 or 2 a.m. that night, with a resultant tiredness and tendency to oversleep the next morning. And so the cycle continues. Establishing regular wake-up times across the whole week (with no more then 1 hour variability across weekdays and weekends) for a period of a few weeks will usually clear up the problem. If this schedule fails to help, a disorder of the sleep-wake cycle might then be suspected.

Difficulty with arising in the morning may be related to a **depressive episode** in which the individual's mood tends to be worse in the morning. However, some forms of depression such as melancholic depression are associated with early morning wakening. A regular sleep-wake cycle can be absent in the case of severe depression.

Long-term **stimulant abuse** needs to be excluded in individuals who present with a longer than 24 hour sleep-wake cycle. Normal sleep-wake cycles can be virtually abolished in a number of **physical conditions** including severe dementia, head injury, other cases of brain damage, and recovery from coma. Irregular sleep-wake cycles are also associated with recovery from **drug or alcohol intoxication**, and **sedative or hypnotic dependency**.

MANAGEMENT GUIDELINES FOR DISORDERS OF THE SLEEP-WAKE SCHEDULE

Education about good sleep habits

Good sleep habits are covered in detail in the handout in Section 9.3.2. In the case of a delayed sleep pattern (i.e., difficulty falling asleep until late), it is advisable to start by establishing strict adherence to regular waking times across each week, with no more than 1 hour's variability across weekdays and weekends. In the case of an advanced sleep pattern (i.e., falling asleep early in the evening), slowly delaying sleep onset 15 minutes at a time can be effective. The regularity of the sleep-wake cycle can be reinforced with normal daytime activity, regular exercise, and meals. Education about good sleep habits is the easiest intervention to implement and adhere to, and some cases do resolve without further intervention.

Chronotherapy for delayed sleep pattern

Chronotherapy involves placing individuals on a 27-hour day so as to progressively delay the usual onset of sleep by about 3 hours each sleep-wake period. This 27-hour day continues until the sleep onset time has been moved 'around the clock' to the time that the individual considers an appropriate bed-time. It is essential that each sleep period be limited to a maximum of 7 or 8 hours and no napping is allowed. This strategy is frequently effective so long as the individual strictly adheres to the waking time so that the sleep-wake rhythm is not allowed to continue to be delayed. If the individual stays up unusually late, such as for a party, the problem may recur and the chronotherapy may need to be repeated. It may also be necessary to repeat the strategy at regular intervals as the sleep-wake schedule may continue to become disrupted. The main disadvantage of this strategy is the disruption caused to daily schedules. For several days it will be necessary to sleep through the day uninterrupted. Hence, appropriate arrangements may need to be made regarding work commitments, or child care.

An alternative and less disruptive method is to keep the individual awake all night for one night over the weekend and then ask him or her to go to bed 90 minutes earlier than usual the next evening. It is essential that each sleep period be limited to a maximum of 7 or 8 hours and no napping is allowed. The individual is instructed to go to bed at this same time for the rest of the week. This strategy can be repeated each weekend to continue the advance shift in sleep onset without the typical 5 to 7 days of weekday disruption of the previous method.

Chronotherapy for advanced sleep pattern

Going to bed 3 hours earlier each night until the sleep cycle is advanced back to a normal bed-time has been effective in a number of cases. For example, if the individual usually goes to bed at 8 p.m., he or she would go to bed at 5 p.m. on the first night of the programme, then at 2 p.m. the following day, and so on until an appropriate bed time is reached. Theoretically this approach is possible but is apparently difficult to implement, particularly in the elderly who are frequently those with an advanced sleep pattern.

Phototherapy

It is thought that the circadian rhythm is affected by exposure to darkness and light. Therefore, manipulating darkness and light (phototherapy or bright light therapy) may be useful in some cases.

Expert referral

If the previously mentioned strategies are not effective, referral or consultation with a sleep disorders unit is advised.

SLEEP-WAKE CYCLE DISRUPTION DUE TO SHIFT WORK

The shift worker's most common complaint is disrupted sleep. Associated problems can include chronic fatigue and daytime drowsiness. Sudden changes in working hours (e.g., starting night shift) place the sleep-wake cycle suddenly out of synchrony with other biological rhythms. This desynchrony causes sleep to be more difficult to initiate, less restful when obtained, and shortened in length. It has been argued that the sleep loss itself, the substances used to enhance sleep (e.g., alcohol and sedatives), and the substances used to enhance alertness (e.g., stimulants, caffeine, nicotine) can all contribute to a shift worker's problems.

The body's ability to adapt to a time shift is in part a function of the direction of the shift. A shift change which delays sleep time 8 hours later can be adapted to in about 3 days, while a shift which advances sleep time 8 hours earlier can take 6-7 days to adapt. A worker with no regular shifts but who has constantly changing or 'on call' schedules will never have a chance to develop adequate synchrony. Furthermore, because some people who do regular night work return to a 'normal' sleeping pattern on days off, their sleep-wake cycle never fully adapts.

Recommendations for shift workers:

- Try to keep regular sleep and meal schedules whenever possible.
- Encourage naps to limit sleep loss.
- Practice good sleep habits, especially reducing alcohol, nicotine, and caffeine consumption.
- If sleeping during the day, ensure adequate darkness and screening from noise and interruptions.

Recommendations for employers:

- Allow workers to change shifts in a phase-delayed direction (i.e., night shift to day shift).
- Allow napping to maintain alertness on long work stints.
- Avoid scheduling people on for excessively long shifts.

9.1.6 SLEEPWALKING

DESCRIPTION

Sleepwalking (or somnambulism) is characterised by an altered state of consciousness which occurs during the first third of nocturnal sleep. The individual sits up or gets out of bed while asleep and walks around. Episodes generally last from several seconds to a few minutes, with some reports of episodes lasting an hour. In children, the majority of sleepwalkers will not leave the bed, but may sit up on the edge of the bed while making repetitive movements. While sleepwalking, the individual has low levels of awareness, poor motor skills, and little reactivity to stimuli in the environment.

Sleepwalking is considered a disorder of arousal, particularly of arousal from the deepest stages of sleep (i.e., stages 3 and 4). During this time, motor behaviours are activated but full consciousness does not return. Individuals who sleepwalk tend to have a family history of such activity and have usually also experienced sleep terrors in the past. This disorder usually has its onset in childhood and generally does not continue into adulthood. Individuals with an onset of sleepwalking in adult life, often following a period of increased stress, are more likely to exhibit associated psychological disturbance than individuals with an onset of sleepwalking in childhood. It is possible for the disorder to occur for the first time in old age or dementia.

DIAGNOSIS

According to ICD-10 the following criteria must be satisfied for a diagnosis of sleepwalking:

- The main symptom involves two or more episodes in which the individual rises from bed during the first third of nocturnal sleep and walks around for a few minutes or up to half an hour.
- During the sleepwalking episode the individual has a blank, staring face, is unresponsive to communications from others, and can only be awakened with great difficulty.
- The individual has no recollection of the episode after waking the next morning or after being woken from the episode during the night.
- After being woken from an episode the individual may initially exhibit confusion and disorientation but, after a few minutes, the individual no longer displays any impairment of mental activity or behaviour.
- There is no sign of an organic mental disorder such as dementia or a physical disorder such as epilepsy.

DIFFERENTIAL DIAGNOSIS

Sleepwalking must be differentiated from **psychomotor epileptic seizures**. These seizures seldom occur only at night. During an epileptic attack, however, the individual is likely to display repetitive movements such as hand rubbing and exaggerated swallowing. An EEG recording can confirm the presence of epileptic phenomena.

MANAGEMENT GUIDELINES

Most children will grow out of sleepwalking as they grow older. Reassurance for both the parents and the child is indicated.

Sleepwalkers should be protected by appropriate locks on the doors and windows so as to stop them endangering themselves by leaving the house. It is also useful to have them sleep on the ground floor to avoid the risk of falling down stairs.

Sleepwalkers should be advised to avoid activities or circumstances that will increase slow wave sleep, such as sleep deprivation and shift work. It is also helpful for sleepwalkers to avoid going to bed with a full bladder, as this may increase the likelihood of nightime arousals.

Severe cases of sleepwalking may be associated with unresolved stresses and problems in an individual's life. Therapy directed at resolving such problems can often alleviate these symptoms.

There are reports of successful resolution of sleepwalking with the use of tricyclic antidepressant medication. This medication may decrease the frequency of these events, either by suppressing arousal or by suppressing the deep stages of sleep.

9.1.7 SLEEP TERRORS

DESCRIPTION

Sleep terrors (also referred to as night terrors) are characterised by extreme nocturnal terror and panic. They are associated with intense vocalisation, extreme body movements, and high levels of activity of the autonomic (involuntary) nervous system (e.g., increased heart rate and respiration). During a sleep terror the individual sits upright in bed (or gets out of bed) and vocalises a panicky scream. The individual may appear to be trying to escape from something and may actually make an escape attempt, thereby placing himself or herself at great risk of injury. Attempts to wake someone during a night terror are ill advised. When other individuals attempt to intervene or communicate with the individual, the panic and fear may increase since the individual is disoriented at this time and has little comprehension of what is going on. After waking, the individual usually has no recollection of the episode. Sleep terrors usually occur during the first third of nocturnal sleep.

The causal factors associated with sleep terrors are the same as those associated with sleepwalking (e.g., genetic, developmental, organic, and psychological factors). Individuals who experience night terrors tend to have a family history of such activity. This disorder usually has its onset in childhood and generally does not continue into adulthood. Individuals with onset of sleep terrors in adult life, often following a period of increased stress, are more likely to exhibit associated psychological disturbance than individuals with an onset of sleep terrors in childhood.

DIAGNOSIS

For a diagnosis of sleep terrors the following criteria must be satisfied:
- There have been two or more episodes during which the individual has risen from sleep with a panicky scream and has displayed intense anxiety, body movements, and high levels of activity of the autonomic nervous system such as rapid breathing, tachycardia (extremely rapid heart rate), dilated pupils, and sweating.
- The episodes usually occur during the first third of nocturnal sleep and last from 1-10 minutes.
- The individual is relatively unresponsive to communications from other people and such communications usually result in several minutes of disorientation and repetitive movements.
- There is minimal if any recall of the event; any recall that is experienced is usually limited to one or two fragments of mental imagery.
- There is no evidence of an organic factor such as a neurological or medical condition, psychoactive substance use, or a medication. There is also no evidence of a physical disorder such as epilepsy or a brain tumour.

DIFFERENTIAL DIAGNOSIS

Sleep terrors must be differentiated from **nightmares**. Nightmares involve limited, if any, vocalisation or body movements. Unlike sleep terrors, nightmares may occur at any time of the night and the individual can usually be aroused easily, at which time he or she is able to give a detailed account of the nightmare experience.

Epileptic seizures also need to be differentiated from sleep terrors. These seizures do not usually occur solely at night time. An EEG recording can help to identify the presence of such seizures.

Panic attacks (where individuals awaken with symptoms such as palpitations, shortness of breath, sweating and extreme fear or terror) may be confused with sleep terrors. The main distinction between a sleep terror and a nocturnal panic attack is that individuals are alert and aware of their surroundings during a panic attack and will have a clear recollection of the episode the next morning.

Post traumatic stress disorder is characterised by a re-experiencing of the traumatic event. These experiences can occur during deep sleep, causing the individual to awaken in a terrified state. However, most of these awakenings are accompanied by verbalisation, emotion, and more dream-like content than is usually seen in sleep terrors.

MANAGEMENT GUIDELINES

Education

Most children will grow out of sleep terrors as they grow older. Reassurance for both the parents and the child is indicated. A guide for helping parents cope with night terrors is reproduced in Section 9.3.3.

Scheduled awakenings

If night terrors are frequent, the individual can be woken about 1 hour after sleep onset. Scheduled awakenings appear to alter sleep architecture and prevent attacks in some people.

Resolve stress

Severe cases of sleep terrors may be associated with unresolved problems or stress. Therapy which is directed at resolving such problems can often alleviate these symptoms.

Medication

There are reports of successful resolution of sleep terrors with the use of tricyclic antidepressant medication and anticonvulsant medication (e.g., carbamazepine). This medication may decrease the frequency of these events either by suppressing arousal or by suppressing the deep stages of sleep.

9.1.8 NIGHTMARES

DESCRIPTION

Nightmares are very vivid and detailed dream experiences that are associated with intense fear or anxiety. The themes of the nightmares usually involve threats to survival, security, or self-esteem. During a nightmare there is a certain amount of activity of the autonomic nervous system (e.g., increased heart rate and respiration) but no vocalisation or body movement. The experience of frequent nightmares in the absence of an underlying mental disorder (such as post traumatic stress disorder) can be associated with a sensitive personality. In children, however, nightmares are more common. They are usually related to a specific phase of emotional development, and are less likely to be associated with psychological disturbance.

DIAGNOSIS

For a diagnosis of nightmares the following criteria must be satisfied:
- At any time during the sleep period or nap (but usually during the second half), the individual awakens with vivid recall of extremely frightening dreams that usually involve threats to survival, security, or self-esteem.
- The individual rapidly becomes alert and oriented after awakening from the dream experience.
- The individual may experience marked distress as a result of the dream experience itself or of the resulting disturbance of sleep.

DIFFERENTIAL DIAGNOSIS

Nightmares must be differentiated from **sleep terrors** (see Section 9.1.7).

A severely traumatic event may be followed by frequent nightmares in which the event is re-lived, which in turn may be a component of **post traumatic stress disorder**.

A sudden increase in the experience of nightmares in late adolescence may be a sign of an impending **psychotic episode**.

Nightmares may also arise from the use of certain **medications** such as fat-soluble beta-blockers, reserpine, thioridazine, certain tricyclic antidepressants, and benzodiazepines. Nicotine patches that are used for smoking cessation also appear to be associated with an increased frequency of nightmares. Abrupt withdrawal of drugs such as non-benzodiazepine hypnotics may also lead to enhanced dreaming since these drugs suppress REM sleep (the stage of sleep during which dreams occur). The subsequent withdrawal from these drugs may lead to REM rebound.

MANAGEMENT GUIDELINES

Desensitisation with muscle relaxation

This treatment is based on the principles of systematic desensitisation and has support in the literature from controlled treatment trials. The treatment protocol usually involves:

Weeks 1-2:   Regular practise of progressive muscle relaxation (see Anxiety Disorders in Chapter 4 for details and a handout). The individual writes down his or her nightmare/s.

Weeks 3-4:   Individuals are given instructions to spend a period of time each day in which they imagine their nightmare and relax whenever the imagined nightmare causes any tension or anxiety. This process is called imaginal desensitisation. Individuals are also required to practise muscle relaxation each night before falling asleep.

Weeks 5-8:   Individuals are requested to practise the imaginal desensitisation once each week, but more often if the nightmares persist.

9.1.9 SLEEP IN THE ELDERLY

POSSIBLE CAUSES OF SLEEP COMPLAINTS IN THE ELDERLY

Sleep complaints have been found to increase significantly in the elderly. This increase can be attributed to four main components:
1. Normal changes to the physiological systems controlling sleep that are part of the ageing process.
2. An increased incidence of specific organic sleep disorders such as periodic limb movements during sleep (PLMS) and sleep apnoea.
3. An increased incidence of medical conditions (e.g., osteoarthritis) and mental disorders (e.g., depression, dementia) that adversely affect sleep.
4. An increased use of a variety of medications, that may either interact with each other, or act differently in the elderly person.

NORMAL AGE-RELATED CHANGES

These changes include:
- A decrease in the amount of deep sleep (stages 3 and 4), and an increase in the proportion of lighter sleep.
- An increase in wakefulness, number of awakenings, and fragmented sleep during the night.

- A perception of decreased quality and quantity of sleep.
- A decreased ability to adapt to changes or interruptions to the sleep-wake cycle (especially where clear day-night differences in light and noise may be diminished).
- A tendency for the sleep-wake cycle to drift towards earlier sleep onset and earlier wakening.

These normal changes usually begin around the age of 50.

DIFFERENTIAL DIAGNOSIS

A thorough assessment of differential diagnoses are very important in elderly individuals who present with sleep complaints. The following questions will need to be considered.

- Have poor sleep habits contributed to the complaint? Common factors include spending excessive time in bed, keeping the radio or television on throughout the night, excessive daytime napping, and lack of exercise.
- Is a sleep disorder present? Consider particularly the possibility of sleep apnoea, periodic limb movements in sleep, and REM behaviour disorder ('acting out' of dreams in REM sleep due to an absence of the normal lack of muscle tone associated with REM sleep).
- Have coexisting medical disorders been adequately assessed and optimally treated?
- To what extent are medications, sedatives, alcohol, caffeine and/or nicotine contributing to the problem?
- Is unrecognised depression or dementia playing a role?
- Have there been any changes or stressors in the individual's emotional life, such as retirement, hospitalisation, or the death of a loved one? Individuals who are coping with recent stressors often have problems falling asleep or staying asleep. These problems can then cause daytime irritability, anxiety, tiredness, slowed cognition, and tearfulness.

MANAGEMENT GUIDELINES SPECIFIC TO PROBLEMS OF THE ELDERLY

The treatment of specific sleep problems in the elderly would be the same as for younger individuals. There are, however, a number of issues that may be specific to the elderly.

If *medications* might be contributing to the sleep problem, a trial reduction or elimination of all but the most necessary medications will be helpful in determining whether any of these substances is affecting sleep. If elderly individuals are on a number of different prescription medications, ideally one physician should manage all the medications. The role of medications in the treatment of medical conditions or a mental disorder should take into account that the half-lives of the drugs may be extended, that the possibility of drug interactions will be increased, and that lower than normal doses may be adequate.

The sleep problems of individuals with *dementia* include increased awakenings and night-time wandering, 'sundowning' (wandering and agitation at sundown), agitation, and confusion. Low-dose antipsychotic medications can be considered for the relief of agitation, but these individuals can be particularly sensitive to the side effects of medications. Safety at night can be improved by providing a night light, lowering the bed to near floor level, removing glass objects from the bedroom, and locking outside doors and windows.

Sleep problems that are the result of a *stressor* will generally resolve with time as the elderly individual adapts to the stress-related event. If the stressor is severe, the period of adaptation may take some time. Treatment strategies for insomnia will be helpful in these cases.

9.2 BIBLIOGRAPHY

Becker, P.M. & Jamieson, A.O. (1992). Common sleep disorders in the elderly: Diagnosis and treatment. *Geriatrics*, *47*, 41-52.

Bootzin, R.R. & Perlis, M.L. (1992). Nonpharmacological treatments of insomnia. *Journal of Clinical Psychiatry*, *53 (Suppl.)*, 37-41.

Driver, H.S. & Shapiro, C.M. (1993). Parasomnias. *British Medical Journal*, *306*, 921-924.

Eisen, J., MacFarlane, J. & Shapiro, C.M. (1993). Psychotropic drugs and sleep. *British Medical Journal*, *306*, 1331-1334.

Kellner, R., Neidhardt, J., Krakow, B. & Pathak, D. (1992). Changes in chronic nightmares after one session of desensitisation or rehearsal instructions. *American Journal of Psychiatry*, *149*, 659-663.

Kryger, M.H., Roth, T. & Dement, W.C. (1989). *Principles & Practice of Sleep Medicine*. Philadelphia: W.B. Saunders Company.

Lacks, P. & Morin, C.M. (1992). Recent advances in the assessment and treatment of insomnia. *Journal of Consulting and Clinical Psychology*, *60*, 586-594.

Parkes, J.D. (1993). Daytime sleepiness. *British Medical Journal*, *306*, 772-775.

Reite, M.L., Nagel, K.E., & Ruddy, J.R. (1990). *The evaluation and management of sleep disorders*. Washington: American Psychiatric Press.

Stradling, J.R. (1993). Recreational drugs and sleep. *British Medical Journal*, *306*, 573-575.

Tyrer, P. (1993). Withdrawal from hypnotic drugs. *British Medical Journal*, *306*, 706-708.

Paperbacks for individuals with sleeping complaints

Bearpark, H. (1994). *Overcoming Insomnia*. Rushcutters Bay, Sydney: Gore & Osment Publications.

Oswald, I, & Adam, K. (1983). *Get A Better Night's Sleep*. Methuen Australia.

9.3 RESOURCE MATERIALS

9.3.1 SLEEP DIARY

Date	Time of getting to bed	Time taken to fall asleep	No. of awake -nings	Time spent awake during night	Time of awakening in morning	Time of getting up	Naps	Exercise (type & duration)	Drugs, alcohol & caffeine	Significant events today
6/2/97	10.45pm	11.30pm	2	30 mins	6.50am	7.15am	2-3pm 7-7.20pm	Walking (30mins)	2 cups coffee, 15 cigs, 1 red wine	Job interview

9.3.2 UNDERSTANDING SLEEP [1]

SECTION 1: WHAT IS SLEEP?

One of the first things to note about sleep is that it is not a uniform process. Just as one can tell the difference between wakefulness and sleep, so can one distinguish between different kinds of sleep, called *sleep stages*. This means that the type of sleep you have when you first fall asleep is in some ways different to the sleep you have after being asleep for some time.

The notion of sleep stages may be easier to understand if you think of the brain as a collection of millions of cells that are sending information from one part of the brain to another. Information such as how things look, sound, and feel is picked up by our senses and sent to the brain to be organised and understood. This allows us to make sense of what we see or hear and to respond sensibly. Thus, while we are awake our brains are very active, since lots of messages are being sent from many different sources. When we fall asleep, however, the pattern of activity in these brain cells gradually changes and becomes slower.

More about the stages of sleep

Sleep is divided into five stages: stages 1, 2, 3, 4, and REM (rapid eye movement). Sleep stages 1 to 4 are used to describe what is commonly considered to be a gradual descent into 'deep' sleep. This descent begins with stage 1 (the lightest stage) and progresses through stages 2 and 3 to stage 4 (the deepest stage of sleep). It becomes more and more difficult to awaken people as they move from stage 1 sleep to stage 4 sleep.

The fifth stage of sleep, REM, is different from the other stages of sleep in a number of ways. The main feature of this stage is that the eyes of the sleeper, which are usually quite still, begin to move in a rapid and jerky manner. For this reason this stage is called rapid eye movement sleep. Stage REM is also the stage of sleep during which people dream. Contrary to popular belief, people do not dream for the whole time that they are asleep. Even people who don't normally remember their dreams are likely to report that they were dreaming if you awaken them from this stage of sleep.

The sleep cycle

During the night we pass in and out of these five stages many times according to a pattern called a sleep cycle. Each sleep cycle lasts about 90 minutes. The typical sleep cycle begins at stage 1 sleep (light sleep) and moves through stages 2 and 3 to stage 4 sleep (deep sleep). The sleep cycle then passes back up through stages 3 and 2 into REM (dream) sleep, where the first cycle ends. In the first cycle of the night most of the 90 minutes is spent in deep sleep (stage 4). However, with each cycle that follows, less and less time is spent in deep sleep while more time is spent in REM and stage 2 sleep. *Nearly all deep sleep is obtained in the first four hours of sleep. Therefore, even if you only sleep for four or five hours a night you get the same amount of deep sleep as someone who sleeps for eight hours a night.*

Another thing to note is that everybody has periods of light sleep and deep sleep each night. People who call themselves 'light' sleepers are probably just be more sensitive to sources of sleep disruption than are other people, so they may awaken to noises that other people sleep through.

---

[1] Adapted from a handout written by Merran Lindsay (1992) for the Clinical Research Unit for Anxiety Disorders at St. Vincent's Hospital, Sydney.

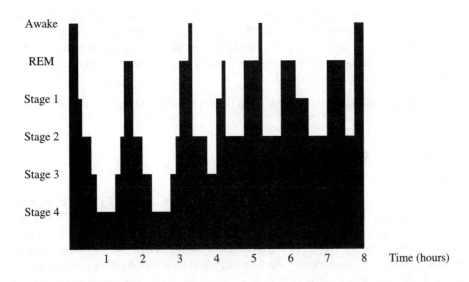

What makes us sleepy?

All human beings have within them a biological clock that acts to regulate such things as body temperature, activity levels, and renewal of body tissues. This internal clock is referred to as a *circadian rhythm*. The term is derived from the Latin 'circa diem', meaning 'about a day', because the rhythm takes around 24 hours to complete. Thus, body temperature reaches its highest and lowest points once every 24 hours. Feelings of alertness and sleepiness tend to result from rises and falls in body temperature. Therefore, people typically feel most alert in the early afternoon when their body temperature is highest and begin to feel sleepy in the evenings as their body temperature falls. By controlling these variations in body temperature, circadian rhythm thus influences our readiness to fall asleep.

The relationship between sleep and circadian rhythm is perhaps best illustrated by the jet lag that occurs when you travel overseas. A different country may have a time schedule that is behind or in front by a few hours. Therefore, you tend to want to sleep at your normal sleep time rather than at the sleep time of your new environment. Usually, by prolonging sleep onset to the appropriate time, you can adjust to the new clock in a matter of days. Delaying sleep in this way forces your circadian rhythm to shift into line with the new environment.

Interestingly, if people are made to live in an environment in which there are no clues to time, such as sunlight and clocks, their circadian rhythm cycles around once every 25 hours. These people go to bed an hour later every night and wake up an hour later every morning. It is not hard to see how free running in this way might interfere with the demands of modern society. For example, we may not attend work at the same hour every day. Thus, to operate on a 24 hour clock, our circadian rhythm must constantly be kept in check by timekeepers such as clocks, regular work hours, meal times, and alarms.

For most people these time keepers are enough to keep the circadian rhythm in check, allowing them to function well within the normal 24 hour time frame. However, under certain conditions this rhythm can get out of step. Instead of your body temperature reaching its highest point in the early afternoon, it may reach this point later in the evening, making it difficult to fall asleep until the early hours of the morning. An example of the type of condition that would bring about this change is when shift work requires a person to stay awake during the night and to sleep during the day. Although at first it may be very hard to stay awake throughout the night, after some time the circadian rhythm will shift into line with this new system. The person will then feel alert during the night and sleepy during the day. Changes in circadian rhythm can also be brought about by daytime napping, a point that will be discussed in more detail in section 3.

Now that you have a better understanding of what sleep is, let us address the question of sleep loss and how it may affect you.

SECTION 2: SLEEPLESSNESS AND SLEEP LOSS

Sleep deprivation studies

The effects of sleep loss on brain and body functioning have been studied carefully over the past 50 years. In most cases these studies have involved keeping people awake for between 70 to 205 hours. Contrary to popular belief, there is no evidence from these studies to suggest that sleep loss causes long term damage to either mind or body. The most common finding is that sleep-deprived people experience extreme sleepiness, have difficulty concentrating, and lack motivation, especially when performing boring and repetitive tasks. However, these symptoms are relatively minor and disappear when the person is allowed to sleep again.

As you might expect, these studies have also shown that preventing people from sleeping for long periods of time becomes more and more difficult as the length of time without sleep increases. Sleep deprived people require constant stimulation to keep them awake, otherwise they fall asleep the moment they are left in peace. The lesson to learn from this is that nature has provided us with an in-built mechanism which ensures that if we really need to sleep we will. Although sleeplessness may cause you to feel listless and irritable, you cannot die from lack of sleep, nor will lack of sleep cause long-term mental and physical damage. If your body really needs sleep, you can be sure that almost nothing will be able to stop it.

When is sleeplessness a problem?

For many people, sleeplessness is a stressful and unpleasant experience. This is often because the time they spend awake during the night is spent worrying. Therefore, these people are not only tired during the day because they have not slept much but also because all their worrying has exhausted them. In this case, sleeplessness is likely to be a problem that needs attention. However, other people find that they feel fine even though they do not get much sleep. In this case sleeplessness is not really a problem at all. You are the best person to judge whether you need to do something about your sleep. When you cannot sleep, lying in bed worrying only makes things worse. A much better way of dealing with insomnia is to get up, and do something that is distracting yet relaxing, such as listening to music. This way, even if you are not asleep, you are resting and you are less likely to feel tired the next day than if you spent half the night tossing and turning in bed. The same rules apply to people who wake up during the night and find they cannot get back to sleep.

Individual differences in need for sleep

The term 'sleep loss', implies people are losing something they should be getting. This is not necessarily the case, as everybody differs in the amount of sleep they need. Some people require only 4 or 5 hours each night, whereas others can sleep happily for 9-10 hours a night. Not only do people differ in the amount of sleep they need, but most people find that as they get older they require less sleep. Very few people find that at the age of sixty they can sleep for as many hours each night as they slept at the age of thirty.

SECTION 3: HOW TO GET A BETTER NIGHT'S SLEEP

The following pages outline good sleep habits and provide guidelines for dealing with common causes of sleep disturbance.

Establish a regular waking time

Establishing a regular sleep-wake pattern is very important, especially waking up at the same time each morning. The time that you wake helps to synchronise your body's circadian rhythms, so try not to vary the time of day that you get up by more than one hour, even across the weekends.

Establish a proper sleep environment

1. Comfort

The discomfort caused by a rumbling stomach, persistent aches and pains, or being too hot or cold, can prevent you from relaxing enough to fall asleep. Therefore it is necessary that all your immediate needs have been met before you try to sleep.

2. Noise

Noise during the night (such as traffic) is another common source of sleep disturbance. Even if you do not awaken and cannot remember the noises the next day, the noises can interfere with your normal sleep pattern. If you sleep in a place that tends to be noisy, try to shut out sound by closing windows and doors, wearing earplugs, or sound-proofing the room.

3. Light

A light room will make it more difficult for you to sleep. If you have trouble sleeping, darken the room to ensure that the morning light does not wake you.

Allow a wind-down time prior to sleep

Make sure that you stop work at least 30 minutes before you go to bed and do something different and nonstressful, such as reading, watching television, or listening to music.

Use your bed only for sleep

Your bedroom should only be used for sleep (and sexual activity). Activities such as eating, working, watching television, reading, or discussing the days problems should be done elsewhere, because their associated arousal may interfere with you getting to sleep. These activities also make you associate your bed with wakefulness and alertness rather than drowsiness and sleep onset.

Coping with worry and anxiety

One of the most common causes of sleep disturbance is anxiety. Many people find it difficult to wind down when they climb into bed at night after a hectic day. Often this is the first chance they have had to think about things that are concerning them. People can find themselves lying in bed worrying about their problems when they would rather be asleep. The feelings of tension and arousal that accompany these thoughts make it more difficult to fall asleep, and people may then begin to worry about their sleeplessness as well as their other problems. If you think you are having trouble sleeping because you are anxious about things that are happening in your life, there are two things you can do to improve your sleep.

Set aside time for problem solving during the day

Bed is not the place for thinking about things that distress you. If you do not normally find time during the day for thinking about things that are happening in your life then you need to set aside a time each day to do so. It should be a time when you are alone. Try to think of ways to resolve your problems. Usually this will require you to make decisions, some of which may be difficult because they concern important features of your life such as family and work. However, in most cases the uncertainty that accompanies difficult decisions is much more stressful and unpleasant than living with the outcome of the decision once the decision is made. Talk to your therapist or health worker if you would like more information about useful problem solving techniques.

Do not stay in bed when you are not asleep

If you have been having problems falling asleep, only go to bed when you are sleepy. If you find yourself still awake and worrying after 10 minutes get up and do something that is distracting yet relaxing, like knitting, listening to music, or reading a book. You may even want to listen to a relaxation tape. Do not return to bed until you feel sleepy again. When you do go back to bed, if you find that you are still worried and sleepless, get out of bed again and do something relaxing until you are sleepy enough to return to bed once more. At first you may find you need to get out of bed a number of times before you are finally able to fall asleep. The important thing is that you will learn to associate your bed with sleep and not with worry. It is also important that you get up at the same time each morning, no matter how long you slept.

Avoid napping during the day

It is not uncommon for people who have had a particularly bad night's sleep to feel sleepy the next day. This daytime sleepiness can make it very tempting for you to take a nap during the day. However, if you have insomnia and nap in the daytime, you make it much more likely that you will have another night of poor sleep. This is because when it comes time for bed you will be less tired and will need less sleep because you have slept during the day. You will probably take longer to fall asleep and you will awaken more frequently during the night. The next day you are likely to feel sleepy again and will be tempted to have another daytime nap.

As you can see, this pattern of napping soon becomes a vicious cycle that makes your original sleeping problem even worse. If you have insomnia, no matter how tired you are during the day, try to avoid daytime naps (unless you are doing shift work). Stick to regular sleep times by going to bed at the same time every night and waking up at the same time every morning. If you cannot get to sleep until later than your normal sleep time, do not sleep late the next morning - get up at your normal waking time. By following these instructions you will help to ensure that your natural body rhythm works *with* you, helping you to sleep at the times you want to sleep.

Avoid caffeine

This drug is found in coffee, tea, cocoa, cola drinks, as well as some over the counter medications. Consuming caffeine before bedtime, or drinking too much caffeine during the day will increase feelings of energy and wakefulness and make it more difficult for you to fall asleep. Any caffeine consumed after about 4 p.m. will still have an effect by the time you go to bed.

The table below shows the average quantity of caffeine in a variety of common drinks.

Caffeine content of common drinks per 150ml cup (One mug = 200-300ml)	
Roasted and ground coffee (percolated)	83 mg
Instant coffee	59 mg
Decaffeinated coffee	3 mg
Tea	27 mg
Cola drinks	15 mg
Milk chocolate (60ml)	40 mg
Cocoa (African)	6 mg
Cocoa (South American)	42 mg

Avoid nicotine

Nicotine stimulates the nervous system by releasing a hormone called 'adrenaline'. Adrenaline acts to arouse the body and mind, making you alert and ready for action. Smoking prior to bedtime increases energy and liveliness at the very time when you want to be relaxed and ready for sleep. So do not smoke for at least an hour before going to bed to allow time for the stimulating effects of nicotine to wear off.

Avoid excessive alcohol

A popular belief about alcohol is that alcohol will help you sleep if you are uptight and anxious. One or two glasses of wine in the evening may help you to relax, but regularly having several drinks in the evening causes you to get much poorer sleep overall. As the alcohol in your system is broken down by your body, you tend to awaken more frequently and you spend less time in the deeper stages of sleep. If you drink regularly you may find that you come to depend on the alcohol to reduce your anxiety and help you get to sleep. Not only will alcohol leave you feeling unrefreshed the next morning (because you are robbed of better quality sleep), but you are likely to have rebound anxiety which will last throughout the day and make it even more difficult to sleep at night. Alcohol is not the solution to sleeping problems so do not drink before you go to bed.

Avoid sleeping pills

The use of sleeping pills (sedative hypnotics) for any length of time causes as many problems as it solves. While sedative hypnotics will help you fall asleep and will decrease your anxiety *in the short term*, these benefits will disappear in the long term if you continue to use the sedatives regularly. You will begin to feel anxious and sleepless even though you are taking the pills. When this happens you will be tempted to take more sleeping pills since doing so will bring back the benefits of the drug. Unfortunately, however, these benefits will not be permanent either so that after a time you again experience the unwanted symptoms of anxiety and sleeplessness. The process that makes you less sensitive to the benefits of the drug over time is called *tolerance*. While sleeping pills are useful for overcoming temporary sleep loss, the development of tolerance means that these drugs do not provide a long term solution to sleeping problems.

Continual use of sleeping pills also has the disadvantage that it becomes increasingly difficult to stop using them because doing so will cause withdrawal effects. The levels of anxiety and sleeplessness that you experience after stopping the drug are likely to be greater than the anxiety and sleeplessness that made you *start* using the drug. Coming off sleeping pills can also cause you to have vivid dreams and nightmares.

If you do not use sleeping pills, or use them only occasionally, take heed of these warnings and do not start using them regularly. If you do use sleeping pills every night to help you sleep, it is recommended that you talk to your family doctor about reducing your intake of sleeping pills over time until you can stop using the pills altogether. Your doctor can help you come off the sleeping pills slowly without causing too many unpleasant side effects. Do not stop taking your sleeping pills without first talking to your doctor.

Take a late snack

A light bedtime snack, such as a warm glass of milk or a banana will help some people get to sleep. These foods are high in an amino acid called tryptophan, which is thought to be involved in the biochemical systems that induce and maintain sleep.

Summary of Good Sleep Habits

1. Go to bed when you are sleepy and get up at the same time every morning. Do not sleep late in the mornings trying to make up for 'lost sleep' and, if you think you have insomnia, do not take naps during the day.

2. Set aside time for problem solving during the day, not last thing at night. Identify any problems that are causing you to be anxious and try to resolve these problems by making decisions.

3. Do not lie in bed worrying for long periods of time. If you cannot sleep, get out of bed and do something that is distracting yet relaxing. Return to bed only when you feel sleepy again.

4. Do not use alcohol to help you sleep.

5. If you experience insomnia, avoid drinking caffeinated drinks after about 4 p.m. and do not drink more than two cups of caffeinated drinks each day.

6. Do not smoke for at least an hour (preferably an hour and a half) before going to bed.

7. Avoid sleeping pills: they do not provide a long-term solution to sleeping problems.

8. If you sleep in a noisy place, try to reduce noise levels by closing windows and doors and wearing ear-plugs.

9. Ensure the room is dark and that the morning light does not filter in. If you have a tendency to *over*sleep, it may be helpful to let the morning light enter the bedroom.

10. Getting to sleep when you are comfortable is much easier than getting to sleep when you are hungry, cold, in some kind of physical pain, or when you need to go to the toilet. Make sure all your immediate needs have been met before you go to bed.

11. Regular exercise during the day or early evening can improve sleeping patterns. Try to avoid exercise late in the evening as this may make it more difficult for you to get to sleep.

12. By doing the same thing every night before you go to bed you can improve your chances of falling asleep quickly. It is a good idea to develop a short routine involving things like washing your face and cleaning your teeth which you can easily perform before going to bed at night.

13. Be aware of things in the environment that may interfere with your sleep. For example, pets can disturb your sleep if they become active during the night or if they prevent you from moving freely in the bed. Also, digital clocks can be distracting if they glow or flash. It is often helpful to face the clock in the opposite direction.

9.3.3 COPING WITH NIGHT TERRORS: A GUIDE FOR PARENTS AND PARTNERS [1]

Normal sleep includes cycles of light sleep, deep sleep, and partial wakefulness. Sometimes dreams, nightmares and night terrors can disturb sleep. These disturbances are particularly common in children aged 2-6 years. However, sometimes these disturbances may continue into adulthood.

What are night terrors?

Night terrors are brief episodes (about 10-20 minutes) of partial wakefulness which occur during deep sleep. These episodes involve thrashing, kicking, rolling movements, and speech that cannot be understood. The individual does not respond to voice, touch, or reassurance. The episodes usually occur within the first two hours of going to sleep.

Important facts about night terrors
- The person will not remember it in the morning.
- Trying to wake the person during the night terror rarely shortens it.
- The person is not ill.
- Night terrors do not have any long term ill effects.
- Night terrors often occur only once a night, and not every night. (In children, night terrors will usually decrease and disappear 3 - 4 months after they start).
- Over-tiredness and changes in routine will make night terrors worse.

What parents or partners can do
- Stay calm during the night terror.
- Restrain the person physically so as to prevent injury.
- Place anything breakable out of reach. If necessary lock doors and windows.
- Waking the individual about 1 hour after sleep onset may help to abort attacks in some people. This method may be useful to try with children.
- Reassure other family members (especially children) that the terrors will do no harm and will go away.
- Remember that the person will have no memory of the episode, either the next day or even straight after the episode.
- Your reaction, and that of other family members, may upset the person who is having the night terrors. Stay calm and reassure the person.
- Try to find out if the person is worried about anything, and see if you can help. With children, maintain their bedtime routine as far as possible. Encourage periods of rest after physical activity.
- Seek professional help if the type or frequency of the night terrors continues.

[1] Adapted from Driver, H.S. & Shapiro, C.M. (1993). Parasomnias. *British Medical Journal, 306,* 921-924.

10
SEXUAL DYSFUNCTION

10.1 SEXUAL DYSFUNCTION

10.1.1 WHAT IS SEXUAL DYSFUNCTION?

Sexual dysfunction refers to the persistent impairment of the normal patterns of sexual interest or response. Naturally, however, there are difficulties with any definition of sexual dysfunction. For instance, the use of the word 'normal' raises the problem of what exactly is considered 'normal' in human sexuality when the range of sexual interest and performance is so wide both across and within individuals. Secondly, it could be argued that the presence of a sexual dysfunction would depend on whether or not the individual or his or her partner considers that a problem exists. Generally, however, sexual dysfunction may involve a lack of interest or enjoyment in sexual activities, the inability to experience or control orgasm, or a physiological barrier (e.g., erectile failure, failure to lubricate) that prevents effective sexual interaction.

Human sexual response involves both psychological and somatic processes hence both processes are involved in sexual dysfunction. It is the clinician's job to determine how each process contributes to the sexual dysfunction so that the individual can be helped to regain or develop an active and fulfilling sex life.

According to World Health Organization's (WHO) International Classification of Diseases, 10th Edition (ICD-10), the following criteria are required for a diagnosis of sexual dysfunction:
- The individual cannot participate in a sexual relationship as he or she would like.
- The sexual dysfunction is frequently present but may be absent on some occasions.
- The dysfunction has endured for at least 6 months.
- The dysfunction cannot be accounted for entirely by a physical disorder, drug treatment, or any other mental and behavioural disorder.

Additionally, DSM-IV requires that the disorder causes significant distress or interpersonal difficulties.

Many individuals with sexual problems do not have a clear-cut ICD-10 or DSM-IV sexual dysfunction. Rather, they may simply be experiencing adjustment difficulties relating to such areas as the timing, frequency, and method of initiation of sexual activity. Such individuals are unlikely to need intensive therapy but may benefit from brief sex education and enhanced communication with their partners. The sex education component of this chapter may be helpful in such cases. For individuals who are experiencing greater distress and difficulty, specialist referral may be required.

10.1.2 COMMON SEXUAL DYSFUNCTIONS AND THEIR TREATMENT

The sexual dysfunctions covered in this chapter include:
- Lack or loss of sexual desire
- Sexual aversion
- Lack of sexual enjoyment
- Failure of genital response (in women and men)
- Orgasmic dysfunction (in women and men)
- Premature ejaculation
- Nonorganic vaginismus
- Nonorganic dyspareunia

LACK OR LOSS OF SEXUAL DESIRE

This disorder is characterised by a lack of pleasure in anticipating sexual activity or by a low urge to engage in sexual activity. Sexual enjoyment and arousal during sex can still be present although the lack of desire makes initiation of sexual interaction less likely. The disorder is said to be a primary dysfunction of the desire phase of the sexual response cycle if the individual has *always* experienced a lack of sexual desire, and is termed a secondary dysfunction of the desire phase if the individual has experienced a marked *decline* in sexual desire. For this disorder to be diagnosed, loss of desire should be the primary problem and not secondary to other sexual problems such as nonorganic dyspareunia or erectile failure.

In clinic samples this disorder is more common among females than males although the incidence in the general population is unknown. The loss of sexual desire is one of the most difficult sexual dysfunctions to treat. This problem may range from a lack of spontaneous interest in sex to a total lack of interest in sex.

It is important to note that an extremely wide range of sexual interest exists in the general population. There is a need to take into account people's previous level of interest, their concern about their level of interest, and their interest in a whole range of sexual activities.

Loss of desire may be associated with all forms of sexual dysfunction since sexual dysfunction leads to a negative sexual experience, thereby reducing anticipation of positive sexual experiences in the future. It will be important to assess for the presence of other sexual dysfunctions before making this diagnosis. In particular, this disorder must be differentiated from sexual aversion and lack of sexual enjoyment which often stems from a traumatic sexual experience in the past, such as rape or molestation. Lack or loss of sexual desire generally involves a lack of interest in sex without the emotional intensity of aversion and fear.

Loss of desire may be situational (e.g., only with a particular partner) or total. If individuals appear to have a total loss of sexual desire (i.e., there is a complete lack of sexual desire in response to any individual or stimulus) then a thorough medical examination can be undertaken to rule out physical causes (e.g., chronic pain, hormonal imbalances, or the effect of drugs or alcohol). A mental status examination and psychiatric history (see Chapter 1: Core Management Skills) would also be undertaken to rule out a depressive episode (particularly if there has been a dramatic change in desire over a short period of time).

Treatment

It is asserted that a lack or loss of sexual desire is one of the most common and most difficult problems to treat. The generalist mental health clinician is unlikely to possess the skills necessary to assess and treat this complex problem. Hence, referral to a clinician who is specialised in the treatment of sexual dysfunction is recommended. When such problems are presented, however, the following issues will be important.

Determine the individual's motivation to seek treatment

Quite often an individual will seek treatment because of pressure from his or her partner. If the individual does not share his or her partner's motivation to deal with the sexual dysfunction, the prognosis is likely to be less favourable.

Provide information

Providing information, particularly about the desire phase of the sexual response cycle will be important for 'normalising' the individual's experience (Section 10.1.5). Additionally, Section 10.3.1, "Common Triggers of Sexual Problems", may help couples identify factors that interfere with their level of sexual desire or interest.

Expert treatment

Treatment of lack or loss of sexual desire involves a thorough assessment and formulation of the problem, dealing with general relationship issues, graded behavioural homework tasks (usually beginning with individual exercises followed by couple exercises), and dealing with other issues as they arise.

SEXUAL AVERSION

Sexual aversion involves strong negative feelings and fear or anxiety at the prospect of sexual interaction with a partner. The fear and anxiety is of sufficient intensity that sexual activity is avoided.

Treatment

As this problem can often have a complicated presentation and history, it is best managed by referral to a clinician who has expertise in the treatment of sexual dysfunction. If this is not possible the clinician should familiarise themselves with the relevant literature and seek expert consultation.

LACK OF SEXUAL ENJOYMENT

In lack of sexual enjoyment, sexual responses occur normally and orgasm can be achieved although there is a lack of appropriate pleasure. Women seem to experience this complaint more frequently than men.

Treatment

As for sexual aversion, this problem can often have a complicated presentation and history. Therefore, lack of sexual enjoyment is best managed by referral to a clinician who has expertise in the treatment of sexual dysfunction.

FAILURE OF GENITAL RESPONSE IN WOMEN

Among females, the main dysfunction of genital response is vaginal dryness or failure of lubrication. This problem may stem from psychological factors (e.g., anxiety), and may also be exacerbated by pathological factors (e.g., infection), or oestrogen deficiency (e.g., among post-menopausal women). It is usually post-menopausal women who report vaginal dryness as being their only sexual complaint. In other cases this dysfunction is usually associated with lack or loss of sexual desire. If the disorder stems entirely from a medical condition, this diagnosis is not appropriate.

Treatment

Treatment for this disorder is aimed at increasing arousal levels during periods of sexual activity, and reducing factors that may inhibit arousal. Techniques for increasing arousal are discussed in the section about orgasmic dysfunction in women (p. 581). In addition to these techniques, the regular or occasional use of lubricating gel may also be helpful. Factors that may inhibit arousal (e.g., lack of privacy, tiredness) are outlined in Section 10.3.1. It will be helpful for the individual to try to identify any such factors that are present and devise strategies for minimising these factors. If these techniques are not successful, referral to an expert sex therapist will be required.

FAILURE OF GENITAL RESPONSE IN MEN (ERECTILE FAILURE)

Erectile failure is when a man is unable to maintain or develop an erection and hence is unable to have coitus or sexual intercourse. This condition may be *primary* (the man has *never* been able to sustain an erection) or *secondary* (the man has been able to sustain an erection in the past but cannot do so now). In addition, the dysfunction may be *total* (the man cannot currently sustain an erection in any circumstance) or *situational* (the man is only unable to sustain an erection in specific circumstances). Primary total dysfunction is relatively rare and usually has a physical basis.

If the individual is able to have an erection in certain circumstances (e.g., with his partner, during masturbation, during the night, or upon wakening) but not in other circumstances, the dysfunction is likely to have a psychological cause. Erectile failure of gradual onset in older men is likely to have a significant physical component.

A thorough medical assessment will be important for determining the role of physical factors often requiring investigation of the blood supply to the penis. Physical factors include physical illness, surgery, drugs, and medication side effects.

It has been suggested that primary dysfunction of genital response can be caused by a highly moralistic, often religious family upbringing in which sexual activity that is engaged in for any purpose other than procreation is considered to be unacceptable and evil. Individuals from such families are generally lacking in sex education and may have been punished for showing an interest in learning about sex. Additionally, individuals are likely to have been punished for masturbating, exploring their bodies, or for premarital kissing or caressing of girlfriends or boyfriends.

Another possible cause of primary erectile failure may be the experience of disastrous adolescent sexual activity. For example, being too anxious or receiving a negative response from a partner. An initial aversive experience may severely undermine sexual confidence and expectations of a more positive experience in the future.

Individuals with a secondary erectile failure may also have had highly moralistic upbringings with little sexual education. However, other factors are probably more closely linked to the dysfunction. Many men develop erectile failure after experiencing other sexual dysfunctions such as premature ejaculation. If a man regularly ejaculates prematurely he is likely to lose self-confidence in his ability as a lover, and hence may worry excessively about his sexual performance. Performance anxiety plays an important role in the development of erectile failure.

If a man's sexual fantasy or his sole sexual experience relates to being a passive partner in a homosexual partnership, the man may develop erectile dysfunction if he enters into a relationship in which he is no longer expected to be the passive partner. In such a case the dysfunction would be considered to be situational and not total.

Alcohol use, stress, and fatigue can also impair erectile ability. Fatigue and large quantities of alcohol have a depressive effect which makes it more difficult for a male to have and maintain an erection. The negative sexual experience that follows may cause stress and performance anxiety in the future, thus contributing to and consolidating the erectile dysfunction.

It is important to note that most men will occasionally be unable to achieve or sustain an erection. Such occasional experiences should be regarded as entirely normal.

Treatment

Physical treatments

The availability of sildenafil (Viagra) has changed the treatment choices for erectile dysfunction considerably. Several clinical and dose-ranging studies have found that Viagra effectively treats a wide range of males with erectile dysfunction. Viagra works by relaxing the blood vessels in the penis when a man is sexually excited, allowing a greater blood flow into the penis, in turn allowing an erection. Other physical treatment include the implantation of a semi-rigid or inflatable penile prosthesis, training in self-administration of intracavernosal papaverine or prostaglandin E_1 injection (a vasodilator) into the penis prior to intercourse, or a vacuum constriction device.

The advantages and disadvantages of these options should be fully discussed with a clinician or physician with expertise in the area of sexual disorders and will not be covered in this chapter. Erectile dysfunction is commonly due to a mixture of organic and psychological causes. For example, in addition to having a mildly impaired physiological capacity to have an erection, the erection may also be vulnerable to psychological factors. Dealing with the psychological factors alone may help the man to gain a full erection.

The range of problems with erectile failure is considerable and it is important the more difficult or complex cases are referred to an expert sex therapist. The following guidelines will help determine whether the problem can be treated by a generalist mental health clinician.

TREAT if problem is:	**REFER** if problem is:
Secondary (i.e., the man has been able to sustain an erection in the past).	*Primary* (i.e., the man has never been able to sustain an erection).
Situational (i.e., the problem occurs in only some circumstances, such as being with a partner), OR *Occasional* (i.e., the problem occurs intermittently).	*Total* (i.e., the problem occurs across all circumstances and on all occasions).
Recent (e.g., weeks or months).	*Long-standing* (i.e., years)
Associated with obvious triggers (e.g., stress).	Not associated with any obvious triggers.

If treatment is appropriate, the following steps are recommended.

Education

An important first step in the education process will be to provide the individual with information about the physical and psychological factors that can contribute to erectile failure. The information contained in Section 10.1.5 may also be helpful.

Self-help exercises

Individuals can be directed to work through the self-help exercises outlined in either of the following two texts. These books are widely available and contain excellent guides to individual and partner exercises. The involvement of the partner in treatment tends to increase success rates.

Zilbergeld, B. (1980). *Men and Sex*. London: Fontana
Williams, W. (1985). *It's Up To You*. Sydney: Maclennan & Petty.

Preparing for relapse

Up to 75% of men will have a recurrence of their problem following treatment. Therefore, an important role of treatment will be to assist men to cope well with relapse. Most recurrences will occur in a temporal pattern (i.e., will occur more at certain times than at others) and will usually improve naturally or with self-initiated recommencement of the treatment techniques described here. The notion that such relapse is normal and to be expected will help to reduce the anxiety and sense of failure that may otherwise prolong erectile difficulties.

ORGASMIC DYSFUNCTION IN WOMEN

In this dysfunction the sexual excitement phase of intercourse proceeds normally but orgasm is markedly delayed or does not occur at all. This condition may be *primary* (the woman has *never* been able to have an orgasm in any situation) or *secondary* (the woman has been able to have an orgasm in the past but cannot do so now). Additionally, orgasmic dysfunction may be *situational* (i.e., only occurs in specific situations) or may be *total* (i.e., occurs across a wide variety of situations). Situational orgasmic dysfunction implies that there is likely to be a psychological cause since orgasm occurs normally at other times. If the dysfunction is total there may be a variety of causes (e.g., psychological, physical). Orgasmic dysfunction is more common in women than in men and is one of the most common sexual complaints among women. However women who do not reach orgasm regularly or ever in sexual activity may not consider it a problem.

Treatment

As with other sexual dysfunctions, there will be a wide variation in the severity of the presenting problem. It is important that the more difficult or complex cases are referred to an expert sex therapist.

In general, the guidelines to follow are:

1. If the problem is one of primary total orgasmic dysfunction and there is an absence of uncomplicating factors (e.g., secondary lack or loss of sexual desire, other sexual dysfunctions, relationship difficulties), then it may be appropriate for the generalist clinician to direct the individual and couple to work through a series of homework exercises.

2. If the problem is secondary or situational, or if complicating factors exist, the individual or couple are best referred to an expert sex therapist.

If treatment is appropriate, the widely available self-help book by Heiman, LoPiccolo, & LoPiccolo (1976) titled *Becoming Orgasmic: A Sexual Growth Program for Women* contains a programme that women and partners will be able to follow at home. It is recommended that the clinician helps the individual or couple work through these exercises. Exercises include:

Directed masturbation

The most effective treatment for lifelong lack of orgasm in women is a directed masturbation programme. The intense orgasm that is usually associated with masturbation increases blood flow to the genital region. An increase in blood flow, brought about by repeated masturbatory orgasms, can increase orgasmic potential. Furthermore, an increased frequency of orgasms leads to a greater anticipation of obtaining pleasure from sexual activity. Therefore, on both psychological and physical grounds, masturbation can be a sensible treatment for orgasmic dysfunction in women.

The directed masturbation technique has had high success rates in a number of uncontrolled treatment studies. The technique allows the woman to redirect her attention to her own physical sensations and sexual feelings. She progresses at her own pace in private, thus ensuring maximum relaxation and minimum pressure.

The programme involves:
- Self examination of the body with the use of hand-held and full-length mirrors.
- Tactual body and genital self-examination to discover pleasurable body and genital sensations.
- Increased manual stimulation of genitals until 'something happens' or the woman becomes tired or uncomfortable (later sessions may include the use of a vibrator if orgasm has not been experienced).
- Partner participation during the later stages of the programme.

Sensate focus for couples

This technique involves giving or receiving pleasurable (initially, not necessarily sexually arousing) caresses in a relaxed and comfortable atmosphere. In the case of orgasmic dysfunction, sensate focus allows a woman to experiment with arousal techniques with her partner.

Kegel's pelvic floor exercises

These exercises are often recommended although there is no research evidence to support their unique contribution to helping a woman achieve orgasm. The exercises will strengthen the pelvic floor muscle and thus increase the woman's ability to recognise sensations of arousal in this region of her body (i.e., the woman will be able to feel her pelvic floor lifting during effective arousal).

Sexual fantasies

It may be important to give the woman permission to make use of sexual fantasies. Books such as "The Joy of Sex" by Alan Comfort, or Nancy Friday's books about female sexual fantasy (e.g., "My Secret Garden", "Forbidden Flowers", "Women on Top") can be helpful and are easily obtained from most bookstores.

ORGASMIC DYSFUNCTION IN MEN

In this dysfunction (also referred to as inhibited ejaculation) the sexual excitement phase of intercourse proceeds normally but orgasm is markedly delayed or does not occur at all. Orgasmic dysfunction may be *situational* (i.e., only occurs in specific situations) or may be *total* (i.e., occurs across a wide variety of situations). Situational orgasmic dysfunction implies that there is likely to be a psychological cause since orgasm occurs normally at other times. If the dysfunction is total, there may be a variety of causes (e.g., psychological, physical, environmental). Orgasmic dysfunction in men is thought to be a relatively rare dysfunction.

Treatment

The treatment of orgasmic dysfunction or inhibited ejaculation in men usually involves:
- Decreasing performance anxiety
- Increasing arousal and physical stimulation

Treatment may also need to involve:
- The reduction (when possible) of environmental factors that might be causing stress, worry, or distraction, and which may subsequently contribute to ejaculatory problems (e.g., lack of privacy, a cold room, see Section 10.3.1).
- Assistance with relationship problems.
- The reduction of psychological inhibition resulting from anxiety or guilt (e.g., memories of previous traumatic or unpleasant sexual experiences).

If significant problems lie in the last two categories, the individual is best treated by a clinician who specialises in sexual dysfunction and/or cognitive therapy. In other and relatively milder cases, the following strategies may be useful.

Education

In addition to the general education section (Section 10.1.5).

• Dispel myths that might be contributing to a man's fear or guilt about sexuality. For example, being overly concerned about a partner's ability to orgasm.

• The physiological refractory period places limits on the male's ability to achieve repeated orgasms. Some men may need education about the refractory period.

• If fear of pregnancy is a source of anxiety for the man, the provision of contraceptives and education about birth control can be helpful.

• The clinician may need to 'give permission' for the man to enjoy his sexual response.

• Large quantities of alcohol can contribute to orgasmic dysfunction such that a man may have difficulty reaching orgasm.

Sensate focus

Because men with orgasmic dysfunction usually have no difficulties in obtaining an erection, somewhat less time can be given to the earlier stages of a sensate focus programme, unless the man is significantly inhibited in activity leading up to intercourse or there are communication difficulties between the couple. If the man still has problems with ejaculation, for instance if he remains unable to ejaculate in the presence of his partner, then expert referral or consultation should be sought.

PREMATURE EJACULATION

While there is no entirely satisfactory definition of premature ejaculation, this dysfunction is commonly described as the inability to control ejaculation adequately for both partners to enjoy sexual interaction. In some cases ejaculation may occur before or immediately after penetration, or may even occur in the absence of an erection. If prolonged stimulation is required for the development of an erection, ejaculation may appear to be premature since the time interval between full erection and ejaculation is shortened. In this case the primary problem is delayed erection rather than premature ejaculation. An assessment of the factors associated with the delayed erection will be required. It is unlikely that premature ejaculation has an organic basis, however, this dysfunction may develop in response to a co-existing organic impairment (e.g., pain).

Rapid ejaculation is common in young men during their first sexual encounters. However, most men will subsequently gain control over their speed of ejaculation.

Premature ejaculation is usually a primary problem (i.e., the man has never learned to gain control over ejaculation). Sometimes a history of rapid masturbation, perhaps accompanied by feelings of guilt, can predispose a man to premature ejaculation when he starts a sexual relationship.

A partner's reaction to premature ejaculation can be crucial. Anger and condemnation from a partner may lead to loss of confidence and increased anxiety, which will cause even more rapid ejaculation. The use of distracting thoughts, anaesthetic creams, or reducing the time spent on sexual activities prior to penetration are not helpful.

Premature ejaculation can occur as a secondary problem during a time of stress, or can occur transiently when a man's frequency of sexual activity is reduced.

Treatment

Again, it will be important for all presentations that are not straightforward (e.g., if associated with orgasmic dysfunction or lack or loss of sexual desire) to be referred to an expert sex therapist. In straightforward cases, most men will be able to gain ejaculatory control with the help of specific exercises.

Education

In addition to the general education issues covered in Section 10.1.5, the clinician may need to deal specifically with issues that contribute to performance anxiety. For example, if either partner holds unrealistic beliefs about the length of time a man is expected to be stimulated or engage in intercourse before ejaculation occurs, then this belief will need to be dispelled. A supportive and reassuring partner can often help to allay fears of negative evaluation.

Specific exercises

Clinicians can help men and their partners by working with them through the self-help exercises outlined in Zilbergeld's *Men and Sex*. The structured exercises outlined in this book move through the stages of masturbation, to manual stimulation, to intercourse. The treatment exercises include:

1. *The stop-start technique (Semans' technique)*
2. *The squeeze technique*
3. *Sensate focus*

Stop-start technique. The stop-start technique developed by Masters and Johnson has been found to be highly effective for the treatment of premature ejaculation. Success rates of up to 90% have been reported. The technique aims to increase the frequency of sexual contact and increase the sensory threshold of the penis.

This technique is best carried out in the context of sensate focus exercises because:

- Some males ejaculate so rapidly that direct stimulation of the penis of any kind can trigger ejaculation straight away. Starting with non-genital caresses will allow the male more time to identify the sensations that occur immediately prior to ejaculation.
- The sensate focus experience tends to limit the number of 'accidental' ejaculations that might discourage some couples in the early stages of treatment.
- The exercises increase communication and co-operation between couples.
- Anxious individuals will find the graded approach less threatening.
- The directive to refrain from direct genital stimulation allows the couple to experience more prolonged, sensuous caresses, thereby increasing the quality of their sex life.

The stop-start technique is incorporated into a series of individual and couple exercises and involves:

1. Stimulation of the penis until high arousal (but not threshold for ejaculation) is reached.
2. Cessation of stimulation (for up to a few minutes) to allow arousal to subside.
3. Repetition (4-5 times) of steps 1 and 2 until ejaculation is allowed to occur.

Squeeze technique. The squeeze technique can be used if control does not develop after several attempts with the stop-start technique. The squeeze technique inhibits ejaculatory reflex and hence reduces the urge to ejaculate.

In this technique, when the man indicates high arousal, he (or his partner) applies a firm squeeze to the head of the penis for 15-20 seconds. The forefinger and middle finger are placed over the base of the glans and shaft of the penis, on the upper surface of the penis, with the thumb placed at the base of the undersurface of the glans (see following diagram).

The squeeze needs to be practised before high arousal occurs to find out how firmly the penis can be squeezed without causing pain.

It will be useful to ensure that the individual and couple realise there may be a few 'failures' with both the stop-start and squeeze techniques but that persistence usually brings success.

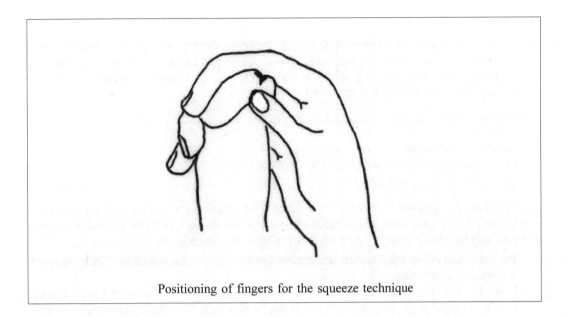

Positioning of fingers for the squeeze technique

NONORGANIC VAGINISMUS

In nonorganic vaginismus, penetration is impossible or painful due to blockage of the vaginal opening. The blockage is caused by spasms of the pelvic floor muscles which surround the vagina. The muscle spasms themselves have usually developed in response to anxiety and fearful thoughts and as such have a psychological rather than a physical basis. Events or thoughts that may be associated with spasms of the pelvic floor muscles include:

- Fear of vaginal penetration with the anticipation of pain.
- Previous rape, attempted rape, or molestation.
- The belief that premarital sex is wrong or sinful. This belief may be so ingrained that, even when intercourse is sanctioned by marriage, it may be difficult to relax physically or mentally during sexual intercourse.
- Childhood punishment for masturbation.
- A fear of sex that is instilled by friends or family following the suggestion that the first experience of intercourse is likely to be painful or bloody.
- Fear of pregnancy and painful labour.

If vaginismus does occur during intercourse the individual will probably experience pain. This pain reinforces the individual's fearful thoughts about intercourse, thereby making the vaginismus worse. Contractions of the pelvic floor muscles may occur as a result of local pain caused by such things as vaginal dryness, recent childbirth, or abdominal or back pain. In this case the pelvic floor spasms are secondary to the local pain and nonorganic vaginismus should not be diagnosed.

Individuals who are suspected of having vaginismus are advised to have the diagnosis confirmed by their general practitioner or gynaecologist. This physical examination will rule out the possibility of vaginal obstruction caused by a growth or tumour, or by the hymen (a membranous fold that may partially or completely occlude the vaginal opening).

Treatment

The treatment of vaginismus is best carried out by an expert sex therapist as vaginismus will commonly involve intensive therapy. With good treatment, vaginismus has a very promising outcome. Approximately 90% of women are able to engage in normal sexual intercourse after an intensive treatment programme such as that described by LoPiccolo.

The management of vaginismus includes three aspects:
1. Education
2. Relaxation techniques
3. Strategies that lead to achieving penetration of the vagina

Education

Individuals with vaginismus have often received little sex education or may have a negative attitude towards sex. Others may have been a victim of sexual assault. In addition to the general educational material provided in Section 10.1.5, the following issues will be relevant.

- The individual is given permission and encouragement to enjoy her sexuality if such enjoyment is culturally appropriate.
- It will be important to dispel the notion that intercourse is the only important part of sexual activity. A small proportion of women will not be able to achieve intercourse. In these cases particularly, it will be important to focus on non-coital aspects of sexual activity such as achieving orgasm through manual or oral stimulation, and enhancing communication, intimacy, and sensuality.
- The clinician needs to ensure that the individual obtains a thorough understanding of *all* treatment options so that she can choose the aspects of treatment in which she wishes to participate. For example, strategies that involve the insertion of objects into the vagina will worsen vaginismus if the woman is reluctant to proceed with this strategy and becomes traumatised by the experience.

Relaxation techniques

Progressive muscle relaxation exercises will lower the individual's general muscle tension and anxiety. In particular, the woman will need to learn to relax muscles around the inner thigh and pelvic area. Kegel's exercises may also assist by increasing control and voluntary relaxation.

Strategies to achieve penetration

The expert sex therapist will direct the women to use the following strategies in a graded approach with the woman taking complete control over the pace of treatment. The woman would start with self exploration and work down the list towards gradual attempts at intercourse. The individual is advised to avoid intercourse until the final level.

- Self exploration.
- Progressive muscle relaxation training and Kegel's Exercises.
- Insertion of graded trainers (made from glass or plastic) or fingers, after engaging in relaxation exercises. Trainers come in a number of sizes. The smallest trainer is about the size of a pencil while the largest trainer is the size of an erect penis. The individual is taught how to painlessly insert the smallest trainer by using lubricating gel and targeted relaxation of the pelvic floor muscles. The individual gradually works towards inserting the largest trainer. The process proceeds gradually as the woman may become discouraged or anxious if the treatment proceeds too quickly for her or if pain or discomfort is experienced.
- Sensate focus exercises.
- Insertion of fingers or graded trainers by the individual's partner.
- Gradual attempts at intercourse with the woman on top, controlling the pace and depth of penetration.

Reassurance for the partner

The individual's partner may also need to be reassured at this time that he or she is not to blame for the disorder. Partners will often feel frustrated, angry, guilty, inadequate, or helpless. The best thing a partner can do is to attend all treatment sessions (if so desired by the index individual), provide support and reassurance for the individual, and co-operate with treatment exercises later in the programme. Partners may also have a sexual dysfunction that requires treatment.

NONORGANIC DYSPAREUNIA

Dyspareunia, or pain during intercourse, may occur in both women and men. In women the pain may be superficial (i.e., located at the entrance of the vagina) or deep in the vagina. This dysfunction should not be diagnosed if there is evidence of a local pathological condition (e.g., infection, tender episiotomy scar if pain is superficial, endometriosis or ovarian cyst if pain is deep). Dyspareunia should only be diagnosed if there is no other sexual dysfunction such as vaginal dryness or vaginismus that is causing the pain.

Dyspareunia in men almost always has an organic cause (such as urethral infection, scar tissue resulting from a sexually transmitted disease, or a tight foreskin). Such organic causes can usually be treated directly. In cases where there is no obvious cause, emotional factors are more likely to be involved.

Treatment

The following guidelines have been directed towards the management of dyspareunia in women, since most cases of dyspareunia in men are caused by organic factors. However, some of the principles can be adapted for the management of males with dyspareunia.

Exclude physical causes of pain

This step will usually involve referral to the woman's general practitioner who can examine her for possible physical causes of pain.

Provide information about adequate arousal

Once a physical cause has been excluded, the most likely cause of 'superficial' pain is inadequate arousal. During full arousal the vulva and labia swell and separate, making penetration of the erect penis comfortable. Additionally, during full arousal the vagina becomes lubricated by the secretion of mucosal fluid. Inadequate lubrication may cause the labia to get caught or may cause local tissue trauma in the form of tiny lesions, both of which can be painful. (N.B.: While inadequate arousal and its associated features can lead to pain during intercourse, dyspareunia cannot be diagnosed if pain is caused solely by lack of lubrication).

If deep pain is experienced by the woman *during intercourse*, the most likely cause is the upwards displacement of the internal organs and supporting ligaments caused by the insertion of the penis or finger. Ovarian compression can occur in such instances and may cause discomfort, especially if the ovary is enlarged and tender around the time of ovulation. With adequate arousal, the outer third of the vagina becomes snug and engorged, while the inner two thirds of the vagina expands and balloons and the uterus is elevated to make room for comfortable accommodation of the penis. If arousal is not adequate, however, the uterus may not rise and pain can occur. Therefore, the couple may find it helpful to ensure that the woman is fully aroused before penetration of the vagina occurs. Techniques for enhancing arousal have been covered in the section on orgasmic dysfunction.

Provide information about suitable intercourse positions

In addition to discussing the importance of adequate arousal, the couple may also be aided by specific suggestions regarding modification of their usual intercourse positions. In particular, it may be helpful for the couple to avoid positions that lead to deep penetration (such as vaginal entry from the rear) and to adopt positions in which the woman is in control of the depth of penetration (woman on top) or in which penetration is not too deep (side by side or 'spoons' position).

Encourage the use of relaxation exercises

Once a woman has repeatedly experienced pain on intercourse, it is likely that she will tense up on future occasions in anticipation of further pain. Such tension may act to *increase* pain since the muscles may be more resistant to penetration. For this reason, relaxation exercises prior to or during intercourse may be helpful. Progressive muscle relaxation prior to sexual activity may allow the women to decrease her general bodily levels of tension, while more specific relaxation exercises immediately prior to intercourse (e.g., Kegel's exercises) may help to relax the muscles around the pelvic region and may enhance arousal. Progressive muscle relaxation is discussed in Anxiety Disorders in Chapter 4 and Kegel's exercises are discussed in Section 10.3.2.

Positive self-talk

Once a woman has acquired a number of coping techniques for minimising the likelihood of pain, positive self-talk may be helpful. Such self-talk could involve the woman reminding herself that *she is in control* of the situation and that she will be the one to determine when penetration is to occur and how deep penetration will be. Pain is not inevitable and can be removed or reduced using the strategies outlined in this chapter.

Pelvic congestion syndrome

If deep pain is experienced in the hours or days following intercourse then a likely cause is 'pelvic congestion syndrome', whereby the congestion of blood in the sexual organs causes a dull, throbbing pain which may be similar to pre-menstrual ache (the mechanism is the same). Backache is common as are urinary symptoms and breast tenderness. Congestion may occur if blood accumulates during arousal and an orgasm does not occur, or is not strong enough to allow the congestion to drain away. The specific suggestion for couples in this case is for them to try to ensure the woman achieves orgasm, either through intercourse, masturbation, or a vibrator, so as to alleviate the congestion of blood in the shortest time possible. If orgasm is not achieved, the blood will eventually disperse but may take a number of hours or even days to disperse completely.

Consider expert referral for difficult or persistent cases

Less commonly, the dyspareunia will be vague and intermittent and may be associated with primary orgasmic dysfunction or other sexual dysfunction. Alternatively, the problem may persist despite the use of the strategies outlined in this chapter. In these cases, intensive therapy may be required and hence may need referral to a clinician who has specific expertise in the management of sexual dysfunction.

10.1.3 BASIC ISSUES IN THE MANAGEMENT OF SEXUAL DYSFUNCTION

WHEN TO TREAT AND WHEN TO REFER

Identify problems that require priority in treatment

Although sexual dysfunction may occur in isolation, it is frequently the case that another co-existing problem is contributing to the dysfunction (e.g., relationship difficulties). Alternatively, the individual may have a psychiatric or physical illness that is interfering with his or her sexual abilities and desire (e.g., a depressive disorder or a sexually transmitted disease).

As always, it is important that the initial interview commences with a full psychiatric history. Such a history will allow the clinician to identify any other signs of distress or illness so that important concurrent problems are not missed.

Other problems may need to be addressed before treatment for a sexual dysfunction is commenced such as relationship discord, psychiatric problems (major depression, generalised anxiety, schizophrenia), and physical problems such as neurological impairment, vascular disease, genital health, and drug effects.

Clinician expertise

The clinician needs to make a professional and ethical decision about whether he or she is qualified to treat the individual or whether it is more appropriate to refer the individual to an expert or specialised agency. This decision will be based on a number of factors including the level of expertise required for the presenting problem, and whether or not the clinician feels comfortable talking about sex and has sufficient knowledge about sexual functioning.

THE PLISSIT MODEL OF TREATMENT

The PLISSIT model is a simple graded counselling model that allows all clinicians to intervene to the level of their expertise.

P	=	Permission
LI	=	Limited Information
SS	=	Specific Suggestions
IT	=	Intensive Therapy - usual point of referral

All health care professionals can develop the expertise required to intervene at the first 3 levels of the model. However, intensive therapy will require specialised clinicians who have expertise in the treatment of sexual dysfunction.

Permission. The first level involves allowing the individual to talk about sex, to ask questions, to be anxious, and to see himself or herself as a sexual being. The clinician acknowledges sex to be a normal and acceptable part of a person's life.

Limited Information (sex education). The second level involves the provision of basic information on the topic of sex and sexuality. Many individuals only require reassurance that they are normal. Therefore, sex education including anatomy, arousal, and the male and female sexual response will be the starting point of any intervention.

Specific Suggestions. The next level involves the clinician making direct suggestions that may include directing the individual to work through exercises in a recommended self-help book.

As the PLISSIT model suggests, the majority of sexual counselling is *educational*. It is therefore important that all clinicians who wish to work in this area have a sound knowledge of human sexuality.

FEELING COMFORTABLE TALKING ABOUT SEX

An important factor in the clinician's decision about whether to treat a sexual dysfunction is whether he or she feels comfortable talking about sex. Helen Kaplan, the author of a number of books on sex therapy, has stated that it can take up to two years of full-time work in the area before clinicians can feel truly comfortable addressing all sexual topics.

Discussing sexual dysfunction and other sex-related issues can be embarrassing for both the clinician and the individual. If the clinician appears to be embarrassed then the individual is likely to sense this embarrassment. Adequate practice and experience on the part of the clinician is highly desirable.

Embarrassment on the part of the individual

Some individuals may understandably be embarrassed about admitting that they have a problem with their sexual responses or behaviours. Individuals may feel that they have failed in some way, or that they are abnormal. Additionally, some individuals, especially the elderly, may be embarrassed to admit that they have sexual desires or that they engage in certain sexual behaviours (e.g., masturbation, oral sex). In such cases the clinician's main goal will be to *generalise* and *normalise* the individual's sexual experiences. For example, when first introducing the topic of sex the clinician could say,

"Many people (in your situation/with your condition/following this operation) have sexual worries." Or *"Often people notice that (depression/this medication) affects their sexual relationship/s. Have you noticed any changes?"*

It is also important for the clinician to:
- Be empathic, non-judgmental, and understanding.
- Pre-empt the individual's embarrassment. Acknowledge that it can be difficult talking about such issues. For example, the clinician may say, *"Most people find it difficult to talk about these things and may feel a bit embarrassed. I'd just like to reassure you that everything you say is confidential within this centre and that I'd like to help you if I can. The first step is to find out exactly what's going on so that we can figure out how to make things right again. Please feel free to be open with me and to ask questions along the way."*
- Reassure the individual that sexual dysfunction or adjustment problems are common and that treatment is available. For example, *"It is common for some people to ..."*
- Explain all behaviours or concepts in *plain, clear, specific* terms. Some individuals will not understand the language normally used by clinicians and may feel embarrassed to admit this. When introducing new terms, ensure that alternatives or explanations are always provided.
- Start with general, non-threatening questions first (e.g., *"Do you have a regular partner?"*) then work up to more specific and potentially embarrassing questions (e.g., *"Do you also experience this problem when you masturbate, that is, when you touch or stimulate yourself?"*).
- Never assume anything (e.g., sexual orientation, number of partners, sexual practices).

SHOULD PARTNERS BE INVOLVED IN TREATMENT?

Partner presence in treatment sessions has been found to enhance marital and sexual satisfaction. The presence of the partner also allows the clinician to assess how well the couple interact and communicate with each other. The partner may also provide important information about the sexual problem. Furthermore, since some partners may feel threatened or anxious about an individual's new behaviours following treatment (e.g., a tendency to initiate sex more frequently, greater interest and knowledge in sex), the inclusion of the partner in all or some of the treatment sessions will help to reduce potential threat and conflict and increase co-operation and support.

In all situations in which the partner does not wish to or cannot attend treatment sessions, it is recommended that, if possible, the clinician has at least one interview with the partner during the assessment phase. It is often worthwhile interviewing the couple together and then chatting briefly with the partner alone. This interview will be helpful for understanding the partner's view of the problem (e.g., attitudes to intervention, the extent of likely co-operation) and the extent of clear communication and conflict between the couple. This interview will also allow both partners to understand and agree upon treatment goals.

Treatment of individuals without partners

Individuals who present with sexual difficulties and who do not have a partner would perhaps be assessed from a different perspective. That is, is the sexual dysfunction simply one example of a general difficulty the individual experiences in establishing and maintaining a relationship? If an individual has recently lost a partner, either through death or separation, assessment would also cover grief reactions. Alternatively, an individual may have experienced a sexual difficulty in a previous relationship but does not currently have a partner or is dating casually.

While there is little support of efficacy, the treatment of individuals who do not have partners is usually brief individual counselling (including a strong educational component) and specific strategies adapted for individuals (e.g., masturbation exercises using the 'stop-start' technique for premature ejaculation). The practical, ethical and legal problems associated with the use of partner surrogates remain unresolved.

10.1.4 TAKING A SEXUAL HISTORY

Taking a sexual history is a specific aspect of general history taking. It will be important to gain a broad understanding of the context of an individual's sexual problem as well as a detailed understanding of the problem itself.

The following guidelines may be useful:
- If a couple has presented together, gather the information for a sexual history from each individual separately (i.e., not in each other's presence).
- Assume the individual has little knowledge of technical terms or of physiological/biological aspects of sex.
- Make sure the individual understands all the terms you are using. If there is any doubt, get the individual to explain his or her understanding of what you mean. The use of anatomical drawings can be very useful (see Section 10.3.3).
- Aim to use neutral language (as opposed to vulgar language) and proper medical terms as long as they are in common usage (e.g., use 'penis' and 'vagina', but perhaps 'lips' rather than 'labia').
- Attempt to get as detailed a description as possible of the individual's problem.

The following areas are important to consider when taking a sexual history:
- Personal and sexual history including the current relationship, early sexual development and experience, and religious and cultural beliefs.
- Medical and psychiatric history including illnesses and operations, mental disorders, and current and recent medication.
- Drug and alcohol use
- The nature and development of the presenting problem

Some useful questions are listed on the following pages.

NATURE AND DEVELOPMENT OF THE PROBLEM

- Is there a problem? Make sure that the 'problem' does not just reflect a lack of knowledge or unrealistic expectations on the part of the presenting individual.
- When and how did the problem begin?
- Did anything noteworthy happen at that time to cause the problem? (e.g., other problems within the relationship, family problems, working too hard, a new job, major life change, financial difficulties, marriage, pregnancy or childbirth).
- What course has the problem taken since it started?
- What factors make the problem worse? (e.g., stress, feelings of depression, medication)
- What factors make the problem better?
- Has the individual tried to solve the problem for himself or herself? How effective have these attempts been?
- What effect has the problem had on the individual's partner or relationship?
- What has prompted the individual to ask for help with this problem *now*?
- If appropriate, the nature and effect of any previous treatment.

CURRENT SEXUAL RELATIONSHIP/S

- Does the individual have a regular sexual partner?
- How did the individual meet his or her current partner?
- What happened the first time the individual had sex with his or her current partner? For example, What led up to the sexual activity? Who initiated the sexual activity? What was the individual's emotional and sexual response? What was the partner's emotional and sexual response? Was the sexual relationship satisfying at any time? Were there any problems early in the sexual relationship?
- What is the individual's current level of sexual activity? Does he or she masturbate?
- How often does the individual actually engage in sexual activity with a partner? Who usually initiates this activity?
- How does the individual describe his or her feelings about a typical sexual encounter (e.g., satisfying, boring, embarrassing, painful, stressful, routine, upsetting). Why does the individual feel this way?
- Is the individual able to communicate with his or her partner about sex? When there are sexual problems, how does the partner respond?
- What is the relationship like apart from the sexual difficulties? For example, affection, arguments, social interests, or friends; Have pregnancy, childbirth, or children affected the relationship? Is the individual committed to the relationship? Is the partner committed to the relationship?
- Is the individual or his or her partner having sex with others?

EARLY SEXUAL DEVELOPMENT AND EXPERIENCE

- At what age was the onset of puberty? For example, in women, how old was the individual when her periods started? Was the individual prepared for this at the time? Can the individual remember how she felt at the time? In men, how old was the individual when he first ejaculated or experienced a wet dream? Was he prepared? What was his reaction at the time?

- Does the individual know (or have an idea about) whether his or her parents have a good sexual relationship? How do the individual's parents express their feelings or attitudes about sex? How do family members show affection?

- Where did the individual learn about sex? Does the individual think their knowledge is adequate?

- When and how did the individual find out about masturbation?

- Were there any upsetting sexually-related events in childhood? (e.g., being caught and shamed in sexual experimentation, exposure to exhibitionism, sexual abuse).

- When did the individual first become sexually attracted to someone? When did the individual have his or her first relationship? When did the individual have his or her first sexual experience? What was that like at the time? Have there been any problems with subsequent sexual experiences before now?

LACK OR LOSS OF SEXUAL DESIRE

- Has the individual completely lost interest in sex, or is he or she sometimes interested? How often does the individual feel the urge to engage in sexual activity? How often does the individual actually engage in sexual activity?

- How often has the individual wanted to engage in sex in the past? (Note any sudden decrease in interest and find out what was happening in the individual's life at the time).

- How frequently does the individual's partner express interest in engaging in sexual activity? Has the partner's interest increased or decreased recently? How does the individual respond when his or her partner wants to have sex?

- Is the lack of desire related only to the individual's current partner or does the individual experience a total loss of interest? Ask about sexual desire in response to sexual day dreams or fantasies (e.g., making love to a stranger); masturbation; attraction to other people; and watching erotic movies, looking at erotic pictures, or reading erotic stories.

- Is the lack of sexual desire an isolated problem or is it associated with other problems? For example, feelings of depression; feeling tired or low in energy; not enjoying things in general; physical illness; medication side effects; consumption of large amounts of alcohol or other drugs such as marijuana or narcotics; a major life event.

- Is the lack of sexual desire associated with pregnancy or childbirth?

- Is the lack of desire associated with changes in the individual's relationship? For example, loss of affection; partner not physically attractive; fights or rows.

- How frequently would the individual like to have sex if he or she did not have this problem? To what extent does the individual wish to increase sexual activity for the benefit of the partner?

Note

For this dysfunction to be diagnosed and treated it must first be clear that there is actually a problem with the individual's level of *desire*. It is important to determine whether the individual's desire is simply directed towards some*one* or some*thing* other than the regular partner or expected gender category. It must also be clear that it is actually *desire* that is decreased not performance ability. Finally it is important to determine whether desire is present but is simply not being *expressed*. The reason for the lack of expression of desire is also important. The following questions will need to be considered by the clinician:

- Is loss of sexual desire the *main* sexual dysfunction or is there another underlying problem? (e.g., erectile dysfunction, anorgasmia, marital conflict)
- What is the individual's definition of sexual desire? Some individuals confuse sexual desire with sexual 'ability' (i.e., ability to have an erection or an orgasm). Desire may be present even if genital responsiveness is absent.
- If the level of desire is low, is the level of desire inhibited by some factor or is it normal for this individual?
- Is there truly a lack of *desire* for sex or merely a fear or reluctance to openly *express* desire, perhaps for fear of being rejected or being labelled as 'oversexed'?
- Is desire present but not acted upon or expressed due to an effort to control the other person by using sex as a bargaining tool?
- Is the presenting problem that one partner desires sex much more frequently than the other partner? A partner who desires sex every day or two may view the index individual who only wants sex once a week as having an abnormally low sex drive. By contrast, if both partners only desire sex once a fortnight, no problem regarding sexual desire is likely to be reported. Therefore, low sexual desire within a relationship can also be viewed as the other partner's *higher* sexual desire. The disorder can really only be diagnosed if the index individual (and not the partner) expresses dissatisfaction with his or her own level of sexual desire.

SEXUAL AVERSION OR LACK OF SEXUAL ENJOYMENT

- What did the individual learn about sex when he or she was growing up? What was discussed? What attitudes did his or her parents have about sexuality? What effect did these attitudes have on the individual? How did the individual's parents express emotion?
- Has the individual had unpleasant experiences with sex? (e.g., sexual assault, sexual abuse, dyspareunia).
- How does the individual feel when his or her partner initiates sex? (e.g., angry, afraid of failure, resignation or indifference, disgust).
- How does the partner feel about the individual's responses?
- Is there anything that makes sex particularly unpleasant or difficult? (e.g., partner's hygiene, possible interruptions, tiredness, other sexual dysfunctions).

FAILURE OF GENITAL RESPONSE

Erectile dysfunction in men

- Has the individual *ever* been able to achieve an erection? (i.e., is the problem primary or secondary?).
- Are there circumstances under which erection can currently occur? (i.e., is the problem total or situational?). If so, under what circumstances does erection occur? (e.g., during the night, upon wakening, when masturbating, with erotic magazines or videos).
- Does the problem occur with all sexual partners?

- If erection does occur, is it full or partial? (Information from the partner will be important). Are there any abnormalities in the shape of the erection? What happens when the individual begins sexual activity with a partner? Who initiates sexual activity and how? Does the individual begin to get an erection at all? What happens to the erection? How long does the erection last?
- Is there any influence of medications, alcohol, or chronic illness?

Women under the age of 45:
- What happens when sexual activity is initiated? Does the individual become sexually aroused?
- Is there a lack or loss of sexual desire?

Women over the age of 45:
- Is the individual menopausal (i.e., could vaginal dryness be caused by an oestrogen deficiency?)

ORGASMIC DYSFUNCTION
- Has the individual *ever* experienced an orgasm or ejaculation? (i.e., is the problem primary or secondary?)
- If male, how long does it take to ejaculate following stimulation or following penetration?
- If female, how long does it take to achieve orgasm following stimulation?
- By which methods can the individual ejaculate or achieve an orgasm? For example, intercourse, manual stimulation from partner, oral stimulation, masturbation, during sleep.
- Does the individual become sexually aroused during periods of sexual activity?
- Is there enough or appropriate stimulation from his or her partner?
- Does the individual ever feel close to orgasm?
- Is anxiety (or another emotion) associated with arousal?
- Does the individual use sexual fantasies during sexual activity?

PREMATURE EJACULATION
- When does ejaculation occur? (e.g., shortly after stimulation commences, immediately after penetration).
- If penetration occurs, how long does it take from the time the individual inserts his penis to the time he ejaculates? Has the delay shortened in time?
- What is the individual's level of satisfaction? How satisfied is his partner? How does his partner react?
- Does the individual ever have to ask his partner to stop touching his penis because he is about to ejaculate?
- How long would the individual like to last before ejaculation? How long would his partner like him to last?
- Has the individual always experienced early ejaculation? What were the individual's early sexual experiences like? (e.g., What partner and situations? Was there a need for rapid ejaculation? What were the individual's emotional responses?)
- How were the individual's early experiences of masturbation? (e.g., guilt, secrecy, need for speedy ejaculation, emotional responses).
- What attempts are made to delay ejaculation? (e.g., distracting thoughts, alcohol).
- What makes premature ejaculation worse? (e.g., tiredness, long or short stimulation, a new partner).
- Is the individual's partner orgasmic by intercourse or other stimulation?

NONORGANIC VAGINISMUS

- What happens when sexual activity is initiated? Does the woman become aroused? Does she become lubricated?
- What happens if penetration is attempted? What is the response of the pelvic floor muscles? Is the woman or her partner aware of muscle spasm? Is there pain? Where does pain occur? Is vaginal penetration ever possible during intercourse?
- Has it been possible for the woman or her partner to insert a finger into the vagina? The woman to insert a tampon? The woman to be vaginally examined by a doctor?
- How does the partner react when the woman's muscles go into a spasm?
- Have there been any unpleasant sexual experiences or precipitating events For example, shame or guilt following sexual experimentation; shame or guilt following exposure to pornography; intrusive medical procedures (e.g., episiotomy); vaginal infection; sexual assault

NONORGANIC DYSPAREUNIA

- Where is the pain? (e.g., for women, at the entrance or deep in the vagina?)
- What type of pain is it? (e.g., sharp, stinging, dull ache).
- Is there evidence of vaginal infection? (e.g., discharge, itch, odour).
- Has there been trauma to the vagina? (e.g., rape, childbirth, episiotomy).
- Is there evidence of urinary tract infection (e.g., pain on passing urine, or dark urine)?
- Is there pain on intercourse even when the individual is sexually aroused?

10.1.5 SEX EDUCATION

The majority of sexual counselling work and the first step in the treatment of any sexual dysfunction is education. The aims of education are to:

1. Normalise the individual's experiences (i.e., help the individual realise that there are many others who have the same needs, problems, and experiences).
2. Reduce anxiety about sex. It will be important to:
   - Provide accurate information about arousal and normal sexual response
   - Dispel sexual myths
   - Dispel unrealistic expectations

Material that can be used by clinicians is outlined on the following pages and covers the following topics:
- The female sexual response cycle
- The male sexual response cycle
- Important information for couples
- Overcoming sexual myths

Handouts featuring diagrams of normal male and female anatomy are found in Section 10.3.3. There are also a number of useful self-help paperbacks listed at the end of this chapter.

THE FEMALE SEXUAL RESPONSE CYCLE

There are a number of distinct phases in the female sexual response cycle. These phases are discussed below.

Desire

Sexual desire refers to fantasies and thoughts about sex, or to the 'urge' to engage in sexual activity. Such experiences typically lead to sexual arousal, although it is possible that physical signs of sexual arousal may occur first and lead to subjective feelings of desire. The frequency or intensity with which an individual likes to participate in sexual activity may be referred to as the individual's sex drive. In both females and males, sexual desire is controlled to some extent by androgen hormones in the blood stream (the hormones, including testosterone, that are responsible for male characteristics). However, environmental and psychological factors (such as thinking about one's partner, or seeing sexy underwear) are also important. In other words, desire is influenced by a willingness to engage in sex and also by biological drive. Desire for sex differs from one individual to the next, although some individuals are clearly distressed by their excessively high or low sexual desire.

Excitement

In the excitement stage the individual begins to develop the following noticeable feelings and signs of sexual arousal.

- A general bodily reaction occurs in which muscle tension increases and blood accumulates in the vessels.
- The labia minora (the inner set of lips around the vagina) increase in size and separate during the excitement phase.
- The accumulation of blood in the vessels of the genitalia causes droplets of a fluid substance to pass through the vaginal wall (the fluid is called a transudate). This fluid is secreted on the inner vaginal lining and marks the beginning of vaginal lubrication. The vagina also begins to darken and redden in colour.
- The clitoris enlarges in size during this phase. The enlargement may or may not be obvious to the human eye.
- The uterus also becomes engorged with blood and rises from its resting position. As the uterus rises a ballooning of the vagina occurs, thus giving the vagina greater length and width to accommodate the penis.

Arousal may wax and wane during the excitement stage and may differ slightly in pattern, intensity, or rapidity from one individual to the next, and from one occasion to the next.

Plateau

During the plateau stage, the accumulation of blood in the genitals reaches a maximum.

- The labia minora become pink, bright red, or deep wine in colour. Generally, the colour is darker and deeper among women who have given birth. Also, the more sexually aroused the individual, the more dramatic is the colour change. Masters and Johnson report that no woman has been known to have an orgasm in the absence of a clearly noticeable colour change in the labia minora.
- The vagina deepens further in colour to a deep red or purple and increases slightly more in length and width.
- During this phase the clitoris retracts back under its hood if stimulation is continued. If the level of stimulation falls the clitoris re-emerges.
- There is a further rise of the uterus.
- There is a marked increase in muscular tension throughout the body.

Orgasm

The female orgasm involves involuntary rhythmic contractions (every 0.8 seconds) of the muscles around the vagina (especially the lower third of the vagina) and the pelvic region. A single orgasm may involve anywhere from 2 to 15 contractions and as such is generally longer in duration than an orgasm in a male. The uterus and rectal sphincter may also contract during the orgasmic phase, and the clitoris retracts under its hood. The orgasm may last for a few seconds or, if sexual stimulation continues, further orgasms may be experienced immediately. (It is interesting to note that males do not generally have repeated or multiple orgasms but usually require a break of anywhere from a few minutes up to a few hours before orgasm can be achieved again). The quality or intensity of the female orgasm may differ according to how the orgasm was achieved. Generally, masturbation or a vibrator produce the most intense orgasms while orgasms experienced during intercourse alone tend to be of a lower intensity.

Resolution phase

During this phase there is a reversal of the bodily changes that occurred during the previous phases. Within about 5-10 seconds the clitoris returns to its normal position and within 10-15 seconds the labia minora return to their usual colour. It may take 10-15 minutes for the vagina and clitoris to return to their normal size and colour and for the uterus to descend to its regular position. If orgasm has not occurred it may take considerably longer, even hours, for all tumescence (swelling) to subside.

Other bodily reactions

Listed below are a number of other changes that occur in the body during the sexual response cycle.

- The female breast enlarges in size, the nipples become erect, and the pattern of veins on the breast becomes more obvious. However, women who have breast-fed may not experience much of an increase in breast size.
- A sex-flush or 'rash' appears across the chest, back, neck, or face in about 75% of women during orgasm and disappears quickly immediately after orgasm.
- A generalised spasm of various muscle groups (including the rectal sphincter) occurs during the orgasmic phase.
- Hyperventilation (overbreathing) begins late in the plateau stage and continues into the orgasmic phase.
- Heart rate and blood pressure increase immediately after the onset of sexual stimulation and rise further as the level of arousal increases.
- Immediately following orgasm, perspiration may develop on the hands and feet or over the entire body, regardless of the amount of physical exertion.

THE MALE SEXUAL RESPONSE CYCLE

Males experience the same phases of sexual response as do females. Each of these phases will be discussed in turn below.

Desire

The basics of the desire phase are described under the female sexual response cycle are equally applicable to males. In males, sexual desire decreases slightly with increasing age. It is not clear, however, whether this decrease in desire is related to the gradual decline of circulating hormones in the blood stream.

Excitement

In the excitement phase the individual begins to develop the following noticeable feelings and signs of sexual arousal.

- The first physiological sign of sexual excitement is penile erection in which the length, diameter, and firmness of the penis increases markedly. During erection there is a retraction of the foreskin. In a prolonged excitement phase the erection may be partially lost and rapidly regained numerous times. A sudden change in temperature, noise, lighting, or a surprise occurrence may cause immediate partial or complete deflation of the penis.
- A general bodily reaction occurs in which muscle tension increases and blood accumulates in the vessels.
- The scrotal sac contracts causing decreased movement of the testicles within. The intricate patterns of scrotal folds are rapidly lost as tension in the scrotum increases.
- Shortening of the spermatic cords causes the testicles to be partially elevated towards the body. If sexual stimulation continues for 5-10 minutes the testes may relax despite the maintenance of sexual excitement since the muscular tension cannot continue uninterrupted for long periods of time. Other factors such as fear, anger, and cold weather may also produce similar elevation of the testes.

Arousal may wax and wane during the excitement phase and may differ slightly in pattern, intensity, or rapidity from one individual to the next, and from one occasion to the next.

Plateau

In the plateau phase, the accumulation of blood in the genitals reaches a maximum.

- The penis increases further in diameter and the colour of the penis may change to a mottled reddish-purple colour.
- The testes become more elevated so that they are situated tightly against the body. If the testes do not elevate sufficiently, full ejaculatory response does not occur. The testes also increase in size, anywhere from 50-100%. Generally, the longer the individual remains in the plateau stage, the more obvious is the increase in testicular size.

Orgasm

Two separate stages can be identified during the orgasm phase - emission and ejaculation. During the emission stage, the vas deferens, seminal vesicles, and ejaculating ducts contract to place semen at the entrance of the urethra. The internal sphincter of the urethra contracts to prevent backwards ejaculation of semen into the bladder.

Ejaculation involves involuntary rhythmic contractions (every 0.8 seconds) of the penile urethra and the muscles in and around the penis. These contractions cause seminal fluid to be ejaculated under pressure from the penile urethra. After an initial 3 or 4 major contractions, the contractions become irregular and weak for several seconds. The rectal sphincter may also contract at this time.

Resolution

During this phase there is a reversal of the bodily changes that occurred during the earlier phases of the sexual response cycle.

- The penis may return to its pre-ejaculatory state very rapidly if the individual removes himself from all stimulation or attempts to urinate. However, if penetration continues or the male remains in close proximity to his partner, the penis usually takes considerably longer to become completely flaccid.

- There is a decrease in tension and contraction of the scrotal sac. Some men experience rapid relaxation of the scrotum while others may not experience full relaxation of the scrotum for a number of hours.
- The testes decrease in size and drop back to their normal, lower position. As with the scrotal sac, some men experience a rapid return to their normal state while others experience a greater delay.

The beginning of the resolution phase is called the refractory period. A male cannot be re-stimulated to a level of high sexual excitement or orgasm until the refractory period has terminated. The refractory period is maintained until the male's arousal level has decreased to the phase of low-excitement. In young males the refractory period (or the time taken to return to the low-excitement phase) may be only a matter of minutes while in older men the refractory period may have a duration of a few hours or even days. Because of the existence of a refractory period, males are unable to have multiple orgasms in quick succession.

Other bodily reactions

A number of other changes occur in the body during the sexual response cycle, these are similar to those that occur in women.

IMPORTANT INFORMATION FOR COUPLES

- Educate both partners about the wide variation in the extent and frequency of feelings of sexual desire from one individual to the next.
- Educate both partners about the importance of the timing of sex. The time of day that suits one partner may not suit the other.
- Help the couple plan their time so that they have regular blocks of time alone in which to relax, enjoy each other's company, and engage in sexual play if desired. It may be necessary to hire a baby-sitter, spend less time with friends, or maybe even put a lock on the bedroom door. Going to bed early and getting up early the next day may be one solution.
- Educate partners about how to refuse sex diplomatically.
- Educate both partners that sex will sometimes be refused and that the refusal is not necessarily an insult or a personal rebuff. It is simply unreasonable to expect that both partners should always feel like sex at the same time.
- If culturally appropriate, encourage partners to accept the use of masturbation or manual stimulation if sexual advances are refused. Remind couples that masturbation does not represent a lack of love or desire for one's partner.
- Assist shy or reluctant partners with learning to initiate sex more frequently. Clear communication between partners will be necessary.
- Educate couples about the fact that sexual desire levels fluctuate over the life span.
- Discuss how sexual desire can be easily affected by physical and psychological factors. Desire can also be significantly influenced by the behaviour of each partner (see Section 10.3.1).
- Encourage partners to communicate their own needs for desire and sexual arousal.
- Encourage partners to show each other what sort of stimulation is required for orgasm to occur (e.g., manual or oral stimulation).
- Educate males that some females may be able to have multiple orgasms (especially if a vibrator is used) and hence may sometimes find it pleasurable if genital stimulation is continued after the initial orgasm.

- Encourage partners to talk about what kinds of caresses they do and do not like immediately before, during, or after orgasm (e.g., genital stimulation after orgasm may be unpleasant).
- One commonly asked question is, *"How do I know if I've had an orgasm?"*. Generally, it can be explained that prior to an orgasm there is a build-up of tension and sexual excitement, which is following by a release of tension during orgasm. After orgasm there is a general feeling of relaxation and an absence of any feelings of annoyance about the discontinuation of stimulation.

What constitutes a 'normal' amount of sexual desire?

The desire for sex differs from one individual to the next, and may even differ within an individual from one month to the next depending on life circumstances. Some individuals may desire sex every day while others may only desire sex once a fortnight or once a month. These frequencies represent a normal and healthy range of sexual desire. Sexual desire is influenced by many factors.

For example, things that will increase sexual desire include a new romance, courtship, and erotic stimuli. Things that will decrease sexual desire include children, negative life events, illness, fatigue, depression, anxiety, and pregnancy.

Section 10.3.1 lists some common triggers that may cause problems with sexual functioning. It may be helpful for individuals to read through this list so as to help them identify any factors that may trigger sexual problems. Strategies can then be devised to minimise the influence of such factors.

Sexual desire and pregnancy

Sexual desire may decrease in the last few months of pregnancy. The cause of the decrease is unclear but may involve numerous factors including psychological causes (e.g., fear of hurting the unborn child, a decrease in perceived sexual attractiveness), physical discomfort, or fatigue. Lack of desire may continue into the first few months of the postnatal period. In addition, the increase in the prolactin hormone during breast-feeding can decrease both desire and lubrication.

Problems with initiation and refusal of sex

One of the most common sexual problems is that one partner tries on many occasions to initiate sexual activity while the other partner repeatedly refuses to participate. Given time, the initiating partner learns not to ask for sex because the requests are never successful. He or she may then become angry, frustrated, insulted, may experience a deflated self-concept, and may begin to feel sexually undesirable. This partner may also become distant, less affectionate, and physical contact may decrease.

It will be important in this situation for the clinician to elicit the cause of the refusal. Having determined the cause, further information may be obtained so as to work out how the problem may best be tackled. Some possible causes of refusal are listed below.

- The initiating partner's timing is unsuitable
- The refusing partner is unwell or stressed (physically or mentally)
- The refusing partner is withholding sex as a means of punishment
- The refusing partner is no longer attracted to the initiating partner
- Sexual interaction is unpleasant or unsatisfying for the refusing partner
- The refusing partner does not want sex as often

Management strategies will depend on the exact cause of the refusal but may include:
- Communication skills training (getting individuals to tell each other what they like – see Core Management Skills in Chapter 1)
- Using new techniques to enhance desire and arousal

- Training in structured problem solving (to assist the couple with finding solutions to new problems when they arise – see Core Management Skills in Chapter 1)
- Increased use of masturbation for the initiating (refused) partner
- The use of manual or oral stimulation by the refusing partner as an alternative to intercourse.
- A change of timing of sexual initiation
- Encouraging the refusing partner to initiate sex when the timing is suitable
- Education about the sexual response cycle and associated issues

Disagreements about sexual activities

Couples sometimes disagree about the kinds of sexual activity in which they will engage (e.g., oral sex). Individuals should never be forced to engage in sexual activities which are uncomfortable or distressing. However, individuals may refuse to engage in certain activities for a variety of reasons, some of which may be unnecessarily rigid. For example, an individual may refuse to have intercourse during a woman's menstrual cycle in the belief that to do so would be messy or unhygienic. Or, the individual may not want to engage in oral sex with a partner because he or she was taught from childhood that the genitals are 'dirty'. Others may feel like perverts if they view erotic movies or magazines.

Sometimes individuals may simply need reassurance that particular behaviours are common and that there is no 'right' or 'wrong'. In other words, they may need to be given 'permission to experiment' with the understanding that it is all right to stop whenever the activity becomes uncomfortable.

OVERCOMING SEXUAL MYTHS

For some individuals, inappropriate sexual beliefs or myths can cause problems within a relationship. Individuals acquire expectations about what sex should be like and how they or their partner should behave. Some of the following myths apply equally to both men and women, while others will be more relevant to one gender than the other. One of the components of education will be to help the individual and his or her partner alter any sexual beliefs that interfere with the individual's enjoyment of sex. The handout in Section 10.3.4 discusses some commonly-held sexual myths.

10.1.6 TREATMENT OF SEXUAL DYSFUNCTION IN THE MULTI-CULTURAL SETTING

Much of the work in the development of treatment strategies for sexual dysfunction has been based on culturally homogenous Western populations. Clinicians will need to be aware of different beliefs and attitudes towards sexual behaviour, and particular care will need to be taken when the clinician and the couple are each from different cultural groups. There may also be major differences within cultural groups; for example, between sexes and social classes.

In a multicultural setting it is not appropriate for the clinician to try to 'demythologise' different cultural beliefs and impose another set of beliefs. The clinician's beliefs will not necessarily be more 'normal' than the individual's beliefs. Instead it will be important that any management strategies *incorporate* rather than *undermine* existing cultural belief systems. Some strategies may have to be modified considerably. The best approach is to ask the client to explain how sexual behaviour is viewed in their specific culture.

10.1.7 SEXUAL FUNCTIONING IN THE ELDERLY

It is a commonly held myth that elderly people do not have sexual desires, are not sexually desirable, and are not sexually capable. While sexual responsiveness may change with age, the majority of individuals (in the absence of organic problems and significant cognitive impairment) are capable of responding sexually and of experiencing arousal and orgasm throughout their lives. The majority of couples will continue to engage in sexual activity. More often, what is lacking is the *opportunity* for sex, particularly if the older individual lives in residential care or with an extended family, or if he or she does not have a partner.

CHANGES IN DESIRE WITH AGE

Some people incorrectly assume that once a woman passes menopause she loses interest in sex. There is, however, no factual basis for this belief. It is widely accepted that the hormone largely responsible for sexual desire in women is testosterone, not oestrogen. Therefore, when a woman goes through menopause and ceases to produce oestrogen, this bodily change has no direct bearing on her level of sexual desire. While it is possible that the frequency or satisfaction of sexual activity may diminish in response to symptoms associated with menopause and ageing (e.g., vaginal dryness, pain caused from arthritis), increased age and menopause per se may not in themselves cause a direct reduction in sexual desire. It is often a woman's *attitude* to ageing and menopause (i.e., psychological factors) that is more likely to be associated with any reduction in sex drive.

Among men there does tend to be a gradual decrease in sex drive with increasing age. There is also a gradual decline in testosterone levels. However, it is not clear whether the changing testosterone level accounts for the slight reduction in sex drive. Regardless, elderly men may certainly possess strong sexual desires. Whether they act on their sexual desires may depend on such issues as psychological factors, the availability of partners, physical health, and so on.

CHANGES IN SEXUAL RESPONDING WITH AGE

In men, there is usually an increased time to achieve a full erection and an increase in duration of the refractory phase. In women, a number of physical changes may accompany menopause. Genital changes include reduced size of clitoral, vulvar and labial tissue and some loss of elasticity and thinning of the vaginal wall. In addition there may be a lack of lubrication or it may take longer for lubrication to occur, which may lead to painful intercourse.

CHANGES IN SEXUAL ACTIVITY WITH AGE

The type of sexual activity tends to change with increasing age. While intercourse tends to decrease, sexual behaviours such as touching, caressing, masturbation, and the use of fantasy become more important. Older people are often unwilling to talk about sexual problems and may need to be asked specifically about them.

MANAGEMENT OF SEXUAL PROBLEMS AND DYSFUNCTION IN THE ELDERLY

The management of sexual dysfunction will be similar to that for other age groups and will include the following issues:

- Education, particularly if the problem is based on misinformation or unrealistic expectations. For example, if individuals are uninformed about the normality of changes with age then apprehension about these changes may lead to anxiety which then may in turn interfere with sexual functioning. Elderly individuals may also believe certain myths (such as the belief that elderly people do not have sex) which may need to be challenged.

- Treatment goals should be in line with the individual's age (e.g., taking into account the increased time to become aroused).
- 'Older' attitudes and values may need to be taken into account (e.g., masturbation or oral sex may be unacceptable).
- Differences in health, or sensory and cognitive functioning may need to be taken into account. For example, information may need to be given more slowly and repeated more often. Written instructions may need to be used more often, and it may be necessary to suggest alternative sexual practices or positions so as to manage pain or restriction of movement.

10.2 BIBLIOGRAPHY

American Psychiatric Association (1994). *Diagnostic and Statistical Manual of Mental Disorders (4th ed.)*. Washington D.C.: American Psychiatric Press.

Andersen, B.L. (1983). Primary orgasmic dysfunction: diagnostic considerations and review of treatment. *Psychological Bulletin*, *93*, 105-136.

D'Ardenne, P. (1986). Sexual dysfunction in a transcultural setting: assessment, treatment and research. *Sexual and Marital Therapy*, *1*, 23-34.

Hawton, K. (1985). *Sex Therapy: A Practical Guide*. Oxford: Oxford University Press.

Masters, W.H. & Johnson, V.E. (1966). *Human Sexual Response*. New York: Bantam Books.

Masters, W.H. & Johnson, V.E. (1980). *Human Sexual Inadequacy*. New York: Bantam Books.

Munjack, D.J. & Oziel, L.J. (1980). *Sexual Medicine and Counseling in Office Practice: A Comprehensive Treatment Guide*. Boston: Little, Brown and Company.

Ross, M.W. & Channon-Little, L.D. (1991). *Discussing Sexuality: A Guide For Health Practitioners*. Sydney: MacLennan & Petty Pty Limited.

Spence, S.H. (1991). *Psychosexual Therapy: A Cognitive-Behavioural Approach*. London: Chapman & Hall.

World Health Organisation (1992). *ICD-10 Classification of Mental and Behavioural Disorders: clinical descriptions and diagnostic guidelines*. Geneva: World Health Organisation.

Recommended self-help paperbacks

Heiman, J., LoPiccolo, L. & LoPiccolo, J. (1976). *Becoming Orgasmic: A Sexual Growth Program For Women*. New Jersey: Prentice-Hall Inc.

Kaplan, H.S. (1989). *How to Overcome Premature Ejaculation*. New York: Brunner/Mazel.

Llewellyn-Jones, D. (1982). *Everywoman: A Gynaecological Guide For Life*. London: Faber & Faber.

Llewellyn-Jones, D. (1986). *EveryMan*. Oxford: Oxford University Press.

Pertot, S. (1994). *A Commonsense Guide to Sex*. Sydney: Harper Collins Publishers.

Valins, L. (1992). *When a Woman's Body Says No to Sex*. Ringwood, Vic.: Penguin.

Williams, W. (1985). *It's Up To You*. Sydney: Maclennan & Petty.

Williams, W. (1986). *Man, Woman & Sexual Desire: Self-Help for Men and Women with Deficient or Incompatible Sexual Drives or Interests*. Sydney: Williams & Wilkins.

Wolfe, J. (1992). *What To Do When He Has a Headache*. Thersons.

Zilbergeld, B. (1980). *Men and Sex*. London: Fontana.

Videos for individuals and clinicians

LoPiccolo, J. & Friedman, J. (1980). *Treating erectile problems*. NY: Focus International.

LoPiccolo, J (1993). *Becoming Orgasmic. A Personal and Sexual Growth Program for Women*. NY: Focus International.

LoPiccolo, J. (1984). *Treating Vaginismus*. NY: Focus International.

10.3 RESOURCE MATERIALS

10.3.1 COMMON TRIGGERS OF SEXUAL PROBLEMS

Psychological factors

- An unsatisfactory relationship
- High levels of life stress or anxiety
- Sexual performance anxiety (caused by having a new partner or a sexual dysfunction)
- Depression
- Excessive monitoring one's own level of arousal during intercourse or the partner's level of arousal
- Guilt about having a sexual relationship (e.g., being under-age, conflict with religious beliefs)
- Self-doubt or low self-esteem
- Fear of pregnancy
- Fear of catching an STD
- A previous negative sexual experience such as rape or child sexual assault
- Lack of knowledge about sexuality and sexual responses

Situational / environmental factors

- Fear of interruptions (e.g., children bursting into the room, parents coming home)
- Guilt about the situation (e.g., partner is under-age, married to someone else)
- Discomfort (e.g., cramped position, hard surface)

Physical factors

- Side effects of medications
- Use of alcohol and other drugs
- Difficulties because of physical illness (e.g., a chronic back problem, haemorrhoids)
- Feeling run down and tired
- Recent childbirth

Factors associated with the partner

- A partner of the non-preferred sex
- A partner who is physically unappealing (e.g., too fat or thin, pimples, body odour)
- A disinterested partner, or a partner who is critical, inconsiderate, or reacts to sexual or other difficulties in a negative and blaming manner
- A partner who is sexually inexperienced or with poor sexual technique
- A partner who prefers sexual activities that are unappealing to the individual (e.g., anal sex, oral sex)

10.3.2 KEGEL'S EXERCISES

Kegel's exercises are simply exercises of the pelvic floor muscle. This muscle can be identified by stopping your urine flow (only do this once or twice to find the right muscle). Try contracting the muscle again. You may not feel the contraction at first, but practice will help the exercise to become routine.

The exercise

1. Contract and relax the muscle as quickly as possible while continuing to breath normally.
2. Contract the muscle, hold for a count of three, then relax, breathing normally.
3. Contract the muscle slowly while counting to three, pulling the muscle upwards with the intake of breath. When you have tightened the pelvic floor, hold to the count of three, then relax the muscle gradually to the count of three.
4. When the muscle is relaxed, on the count of three bear down as if you are trying to push something out of your vagina.

How often should the exercise be practised?

Practise the exercises for a few minutes every day. Exercises 1 and 2 should initially be carried out ten times each, building up to 30 times each over 4-6 weeks. Exercises 3 and 4 should initially be carried out five times each, working up to 20 times each over 4-6 weeks.

10.3.3 MALE AND FEMALE SEXUAL ANATOMY

FEMALE SEXUAL ANATOMY (external)

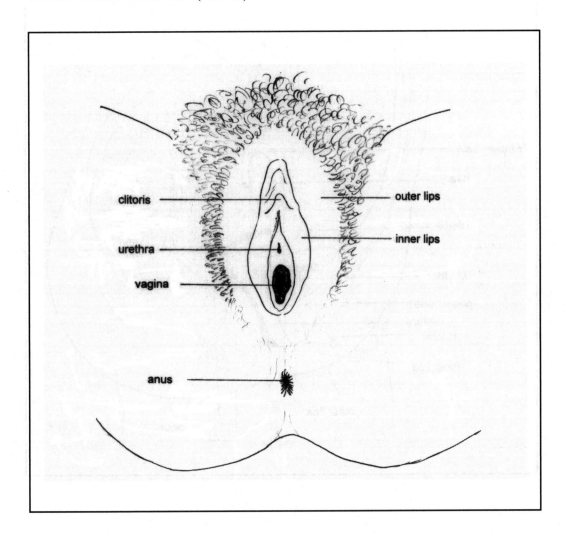

FEMALE SEXUAL ANATOMY (internal)

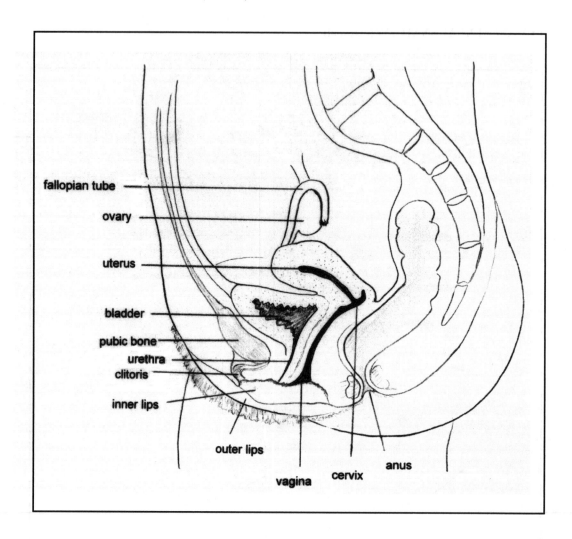

MALE SEXUAL ANATOMY (internal and external)

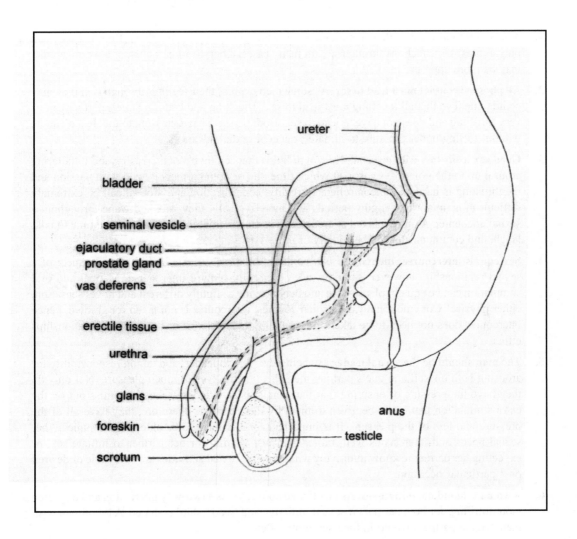

10.3.4 COMMON SEXUAL MYTHS

1. **Men should not express their emotions.** As a result of this myth, some men find that they can only express their feelings through sex. In many cases, a heart-to-heart chat, or a warm cuddle, may be more appropriate.

2. **All physical contact must lead to sex.** As some men express their feelings through sex, they may come to believe that all touching must lead to sex. Touching and cuddling one's partner can be very fulfilling and does not have to lead to sex. Both partners have the right to touch and cuddle without feeling under pressure to initiate or accept sexual advances.

3. **Good sex leads to a wild orgasm.** This myth holds that sex involves increasing and unfaltering arousal up to the point of orgasm, at which time one or both partners is wild with passion and the thrusting is hard and uncontrolled. In reality, concentration and arousal can be extremely difficult to maintain for lengthy periods and more typically they wax and wane throughout a sexual encounter. A more relaxed approach to sex, in which both partners take the time to talk, laugh, and communicate, can be equally or more satisfying.

4. **Sex equals intercourse.** Intercourse can certainly be a pleasurable and important aspect of a sexual relationship, however, sex does not necessarily require intercourse. Manual and oral stimulation can be equally pleasurable and may provide a slightly different and novel sensation, either physically or emotionally. In lesbian couples, intercourse is not taken for granted, hence intercourse does not need to be taken for granted in heterosexual or homosexual relationships either.

5. **The man should be the sexual leader.** By being the 'sexual leader' and taking responsibility for arousing both oneself and one's partner, men cheat themselves of much pleasure. Not only do they have the pressure of ensuring that the woman is satisfied, but they also miss out on the extra stimulation that could be given to them by their partner. Therefore, they have all of the pressure and less of the pleasure. It is important for a woman to be able to communicate her sexual needs and interests as well, rather than just waiting for her partner to initiate sex, or expecting her partner to know intuitively what specific sexual activities are enjoyable or desired on a particular occasion.

6. **A woman should not initiate sex.** As mentioned above, sex is a two-way interaction and it is often more fulfilling for both partners if sexual initiative and 'leadership' is shared. A lot of men wish their female partners would initiate sex more often.

7. **A man feels like sex at any time.** While men accept that women do not always feel like sex, some men hang onto the myth that they should feel like having sex whenever the occasion arises. However, the fact is that life is often hectic, stressful, and tiring, and that men do not always feel like sex at any time of the day. While they may be *capable* of having sex at any time, they may not necessarily *want* to have sex at any time and should not feel obligated to have sex at any time. It is all right for a man to say, "Not tonight, darling. I'm feeling a bit too tired. Let's just cuddle."

8. **A woman should always have sex when her partner makes sexual approaches.** In western cultures, it is not a woman's 'duty' to have sex with her husband. A woman should feel able to say no to sex when she does not feel like it.

9. **Sex happens automatically.** This myth asserts that we should not have to learn about sex or ask our partner about what they like because sex is something we should instinctively know about. Most of what we know about sex is learned from the media, our parents, and our friends. Much of this information promotes biased or unrealistic beliefs that may actually interfere with our enjoyment of sex. Good sex may involve *re*-learning much of what we know and assume. However, with practice, this new knowledge will become natural and our sex lives and relationships will be enhanced.

10. **A 'respectable' woman should not enjoy sex too much and should certainly never masturbate or use a vibrator.** A respectable woman of any age is a sexual being. She should feel free to experiment sexually in any way that feels comfortable. Enjoyment of sex is healthy, natural, and to be encouraged.

11. **All other couples have sex several times a week, always orgasm every time they have sex, and orgasm simultaneously.** Firstly, this is not a factual statement. Secondly, while this description of sex may hold in the early stages of a relationship, it becomes less true as a relationship progresses. Couples may be left with a set of unrealistic expectations that may trigger or exacerbate sexual problems.

12. **There must be something wrong with the relationship if sex is not good.** While a bad relationship is unlikely to have good sex, the reverse is not true. A loving couple with a stable and communicative relationship may have specific sexual difficulties. Remember that good sex does not always happen automatically and that some degree of learning or re-learning may be required.

11

PERSONALITY PROBLEMS

11.1 PERSONALITY PROBLEMS

11.1.1 GENERAL ISSUES

Sometimes an individual who seeks assistance from a mental health professional will be difficult to help because his or her personality interferes with the treatment process. Personality can be thought of as patterns of thinking, feeling or behaving that is persistent across time and situations. Personality is the expression of an individual's characteristic lifestyle and mode of relating to others.

Depending on the particular personality problem, individuals may be more or less likely to complain about their personality traits and seek help from mental health professionals (e.g., avoidant or dependent personalities are perhaps more likely to seek help than are people with paranoid or schizoid personalities). However, mostly individuals will present to a community mental health centre during the course of another disorder or mental health problem. It is often the case that the individual's personality interferes with treatment for the other mental health problem. Therefore, the clinician needs to have an understanding of some useful strategies for handling difficult personalities.

The aim of the current chapter is twofold. This chapter aims to:
1. Enable clinicians to readily recognise various personality problems that may interfere with the effective management of other mental health problems.
2. Suggest strategies and management guidelines that can help prevent or minimise management problems that arise from these difficult personality types.

The personality types covered in this chapter are:
- The paranoid person
- The withdrawn person (including schizoid and anxious personalities)
- The potentially violent person
- The impulsive or emotionally unstable person
- The antisocial person
- The histrionic person
- The dependent person
- The obsessional person
- The passive-aggressive person

In a number of sections, reference is made to certain categories of 'personality disorder' as described in the diagnostic classificatory systems of ICD-10 or DSM-IV. According to ICD-10, a personality disorder represents an extreme deviation from the way an average person in a particular culture perceives, thinks, feels, and relates to others. The disorder involves deeply ingrained and enduring patterns of behaviour that are manifest as inflexible responses to a wide range of social and personal situations. The disorder may cause distress to the individual and create problems in social functioning or performance.

The reference to personality disorders in this chapter does not imply that the concept of personality 'disorder' is unequivocally correct. Rather, personality disorders are referred to because they are a useful and recognised way of illustrating how various constellations of enduring behaviours tend to cluster together. In all cases the concept under discussion (e.g., paranoia, dependency) might be better viewed as a process and not as a diagnostic label. These concepts can aid the clinician's understanding and management of such individuals.

When evaluating an individual's personality style it is always important to ensure that the behaviour is in fact enduring and pervasive. For instance, ensure that any 'difficult' behaviour is not just the individual's reaction to a particular situation or perception. If an individual feels that he or she has been hard done by or mistreated in some way by staff at the community mental health centre then his or her behaviour may be situational rather than part of an enduring personality pattern. It is often useful to get individuals to describe their behaviour across a number of different settings. For example, *"Do you also get angry with people at your work place?"* or *"Do you also have difficulty with making decisions at home?"*

It is also important to make sure that what the clinician may interpret as a difficult personality is not just the result of a symptom-based disorder. For example, there are individuals with depressive or phobic disorders who might be viewed as having dependent personality traits, however, these 'traits' disappear when the depression or phobia is effectively treated.

It needs to be noted that the *most difficult people* are usually those who have comorbid diagnoses in which one or more personality problems may be present in conjunction with another mental disorder (e.g., someone who has borderline personality disorder, schizophrenia, and a substance abuse problem). Such individuals are likely to be extremely distressed and will constitute serious management difficulties.

Given that the treatment of personality disorders is complex, of varying effectiveness, and requires the presence of a clinician who has expertise in this area, it is probably not within the generalist community clinician's role to provide treatment that aims to 'cure' the personality disorder. Sometimes, however, even generalist clinicians who have years of clinical experience may become unwittingly involved in long term counselling of people who have severe personality problems. Some reasons for this involvement may stem from:

- The clinician's strong desire to help.
- The clinician's insufficient knowledge about the limitations of his or her counselling models, or diagnostic and therapeutic skills.
- Unrealistically high expectations about what may be achieved with a particular individual under their care.
- The engaging dependency, high levels of distress, and manipulative or persistent behaviours of some individuals.

Unless clear boundaries are devised and a limit setting approach is utilised, clinicians may sometimes find that they can become more involved than is comfortable. In extreme situations the clinician may inadvertently foster situations that are abusive to himself or herself, and to the health centre.

A final caveat is that in all cases where an individual's personality difficulties are extreme enough to seriously impede management of a mental disorder, referral to a clinician with experience and expertise in dealing with such problems is recommended. In other cases, if the problem for which the individual originally sought help is relieved but the individual remains handicapped by his or her personality, consultation or referral is again recommended.

11.1.2 THE PARANOID PERSON

HOW TO RECOGNISE THE PARANOID PERSON

These individuals will vary in their degree of paranoia, ranging from a mildly suspicious attitude in some, through to the extreme of a delusional disorder (a disorder in which a delusion is the only or most prominent clinical characteristic) in others. Since paranoid individuals are by nature suspicious of others, they do not often present voluntarily for mental health care.

For some individuals, particularly the dementing elderly, paranoia may be the presenting complaint. These individuals are most likely to present following requests by family and friends. Paranoia may also be one of the many difficult symptoms associated with a diagnosed mental disorder such as schizophrenia, affective illness with psychotic symptoms, paranoid delusional disorder, paranoid personality disorder, or schizotypal personality disorder. Paranoid thinking can also occur in association with many physiological and psychological disturbances such as brain injury, abuse of stimulants or hallucinogenic drugs, dementia, and cultural isolation. Lastly, paranoia may be a personality trait characterised by social isolation, hypersensitivity, and suspiciousness that may lie inside or outside the range of 'normal' behaviour.

Paranoid behaviour may be recognised by the individual's:
• General suspiciousness.
• Fears and beliefs that he or she is being persecuted, taken advantage of, or wronged in some way.
• Inability to trust or confide in others.
• Hostility if it is perceived that others are prying or scheming against the individual.
• Hostile or adversarial relationships.
• Reluctance to sign any sort of paperwork.
• Excessive concern about confidentiality.
• Refusal to accept medication or other forms of treatment due to suspiciousness or lack of trust in the clinician's motives.
• History of repeated terminations of employment.

As with all individuals who have difficult personalities, clinicians may find that their own reactions will help them recognise paranoid individuals. Paranoid individuals usually elicit in the clinician feelings of incompetence, inadequacy, nervousness that the individual might make trouble, and even strong dislike, which may then lead to feelings of guilt.

It has been suggested that paranoid individuals elicit such feelings in clinicians because it is the paranoid person's goal to confirm his or her suspicious and mistrustful view of the world. The core identity of these individuals may be weak and vulnerable but, rather than accept such a belief about themselves, they perceive their discomfort as arising from the actions and motives of others. A greater understanding of such processes by clinicians may lead to greater tolerance on the part of the clinician and a greater confidence in their own ability to handle individuals with paranoid traits.

HOW TO MANAGE THE PARANOID PERSON

Generally, paranoid individuals will be reluctant to present for treatment unless they experience a crisis of some sort or are persuaded by family and friends to seek assistance. Furthermore, since paranoid thinking is likely to be heightened by stress, these individuals may be even less likely to trust mental health professionals at this time.

The approach to managing paranoid behaviour will be different depending on the cause of the paranoia. In some instances paranoid behaviour is temporary and may be markedly reduced or alleviated with psychotropic medication (e.g., among individuals who have schizophrenia, psychotic depression, or severe mania). If paranoia is severe, the first step in management is to ensure the individual is seen by someone who is experienced in the assessment and diagnosis of mental illness. It may be possible to treat the underlying illness, thereby reducing the paranoid behaviour.

Among other individuals the paranoia may be more permanent and less responsive to psychotropic medication, for example in paranoid or schizotypal personality disorders, or in treatment resistant schizophrenia. In these cases, clinicians are advised to learn to cope with the individual's paranoia and to assist the individual with other life problems as appropriate. The guidelines below provide some useful information for dealing with paranoid behaviour.

The therapeutic relationship

It will be difficult to establish a therapeutic relationship since individuals may be suspicious of the clinician and fear close relationships. From the outset it will be important for the clinician to clarify the respective roles of clinician and client. This clarification means clearly specifying the structure of the relationship such as timing and duration of appointments, what to do in emergencies, clinician availability, and the provision of medication. The clinician is best to pay attention to any minor distortions the paranoid individual may make regarding expectations and feelings about the working relationship. The clinician is advised to clarify things before major problems develop.

It is important that the clinician does not try to be too friendly or inquisitive but rather maintains a formal, respectful, honest, open, and professional attitude. Humour, over-familiarity, and untoward warmth are to be avoided. The therapeutic relationship cannot be rushed and may take years to develop. Some individuals will only be seen for short-term crisis intervention thus limiting the opportunity for development of a therapeutic relationship. Other individuals will be long-term clients, thereby allowing for the development of a somewhat stronger relationship over time.

The development of a relationship may also be hindered by the paranoid person 'testing out' the clinician to see whether or not he or she is genuine. Such tests will include accusations against the clinician, or the individual belittling or devaluing the clinician. These difficulties are to be anticipated and tolerated by the clinician if the relationship is to have any chance of success.

Listen to and evaluate the individual's concerns

Allow the individual adequate opportunity to air his or her grievances and concerns. Be objective and try to verify the individual's statements wherever possible by speaking with the individual's family, friends, neighbours, etc. Obtain the individual's permission to speak with these people before proceeding.

Accept but do not confirm the individual's beliefs

Accept the individual's beliefs as being real to him or her but do not confirm or argue with the beliefs. Gentle reality testing may be useful if approached carefully. In other words, the clinician can firmly and actively assist paranoid individuals to examine other possible interpretations of the actions of others. In the long term this process of looking at alternative explanations may allow the paranoid individual to question some of his or her conclusions and thus begin to change his or her view of the world. For example, the clinician may say:

"You say you're worried that I might show these treatment notes to your wife. We have a policy of not allowing anyone outside this clinic (or office etc.) to see people's notes without their permission. Is there a particular reason why you feel you can't trust us with your notes?"

"We've been giving you your medication for 3 months now. We haven't poisoned you yet. Is there any reason why you feel we're going to poison you now?"

The urge to directly confront the paranoid individual's beliefs should be avoided for two reasons:

1. The paranoid individual is likely to reject any information which counters his or her suspicious view of the world.
2. If the clinician pressures the individual too vigorously the clinician may then become the target of the original suspicious idea or of the perceived conspiracy against the paranoid individual.

Plan clear and mutual goals

It will be helpful to develop clear goals when engaging in any form of intervention with the individual. It will also be necessary to ensure that the individual agrees with these goals. Interventions that are carried out must be clearly related to the specified goals so as to alleviate suspicion about the reason for various treatments. The most useful approach is, *"How can we work this out together?"*, thereby aiming for the establishment of a working alliance.

Explain *everything*

Always provide the individual with a complete and detailed explanation of all treatment strategies. Individuals are likely to be extremely inquisitive, even obsessional, about understanding the most minute details of treatment since they will be suspiciously searching for the clinician's 'hidden agenda'. Be honest and straightforward when discussing treatment strategies.

When treatment involves medication, clear explanations are especially important. The paranoid individual will be particularly alarmed by unexpected medication side effects which can subsequently result in non-adherence. Since paranoid individuals tend to be hypervigilant, even the smallest physical sensations can be interpreted in a threatening manner. Asking these individuals about their preferences and allowing them to regulate certain medications within set limits will allow them to experience partial control of the situation.

In addition, it may be sensible to talk about the therapeutic effects of medication on a slightly pessimistic rather than an overly optimistic note (e.g., *"It's possible that the medication will do nothing for you but it's also possible that the medication may give you some relief. Perhaps you could stick with it for a while longer, that way, if there's no benefit from the medication, at least you'll know you've tried it and that you're not missing out on anything good."*) By adopting this approach, if the medication does not produce great benefit, or if the medication causes unpleasant side effects, the clinician is less likely to lose the individual's trust. When it comes to antipsychotic medication, individuals tend not to believe that they need this medication, therefore, it will be particularly useful to adopt a slightly pessimistic view.

Empathise with the individual's anxiety

Paranoid individuals tend to be anxious. They may sweat, flush, shiver, or show other signs of anxiety. It will be important for the clinician to recognise these signs of anxiety and empathise accordingly. For example, the clinician could say something like:

"I realise it can be a bit unsettling to talk to a stranger about your life and activities. Most people feel a bit anxious in this sort of situation. If you're unsure about anything, or have any questions you want answered, please ask me."

Share your information with the individual

The individual will want to know about every issue that affects him or her. When sending paperwork such as referral letters, mail the letter to the individual and let him or her forward the letter to the specialist, or, send the letter to the specialist and a copy to the individual. Where appropriate, share any communications you have received about the individual, and allow the individual to read all treatment notes and other communications. By sharing with the individual all information relating to him or her, the clinician can be seen to be honest and open, thus facilitating the therapeutic relationship by building trust.

Having said this, however, a note of caution is also needed. Sometimes communications from other clinicians are not meant for the individual's eyes and as such may cause unhelpful consequences if seen by the individual. If the other clinician knew that the individual was going to read the letter, he or she may have phrased the letter differently. Generally, when writing letters about patients, a clinician is wise to *assume* that the patient may see the letter at some stage and is advised to write the letter accordingly. However, if the other clinician has not followed this strategy, you may be in a tricky situation. You will need to use your discretion in such cases. Remember, however, that if you choose to keep correspondence from the individual you will need to think carefully about where you will file the letter and what the consequences may be if the individual reads the letter at some stage in the future.

Take careful notes

Paranoid individuals may be very litigious, therefore, it is useful to document meticulously all interactions where appropriate.

Help with the 'here and now'

The aim of treatment is not to cure the paranoia but to help the individual deal with everyday life problems. Focusing on the 'here and now' is probably the most useful approach depending on the severity of the paranoia. Long-term mutual goals may be appropriate for some individuals but not for others.

Avoid group programmes

Group programmes are probably not appropriate for paranoid individuals unless their paranoia is very mild. To begin with, individuals are unlikely to participate or will drop out early. If they do participate, individuals are likely to remain very suspicious and thus gain little from the group programme. If individuals are only mildly paranoid and are able to stick with the group, the experience of sharing their feelings with others may be useful in terms of gaining trust and becoming more open with others.

Assessment of dangerousness

Paranoia combined with violent behaviour can be a dangerous combination. If the clinician is at all worried about the dangerousness of the individual the guidelines in Section 11.1.4: The violent person, should be consulted.

SPECIAL CASE: PARANOIA IN THE ELDERLY

Paranoid symptoms become more prevalent with increasing age. Some reasons for this paranoia are given below.

- With increasing age individuals may become less in control of their lives due to difficulties such as loss of mobility or decreased cognitive functioning. Carers often assume greater control of the individual's life, therefore, it is not surprising if the individual starts to blame others when things go wrong.
- If individuals become forgetful with age it is less threatening for the individual to blame others for misplacing or stealing things than to acknowledge a failing memory.
- Impairments with hearing or vision may lead to misinterpretation of what is heard or seen.
- Paranoia may be especially noticeable in those individuals who are dementing or taking numerous medications.
- Keep in mind that some elderly people are abused, tricked by family or greedy children, or are victimised by others who believe these individuals are too feeble to protest. Sometimes the individual's paranoia may be justified.

How to deal with paranoia in the elderly

- Acknowledge the individual's fears and beliefs without reinforcing these ideas. For example, you may say, *"I understand that you're upset because you believe that...."*
- Try to determine whether there is any basis to the complaints. Consult with one or more family members or carers, preferably with the individual's permission.
- Conduct a Mini Mental State Examination with the individual if he or she consents so as to ascertain the possibility of mental impairment such as dementia (see Chapter 1: Core Management Skills). If the individual does not consent, try to engage the individual in casual conversation about topical issues such as the weather, current affairs, the season of the year, or daily events so as to obtain information about the individual's memory and judgement. Note also the individual's grooming, speech, behaviour, and hearing.
- Offer a complete and detailed explanation for all treatment strategies.
- Encourage the individual to retain as much control over his or her life as possible and offer the individual choice with treatments or daily living where appropriate.
- Ensure that all sensory deficits (e.g., hearing and sight) are corrected wherever possible.
- Talk to the individual's general practitioner or psychiatrist about medication so as to ensure that medications which affect cognitions are kept to a minimum.

If the individual's paranoia is severe, persistent, or worsening, it may be necessary to refer the individual for specialist assessment for psychiatric illness (e.g., dementia, late-onset schizophrenia, depression with psychotic features).

11.1.3 THE WITHDRAWN PERSON

CAUSES OF WITHDRAWN BEHAVIOUR

Interviewing an individual who is withdrawn and silent can be a frustrating experience. As with all problem behaviours, it is important to consider the meaning of the difficult behaviour.

Firstly it is important to exclude a physical cause or mental disorder that could be causing the withdrawn behaviour. Some possible physical or mental causes of withdrawn behaviour are:

- Delirium
- Head injury or stroke resulting in aphasia (i.e., loss of ability to comprehend or express speech or written language)
- Drug or alcohol abuse
- Depression
- Psychosis
- Developmental disability
- Specific skills deficits e.g., hearing impairment

Other causes of withdrawn behaviour may include:

Being intimidated by a new environment

If the individual is scared, angry, or intimidated then understanding and reassurance are indicated.

Language difficulties

For example, is the individual reluctant to talk because he or she is unsure of what you are saying or is unsure about how to respond to your questions? A translator service may be helpful even if the individual has a rudimentary grasp of English.

Enduring personality traits

If it appears that the individual's withdrawal is a long-standing feature of his or her personality, future management of the individual may be enhanced by a greater understanding of what underlies the individual's withdrawal.

Generally, if the withdrawal is part of an enduring personality trait, the individual will show characteristics of one (or more) of the following personality types:

- The individual may be paranoid or suspicious and hence reluctant to talk (see the section relating to the Paranoid Person discussed previously).
- The individual may have schizoid personality traits (see section following).
- The individual may have avoidant or anxious personality traits (see section following).

THE SCHIZOID PERSON

The extreme version of the schizoid trait is schizoid personality disorder – a rare disorder that is diagnosed infrequently in clinical settings. The core features of a schizoid personality are indifference to others and a lack of genuine emotional response when relating to others.

How to recognise the schizoid person

A clinician will recognise a schizoid personality by the following characteristics:

- A preference for solitary activities.
- A lack of close friends or confidants and a lack of desire for developing such relationships and friendships.
- Mundane and unremarkable behaviour and appearance.
- Aloofness; lack of responsiveness (even towards the clinician's attempts to make the individual feel comfortable); and a lack of warmth or humour in the interview. Schizoid individuals will rarely smile or nod during such an interaction. These individuals will also report that they do not experience any strong emotions such as anger, sorrow, or joy.
- A reluctance to talk about their problems. Sometimes these individuals will deny that they have any complaints, despite the concerns of others.
- These individuals will often function adequately in occupations that allow them to keep to themselves.

The schizoid individual will rarely initiate contact and therefore it is more usual that someone else who is concerned about the individual will seek professional attention on the individual's behalf. Alternatively, relatives or friends may seek professional help for themselves if their own lives have been disrupted because of a schizoid individual's functioning. For example, a family member who may have previously compensated for the schizoid person's withdrawn behaviour may now be unable to do so, therefore allowing disruption to develop within the family.

Sometimes a change in a schizoid individual's life circumstances will cause such distress that the individual will seek help on his or her own behalf. For example, the individual may have a change in employment or in housing that results in increased interaction with others. Or, there may be a change in physical health that interferes with the individual's usual routine or which leads to increased interactions with others.

In either case, given the long-standing nature of the individual's social withdrawal, the question to unravel is, what has happened recently to cause such distress that this individual (or his or her relative/friend) has found it necessary to seek professional help?

- If the individual or relative has developed an episode of acute anxiety or depression as the result of a crisis, specific treatment for these symptoms may be required.
- A problem solving approach may be needed to rectify the current crisis and subsequently resolve distress.

How to manage the schizoid person

Proven effective treatments that attempt to change schizoid personalities have yet to be documented. However, there are a number of strategies that may help to make the interaction more tolerable for both the clinician and the individual.

- These individuals often resist treatment for any ongoing mental disorder and keep the clinician at a distance. However, this is not necessarily true for all schizoid individuals since some individuals may have comorbid dependent (or other) traits that actually promote involvement.
- In the therapeutic relationship, sensitivity and tact will be important. The clinician will need to be tolerant of long silences and will need to allow time for trust to develop. The clinician's feelings of frustration or boredom may be used constructively if it is recognised that these feelings may be an index of what the individual is suffering or may be an indication of what the individual has most difficulty discussing.

- Do not attempt any lasting change in social behaviour. However, increased social activity could be encouraged if kept within the individual's tolerance levels (e.g., joining a chess club or attending evening classes where interaction with others is minimal).

THE AVOIDANT PERSON

The extreme version of the avoidant trait is the anxious or avoidant personality disorder. This type of personality is characterised by marked anxiety about being negatively evaluated, rejected, or humiliated by others. Anxiety underlies this personality type and it has been argued that this personality is a severe, long-standing, and more generalised variant of social phobia. Social phobia, covered in Chapter 4, is also characterised by a fear of negative evaluation that leads to excessive anxiety and/or avoidance of a number of situations. However, in the case of social phobia, the fear is more likely to be limited to a number of specific situations (e.g., speaking to groups of people, eating in public) as opposed to being a pervasive feature of an individual's personality as is the case in avoidant personality disorder. For example, the individual with social phobia will usually be untroubled in his or her close personal relationships and generally has good occupational functioning, so long as the job does not require the individual to perform in front of people on a regular basis.

How to recognise the avoidant person

The clinician will recognise an avoidant person by the following characteristics:

- The individual may appear nervous and uncomfortable in the interview and may exhibit poor eye contact, stammering, blushing, or other signs of anxiety. These signs may diminish as the individual grows more at ease with the clinician.
- The individual will report that he or she is often anxious when interacting with others. If asked more about this anxiety, the individual may acknowledge a fear of rejection, criticism, or disapproval from others. However, many avoidant individuals may not be aware of this underlying fear and will be unable to offer any explanation for their anxiety.
- In addition, the individual may be unwilling to get involved with others unless it is certain that he or she will be liked by them. The individual may even fear that he or she will be shamed or ridiculed by others.
- The individual may believe that he or she is socially inept, personally unappealing, or inferior to others - hence deserving of the criticism, rejection, or disapproval that he or she fears will occur.

As a result, these individuals will avoid situations that involve contact with others (such as social events or interactions at their work) and may be fearful of entering into close or intimate relationships.

N.B.: The core difference between the avoidant personality and the schizoid personality is that people who are avoidant have a longing to relate to others but are inhibited by their fear of rejection, while the schizoid person has little interest in other people.

Avoidant individuals may have some difficulty in presenting to a community mental health centre because of their fear of negative evaluation. However, if the avoidant personality trait is not too severe or if individuals are very distressed, they may seek help. Sometimes individuals will present with one area of difficulty but their histories will reveal a more pervasive pattern of fear of criticism or disapproval. For example, an individual may initially complain of a specific social phobia such as a fear of talking to people, addressing meetings at work, or attending lectures at college. Or, an individual may seek help for feelings of depression that are secondary to his or her personality difficulties.

How to manage the avoidant person

There is some evidence in the literature which suggests that avoidant personality disorder will respond to psychological intervention to the extent that some of the distress and avoidant behaviour suffered by these individuals can be reduced. The evidence also suggests, however, that this cognitive-behavioural therapy needs to be intensive, is difficult to implement, and requires considerable expertise. If amelioration of the personality problem is the aim of therapy then referral to, or consultation with, someone who has expertise in this form of therapy is advised.

However, the following guidelines may help the clinician with the management of individuals who have milder avoidant traits.

1. Given the individual's hypersensitivity to negative evaluation, it is important to be accepting, non-judgmental, and understanding at all times. A pushy, fast-talking, or abrasive clinician will make the avoidant person very uncomfortable and likely to drop out of treatment.

2. Be sure that the individual is not agreeing with everything that is suggested just because of his or her need for the clinician's approval. Be careful not to 'bulldoze' the individual into agreeing with every suggestion and make sure that a 'negative' response from the individual is not met with criticism. For example, if the individual says something with which you do not agree, or which you believe to be incorrect, you may respond with a comment such as: *"That's one way to look at it. What do you think about XYZ as another point of view?"*. Allowing the avoidant individual to guide the pace of treatment may reduce the risk of him or her dropping out of treatment.

3. Simple anxiety management procedures such as breathing control, relaxation, and graded exposure can be quite useful for helping an individual cope with tasks and situations that he or she finds difficult. (See Section 4.4.2: Management guidelines for social phobia).

4. If it is apparent that the individual lacks skills in communication or assertiveness and that these difficulties are making anxiety worse, training in these areas may also be helpful.

11.1.4 THE VIOLENT PERSON

GRADES OF VIOLENCE

A violent act may be defined as an act intended to cause physical or psychological injury to another human. There are a number of grades of violence. These grades in order of increasing concern and severity are:

1. Verbal abuse, shouting (e.g., "You can go and get stuffed" or "Everyone here gives me the shits.").
2. Verbal menacing ("I'll come and get you" or "You're dead.").
3. Aggression towards property (e.g., throwing objects in the waiting room or kicking walls).
4. Physical fighting (e.g., an unprovoked punch or a one-off reactive punch).
5. Sustained violence (rare) or premeditated violence using an implement (e.g., club, knife, gun).

While violence itself is easy to recognise, it is not always so easy to recognise the warning signs that *predict* an impending violent outburst. This section outlines some of the common warning signs of violence as well as discussing causes of violence, general safety tips, preventing and managing violent outbursts, and managing potential violence against others.

PREDICTING VIOLENCE

Before interviewing an individual who is unknown to you, it may be helpful to review old notes or discharge summaries (if available) in search of reports of previous violence or imprisonment.

Signs of potential violence include:

Physical appearance
- Being intoxicated or under the influence of drugs (especially in young men)
- Bizarre, bloodstained, dishevelled, or dirty appearance
- Carrying a (potential) weapon

Activity levels & posture
- Pacing, restlessness, agitation, tapping feet (exclude akathesia), inability to sit still
- Clenching of fists or jaws
- Difficulty controlling movements
- Hostile facial expression with sustained eye contact
- Increasing activity levels during interview
- Standing up frequently or entering "off-limits" areas uninvited

Mood
- Angry, irritable, short-tempered, anxious, tense, distressed, labile, not in control of emotions

Speech
- Loud or slurred
- Content of speech is sarcastic, abusive, swearing, or threatening

Clinician's reaction
- Fear, anger, anxiety, frustration, uneasiness, avoidance

The first few minutes of an interview can provide a great deal of information about the individual's potential for violence. There are a number of signs that may alert the clinician to the possibility of an violent outburst. Although these signs may not be immediately present, the signs may appear or escalate during the interview process. The clinician must be constantly on the lookout for behavioural changes that signal increasing agitation or aggression. By recognising these signs early in the interview it may be possible to defuse violence before it gets out of hand. Common signs of impending violence are outlined above.

Other information to obtain

- Does the individual have a history of violent or impulsive behaviour or a criminal record? (e.g., destruction of property, reckless driving, rape, assault, etc.). The more severe a previous act of violence, the more likely is future violence. Also, it is important to note whether the individual was actually imprisoned or was simply sentenced and perhaps fined or put on a good behaviour bond. If imprisoned, the duration of imprisonment gives an indication of the severity of the offence.
- Has the individual been drinking or taking drugs? If so, what?, how much?, and how recently?
- Does the individual have an existing psychiatric or medical illness?

CAUSES OF VIOLENCE

It is desirable to understand something about possible *causes* of violence before trying to *manage* potential violence. One category of violence may result from the perception of a power imbalance. Here the individual uses violence to restore a perceived lack of power, for example, "You have more money than me, I will use my fist/knife/gun to get your money." Such *cold* violence is not a central concern of mental health professionals, lying more in the province of law an order, sociology or politics.

Another category of violence that is of more concern to mental health professionals is that which is a response to psychological "hurt". In this case, *hot* violence may occur, perhaps in an attempt to "share the hurt around" or to retaliate ("I hurt and now you hurt too"). This hurt may arise in a range of psychological states including rage, paranoia or psychosis. For example, anger or rage may follow a life event where one perceives that one has been wronged or insulted. Other factors that may influence the likelihood that violence will result include the individuals level of impulse control, their ability to verbalise their problems or feelings, their ability to emphasise with their potential victim or to be influenced by their perception that injury to others is a wrongful act. Other important factors are alcohol, amphetamines, and the availability of a weapon.

Situational factors such as a noisy waiting room, or a long wait, fear of unknown people or a new environment, excessive hear or pain, may increase the potential for violence. Here the violence is *reactive* and usually stems from fear or frustration. This form of violence responds best to an empathic approach and an attempt to build rapport and diminish factors in the environment that are threatening or unpleasant.

If the violence is more *goal-directed* but if the individual is not too violent (e.g., aggression is limited to verbal abuse or menacing), it may be possible to calm the individual enough to explore the situation and examine how the individual perceives himself or herself to have been wronged. If explanations for events and for other people's behaviours can be provided, the potential for violence may be lessened somewhat. At other times, however, it may be that the individual cannot be calmed. If so, it may be necessary to ask the individual to leave. In other situations it may be best for the *clinician* to leave and call in support. However, this option may be precluded if the individual is a danger to the community or to himself or herself, in which case the best options may be seclusion, restraint, or medication.

Psychiatric illness and violence

Most mentally ill people do not exhibit overt aggressive or violent behaviour. However, violent behaviour may sometimes be associated with various categories of psychiatric illness. These categories of psychiatric illness are discussed on the following page.

Psychotic disorders

Disorders such as schizophrenia, bipolar disorder (manic episode), and schizoaffective disorder (manic episode) may all be associated with violent behaviour. The presence of persecutory delusions, in which individuals falsely believe that people are trying to harm them, may lead to violent (usually fearful and self-protective) outbursts. Violence in psychotic individuals may appear to be unprovoked and it may be difficult or even impossible to influence such behaviour through verbal interventions alone. What may appear to be unprovoked violence may have been provoked elsewhere or earlier in the day. Unprovoked violence may also be associated with the presence of command hallucinations, such as voices telling individuals to harm themselves or others. Additionally, transient psychosis may occur in paranoid and schizotypal personality disorders and may possibly lead to violent outbursts as a result of delusions or command hallucinations.

Organic mental disorder

Individuals who are delirious or demented may exhibit violent behaviour. Often the violence is accidental and may result from the individual lashing out indiscriminately or falling over. This behaviour is usually sudden, unpredictable, and disorganised. It is also fluctuating and may settle as quickly as it comes on. During episodes of violence, individuals are likely to be non-responsive to verbal interventions alone.

Psychoactive substance abuse

Individuals who are intoxicated or have been taking psychoactive drugs (prescription or non-prescription) may become violent and display poor impulse control, particularly if suffering from withdrawal symptoms. Amphetamines and cocaine are often associated with violent episodes. Aggression may be particularly likely among addicts if demands for further drugs or medication are refused. A community mental health worker has no duty to formally assess an individual who is intoxicated. In fact, as violence in such individuals is unpredictable, it is best that the individual is firmly told, *"We can't talk to you when you're drunk - but we would be happy to help you when you're sober."* A safe environment may need to be provided for the intoxicated individual who can be assessed when the effects of alcohol have worn off.

Developmental disabilities

Individuals who are developmentally disabled may have poor impulse control and poor coping strategies. When stressed, these individuals may become violent. The aggression is usually unplanned, may be very unpredictable, and is frequently directed towards objects rather than people.

Personality disorders

One of the diagnostic criteria for antisocial (dissocial) personality disorder is poor control of aggression. Angry outbursts are also associated with emotionally unstable personality disorder (impulsive and borderline types), although the violence is generally more self-directed. These individuals will frequently use the threat of violence or self-harm as a way of manipulating others.

MEDICAL ILLNESS AND VIOLENCE

There are numerous medical conditions that are associated with intentional or accidental violence, some of which are listed on the following page. Many, but not all, of such medical conditions are treatable and reversible. Any cause of confusion, either acute (delirium) or chronic (dementia), may be associated with violent behaviour. The more physically unwell the individual, the less likely it is that he or she will be aggressive.

A thorough medical check-up may help to determine the cause of ongoing violent behaviour.

GENERAL SAFETY TIPS

The most important factor when dealing with a potentially violent individual is to maintain personal safety at all times. The following tips are important for enhancing personal safety.

Never turn your back on the individual

A violent outburst can occur in a split second. Continuous observation of the individual is imperative but avoid direct eye contact. Don't walk ahead of the individual and stand at least a punch distance away. Consider personal safety at all times.

Let the patient talk

Avoid interrupting the patient. If an interruption is necessary ensure that it is done quietly and calmly.

Ensure a safe escape route

The environment of the community centre is extremely important in terms of minimising violence. Many experts recommend that, in the interview room, the individual should remain closest to the door. However, there is apparently no consensus on this topic. Generally, unless violence is premeditated or goal-directed, the distressed individual would rather escape than fight. Violence often occurs because the individual feels threatened, cornered, and not in control. By providing the individual with a safe escape route (i.e., an unobstructed exit), you minimise the chance of a violent outburst. If the individual feels cornered or has trouble finding an exit, his or her aggression levels are likely to rise and innocent bystanders may become the object of the individual's frustration.

Other experts argue that the *clinician* should remain nearest the door so that he or she can escape if the individual becomes violent. Ideally, both the individual and the clinician would have equal access to a safe exit, preferably separate exits. If this set-up is not possible then it is recommended that the clinician remains nearest to the exit, or that the interview room door is left open, or that the room has an observation panel that allows a clear view from, say, the secretary's desk outside.

Structuring the environment

In addition to the provision of safe escape routes, other environmental factors can minimise violence and increase safety during actual or impending violent outbursts. It is important that interview rooms and reception desks have a discreet buzzer or intercom that can be used to summon immediate help when needed. It is also preferable if other staff members are clearly visible or at least seen to pass by the room at frequent intervals so as to deter violence and to provide help if needed. Forewarn other staff to be nearby and available if there is a chance of aggressive behaviour. If help is required, predetermined code words may be spoken to obtain this assistance with minimum fuss (e.g., "Kate, can you get Mr Simpson's red file for me please?"). Also, interview rooms should have *externally* locking doors to ensure that help cannot be locked out and that the individual can be locked in if necessary. Doors should preferably be kept open during interviews so that the individual does not feel trapped and so that help is easily visible and available. However, confidentiality issues also need to be considered.

Look for anger

Look for signs such as a red face, rising voice, focussing/narrowing of gaze, and tensing of muscles.

Don't be a hero

Do not try to handle a violent individual on your own. Get help from anywhere you can, leave the room, or ask the individual to leave. Think SAFETY FIRST.

Weapons

NEVER try to disarm an individual who has a weapon. If the individual claims to have a weapon, take his or her word for it and GET OUT. If you *suspect* that the individual has a weapon, GET OUT. If you cannot keep the individual in safe seclusion, GET OUT of the room or building. Make sure that other staff and waiting patients are informed and escorted to a place of safety such as another room or another building. Call security or the police immediately.

If you cannot escape

- Stay calm.
- Try to get help if possible.
- Do not wrestle with the aggressor.
- Adopt a passive and non-threatening body posture (e.g., hands by side with empty palms facing forward, body at 45° angle to aggressor, minimise eye contact).
- Be observant.
- Be prepared for rapid self-protection if necessary.
- Obey the individual's instructions and try not to upset him or her.
- Generally it is recommended that 'hostages' do not speak unless spoken to. However, it is also suggested that it is better to keep the individual *speaking* rather than *acting*. Therefore, the best option may be to speak as little as is required to keep the individual speaking or preoccupied and not acting.
- If the individual starts to calm down a little and the timing is appropriate, it may be possible to suggest that the individual puts the weapon on the table or in another safe place. If the individual agrees, do NOT attempt to grab the weapon but rather play for time until help arrives. If help cannot be notified, talk empathically with the individual in order to continue to defuse the situation. However, do not agree with ludicrous delusions. It may help to say something such as, *"I can see you're upset by this belief. Maybe it's true, maybe it's not."*
- Use surrounding objects and furniture as shields if violence occurs.
- Escape if a safe opportunity arises.

It must be emphasised here that there is no single way to react and that the clinician should use his or her expertise to choose the most appropriate plan of action. The main point to remember though is: do not wrestle or argue with the aggressor.

Remove 'dangerous' clothing

Scissors, knives, or any other unnecessary objects that can be picked up and thrown (e.g., glass ashtrays) should not be kept in the interview room. Intentional or unintentional injury may occur if a violent individual catches hold of various items of clothing. Some items of clothing that may need to be removed prior to interviewing a potentially violent individual include: glasses; earrings; necklaces; other pieces of jewellery; neckties; pens or pencils (from pockets); and cigarette lighters.

PREVENTING AND MANAGING VIOLENT OUTBURSTS

By recognising signs of impending violence early in the interview it may be possible to defuse it before the individual loses control. The following strategies may be useful for this purpose. If one strategy does not appear to work or is clearly inappropriate, go on to the next strategy. It will be important to constantly monitor the individual's responses and to adopt different strategies accordingly.

Inform the individual about anticipated delays

People do not like to be kept waiting. If you anticipate a delay before being able to see the individual, inform the individual of the extent of the delay, be apologetic, and offer appropriate resources (e.g., magazines, television, a drink, sweets, a bathroom, etc.). Simple consideration can help reduce hostility.

Avoid excess stimulation

Noisy waiting rooms, loud music, or bright lights can overload an already tense or disturbed individual.

Personal space and body posture

The following points are worth noting:
- Have minimal eye contact with potentially violent people. Direct eye contact is confronting.
- Allow the individual adequate personal space (up to 6 metres if necessary).
- Keep your hands visible and preferably open by your sides with your palms facing the individual. This will assure the individual that you are not concealing a weapon.
- Try to maintain open body posture (i.e., keep your legs uncrossed and do not fold your arms across your chest as this posture will signal an unwillingness to be open to the other's ideas).
- Stand at an angle to the person so as to appear less confronting.
- Do not stand if the individual is sitting or you will appear threatening.
- Movement towards the individual may be perceived as a threat so keep your distance when violence is escalating. Move backwards or sideways if you move at all.

General counselling skills

It is easy to become frustrated and annoyed with individuals who are violent, therefore, attention to appropriate counselling skills will be particularly important.

- Maintain respect for the individual.
- Remain calm and patient.
- Try to see things from the individual's point of view and acknowledge his or her feelings. The feelings are real, even if inappropriate or unreasonable.
- Allow the individual a chance to talk freely about his or her concerns.
- Show that you are willing to help where possible.
- Speak firmly, slowly and clearly but with normal tone and intensity - raising your voice will enhance the individual's fear and hostility. Avoid sounding accusatory or punitive.
- Decrease eye contact if violence escalates.
- Do not take the individual's comments personally. Abusive statements may be the only way the individual can express his or her feelings at the time.
- Use open-ended questions (e.g., How?, When?, Why?, What?, etc.) if you want to promote feedback and use closed questions that lead to yes or no answers (e.g., "Do you...?", "Have you...?", etc.) when you want to obtain direct answers to questions.
- Try to be honest with the individual and do not make promises you cannot keep.
- Offer refreshments where appropriate (e.g., a cool drink that cannot cause a burn injury if thrown) so as to communicate a willingness to consider the other person's needs and a desire to co-operate in a friendly manner. However, if made at an inappropriate time, this offer may communicate a desire to avoid dealing with the individual's problem thus angering the individual further. Timing is crucial.

Community visits

If you are required to visit the individual at home, especially if uninvited, remember that you are entering the individual's territory and that the individual is likely to feel threatened. Acknowledge the individual's territorial rights and respect his or her personal space and possessions. Always ask whether you may enter the house, sit down, use the telephone, and so on. By doing so you will allow the individual to retain a sense of control and thus will reduce perceived threat.

Another important point about community visits is that you may not know your way around the house, therefore, escape may be difficult. If your instinct warns you that the individual may be dangerous, ask if you can stand outside and talk to the individual. Otherwise, ASK THE POLICE TO ACCOMPANY YOU INSIDE. Refer to your community centre's internal protocol on violence to obtain further advice about this issue.

Provide adequate education

Often individuals are frightened by symptoms of their illness, by being in a new environment, or by general medical procedures. Fear can lead to violence, so it is important to help reduce levels of fear. One way of doing so is to provide the individual with education about relevant issues (e.g., the purpose of the community centre, the names and roles of clinicians who are present, symptoms of the illness, medication being offered). Helping the individual to understand the causes and consequences of the present situation may decrease levels of fear to a more tolerable level for all concerned. The presence of trusted family members or friends may also reduce fear. Note also that staff members should carry an identification card at all times.

Provide supportive feedback

With some individuals who are a bit agitated and likely to become violent, supportive feedback may help to defuse escalating aggression. Supportive feedback involves noting the individual's non-verbal cues and feeding your impression of these cues back to the individual. The examples below illustrate how this technique may be used.

"You seem to be a bit agitated. Perhaps you can tell me why you're feeling agitated, then I may be able to help you in some way."

"I can see that you're very angry about .. Tell me what you would like me to do to help you."

"I can see that you're very upset about something. Tell me what's upsetting you?"

This technique should be used right from the start of the interview and will be useful even in the absence of potential violence. The open-ended questions encourage the individual to say whatever is on his or her mind and require more than a monosyllabic yes or no answer. However, sometimes this approach may backfire and act to infuriate the individual further. If such a response occurs it will be important to move on to a different technique such as limit-setting, time-out, or restraint.

Try to provide the individual with choice

Individuals may become violent if they feel they are not in control of their situation. Even if individuals are not entirely happy with the alternatives being offered, the very fact that they are allowed to make a choice may help alleviate some of their distress. For example, you may say to an individual:

"I can see that you're extremely distressed and agitated by the voices you're hearing. I can help you to feel better by giving you your usual tablets. You always tell me that the pills make the voices quieter. If you don't want me to help you in that way then you are free to leave here and go home. The choice is yours. Tell me what you'd like me to do."

Limit-setting

By setting a limit within a given situation you are making clear the requirements under which you can work. Many individuals struggle to avoid becoming aggressive, therefore, by setting clear limits you show the individual that you will not tolerate aggression and that you will help the individual to remain calm. Thus limits can act to decrease the individual's anxiety about losing control. Limit-setting may be especially effective if you acknowledge the individual's present emotions, thereby providing a rationale for why limits are being set. Some examples of limit-setting are illustrated below:

"I can see that you're very angry and it's not surprising given your circumstances this evening. I'd like to help you but I cannot do so if you lose your temper. First of all I'd like you to sit down, then you can tell me how I can help."

"You're obviously very annoyed about something. I can see that you feel like hitting something and I'm a bit scared that you may hit me. I'm going to ask the police officer to stand in the room with us. I'd like you to take a seat and then you can tell me what you're annoyed about."

"I'd like to help you but I can't do so if you yell at me. Either you stop yelling and talk to me calmly or I'll have to leave you alone until you have calmed down."

It is quite common for individuals to test the limits you have set. In this case it is usually worth restating the limits firmly. Sometimes, however, individuals simply lose control and surpass the limits. When setting limits, if you have offered alternative outcomes and the individual does not comply with the limits, it is important that you are prepared to go through with the alternative (e.g., restraint, calling the police, leaving, etc.). If you have not made explicit the alternative outcomes and the individual continues with the unacceptable behaviour, it is time to move immediately on to the next strategy - either time-out, restraint, or medication.

Time-out may involve asking the individual to walk around the block for 10 minutes until he or she has calmed down. When the individual returns, make sure you are ready to interview him or her without delay. Alternatively, time-out may involve leaving the individual alone in an unlocked room for a few minutes. It should be clear to the individual that this strategy is not a form of punishment. For example, you could say to the individual, *"I can see that you're very angry at the moment. We're not getting anywhere like this so I'll leave you alone for a while and let you calm down a little"*. This strategy may be effective providing the individual is not agitated to the point of being dangerous. Inform the individual that you will be back in about ten minutes. If the individual appears calmer after this time you can continue with the conversation.

Sometimes the individual does not calm down but instead exhibits escalating aggression. If the strategies listed so far have been tried or are clearly impossible, it may be necessary to leave the individual. Health professionals should not take risks of being attacked. If you judge that the person is dangerous you should only continue the interview when supported by other staff. If in doubt seek support from the police or from security staff. The presence of additional staff may itself settle the individual's behaviour, when he or she realises that violence is pointless and will not be tolerated. If possible the individual should then be persuaded to move to a location where there are more staff.

Sometimes it will not be possible to wait for the police or security staff, in which case community doctors and staff may wish to take responsibility for restraining the individual. Staff should not restrain an individual unless they have been trained to do so, or unless there is either no other more appropriate course of action and there are sufficient people for it to be done in safety.

Medication can be helpful, especially when the aggression is driven by delusional thinking. It is virtually impossible to implement this unless the patient agrees. If they do not, and are deluded or manic, one should consider detaining them in hospital under the relevant Mental Health Act. In this situation the aggression can be contained and medication can be administered, despite the individual's refusal.

WHAT TO DO AFTER A VIOLENT OUTBURST

Immediately following the violent act, the staff members involved will require support which may include being taken to Accident and Emergency or taken home. After any level of violence, a record should be made in the individual's file. The following procedure is recommended:

1. In a prominent position inside the file (NOT on the front cover) record the following note: *see (date)* and give date of documentation of the violent episode.
2. In the individual's notes on that date, give a detailed record (at least half a page) of the violence. Include:
   - The grade or severity of the violence
   - The circumstances in which the violence occurred (e.g., note whether the individual was psychotic, drunk, etc.)
   - Whether the violence was provoked

This note and the detailed description of the violent act means that all workers who have dealings with this individual will be aware of past violence and will know where to look to obtain a description of the violent incident.

If violence has occurred it is usually helpful for participants to discuss their experiences of the incident. Debriefing best takes place between two and seven days following the incident. Staff should get together and talk about what happened, how they felt, what went wrong, what went right, and how to handle such situations more effectively in the future. The new information should be shared with the staff who were not directly involved in the discussion.

It may also be helpful to discuss the incident with the individual once he or she has recovered. The individual is likely to feel quite shaken after such an event, especially if restraint and medication were required. If the violent incident was out of character for the individual, he or she may have trouble understanding why the violence occurred. If the violence was part of a pattern of aggressive behaviour, the individual may at this stage be more willing to accept help for his or her violence.

MANAGING POTENTIAL VIOLENCE AGAINST OTHERS

Potentially violent individuals raise problems for clinicians, both in terms of legal duty and clinical responsibility.

The Tarasoff decision issued in California in 1976 held that the clinician, therapist, or health professional has a duty to protect a person whom the patient threatens to harm. In the U.S. the Tarasoff decision has become a national standard for psychiatric practice and it is generally accepted that this duty also applies internationally.

If the clinician believes there is a reasonable chance that an individual will harm someone and has named that person, then the clinician has a duty to warn that person or contact the local police to warn that person.

There are practical steps that clinicians can take to ensure that they act most appropriately in terms of both legal duty and clinical responsibility. These steps are outlined later in this section.

Assessing potential violence

It is impossible for any clinician to be able to assess with one hundred percent accuracy the likelihood of rare events such as serious violence. However, the following variables are known to be associated with potential violence:

- A history of violence (the single strongest predictor)
- Being male
- Moving house frequently
- Being unemployed
- Living or growing up in a violent subculture
- Abuse of drugs or alcohol
- Low intelligence
- Coming from a violent family
- Having weapons available
- Having victims available
- History of poor impulse control

The most important predictive clinical variable, however, is motive. If you suspect violence, ask the individual the following questions:

- *Are you angry at anyone?*
- *Are you thinking about hurting anyone?*

If the answer to either of these questions is positive then you also need to ask:

- *Who are you angry at, or thinking about hurting?*
- *When do you think you might hurt (the person mentioned)?*
- *Where will you do this?*
- *How long have you been thinking this way?*
- *Are you able to control these thoughts about hurting (the person mentioned)?*
- *Do you think you would be able to stop yourself from hurting (the person mentioned) if you wanted to?*
- *For how long do you think you can control your thoughts about hurting (the person mentioned)?*
- *Have you ever purposely hurt someone in the past?*
- *(If the answer to the previous question is negative) "How close have you come to hurting someone in the past?*

In particular, you also need to consider:

- The individual's history of violence (fights, hurting others, trouble with the police).
- Factors that may weaken self-control (e.g., psychotic illness, paranoid thinking, organic personality disorder such as a frontal lobe syndrome or a limbic epilepsy syndrome, drug or alcohol abuse).
- History of impulsive behaviour. In addition to violence, drug abuse, or alcohol abuse, also consider stealing, shoplifting, sexual indiscretions, binge eating, suicide attempts or threats.
- Lastly, assess the level of intent (as you would with the assessment of suicidal thoughts). For example, specific intent stated in the active voice is more serious than a general threat in the passive voice. It is important to distinguish between levels of increasing concern. For example:
  - *I wish he were dead.*
  - *I'd like to kill that bastard.*
  - *I'll stick a knife in Joe Bloggs if he comes near my house again.*

In general, always try to find out as much as possible about the individual's thoughts and state of mind. At the very least find out as much as you need to know to assess whether violence is likely.

Rules for dealing with potential violence

A thorough and adequate assessment should allow the clinician to determine whether a particular individual is one of those uncommon cases for whom potential violence is a concern. In such cases the clinician has a legal and ethical obligation to the individual as well as to potential victims of violence to try to prevent the violence. It is highly unlikely that the individual will be entirely happy or comfortable with his or her own violent thoughts or actions. Whatever subsequent course of action a clinician may decide to take, there are a number of practical 'rules' to keep in mind.

Discuss your concerns and your intended action with the potentially violent individual

Where possible it is usually best to tell the individual that you are concerned about his or her threats. You may then tell the individual that it is your duty and your intention to tell the third party about the threats that have been made against him or her. However, if you believe that discussing such concerns and intentions with the violent individual will put you at risk then you should warn the third party without informing the violent individual.

Some clinicians are afraid that telling an individual of their intention to warn a third party about potential violence will damage the therapeutic relationship. However, past cases indicate that the therapeutic relationship was rarely damaged if clinicians discussed with the individual their intention to warn the third party about the threat of violence. It was usually when such a discussion with the individual did *not* take place that the case often ended badly. The clinician who takes an individual's threats seriously and discusses a proposed course of action with the individual demonstrates concern for that individual. Such concern may in fact strengthen the therapeutic relationship. After all, being imprisoned for several years for a murderous assault also hinders a therapeutic relationship!

If in doubt, seek consultation with a supervisor or with the mental health team

Questions about assessment and appropriate action will often be clarified through the process of review and discussion with another person. When there is immediate concern, get immediate consultation, even if the consultation is informal or over the telephone. Informal consultation is better than none at all.

Keep careful, detailed, written notes (including notes about the results of review or consultation)

These notes are essential for minimising the risk of malpractice suits against the clinician if violence does occur. Notes should include full and complete documentation of:
- What the individual said (quotes made by an individual during an interview are best)
- What you observed
- What you thought about
- What you concluded about the likelihood of violence
- Your proposed course of action
- The reasons why this proposed course of action is likely to be effective or at least better than any other choice
- A justification of why you breached patient confidentiality by informing a third party
- Why you chose not to place a disproportionate weight on what the individual actually said

The course of action the clinician decides to follow is based on the estimated likelihood of violence.

Protecting a third party against violence

If the clinician believes that there is real likelihood of violence then he or she should consider immediate action.

If the individual satisfies the criteria for 'mental illness' or 'mental disorder' under the most mental health acts hospitalisation (voluntary if possible, involuntary if not) will be the intervention of choice.

If the individual does not meet the criteria for sectioning under the Mental Health Act (e.g., an individual with long-standing delusional jealousy) then the clinician should act to protect the person who is the target of the threat. The law requires that evidence of domestic violence or child abuse is to be reported to the appropriate authorities. The potentially violent individual can be informed of the clinician's course of action and, in many cases, it will be appropriate to carry out such warnings in the presence of the individual. This will ensure that the way the clinician talks about the individual is measured and considered, and will also minimise the chance of the individual developing paranoid ideas about the content of discussions that have taken place in his or her absence.

If the person who is the target of the threat cannot be contacted immediately then the clinician should inform the police. Once the police are informed of such a threat of violence, they too have a duty to warn that person of the risk of violence.

LONG-TERM MANAGEMENT OF VIOLENCE

This chapter does not deal with the modification of long-standing and recurrent violent behaviour. If the aggression is mild it may be helpful to provide the individual with assertiveness training (see Chapter 1: Core Management Skills). Otherwise, the clinician is advised to refer the individual to specialists who are trained to deal with this problem.

11.1.5 THE IMPULSIVE OR EMOTIONALLY UNSTABLE PERSON

The ICD-10 lists emotionally unstable personality disorder among its disorders of adult personality and behaviour. This personality type may be described as 'impulsive' or 'emotionally unstable' and is referred to in DSM-IV and much of the psychiatric literature as borderline personality disorder.

Emotionally unstable personality disorder is characterised by the following features:
- Affective instability or highly reactive and sudden mood swings. The individual may experience intense feelings of dysphoria, irritability, or anxiety that may last for only a few hours and rarely for more than a few days.
- A tendency to act impulsively without consideration of the consequences of those actions. In many cases the impulsive behaviour will cause potential harm to the individual. Examples may include excessive spending sprees, sexual indiscretions, drug or alcohol abuse, reckless driving such as when under the influence of alcohol, shop-lifting, or binge eating. In other words, these individuals will sometimes act as if there were 'no limits' to their behaviour.
- Poor ability to plan ahead and to solve problems.
- Poor tolerance for frustration, which may lead to outbursts of intense anger or to the experience of constant angry feelings. There may also be an inability to control anger, leading to temper tantrums or outbursts of aggression.
- In some individuals, their self-image, goals, and personal preferences (including sexual) will be unclear or disturbed. There may be accompanying feelings of chronic emptiness. In addition, these individuals may have a tendency to become involved in intense and unstable relationships. Repeated emotional crises in those relationships may be associated with excessive efforts to avoid abandonment. For instance, an individual who longs for closeness in a relationship may behave in a way that alienates the other person, then, in a panic, may try to draw the other person back. Self-harm and repeated suicidal threats or gestures may also occur, sometimes in the context of a relationship crisis.

An individual who lies at the severe end of the emotionally unstable personality dimension will be very difficult to manage. The individual's maladaptive personality traits will significantly impede progress with treatment for other mental disorders he or she may have. Although there is little empirical evidence to support any one treatment as being effective for resolving the underlying difficulties associated with this type of personality, it is generally believed that long-term psychotherapy by an experienced clinician can be beneficial for helping individuals learn to control maladaptive behaviours and to mature.

Generally, this form of psychotherapy would not be delivered in the community mental health service setting. Rather, a clinician's time would probably be more usefully spent dealing with any other co-existing mental health problems or crisis situations the individual may experience. In order to maximise treatment for these other problems, the clinician needs to be efficient at managing the individual's difficult personality behaviours so that these behaviours do not interfere excessively with treatment. The following guidelines are designed to assist clinicians with the effective management of individuals who have milder impulsive or emotionally unstable personality traits.

HOW TO RECOGNISE THE EMOTIONALLY UNSTABLE PERSON

There are no 'typical' presenting complaints of individuals with an emotionally unstable personality. Rather, individuals are likely to present with a range of mental health problems such as depression, anxiety, or psychosis. There is not usually any immediately identifiable feature suggestive of this personality type, however, a number of features may become evident in time. These features include:

- A predominantly angry affect and a history of anger.
- Overdoses in the context of perceived relationship difficulties, rejections, and losses.
- Terror of being left alone.
- Clinging dependency, either hostile or despairing.
- An observable pattern of impulsive behaviour, unstable relationships, or recurrent suicidal or self-mutilating gestures (these features may be apparent from the history that is gathered at the first interview).

HOW TO MANAGE THE EMOTIONALLY UNSTABLE PERSON

Given the complexity of the personality difficulties, the following strategies must be seen as merely general guidelines that clinicians may find useful when dealing with these individuals. In reality there are no simple algorithms about how to best manage these individuals - only that at all times clinicians must be firm, fair, and consistent.

Setting clear limits

It is important that clear limits are set and that the individual understands that the clinician is in 'control' of the parameters and boundaries of management. Otherwise the clinician will run the risk of having the individual inappropriately manipulate treatment goals and progress. A typical scenario is where, from session to session, new 'crises' develop that interfere with the contracted management plan. In such cases it often becomes difficult to get the individual back on track. The individual may demand immediate relief for his or her 'crisis' and may refuse to use a problem solving approach, even when a problem solving approach may actually be ideal for resolving the current crisis. In other words, while the clinician may have a clear formulation of the problem and a clear idea of how to conduct the session, he or she may be quite successfully 'controlled' by the individual if clear limits have not been set. Hence, the clinician may find that he or she is undertaking a series of crisis interventions rather than addressing the ongoing problem/s for which the individual initially sought help. Some guidelines for limit setting are given below.

- Have a very clear management plan (i.e., outline exactly what is planned, how many sessions it will take, or how frequently the individual will be seen).
- Make a contract with the individual about the management plan and then stick by the contract. Make sure that the contract is mutually agreed upon by all parties involved and that the contract specifies achievable goals and the strategies available for achieving them.
- Include an agreement about contact between scheduled sessions in the contract. For example, the agreement may only allow unscheduled appointments under specific circumstances and limit telephone contact.
- Provide explicit and clear guidelines about the expected behaviour of individuals. For example, that the individual will not be seen if he or she is intoxicated, or that aggressive behaviour such as shouting or verbal abuse will not be tolerated. It is important that the clinician tells individuals exactly what will happen under such circumstances - and then sticks by what has been said. It is not unusual for these individuals to test the clinician to see whether he or she is consistent with the limits that have been set.

CRISIS MANAGEMENT

Although it is important to establish and follow a clearly defined management plan, despite the best of intentions there will be times when other crises will inevitably interfere with this plan. In some cases involving 'parasuicidal, borderline' individuals, certain behaviours or 'crises' may need to take precedence over the ongoing management plan or other goals that the clinician and individual have agreed to work on. These behaviours are hierarchically ordered by importance as follows:

1. Suicide threats, suicide attempts and other life-threatening behaviours.
2. Behaviours that interfere with the process of treatment (e.g., missing sessions, being overly demanding, angry outbursts, repeated admissions to hospital).
3. Behaviours that seriously interfere with the individual's quality of life (e.g., substance abuse, antisocial behaviours).

The session focus depends on the individual's behaviour in each of these areas since the last session. For example, if a suicide threat has occurred since the previous session, the first task of the current session is to apply problem solving strategies to the suicidal behaviour. Dealing with the suicide threat overrides all other concerns, including behaviours interfering with the conduct of therapy. (N.B.: Suicide attempts are discussed in greater detail under the next heading). If a clinician decides to work under this model then, as with any other management plan, the hierarchy needs to be discussed explicitly with the individual so that he or she fully understands the approach that the clinician will be taking.

Suicidal threats, gestures, or attempts

The rate of suicide completion for individuals with this personality type, although lower than schizophrenia and affective disorder, is substantial and thus all suicide attempts need to be taken seriously even if they appear manipulative and unlikely to have been lethal. As suggested above, the first target of management will always be high risk suicidal behaviours. It has been argued that one of the best predictors of suicidal behaviour is previous suicide attempts. There is some suggestion that problems in interpersonal relationships, depression and substance abuse are also risk factors in this population.

Suicidal threats or ideation need to be immediately and actively assessed as outlined in Section 1.1.3: Suicide Assessment and Management (see Chapter 1). Once the individual's safety is assured, the goal of any intervention will be the replacement of suicidal behaviours with more adaptive ways of solving problems. As with all suicidal behaviour, if the suicide attempt appears to be an inappropriate method of solving a problem (rather than being solely an attempt to manipulate others), then a structured problem solving approach will be very helpful. There are now a number of studies which suggest that problem solving is effective for decreasing further suicidal behaviour in individuals who repeatedly attempt suicide. Further discussion of the problem solving approach can be found in Chapter 1: Core Management Skills.

There are a number of advantages to targeting suicidal behaviour as a priority for management. Firstly, making suicidal behaviour a management priority reduces the likelihood of future suicidal behaviour; secondly, it communicates that the clinician takes such behaviour very seriously; and thirdly, the individuals themselves soon learn that if they engage in such behaviour, they will spend their time with the clinician discussing this behaviour and applying the problem solving model rather than being able to spend time on other topics. Fortunately, suicide completion in these individuals becomes less likely as they get older.

Other problem behaviours

Problem solving is also an effective approach for dealing with other problem behaviours, such as those that interfere with the progress of treatment or seriously interfere with the individual's quality of life. Also important is clear communication about why the clinician believes that these behaviours need to be changed. For example, it is useful to draw the individual's attention consistently and repeatedly to the adverse consequences of his or her behaviours, such as drug abuse or angry outbursts. Often behaviours are linked to each other; for example, individuals who harm themselves often only do so when they are under the influence of drugs or alcohol.

A problem solving approach is particularly effective as it helps to balance empathy and concern with the notion that the individual is ultimately responsible for his or her own behaviour.

Use of medication

A couple of drug trials published in the literature suggest that antidepressant medication, and to a lesser extent antipsychotic medication, may provide relief for symptoms of anxiety and depression in individuals with emotionally unstable personalities. However, it is dangerous to apply a blanket rule to the use of antidepressants in such cases since it is possible that the medication may make the individual worse. Generally, antidepressants would only be prescribed if the individual also satisfied criteria for major depression.

Establishing a team approach

Sometimes these individuals will present in crisis either to the mental health centre's intake service, to a hospital casualty or psychiatric ward, or they may call the crisis or extended hours team. If such presentations are frequent, it will be important to establish a protocol with all parties who might be involved so as to clarify the course of action that should be taken when such contact recurs. Clear communication between staff of various teams will minimise the risk that the individual will play staff members off against one another (see also the "Effect on mental health professionals" on the following page).

The protocol should include details about:
- When the primary clinician should be contacted
- When a crisis visit should occur
- When hospital admission should occur
- What strategies or interventions should occur during the crisis contact
- Strategies for handling self-destructive or threatening behaviour

The protocol should also include the name of the primary clinician and details of any contracts made between the clinician and the individual which outline the action that is to be taken during crisis situations (e.g., that 'crisis' contacts may not necessarily result in admission to hospital, nor even result in a visit by the crisis or extended hours team). Ideally the contract with the individual should clarify that 'crisis' contacts will usually be brief, focused, and goal-orientated.

The following guidelines and strategies may be useful for establishing such a protocol:
- Try to avoid getting angry or irritated with the individual (or at least if you do feel angry or irritated, try to remain outwardly calm and objective). Aim to be firm yet caring and do not argue with the individual.
- Remind the individual of any contract that has previously been agreed upon with his or her primary clinician, and reiterate the details of the contract.
- Establish the validity of any possible injury or overdose.

- Establish the current risk of imminent harm to self or others. There may be occasions in which the individual may not be capable of imposing limits on his or her own behaviour and therefore may need to have limits set by some external structure.
- Hospitalisation should be avoided unless the individual is suicidal or homicidal and there is no other means for helping the individual control his or her behaviour.
- Involve the individual in a common sense discussion of the realities of the crisis situation and the limitations of the resources of the mental health team, crisis team, and individual clinicians (e.g., time, capacity to tolerate abusive or unfair behaviour).
- Ideally, give the individual some responsibility for the resolution of the crisis.
- In general, medication is not an option unless in the context of ongoing management. Benzodiazepines are contraindicated because of the risk of behavioural dyscontrol and the potential that they will be abused.

Effect on mental health professionals

Individuals who are 'impulsive' or 'emotionally unstable' will evoke reactions in most clinicians who deal regularly with them, including feelings of frustration and anger. Thus the clinician needs to become aware of his or her own negative feelings and to avoid acting on them. For example, the clinician may try to justify 'finding a reason' to stop seeing the individual or to cause the individual to seek treatment elsewhere.

On occasions, these individuals will cause problems among a mental health team because of the way their personality traits cause them to relate to others. Typically these individuals evoke strong reactions in health professionals who are subjected to either the 'best' or 'worst' side of their behaviour. For example, poignant requests for help or the sharing of 'secrets' can cause these individuals to appear very appealing to some staff, while other staff members only get to see the worst of their aggressive or demanding behaviour. Therefore, in situations in which a number of team members are likely to be in contact with such individuals, the common management philosophy and protocol of encouraging open communication and frequent case discussion between all team members will be very important.

Additionally, it is suggested that staff process meetings are *essential* for providing staff members with the opportunity to ventilate their feelings and obtain support and feedback from their co-workers. It can be extremely exhausting and emotionally draining dealing with individuals who have a personality problem. By sharing common experiences, or relating particularly bad experiences, staff members can offload some of their frustration, anger, or feelings of demoralisation. Additionally, staff can share any *positive* outcomes they have experienced. Therefore, such meetings serve to help staff members cope with the demands placed on them by people with personality problems, and may also facilitate the transfer of education and knowledge from one staff member to another.

11.1.6 THE ANTISOCIAL PERSON

This type of personality is variously referred to in the literature as antisocial personality, sociopath, or psychopath. Similarly, ICD-10 Dissocial Personality Disorder describes an enduring pattern of behaviour characterised by gross indifference to prevailing social norms. Features of this personality type include:

- Callous disregard for the feelings of other people
- Irresponsibility, and disregard for rules and regulations
- An inability to maintain relationships for any length of time, despite having no difficulty in starting relationships with others
- Low tolerance levels leading to frustration, aggression, or violence
- An inability to experience guilt or remorse
- A tendency not to learn from experience, particularly punishment
- A tendency to blame others or offer rationalisations for their own antisocial behaviour

There is a great deal of controversy in the psychiatric literature as to whether or not such a pattern of behaviour should be considered a mental disorder and whether or not it should be located within the province of mental health. There is no evidence in the literature of effective treatment for antisocial personality. However, given that such individuals can be extremely manipulative, early recognition and strategies for effective management of this behaviour will be useful. Such strategies may help to minimise any difficulties the clinician experiences when interacting with these individuals during the ongoing management of other mental health problems.

HOW TO RECOGNISE THE ANTISOCIAL PERSON

The most obvious way to pick up clues that one might be dealing with an antisocial personality is through the individual's history. A history of being in trouble with authorities (e.g., teachers when at school or the police), drug or alcohol abuse, lack of long term relationships, and the absence of a stable address or employment, should make a clinician wary. On the other hand, antisocial persons can be outwardly successful individuals in business, operating successfully yet ruthlessly on the edge of the law. In such cases a clinician could ask:

- *Have you ever had any legal difficulties?*
- *What sort of financial difficulties have you had?*

During the interview, the clinician can take note of the following:

- Rationalisations and excuses the individual may make for past antisocial behaviours. For example, *"Well, I did lose my license for drink driving, but everyone does it, don't they. I was just unlucky enough to get caught."*
- Statements that the individual will never become involved in such behaviour again and that it was *"all a mistake"*.
- Unwarranted flattery of the clinician. For example, telling the clinician that he or she seems especially talented or understanding of the individual's problems.
- Inconsistencies in the individual's history, such as when his or her story does not seem to 'add up'.

Antisocial individuals can present to mental health settings in a number of ways. Some common presentations are outlined below.

- Previous antisocial behaviour is often easily identified at the first contact with the individual. These individuals may come to seek help from the centre through a court referral, a lawyer, or may occasionally be self-referred. The individual may report that his or her reason for seeking help from the community mental health centre is because he or she is in some sort of legal trouble and wants the mental health professional to help solve the dilemma. Although this intention may not be stated explicitly at the beginning of the interview, when questioned, the individual will usually not deny this intention and will present a sincere request for help.

- Sometimes such individuals will instead present with a 'psychological problem' of some concern. However, a careful and detailed diagnostic interview will reveal that the supposed problem comes across as being inconsistent. For example, the individual may present with a claim of 'hearing voices' but the voices are neither frightening, nor externally experienced, or in some other way are not consistent with the usual clinical pattern. In such cases the individual may be attempting to manipulate the clinician into helping him or her out of a particular difficulty.
- Sometimes these individuals will present with genuine distress due to other, often multiple, mental disorders. These individuals do tend to experience mental disorders at a rate higher than the general population, especially mania, schizophrenia, and drug or alcohol abuse.

HOW TO MANAGE THE ANTISOCIAL PERSON

If the clinician suspects that he or she might be dealing with an individual who has antisocial traits, the following interview guidelines may be helpful:

- Ensure that the individual's reason for seeking help has been clearly identified. The following questions outlined by Lazare and colleagues might be helpful:
  "Why did you come to the centre?"
  "Why did you decide to come today instead of last week or next week?"
  "What do you hope I or the community health centre can do for you?"
  "What do you think is the cause of your difficulties?"
  "If you had not come for help, what do you think would have happened to you?"

  By establishing the individual's agenda early in the interaction, a clinician may prevent the individual from feeling the need to present a 'psychological problem' in an attempt to be taken seriously.

- Begin from the standpoint that the majority of requests are legitimate. If the clinician comes to understand exactly what the individual wants (and the individual knows that the clinician is aware of the request) the clinician is then in the best position to negotiate what he or she can do for the individual, depending on the appropriateness of the request. For example:
  "From what you have told me you seem to be suffering from a disorder that we can help you with. I'll make an appointment for you to see a doctor who might talk to you about taking some medication." OR
  "I can see that you'd like to be admitted to hospital because you're feeling overwhelmed but I don't think hospitalisation is appropriate for you at the moment. However, I could arrange for someone in our team to visit you regularly over the next couple of days until you feel more in control." OR
  "We don't hand out sedatives to people at this centre. I could perhaps help you if you were prepared to tell me why you think you need this medication. But otherwise there is nothing I can do for you."

- Take as full a history as possible. A clear understanding of events that have happened in the past may assist the clinician with his or her judgements about future events or crises and with possible steps that might be taken to avoid these crises. While the history is being taken, the clinician will also have the chance to develop rapport with the individual and identify his or her reason for seeking help.

- Do not accept all information at face value. Seek further evidence that may support the individual's statements. For example, if the individual states that he or she is depressed, the clinician should seek out symptoms that would normally be associated with depression. However, open questions such as *"And what other problems have you been experiencing? What have you been doing with your time?"* will be preferable to closed questions such as *"And have you also lost interest in the things you normally enjoy?"* that may act as leading questions to individuals who are trying to convince you that they have a mental disorder.

- Aim to create an open and trusting relationship. Speak frankly in a warm and accepting manner, and encourage the individual to tell the truth if it is obvious that he or she is lying.

- Set clear limits (see discussion of limit setting in the management guidelines of the emotionally unstable personality).

- If the individual presents with genuine symptoms of a mental disorder then he or she should be offered treatment. Unfortunately, these individuals are difficult to treat and there is evidence that, when treated for a mental disorder, they tend to do significantly worse than others who do not have this personality trait.

- Do not expect to like these individuals. By their very nature they can be manipulative, exploitative, impulsive, and even aggressive. A calm demeanour and an understanding of why these individuals may be eliciting such negative feelings in the clinician may possibly help. The skill lies in accepting these demanding and potentially unpleasant individuals without accepting their demanding and unpleasant behaviour. Some of the guidelines outlined in the section on the aggressive person may also be of use.

- Assist with problem solving strategies for crises, particularly if the current crisis appears to have led to the onset or worsening of psychological symptoms, or even to a worsening of antisocial behaviour itself. For example, a physical illness or social problem or an increase in drug or alcohol abuse will all lessen an individual's ability to cope and hence will increase the likelihood of antisocial behaviour. Practical assistance can be offered for social problems.

- Do not expect to be able to 'rehabilitate' these individuals. There is no evidence that even intensive, institutional programmes for antisocial individuals are effective in changing their behaviour. However, there is evidence that approximately 50% of individuals who appear to have met criteria for an antisocial personality disorder in their teens or twenties will no longer meet criteria after the age of 30, with 80% no longer meeting criteria at age 45. It is therefore the role of the clinician to treat concurrent mental disorders and to help with managing intervening crises so that these individuals (and the clinicians) survive long enough for the antisocial personality traits to be given a chance to remit. Those 20% who do not remit remain a serious problem for society.

11.1.7 THE HISTRIONIC PERSON

This type of personality, while not presenting the same level of difficulties in management as the emotionally unstable or antisocial personality, can still challenge the patience of even the most experienced clinician.

This personality type as described in this chapter is based on the ICD-10 histrionic personality disorder which is characterised by a number of the following features:
- Dramatic, theatrical and exaggerated emotional expression
- A tendency to be suggestible and easily influenced by others
- Shallow and rapidly shifting emotions
- Continual seeking of excitement
- A need to be the centre of attention
- Inappropriate seductiveness in behaviour and appearance
- Over-concern with physical attractiveness

HOW TO RECOGNISE THE HISTRIONIC PERSON

Individuals with histrionic personalities are usually easily recognised in the clinical interview. They present dramatically, tend to exaggerate their emotions, and generally direct their efforts toward capturing the clinician's attention and approval. Even the most mundane information can be presented in a lively fashion.

In addition, individuals' behaviours may include inappropriately exaggerated smiles and elaborate hand gestures and the content of their speech will often be vague, impressionistic, and lacking in detail. Furthermore, they may display inappropriate sexually seductive behaviour. (Some guidelines for the management of sexually seductive behaviour are outlined later in this section). Unlike individuals who are manic, histrionic individuals will not exhibit 'bizarre' behaviour, disordered thinking, delusions, hallucinations, or flight of ideas.

In some individuals, histrionic behaviour may be a method of getting their own way and attempting to manipulate others. These individuals will appear to be self-centred and become uncomfortable when they are not in control of other people's attention. In other individuals, the histrionic behaviour may represent an attempt to gain reassurance and approval from others. In their eagerness to please they will actively avoid any interpersonal conflict.

HOW TO MANAGE THE HISTRIONIC PERSON

As with all of the 'dramatic' personalities, histrionic personality traits appear to diminish with age as individuals mature.

One of the more common presentations and reasons for which histrionic people may seek help is depression. This disorder will need to be actively treated.

The skill in management is for the clinician to avoid becoming distracted or annoyed by the behaviour of these individuals (or at least to avoid showing his or her annoyance). It will be important for the clinician to remain consistently calm and attentive in the face of histrionic behaviour and to consistently guide the individual back to the focus of the session. The clinician can also gently but firmly question the individual when he or she is making generalisations, being overly impressionistic, or overly catastrophic. For example, the clinician may say, *"I can tell that it must have been distressing for you, but can you tell me from the beginning exactly what happened?"*

Do not reward histrionic behaviour

It will be important that the histrionic behaviour itself is not rewarded or reinforced. For example, if the individual feels that he or she is not getting the amount of attention from the clinician that is desired, the individual may engage in more dramatic behaviour, such as weeping or wailing, fainting, or becoming overly distraught. Rather than reinforce this behaviour by making a fuss and giving the individual more attention, it might be useful for the clinician to calmly instruct the individual about strategies that might calm him or her, such as sitting still and breathing slowly. The clinician may then state that he or she will leave the individual to calm down and will return to complete the session when the individual has indeed calmed down. When the consultation is recommenced, the focus can return to the topic that was being discussed rather than to the histrionic behaviour itself. For example, the clinician may say, *"Before you became upset we were talking about your feelings of depression - I'd like to talk about these feelings some more so I might better help you with your current problems."*

Learn how to deal with sexually seductive behaviour

An individual who is behaving in a sexually seductive manner may:

- Enter the clinician's personal body space
- Make frequent or lingering body contact (i.e., touch the clinician)
- Offer numerous compliments, many of which are inappropriate
- Maintain prolonged eye contact
- Wear seductive clothing (e.g., an unbuttoned shirt, a short skirt, skimpy clothing, etc.)
- Adopt a seductive body posture or make seductive gestures (e.g., wink at the clinician, purposely sit with underwear exposed, etc.)
- Ask questions about the clinician's personal life
- Make sexually suggestive comments
- Express the desire to meet socially with the clinician

When considered in isolation, the above-mentioned behaviours are not necessarily indicative of sexually seductive behaviour (e.g., eye contact could be prolonged as a result of aggressive behaviour, or, the individual may intrude on personal body space due to cultural differences). However, when a number of these behaviours are displayed simultaneously the message becomes more clearly one of sexual interest. Also problematic is the expression of non-sexual interest (e.g., the desire to be friends).

The following suggestions for dealing with sexually seductive behaviour may be used as appropriate. These suggestions are not only useful for individuals who have histrionic personalities but are equally applicable to individuals who display sexually seductive behaviours in the context of other mental health problems (e.g., mania, intoxication).

Ignore the behaviour

This strategy is most appropriate if the behaviour stems from a time-limited cause (e.g., mania or intoxication). It may also be useful if the behaviour is relatively non-threatening in nature; that is, if the behaviour is fairly passive and the individual does not make intrusive physical advances (e.g., the individual pays numerous compliments, winks, subtly exposes underwear). If the behaviour is more intrusive (e.g., repeated physical contact, vulgar suggestive comments, removal of clothing), an alternative strategy may be needed.

Examine your own behaviour

It is always important to assess whether you may have unwittingly given the individual the wrong impression. Individuals who are receiving help for psychiatric problems are likely to be vulnerable and in search of approval and acceptance. If the clinician wears revealing clothing, makes physical body contact, or makes comments about his or her personal life, the individual may understandably come to believe that the clinician is attracted to him or her.

Although the sharing of personal anecdotes may be an effective 'strategy', (especially in long-term case management where rapport and genuine concern usually develops) it is easy for this strategy to backfire if not used with caution. Clinician clothing that is revealing (e.g., low-cut shirts or exposed cleavage, mini skirts, singlet tops, etc.) is inappropriate in a professional care-giving relationship. Also, do not initiate discussions about the individual's sex life if there is no therapeutic indication for doing so.

Clarify the situation

The best approach may be to comment on your perceptions in a non-punitive manner at the time an inappropriate incident occurs. For example, you could say, *"Bill/Jill, for me to be able to help you as much as possible, I need to be able to think objectively about your problems, and if we became too close, like your friends or family, I won't be able to do that. So we need to keep a little distance; that is, keep the relationship a professional one so that I can help you as much as I can"*. By phrasing the comment in this manner you allow the individual to save face as well as making your point clear at the same time.

If the individual makes obscene suggestions, it will be sensible to tell him or her that such behaviour is inappropriate and unacceptable and that you will not see him or her if such behaviour occurs again (even if he or she is psychotic). Basically, the more unacceptable the behaviour, the more stern and no-nonsense you need to be.

It may also be necessary to clarify how you like to be addressed by the individual. For example, if you are female and object to having men call you "love", make your feelings clear early in the relationship. Perhaps you could start by saying, *"I don't really like to be called "love". I'd feel much more comfortable if you'd call me Heather or Ms Thompson."* If the individual ignores your request you may need to become more stern on the next occasion.

Leave the door open

If the individual's behaviour makes you feel uncomfortable it may be useful to open the door. The individual may be less inclined to display underwear or touch you if others can see what he or she is doing.

Arrange for a chaperone

If you do not trust the individual to behave appropriately, or if you have reason to believe that the individual may misinterpret conversations or events as having a sexual content, it may be sensible to have a chaperone in the room with you. However, it is advisable to explain to the individual *why* you have asked the chaperone to be present.

Leave, or ask the individual to leave

If the individual continues to act inappropriately it may be necessary to ask the individual to leave. If you are on a community visit and in the individual's territory, it is obviously *you* who will have to leave. It may be necessary to refer the individual to another clinician if you feel that it is impossible or intolerable to continue working with the individual.

11.1.8 THE DEPENDENT PERSON

HOW TO RECOGNISE THE DEPENDENT PERSON

Characteristic attributes of dependent individuals include:

- A strong need for reassurance.
- An inability to be reassured.
- A tendency to seek frequent contact.
- Excessive and ingratiating thankfulness to the clinician for his or her assistance, thereby boosting the clinician's ego and engaging the clinician's vanity and vulnerability (i.e., the clinician's 'need to cure').
- Avoidance of, or long-standing problems with, decision-making.
- Failure to improve and a tendency to present with *more* problems as treatment progresses.
- Reluctance to consider termination of treatment or contact.

HOW TO MANAGE THE DEPENDENT PERSON

The following approach will be necessary and useful for the management of individuals who are overly dependent:

Ensure treatment is well-structured

It is important that treatment is seen to be well-structured with clear goals and plans for each interaction. By being organised and firm you are providing clear boundaries and outlines for treatment. Negotiate the number of sessions that you expect will be required for dealing with the individual's problems. Do not agree to conduct further sessions unless you believe these sessions are really necessary. If the individual requires long-term management, set clear limits and rules for these interactions.

Set limits and rules

It will be useful to make rules about how frequently you will see the individual, and about the extent of contact you will have with the individual between sessions. When setting rules and limits it is best to involve the individual in the negotiation process. Do not simply lay down rules without discussion. Once the limits and rules have been agreed upon they should be made into a detailed and specific written contract. Ensure that the individual clearly understands the contract at this time and that he or she understands the *reason* for the contract (i.e., that the contract will foster greater independence and self-confidence, which will be of benefit to the individual, and that you have limited time to spend with each individual).

Provide training and encouragement for decision-making

Do not make decisions for the individual but encourage the individual to make his or her own decisions, both within and outside of treatment sessions. Initially the individual may be encouraged to make small decisions, thus promoting confidence. The individual may then work towards making more important life decisions. Training in the structured problem solving method will be useful. This method is described in detail in Chapter 1: Core Management Skills.

Set homework tasks

Independent and responsible behaviour may be encouraged by setting relevant homework tasks to be completed between sessions. The homework tasks should be *achievable* and *clearly specified*. For example, the individual may be required to go to a movie alone or, without assistance, to select the menu and purchase the relevant ingredients for an upcoming dinner party.

Promote outside interests

Outside interests that will promote independence are to be encouraged. For example, joining a social club may actually *foster* dependency on others while taking up a solo hobby such as swimming or painting may *encourage independence*.

Provide insight

Dependent individuals may not realise the extent of their reliance on others. By gently making them aware of their dependency needs you may help them realise that they would benefit from learning greater independence. For example you may say, *"I can see that you have difficulty with decision-making"* or *"I get the impression that you need a lot of reassurance from others"*.

Limit reassurance to that which is appropriate

Dependent individuals seek repeated reassurance yet fail to benefit from such reassurance. It may be useful to inform the individual that your reassurance is not going to be helpful. You may use examples of previous interactions with the individual in which copious reassurance was given with no noteworthy or long-lasting benefit being obtained. Ensure that your contract with the individual incorporates the rule that you will not give excessive reassurance, then make sure you *follow* the contract.

Use the individual's behaviour to your advantage

Be aware of the effect the individual's behaviour may have on you. Do not try to live up to his or her unrealistic and idealistic expectations of you. Instead, use the individual's feelings about you to your advantage. For example, you may say, *"I'm glad we get on well and that you feel you can trust me. Now, I feel it would be of great benefit to you if you ..."*

11.1.9 THE OBSESSIONAL PERSON

HOW TO RECOGNISE THE OBSESSIONAL PERSON

The obsessional person's behaviour is characterised by:
- Problems with doubt and excessive cautiousness.
- Preoccupation with details, rules, lists, organisation, or schedules.
- Perfectionism.
- A tendency to be overly conscientious and scrupulous.
- A tendency to be rigid and stubborn and to insist that others do things exactly as directed.
- A tendency to be a workaholic, devoting oneself almost entirely to work related tasks to the exclusion of leisure activities.

These attributes commonly interfere with an individual's social and interpersonal relationships but interfere less often with an individual's work role. Individuals themselves will rarely complain of their obsessional personality but may seek help because of a concurrent mental health problem, problems in their interpersonal relationships, or because changes to their work have caused their indecisiveness and perfectionism to interfere with their ability to function at work.

You can recognise an obsessional person by the following attributes and behaviours:
- Note taking
- Asking excessive questions
- Over-monitoring of treatment and progress and showing excessive attention to detail
- Requests for frequent consultations about the relevant problem and its treatment

Major depression is commonly comorbid with an obsessional personality and may be the problem for which the individual is presently seeking treatment.

HOW TO MANAGE THE OBSESSIONAL PERSON

- Plan treatment in consultation with the individual. This collaborative relationship will allow the obsessional individual to maintain a sense of control, which will thereby alleviate excessive anxiety.
- Aim to help individuals use their obsessional personality traits more constructively rather than to change them. For example, encourage them to direct their diligence towards tasks that will help their progress (e.g., daily relaxation sessions).
- Give clear and specific instructions. For example, you may say, "Check your medication side effects every three days" rather than saying "Check your side effects" as the latter may lead the obsessional individual to conduct unwarranted hourly checking of side effects and symptoms.
- Help the individual to become more aware of their tension levels. Training in relaxation methods (see Chapter 4) may help the individual cope better with situations that produce excessive anxiety (e.g., having to leave work tasks incomplete until the next day).
- Target additional problems to which these individuals may be more vulnerable because of their personality trait. For example, in the context of management of a major depressive disorder the obsessive individual may need extra help with expressing positive emotions and expressing anger. (For information about assertiveness training see Chapter 1). Individuals may also need help with allowing themselves to engage in activities that lead to satisfaction and enjoyment. (For information about increasing pleasant activities see Chapter 3: Affective Disorders).

11.1.10 THE PASSIVE-AGGRESSIVE (YES, BUT...) PERSON

HOW TO RECOGNISE THE PASSIVE-AGGRESSIVE PERSON

The following attributes are characteristic of the passive-aggressive person:
- Often running late for appointments
- Ready to criticise or challenge the clinician's knowledge or advice
- A tendency to attribute blame for everything to other people
- Does not complete homework tasks but instead offers a myriad of excuses ("Yes, but...")
- Resents any demands placed on him or her
- Will procrastinate with the decision about whether or not to attend for treatment

HOW TO MANAGE THE PASSIVE-AGGRESSIVE PERSON

Obtain treatment history

Obtain a history of the individual's previous treatments by asking the individual about the treatments and by getting a copy of the treatment notes (with the individual's permission) from other clinicians where appropriate. From the previous treatment information, find out about everything that has NOT worked in the past.

Be direct and honest

When recommending treatments, a straightforward approach is required. Tell the individual about the range of treatments you are prepared to offer and inform the individual that you can offer nothing else if he or she does not wish to co-operate with the suggested treatments. You can still give the individual options within the treatments whenever possible, however, once a decision about treatment is made, the individual is expected to commit wholeheartedly. Remind the individual that if he or she does not wish to make the most of treatment, the individual will be wasting his or her own time.

Set limits

Be very clear and explicit about which behaviours you will and will not tolerate. In conjunction with the individual, set very clear written limits and rules that have specific consequences attached to them. Ensure that the individual understands the limits and the consequences and that both parties sign the contract. An example of a rule may be that if the individual is more than five minutes late for an appointment you will not see him or her at that time and that another appointment will have to be made. If more than three appointments are missed you will refer the individual to another clinician. You may have a similar rule if the individual habitually reschedules appointments. When discussing such limits with the individual, present these limits in an empathic and non-punitive manner. For example, you could say, *"If you are more than X minutes late we do not have time to work effectively."*

Individuals are likely to test your limits so it will be important to be consistent and firm otherwise you will find that *the individual will control you.* Ensure that you follow through with all stated consequences if limits are exceeded.

Clarify consequences and/or provide choice

Sometimes it may be helpful to clarify the consequences of the individual's behaviour. For example, you may say, *"If you continue to skip appointments I'll have to stop seeing you. You'll probably end up going to someone else and doing the same thing over again. In the end you'll be wasting your own time and not getting any better. However, if you work **with** me on this problem, together* *we may be able to help you feel a bit better. Then you can be pleased with yourself for your achievement"*. Using this approach you frame the problem in terms of how the individual's behaviour will affect him or her, thus encouraging the individual to directly examine the outcome of his or her own behaviour.

Recognise your own frustration

A major difficulty with treating passive-aggressive individuals is with the feelings these individuals arouse in the clinician. Use these feelings of annoyance to help you recognise passive-aggressive traits. Your feelings of frustration and annoyance may also be used to help you develop a plan for dealing effectively with the individual's behaviour. If your personal feelings towards the individual get in the way of treatment there are three options available.

1. Discuss your feelings with the individual. For example, you may say, *"I find that I become very frustrated when we make agreements and they aren't fulfilled. Your treatment is compromised when we're annoyed with each other. If we can't work together more comfortably I'll have to refer you on to another clinician"* or whatever alternative is appropriate.

2. If animosity between you seems beyond repair, you may wish to refer the individual immediately to another clinician without an attempt at reconciliation.

3. If your job requires you to continue offering help to an individual who is ambivalent about accepting treatment (e.g., in outreach or mobile treatment teams) accept the ambivalence, do not take the individual's response personally, but simply be prepared to provide assistance when needed. The goal for treatment in this case is more likely to be crisis intervention rather than rehabilitation.

Whichever option you choose, do not allow yourself to accept responsibility inappropriately for treatment failure.

11.2 BIBLIOGRAPHY

Alden, L. (1989). Short-term structured treatment for avoidant personality disorder. *Journal of Consulting & Clinical Psychology*, *57*, 764-765.

Beck, J.C. (1987). The potentially violent patient: legal duties, clinical practice, and risk management. *Psychiatric Annals*, *17*, 695-699.

Cahill, C.D., Stuart, G.W., Laraia, M.T. & Arana, G.W. (1991). Inpatient management of violent behavior: nursing prevention and intervention. *Issues in Mental Health Nursing*, *12*, 239-252.

Cowdry, R.W. & Gardner, D.L. (1988). Pharmacotherapy of borderline personality disorder: alprazolam, carbamazepine, trifluoperazine and tranycypromine. *Archives of General Psychiatry*, *45*, 111-119.

Hanke, N. (1984). *Handbook of Emergency Psychiatry*. Lexington, MA: The Collamore Press.

Hillcrest Hospital Nursing Service (1991). *Guidelines for the Management of Aggression*. Adelaide: Hillcrest Hospital Nursing Service.

Hume, F. (1993). The management of the violent and aggressive patient. *Australian Prescriber*, *16*, 90-92.

Jobe, T.H. & Winer J.A. (1988). In J.A. Flaherty, R.A. Channon, & J.M. Davis (Eds.), *Psychiatry: Diagnosis and Therapy*. Connecticut: Appleton & Lange.

Lazare, A, Cohen, F., Jacobson, A.M., Williams, M.W., Mignone, R.J. & Zisook, S. (1972). The walk-in patient as a 'customer': A key dimension in evaluation and treatment. *American Journal of Orthopsychiatry*, *42*, 872-883.

Linehan, M.M., Armstrong, H.E., Suarez, A., Allmon, D. & Heard, H.L. (1991). Cognitive-behavioural treatment of chronically parasuicidal borderline patients. *Archives of General Psychiatry*, *48*, 1060-1064.

Menninger, W.W. (1993). Management of the aggressive and dangerous patient. *Bulletin of the Menninger Clinic*, *57*, 208-216.

Quality Assurance Project (1984). Treatment outlines for the management of schizophrenia. *Australian and New Zealand Journal of Psychiatry*, *18*, 19-38.

Quality Assurance Project (1985). Treatment outlines for the management of obsessive-compulsive disorder. *Australian and New Zealand Journal of Psychiatry*, *19*, 240-253.

Quality Assurance Project (1991a). Treatment outlines for borderline, narcissistic and histrionic personality disorders. *Australian and New Zealand Journal of Psychiatry*, *25*, 392-403.

Quality Assurance Project (1991b). Treatment outlines for antisocial personality disorder. *Australian and New Zealand Journal of Psychiatry*, *25*, 541-547.

Rada, R.T. (1981). The violent patient: rapid assessment and management. *Psychosomatics*, *22*, 101-109.

Salkovskis, P.M., Atha, C. & Storer, D. (1990). Cognitive-behavioural problem solving in the treatment of patients whom repeatedly attempt suicide: A controlled trial. *British Journal of Psychiatry*, *157*, 871-876.

Sparr, L.F., Boehnlein, J.K. & Cooney, T.G. (1986). The medical management of the paranoid patient. *General Hospital Psychiatry*, *8*, 49-55.

Stevenson, S. (1991). Heading off violence with verbal de-escalation. *Journal of Psychosocial Nursing*, *29*, 6-10.

Tardiff, K. (1988). Management of the violent patient in an emergency situation. *Psychiatric Clinics of North America*, *11*, 539-549.

Tardiff, K. (1992). Mentally abnormal offenders: evaluation and management of violence. *Psychiatric Clinics of North America, 15*, 553-567.

Turnbull, J., Aitken, I., Black, L & Patterson, B. (1990). Turn it around: short-term management for aggression and anger. *Journal of Psychosocial Nursing, 28*, 7-13.

INDEX

PSYCHOLOGICAL MEDICINE
a companion to Management of Mental Disorders

Edited by Pierre Beumont, Gavin Andrews, Philip Boyce, and Vaughan Carr.
World Health Organization for Mental Health and Substance Abuse, Sydney.

The Management of Mental Disorders is guide to the recognition and management of individuals with mental disorders. The text also contains a series of resource materials, including interview schedules and assessment instruments for the clinician, and educational handouts and homework exercises for patients. As such the Management of Mental Disorders is intensely practical, avoiding discussion of theoretical issues or current controversies.

This book, Psychological Medicine: a Companion to Management of Mental Disorders, is the antidote. It contains formal discussions and practical advice about psychopathology, consultation and liaison psychiatry, child and adolescent psychiatry, and psychiatry of old age – topics not covered in the original text. It also contains concise essays on critical topics, well referenced self-directed learning guides on common disorders, and self-assessment case studies with model answers.

ORDER FORM

Name: _____

Organization: _____

Address: _____

Phone: _____

Fax: _____

Cost: $75 (Australian dollars; includes postage)

Please send me _____ copies of Psychological Medicine. Total enclosed $_____

Cheques (in Australian dollars) to be made payable to: WHO Collaborating Centre

Please return cheque and order form to: Jennise Sami
299 Forbes Street
Darlinghurst, NSW, 2010
Australia

Enquires: orders@crufad.unsw.edu.au

TREATMENT OF ANXIETY DISORDERS
a Clinician's Text and Treatment Manual

Gavin Andrews, Rocco Crino, Caroline Hunt, Lisa Lampe and Andrew Page.
Cambridge University Press: London.

Anxiety disorders are among the commonest conditions presented to psychiatrists and clinical psychologists, and recent years have seen the development of increasingly specific treatment strategies, using both drugs and cognitive behavioural approaches. Treatment of Anxiety Disorders provides clinicians with and authoritative review of the epidemiology, etiology, and evaluation of anxiety disorders, as well as manuals for conducting a comprehensive and effective cognitive behavioural programme for the common anxiety disorders.

Clinicians at all levels of expertise can use the volume in a variety of ways, as an introduction for those new to the field, as a reference, for planning treatments, or for clinical problem-solving. Treatment of Anxiety Disorders offers both a theoretical overview and a framework to help psychiatrists and clinical psychologists, whether experienced or not, build successful treatment programmes.

Contents

Order from your local bookshop

The Diagnosis and Treatment of Anxiety Disorders – Videos

World Health Organization for Mental Health and Substance Abuse, Sydney.

Two professionally made, fully scripted 30 minute videos for clinical teaching – suitable for under-graduate and post-graduate students, and for hospital inservice training. Each VHS video contains a number of five to six minute self-contained segments that can be used in lectures or as stimuli for small group discussions.

In the first video, actors portray typical presentations of people with the common anxiety disorders: panic/agoraphobia, social phobia, obsessive compulsive disorder, generalized anxiety disorder, and post-traumatic stress disorder. An expert introduction preceedes each vignette. In the second videotape the commonly used cognitive behavioural techniques are illustrated; hyperventilation in the patient with panic disorder/agoraphobia, cognitive restructuring in the person with social phobia, graded exposure and response prevention in the person with obsessive compulsive disorder, structured problem solving in generalised anxiety disorder, and a combination of all techniques in the person with post traumatic stress disorder.

ORDER FORM

Name: _____

Organization: _____

Address: _____

Phone: _____

Fax: _____

Cost per set of videos: $150 (Australian dollars; includes postage)

Please send me _____ sets of videos. Total enclosed $_____

Cheques (in Australian dollars) to be made payable to: WHO Collaborating Centre

Please return cheque and order form to: Jennise Sami
299 Forbes Street
Darlinghurst, NSW, 2010
Australia

Enquires: orders@crufad.unsw.edu.au

Counselling and Management Skills in Clinical Practice – CDRom

Gavin Andrews and Caroline Hunt.
World Health Organization for Mental Health and Substance Abuse, Sydney; and School of Psychiatry, University of NSW, St Vincent's Hospital, Sydney.

This interactive compact disc should enable clinicians to learn or refresh their knowledge of five basic clinical skills – interview skills, patient education, prescribing, structured problem solving and hyperventilation control.

In the first case, Jill's acute stress-related depression is relieved by medication and resolved by structured problem solving. Managed differently she could continue to regard herself as weak and unable to cope.

In the second case, Bob has avoided treatment for his severe depression for some years, but the doctor teaches him about the seriousness of his illness, about the need for medication and the value of psychological techniques. Managed differently he could well suicide.

In the third demonstration case, Sophie's panic attacks would progress to disabling agoraphobia if the doctor had not educated her about the flight or fight response and the nature of panic, and how she could control her hyperventilation and thereby moderate the severity of her panic attacks.

The fourth case is more complex. Susan is often emotionally distressed, jumps to conclusions, and always imagines the worst. The psychologically aware doctor uses techniques of hyperventilation control and problem solving to deal with the current crisis. Managed differently she could continue to focus on her somatic symptoms as a defense against dealing with her problem with her daughter.

The interviews presume that the doctor knows each patient and thus has background knowledge. The demonstration cases are designed for teaching, and while the clinical material is correct, each interview is simplified to allow the relevant teaching material to be emphasized.

ORDER FORM

Name: _____

Organization: _____

Address: _____

Phone: _____

Fax: _____

Cost: $110 (Australian dollars; includes postage)

Please send me _____ CDRoms. Total enclosed $_____

Cheques (in Australian dollars) to be made payable to: WHO Collaborating Centre

Please return cheque and order form to:

Jennise Sami
299 Forbes Street
Darlinghurst, NSW, 2010
Australia

Enquires: orders@crufad.unsw.edu.au

ACUTE INPATIENT PSYCHIATRIC CARE:
A Source Book

World Health Organization for Mental Health and Substance Abuse, Sydney.

Acute Inpatient Psychiatric Care is a source book for the staff of all inpatient units. It was conceived as a brief Best Practice Protocol but it rapidly became obvious that there were no widely available guides to practice and what most units required was access to discussion documents about the role of such units. Guided by a multidisciplinary expert committee and advised by documents from many inpatient units, and with advice from carers and consumers, providers and funders, the research team have assembled an invaluable source book.

The nature of inpatient care, pathways to care and the alternatives, factors influencing the decision to admit are all discussed. But the real job of such units is the efficient and compassionate treatment of people who are seriously ill. The main body of the book is concerned with such issues - admission, emergency treatment, patients needing special care, and the organisational requirements to facilitate all this. The strength of the book is also in the resource materials provided, specimen policy and procedure manuals, assessment criteria for a range of situations, and information sheets for consumers. The focus of this book is problem-specific as opposed to diagnosis-specific care. Many decisions are made in an acute setting before a firm diagnosis has been established and this book recognises the need to deal with problems rather than diagnoses. For six months before publication this book has been trialed in a number of inpatient units across the country and has been extensively revised in the light of the comments received.

ORDER FORM

Name: _____

Organization: _____

Address: _____

Phone: _____

Fax: _____

Cost: $80 (Australian dollars; includes postage)

Please send me _____ copies of Acute Inpatient Psychiatric Care. Total enclosed $_____

Cheques (in Australian dollars) to be made payable to: WHO Collaborating Centre
Please return cheque and order form to: Jennise Sami
299 Forbes Street
Darlinghurst, NSW, 2010
Australia

Enquires: orders@crufad.unsw.edu.au

CIDI-Auto 2.1 – A Computerized Composite International Diagnostic Interview

The CIDI is a comprehensive, fully standardised interview that can be used to assess mental disorders according to the definitions and criteria of ICD 10 and DSM-IV (see *British Journal of Psychiatry*, *159*, 645-658; *International Review of Psychiatry*, *3*, 265-278; *Social Psychiatry and Psychiatric Epidemiology*, *33*, 80-88). It was developed as a collaborative project between the World Health Organization and the US National Institutes of Health. The CIDI has been designed to for use in a variety of cultures and settings. It is primarily intended for use as an epidemiological tool, but it can be used for other research and clinical tasks.

A computerized version of the CIDI, the CIDI-Auto 2.1 has been developed and can be self-administered or administered by an interviewer. The program is supplied on a single 3.5" disk and is accompanied by a manual and a VHS videotape which details installation and operation of the program. The program will run on any IBM compatible machine supporting DOS version 3.0 or later. Data output contains question responses. Data are scored according to both ICD 10 and DSM-IV criteria. The program is licensed to an individual at an address/institution. The licensee may make copies and distribute them to colleagues at that address/instituion. The licensed user remains responsible for all uses of all copies of his/her copy of the program.

ORDER FORM

Name: _____

Title: _____

Organization: _____

Address: _____

_____

The program lists the title, name and institution (or address) of the licensee being the person responsible for confidentiality. Licensee (Title, Name and Institution or Address (80 characters)):

_____

_____

_____

Cost for new licensees: AUD$700, US$500, or Stg£320

Cheques to be made payable to: WHO Collaborating Centre

Please return cheque and order form to: WHO CIDI Training and Reference Centre
299 Forbes Street
Darlinghurst, NSW, 2010
Australia

Enquires: cidi@crufad.unsw.edu.au or www.crufad.unsw.edu.au/cidi/cidi.htm

Management of Mental Disorders Order Form
United Kingdom Edition

To obtain additional copies of this book, please remove or photocopy this order form.

Please note this book is only obtainable from the publisher's agents and is not available via Bookshops or via the Internet.

Please send me _____ copies of Management of Mental Disorders latest edition at £30 (Thirty pounds sterling UK), inclusive of Postage and Packing.

UK Customers representing official bodies, may send an official purchase order and the books will be supplied on an invoice basis.

All other customers should send a cheque drawn on a UK Bank in pounds sterling, an Intenational Money Order or pay by Credit Card, books will be despatched on receipt of your payment, together with a receipt.

ORDER FORM

Name: _____

Delivery Address: _____

_____

Daytime Tel.No: _____

Post Code: _____

Country: _____

Payment enclosed cheque _____ IMO _____

Please charge my   VISA ☐   Mastercard ☐

Card No _____ Expiry Date _____

Card Holders Address if different from above _____

_____

Please send your order to Management of Mental Disorders, PO Box 55, Aldershot, Hampshire, GU12 4FP, United Kingdom

If paying by credit card you may telephone your order to (+44) 1252 322252 or fax to (+44) 1252 322315